Contending Legitimacy in World Politics

Legitimacy, along with security and democracy, is arguably one of the most widely used global buzzwords of the new millennium. Yet, the idea of political legitimacy is not new and has been constructed in different ways at different moments in history. This book problematizes this notion, from various contextual standpoints, disciplinary and theoretical perspectives. Taking a comparative, transnational and bottom-up approach to the study of political legitimacy, this book sheds light on multiple perceptions by different actors (institutions, civil society, majoritarian and minority subjects), analysing the notion of political legitimacy from a critical perspective. Questioning received wisdom or one-size-fits-all analyses, it leads to a reassessment of the link between legitimacy and sovereignty, and emphasises the demand by transnational civil society to go beyond identity politics, which produce logics of violence.

This book was originally published as a special issue of *Global Discourse*.

Bronwyn Winter is Deputy Director of European Studies at the University of Sydney. Her publications include *September 11, 2001: Feminist Perspectives* (Spinifex 2002), *Hijab and the Republic* (Syracuse UP 2008), and *Women, Insecurity and Violence in a Post-9/11 World* (Syracuse UP 2017).

Lucia Sorbera is Senior Lecturer in the Department of Arabic Language and Cultures at the University of Sydney. Her publications include 'Challenges of thinking feminism and revolution in Egypt between 2011 and 2014', in *Post-Colonial Studies*, 17, 1 (2014); 'Early Reflections of an Historian on Feminism in Egypt in Times of Revolution', in *Genesis*, XII/1 (2013); 'Between Cooptation and Resistance: Women's Leadership and Gender Discourse in Contemporary Egypt', in Luca Anceschi, Gennaro Gervasio, Andrea Teti (eds.), *Hidden Geographies. Informal Powers in the Greater Middle East* (Routledge 2014).

Contending Legitimacy in World Politics

The State, Civil Society and the International Sphere in the Twenty-first Century

Edited by
Bronwyn Winter and Lucia Sorbera

Routledge
Taylor & Francis Group

LONDON AND NEW YORK

First published 2018
by Routledge
2 Park Square, Milton Park, Abingdon, Oxon, OX14 4RN, UK

and by Routledge
711 Third Avenue, New York, NY 10017, USA

Routledge is an imprint of the Taylor & Francis Group, an informa business

Introduction, Chapters 1–4 & 6–18 © 2018 Taylor & Francis
Chapter 5 © 2018 Thomas Clément Mercier. Originally published as Open Access.

British Library Cataloguing in Publication Data
A catalogue record for this book is available from the British Library

ISBN 13: 978-1-138-04146-2

Typeset in Myriad Pro
by RefineCatch Limited, Bungay, Suffolk

Publisher's Note
The publisher accepts responsibility for any inconsistencies that may have
arisen during the conversion of this book from journal articles to book chapters,
namely the possible inclusion of journal terminology.

Disclaimer
Every effort has been made to contact copyright holders for their permission to
reprint material in this book. The publishers would be grateful to hear from any
copyright holder who is not here acknowledged and will undertake to rectify
any errors or omissions in future editions of this book.

Contents

CONTENTS

Citation Information

The chapters in this book were originally published as a special issue of *Global Discourse*, volume 6, issue 3 (2016). When citing this material, please use the original page numbering for each article, as follows:

Introduction
Introduction
Bronwyn Winter and Lucia Sorbera
Global Discourse, volume 6, issue 3 (2016), pp. 325–329

Chapter 1
Debating legitimacy transnationally
Anna Meine
Global Discourse, volume 6, issue 3 (2016), pp. 330–346

Chapter 2
Reply: Legitimacy and the shadows of universalism: a response to Meine's 'Debating legitimacy transnationally'
Jessica Whyte
Global Discourse, volume 6, issue 3 (2016), pp. 347–351

Chapter 3
The discursive (de)legitimisation of global governance: political contestation and the emergence of new actors in the WTO's Dispute Settlement Body
Michael Strange
Global Discourse, volume 6, issue 3 (2016), pp. 352–369

Chapter 4
Reply: Political contestation and the emergence of new actors, but who governs? A response to Michael Strange
John Mikler
Global Discourse, volume 6, issue 3 (2016), pp. 370–373

Chapter 5
Resisting legitimacy: Weber, Derrida, and the fallibility of sovereign power
Thomas Clément Mercier
Global Discourse, volume 6, issue 3 (2016), pp. 374–391

Chapter 15

Body politics and legitimacy: towards a feminist epistemology of the Egyptian revolution
Lucia Sorbera
Global Discourse, volume 6, issue 3 (2016), pp. 493–512

Chapter 16

Reply: De-orientalizing sexual violence and gender discrimination in Egypt
Nancy Okail
Global Discourse, volume 6, issue 3 (2016), doi.org/10.1080/23269995.2016.1253288

Chapter 17

Women's human rights and Tunisian upheavals: is 'democracy' enough?
Bronwyn Winter
Global Discourse, volume 6, issue 3 (2016), pp. 513–529

Chapter 18

Reply: A reply to 'Women's human rights and Tunisian upheavals: is "democracy" enough?'
by Bronwyn Winter
Hajer Ben Hadj Salem
Global Discourse, volume 6, issue 3 (2016), pp. 530–534

For any permission-related enquiries please visit:
http://www.tandfonline.com/page/help/permissions

Notes on Contributors

M. Leann Brown is an Associate Professor at the Department of Political Science, University of Florida, USA.

Kathryn Crameri is an Honorary Professorial Research Fellow at the University of Glasgow, UK, where she was formerly Head of the School of Modern Languages and Cultures.

Giulia Daniele is a Postdoctoral Research Fellow at the Centro de Estudos Internacionais, Instituto Universitário de Lisboa (ISCTE-IUL), Portugal.

Neil Davidson is Lecturer in Sociology at the School of Social and Political Science, University of Glasgow, UK.

Anna Meine is a Lecturer at the Institute of Social Sciences, University of Siegen, Germany.

Thomas Clément Mercier recently completed a PhD at the Department of War Studies, King's College, London, UK.

John Mikler is an Associate Professor at the Department of Government and International Relations, School of Social and Political Sciences, the University of Sydney, Australia.

Nancy Okail is the Executive Director of the Tahrir Institute for Middle East Policy, Washington DC, USA.

Paul Rekret is Associate Professor of Politics at the School of Communications, Arts & Social Sciences, Richmond – the American International University, London, UK.

Matthieu Rey is a Faculty Member at Collège de France, Paris, France.

Hajer Ben Hadj Salem is an Assistant Professor at the Department of English for International Relations, High Institute of Humanities of Tunis, Tunisia.

Lucia Sorbera is Senior Lecturer in the Department of Arabic Language and Cultures at the University of Sydney, Australia.

Aurora Sottimano is Visiting Lecturer, ISCTE-IUL, Centro de Estudos Internacionais (CEI), Lisbon, Portugal, and Senior Fellow of the Centre for Syrian Studies, St Andrews University, Scotland. In January 2018 she takes up a post as Lecturer in International Studies at Leiden University Institute for Area Studies, Netherlands.

Michael Strange is Reader in International Relations at the Department of Global Political Studies, Malmö University, Sweden.

Lana Tatour is a Fellow at the Australian Human Rights Centre, University of New South Wales, Sydney, Australia.

Jessica Whyte is Senior Lecturer in Cultural and Social Analysis at Western Sydney University, Australia.

Bronwyn Winter is Deputy Director of European Studies at the University of Sydney, Australia.

Rüdiger Wurzel is Professor of Comparative European Politics and Jean Monnet Chair in European Studies at the School of Law and Politics, University of Hull, UK.

Introduction

Bronwyn Winter and Lucia Sorbera

Legitimacy, along with security and democracy, is arguably one of the most widely used global buzzwords of our new millennium. The most dramatic focus of the battle for political legitimacy has been the Middle East and North Africa in the wake of the 2010–2011 Arab uprisings, yet that battle began well before the Tunisian trigger event on 17 December 2010, when street vendor Mohamed Bouazizi self-immolated in Sidi-Bouzid. It has been waged, often violently, in countries as diverse as Algeria, Turkey, Iran, Iraq, Morocco, Palestine and Israel since at least the 1990s and in many cases earlier.

Intellectuals have long been targeted by authoritarian regimes whose legitimacy they challenge, and those targetings are impacting directly on us as we prepare this special issue of *Global Discourse*. Severe restrictions of academic freedom are experienced by our colleagues in Egypt, where strategies of intimidation of academics, journalists and intellectuals range from bans on entering the country (for those living abroad) to bans on travelling, intimidation, attempts to co-opt and even forced disappearances, detentions, torture and assassination. While the period from 2011 to 2013 witnessed an eruption of freedom and pluralism in Egypt, since 2013 there has been a restriction of the public sphere under neo-authoritarian rule (Jaquemond 2016; Fahmy 2016). However, Egypt is not the only country where academic freedom is under threat. Turkish colleagues are being persecuted by their government for speaking out against the latter's treatment of Turkey's Kurdish citizens. Several international petitions in protest have been launched in both cases. Within the international political science community, the decision by the executive of the International Political Science Association, concerned about the security of delegates, to relocate its 2016 conference from Istanbul to the Polish city of Poznań has sparked considerable controversy, having been seen by some Turkish colleagues as desolidarisation and by others as a signal of solidarity. Even within our own intellectual communities, legitimacy has become a vexed question.

It would be an error, however, to consider that the question of political legitimacy is simply a 'Middle Eastern and North African' problem. Debates over legitimacy have been waged in recent years in places as distant and different from each other as Argentina, Japan and the Philippines. Moreover, these debates have gripped the West since the beginning of our millennium as the 'War on Terror' waged by the US state and its allies in Afghanistan, Iraq and Southeast Asia has been challenged. More recently, the Global Financial Crisis, the World Social Forum and Occupy movements and Indignados movements in North America and Europe – and their recent reawakenings in France as 'Nuit

Debout' – have led to questioning of the legitimacy of global capitalism and its echoes in the neoliberalisation of national institutions. Most recently, the legitimacy of the European Union's responses to the Syrian refugee crisis and to terrorist attacks in Paris and Brussels – a permanent 'state of exception' (Agamben 2003) – has been called into question – as has the legitimacy of the EU itself, as the 23 June 2016 'Brexit vote' has driven home.

Yet, the idea of political legitimacy is not new and has been constructed in different ways at different moments of modern history. Moments of great upheaval or structural change have been significant in shifting meanings of legitimacy, such as during the passage from the *Ancien Régime* to the First Republic in France, or at the moment of debates over succession to the Prophet in the Islamic world. State and non-state actors alike assert their own legitimacy and denounce the illegitimacy of their rivals.

The very term 'legitimacy' is polysemic. Although it derives etymologically from the Latin term *legitimus*, itself derived from *lex* (law), it has developed sociological, political and ethical connotations well beyond the juridical sphere. Today, 'legitimacy' variously denotes what is lawful, authorised or willed (by states, by various institutions, by 'the people', however constructed); accepted as conforming to agreed standards and practices; justified or reasonable (by various political, legal, cultural, social or ethical yardsticks) or indeed authentic – or all of these things at once. It imparts significant moral clout to any social or political actor that is perceived to be characterised by it. In our modern world, legitimacy is frequently allied to claims of national sovereignty and electoral mandates. Once posited, legitimacy is tacitly assumed to inhere in the action or institution so described and to need no further justification – or indeed, definition. Yet clearly, as the above examples show, what is legitimate for one will be illegitimate for others, and claims to democratic legitimacy of sovereign (or aspiring) states are no longer self-evident.

The contributors to this issue of *Global Discourse*, then, problematise this notion, from various contextual, standpoint, disciplinary and theoretical perspectives. Why does the idea have such quasi-unimpeachable moral weight? Who is using the term, to what end, in what contexts? Within what logical, political, legal, economic, cultural or ideological frameworks are actions deemed to be legitimate or illegitimate? How do factors such as gender, culture, religion and socioeconomic or geopolitical status impact on how legitimacy is determined? Can one ever speak of an absolute legitimacy or illegitimacy? Or is legitimacy always contextual and contingent?

As can be expected, the role of the state looms large in all contributions, whether they are examining the functioning of states and their institutions, the state in relation to civil society or to subnational claims for self-determination, within a context of international or regional regulation, or indeed the state *qua* state, as a locus of legitimacy by definition. Anna Meine (2016) and Michael Strange (2016) ask how legitimacy is to be understood, politically and juridically, in a transnational context. Taking a relational approach, Meine (2016) examines the problems raised in considering legitimacy beyond the state, notably as concerns norms and as concerns democratic processes. Building on Linda Lyu's critical approach to the politics of universalism in the Declaration of Human Rights, Jessica Whyte's (2016) response to Meine emphasises that forms of resistance to the norm are emerging from outside Europe and America, and she suggests to overcoming colonial theoretical paradigms to further enrich the debate about transnational legitimacy. Michael Strange (2016) then discusses critiques of the World Trade Organisation's claims to legitimacy through an examination of its dispute-settlement body and the discursive role of non-state actors, notably as concerns environmental and consumer protections. In reply, John Mikler (2016) argues that non-state actors have not managed to fundamentally change the conversation between the WTO and its state members.

Thomas Mercier's (2016) article focuses on the legitimacy of the state *qua* state, with his Derrida-inspired discussion of the assumed relationship between legitimacy and sovereignty through the performative articulation of 'legitimacy' as a self-positioned sovereign authority. He contests this assumed relationship, which he suggests is dominant in International Relations theory, and posits a different articulation of legitimacy which lies in resistance to this performed sovereignty. In reply, Paul Rekret (2016) argues that such resistance nonetheless remains within the logic of the very sovereignty it contests and that overcoming this problem necessitates further reflection on the historical conditions in which the modern state came into existence.

The following two articles take a European focus. The first, by Leann Brown (2016), looks at European Union environmental policy. Brown argues that there is not one absolute yardstick of legitimacy in this area but 'several evolving and interacting bases of legitimacies' associated with different evaluation criteria, themselves in turn associated with different stakeholders. Rudi Wurzel (2016) welcomes this analysis as timely and insightful, although notes that the association of different types of legitimacy with different moments in the evolution of the EU can be problematic. He also suggests that perhaps Brown is over-optimistc in her conclusions, and draws attention to external actors' evaluations of the legitimacy of EU environmental policy. Kathryn Crameri (2016) shifts the focus from EU-wide to subnational level, by examining the cases for and against a referendum on Catalan secession from Spain as two opposing legitimacy claims. In response, Neil Davidson (2016) reflects more closely on the Scottish case, to which Crameri also refers, in particular as regards the political and legal bases of nations and nationalism.

The four remaining articles in this special issue focus on the Middle East and North Africa, which is no doubt unsurprising, given the ongoing and often long-standing political contestations within this region, which have had often dramatic and indeed tragic impacts for populations. Aurora Sottimano's (2016) article discusses various legitimacy claims within the Syrian civil conflict, in particular those made by the Assad regime and by external actors intervening in the country. Sottimano argues that the very notion of legitimacy within this context 'is misleading because it downplays those power practices of discipline and normalisation which shore up the Syrian authoritarian regime and enforce compliance and acquiescence.' Mathieu Rey (2016) agrees with this analysis, and he enriches the study of the Syrian crisis, situating it in a broader historical and regional perspective, where the 2003 invasion of Iraq was a turning point. Both Sottimano and Rey emphasise that the category of sectarianism is misleading and does not shed light on the Syrian case. They invite us to focus our political analysis on structural elements and discursive logics. In contrast, Giulia Daniele (2016) takes not the state but oppositional movements as her starting point. Her discussion of the Israeli left suggests that its claims to oppositional legitimacy are undermined by its lack of attention to the most marginalised groups, representing and promoting issues of intersectional injustice. Daniele's analysis, which is grounded in feminist postcolonial theories, is questioned by Lana Tatour (2016), whose focus is rather on demands for decolonisation and deracialisation.

The final two articles in this issue are authored by its co-editors. They focus on the two key sites of the Arab uprisings and their aftermath: Egypt and Tunisia, in particular as concerns the experience of, and outcomes for, women. Tunisia was the trigger site for the uprisings, and the ostensible 'success story' of the 'Arab spring,' while Egypt became internationally emblematic of both the Arab world's revolutionary potential and the violence of counterrevolution. Yet, Lucia Sorbera's (2016) article on Egypt and Bronwyn Winter's (2016a) article on Tunisia reveal some remarkable similarities between the two countries, and show that the legitimacy of states is always questionable when the full effects of citizenship are not enjoyed by women. Sorbera and Winter both focus on women's political participation and violence against women as key yardsticks by which the success or otherwise of revolution, and the legitimacy or otherwise of states, can be assessed. Winter's feminist approach to the concepts of democracy, human rights, legitimacy and women's rights is further elaborated by Hajer Ben Hadj Salem (2016), whose response to Winter's article is grounded in empirical studies published by Tunisian leading feminist organisations. Building on these data, Ben Salem's response confirms the link between violence against women and lack of political representation. In addition, the two scholars share a critical vision on women's participation in patri-archal organisations, such as the Islamist parties.

The book reviews, by Lori Allen (2016) (*The Human Right to Dominate* by Nicola Perugini and Neve Gordon [2015]), Angela Joya (2016) (*The Muslim Brotherhood: evolution of an Islamist Movement* by Carrie Rosefsky Wickham [2013]), Mauro Moretti (2016) (*Il Nemico in Politica. La delegittimazione dell'avversario nell'Italia contemporanea*, by Fulvio Cammarano and Stefano Cavazza [2010]), Cai Wilkinson (2016) (*Sex, Politics, and Putin: Political Legitimacy in Russia*, by Valerie Sperling [2014]) and Bronwyn Winter (2016b) (*Jewish Voices in Feminism: Transnational Perspectives* by Nelly Las [2015]), survey the breadth of the literature on legitimacy, highlighting a range of contexts within which the concept is deployed and contested.

Taking a comparative, transnational and bottom-up approach to the study of political legitimacy, this special issue sheds light on multiple perceptions by different actors (institutions, civil society, majoritarian and minority subjects), analysing the notion of political legitimacy from a critical perspective. Questioning received wisdom or one-size-fits-all analyses, it leads to a reassessment of the link between legitimacy and sover-eignty, and emphasises the demand by transnational civil societies to go beyond identity politics, which produce logics of violence.

References

Agamben, G. 2003. *Lo stato di eccezione*. Torino: Bollati Bolinghieri.

Allen, L. 2016. "Review of *The Human Right to Dominate,* by Nicola Perugini and Neve Gordon." *Global Discourse* 6 (3): 535–537.

Ben Hadj Salem, H. 2016. "Reply to 'Women's Human Rights and Tunisian Upheavals: Is "Democracy" Enough?' By Bronwyn Winter." *Global Discourse* 6 (3): 530–534.

Brown, M. L. 2016. "The Evolving and Interacting Bases of EU Environmental Policy Legitimacy." *Global Discourse* 6 (3): 396–419.

Cammarano, F., and S. Cavazza. 2010. *Il Nemico in Politica. La delegittimazione dell'avversario nell'Italia contemporanea*. Bologna: Il Mulino.

Crameri, K. 2016. "Do Catalans Have 'The Right to Decide'? Secession, Legitimacy and Democracy in Twenty-First Century Europe." *Global Discourse* 6 (3): 423–439.

Daniele, G. 2016. "Looking for a New Legitimacy: Internal Challengeswithin the Israeli Left." *Global Discourse* 6 (3): 470–486.

Davidson, N. 2016. "Scotland, Catalonia and the 'Right' to Self-Determination: A Comment Suggested by Kathryn Crameri's 'Do Catalans Have the "Right to Decide"?" *Global Discourse* 6 (3): 440–449.

Fahmy, K. 2016. "Giulio and the Tragic Loss of Academic Freedom." *Mada Masr*, February 7. www.madamasr.com/opinion/poliitics/giulio-and-tragic-loss.html.

Jaquemond, R. 2016. "Ahmed Naji, the Use of Life and the Zombies. " *Mada Masr*, February 23. Accessed February 23, 2016. http://www.madamasr.com/opinion/culture/ahmed-naji-use-life-and-zombies.

Joya, A. 2016. "Review of *The Muslim Brotherhood: Evolution of an Islamist Movement*, by Carrie R. Wickham." *Global Discourse* 6 (3): 541–543.

Las, N. 2015. *Jewish Voices in Feminism: Transnational Perspectives*. Lincoln: University of Nebraska Press.

Meine, A. 2016. "Debating Legitimacy Transnationally." *Global Discourse* 6 (3): 330–346.

Mercier, T. C. 2016. "Resisting Legitimacy: Weber, Derrida, and the Fallibility of Sovereign Power." *Global Discourse* 6 (3): 374–391.

Mikler, J. 2016. "Political Contestation and the Emergence of New Actors, but Who Governs? A Response to Michael Strange." *Global Discourse* 6 (3): 370–373.

Moretti, M. 2016. "Review of *Il Nemico in Politica*, Edited by Fulvio Cammarano & Stefano Cavazza." *Global Discourse* 6 (3): 538–540.

Perugini, N., and N. Gordon. 2015. *The Human Right to Dominate*. Oxford: OUP.

Rekret, P. 2016. "The Sovereignty of Sovereignty and the Restricted Object of Critical IR." *Global Discourse* 6 (3): 392–395.

Rey, M. 2016. "Reply to 'Building Authoritarian "Legitimacy": Domestic Compliance and International Standing of Bashar al-Asad's Syria' by Aurora Sottimano." *Global Discourse* 6 (3): 467–469.

Sorbera, L. 2016. "Body Politics and Legitimacy: Towards a Feminist Epistemology of the Egyptian Revolution." *Global Discourse* 6 (3): 493–512.

Sottimano, A. 2016. "Building Authoritarian "Legitimacy": Domestic Compliance and International Standing of Bashar Al-Asad's Syria." *Global Discourse* 6 (3): 450–466.

Sperling, V. 2014. *Sex, Politics, and Putin: Political Legitimacy in Russia*. Oxford: OUP.

Strange, M. 2016. "The Discursive (De)Legitimisation of Global Governance: Political Contestation and the Emergence of New Actors in the WTO's Dispute Settlement Body." *Global Discourse* 6 (3): 352–369.

Tatour, L. 2016. "The Israeli Left: Part of the Problem or the Solution? A response to Giulia Daniele." *Global Discourse* 6 (3): 487–492.

Whyte, J. 2016. "Legitimacy and the Shadows of Universalism: A Response to Meine's 'Debating Legitimacy Transnationally'." *Global Discourse* 6 (3): 347–351.

Wickham, C. 2013. *The Muslim Brotherhood: Evolution of an Islamist Movement*. Princeton, NJ: Princeton University Press.

Wilkinson, C. 2016. "Review of *Sex, Politics, and Putin: Political Legitimacy in Russia*, by Valerie Sperling." *Global Discourse* 6 (3): 544–545.

Winter, B. 2016a. "Women's Human Rights and Tunisian Upheavals: Is 'Democracy' Enough?" *Global Discourse* 6 (3): 513–529.

Winter, B. 2016b. "Review of *Jewish Voices in Feminism: Transnational Perspectives*, by Nelly Las." *Global Discourse* 6 (3): 546–549.

Wurzel, R. 2016. "The Evolving and Interacting Bases of EU Environmental Policy Legitimacy: A Reply to Brown." *Global Discourse* 6 (3): 420–422.

Debating legitimacy transnationally

Anna Meine

ABSTRACT

As modes and institutions of governance proliferate beyond the state, legitimacy has become a key concept for assessing, supporting or contesting not only the domestic but also the international political order. Often, however, it tends to be used as an umbrella term encompassing different standards of evaluation. How we are to understand legitimacy beyond the state systemically and to relate the different discussions on legitimacy to each other or to the legitimacy of our political order in its entirety are questions yet to be answered.

Against this background, I aim to systematise the underlying issues and questions discussed in contemporary politics and in academic debates by means of a relational conception of political legitimacy. This conception stresses the importance of a constructive relation between institutions and those subject to them, i.e. between objects and subjects of legitimacy. They form the frame of the norms and processes, implied in conceptions of legitimacy. By foregrounding this relation, it becomes visible that debates on norms and processes, which transcend the state, implicate uncertainties, if not struggles about the subjects and objects of legitimacy. Thus, making explicit and discussing openly who the subjects of legitimacy are and how they are or should be related to the objects of legitimacy constitutes a jurisdictional challenge. This is a challenge we have to face if we accept and apply legitimacy as a valid standard for transnational politics. In addition, determining the subject of legitimacy constitutes a conceptual and political challenge, which becomes especially relevant when debating legitimacy transnationally. While both challenges call for broadening and deepening our understanding of legitimate political orders as well as legitimate second-order decisions, the latter, in particular, constitutes a meta-jurisdictional task when thinking about and debating the legitimacy of political orders.

1. Introduction: legitimacy as transnationally contested standard

What are the standards by which UN and EU refugee politics should be evaluated? How should decisions be made within the International Monetary Fund (IMF) and World Trade Organisation (WTO)? Should civil society actors be included in processes of decision-making beyond the state? These are some of the many questions, which arise as institutions of governance proliferate not only nationally but also inter-, trans- or even supranationally and as their existence and working become politicised and contested. The upsurge of political as well as academic debates illustrates that legitimacy has become a key concept for assessing and judging, supporting or contesting actors, institutions and processes of transnational politics. Not solely territorial nation-states but international institutions and governance mechanisms as well are increasingly considered as mechanisms of rule in need of legitimation.[1]

Two types of discussions characterise the discourse on transnational legitimacy in political science. On one hand, it is disputed whether democratic legitimacy can be maintained beyond the state and whether distinct norms should constitute the standard of legitimacy transnationally (e.g. Buchanan and Keohane 2006, 417–436).[2] On the other hand, many academic contributions assess the legitimacy of specific institutions, policies or actors without discussing the political order in general.[3] Legitimacy tends to be used as an umbrella term, encompassing a myriad of different issues as well as different standards of evaluation. Yet, while the different issues are worth discussing, their interrelation and broader significance remain unclear. How we are to understand legitimacy beyond the state more systemically and how we are to relate the different aspects and discussions to each other or to the legitimacy of our political order in its entirety are questions yet to be answered.

Against this background, I aim to uncover and systematise the underlying issues and questions discussed in contemporary politics as well as in academic debates on legitimacy by means of the conception of political legitimacy itself. The relational conception of political legitimacy, which I consider to lie at the heart of twentieth century conceptual thinking about legitimacy in political science and theory, denotes a constructive relationship between a subject and an object of legitimacy. Emphasising this relation provides the means to better understand, relate and systematise the theoretical and normative challenges at hand. Not only are norms and modes of governance subject to contestation but also, fundamentally, the underlying relations between subjects and objects of legitimacy are in dispute. Thus, making explicit and discussing openly who the subjects of legitimacy are and how they are or should be related to the objects of legitimacy presents a major jurisdictional challenge we have to face if we accept and apply legitimacy as a valid standard for transnational politics. At the same time, legitimately determining the subject of legitimacy constitutes an additional conceptual as well as a political challenge. The notion of 'horizontal legitimacy' (e.g. Schmelzle 2007), which considers questions of inter-personal relations between members of a democratic collective as a new dimension of legitimacy, does not reach the heart of this challenge. In order to discuss and decide on the frame of a political order, it is necessary to develop an understanding of legitimate meta-jurisdictional will-formation and decision-making based on the relational conception of legitimacy itself. Making this argument, I try to provide a frame within which we can constructively relate the various, highly variable and often highly specific debates we witness and, thereby, understand what is at stake when we argue about the legitimacy of specific bits and pieces of the developing system of governance and rule in and beyond the state.

2. Legitimacy: relational structure as conceptual core

Conceptions of legitimacy highlight different aspects and pursue different aims. However, they all contain information on the object, on norms and/or processes and on the subject of legitimacy. While the subject often remains implicit and norms and processes constitute the main points of contention (see below), the object to be legitimated, though differently denominated in the literature, is always present. Beetham (1991) discusses relations of power, Weber (1978, 212) speaks of authority or rule and Easton (1965, 285) and Luhmann (1983) theorise the political system. But what is at stake here? Buchanan argues that the object of legitimacy is 'the attempt to exercise a monopoly, within a jurisdiction, in the making, application and enforcement of laws (2002, 689–690). Schmelzle (2012, 420, 432–433) convincingly specifies that, fundamentally, the right to govern, which follows from legitimacy, refers neither to a claim to obedience nor to a permission to exercise coercion, but to the competence to set and change binding norms, and thereby the rights and duties of its subjects. Thus, legitimacy refers to the justification of second-order rights. I agree with Schmelzle that authoritative political institutions constitute the object of legitimacy. Yet, in addition, I argue that, at its core, legitimacy refers to the justification of the underlying asymmetric relations between authoritative institutions or their representatives on the one hand and those affected by or subjected to the generated norms on the other. The asymmetric character of this relationship follows directly from the former's competence to set binding norms, but it is only problematic and in need of justification as it restricts the latter's individual autonomy and equality. It is Beetham's (1991, 15–20) multidimensional conception of legitimation, which precisely highlights this fundamentally relational structure and helps to trace it throughout the literature, and elaborates the repercussions of this insight on the different dimensions of legitimacy, i.e. legal validity, publicly voiced consent and justification in terms of the moral convictions of rulers and ruled.

Legal validity and consent are dominant elements of descriptive, sociological or functional conceptions of legitimacy, which focus on compliance and, fundamentally, on legitimacy's function as a means for furthering stable political rule (Peter 2014). In his study, Weber (1978, 213–215; 2004) observes that a general belief in the legitimacy of a system of rule cannot be based on economic, affective or habitual reasons to comply with domination alone, but depends on rational, traditional or charismatic foundations. Easton (1965, 278–309) argues that the belief in legitimacy as 'the conviction on the part of the member [of the political system, A.M.] that it is right and proper for him to accept and obey the authorities and to abide by the requirements of the regime' (278), which may be based on ideological, structural or personal reasons, forms a part of the input, a political system needed in order to persist. Luhmann (1983), in turn, emphasises procedures, e.g. legislative or judicial processes, as mechanisms of self-legitimation by the political system itself, which generate compliance and thus contribute to maintaining the system. These different examples illustrate that legal validity and the belief in the legitimacy of a political system are crucial for the continued existence of authoritative political institutions. Yet, although all three authors implicitly presuppose a normative background consensus, which guarantees the smooth functioning of political institutions, they do not explicitly discuss the normative content of legitimacy. Thus, Beetham's

(1991, 11) criticism of Weber, whom he accuses of ignoring the central element of legitimacy, i.e. the justification of relationships of power in terms of people's beliefs, applies to Luhmann's and, in alleviated form, to Easton's contributions as well. The relation between object and subject of legitimacy is misconstrued and the normative or critical potential of the concept abandoned if legitimacy is reduced to a function of the political system, which, as in Luhmann's case, the system itself might even provide for.

Normative conceptions of legitimation and legitimacy, in turn, focus on analysing and discussing the justification of asymmetric relations of rule beyond legal validity and understand legitimacy as an end in itself. In contrast to procedural conceptions (see below), substantive accounts ask for the qualitative norms constituting standards of legitimacy. Buchanan's proposition to understand 'at least the most basic human rights of all those over whom it [i.e. a wielder of political power, A.M.] wields power' (2002, 703), i.e. the respect of individual liberty and equality, as the core criterion of legitimacy, is a case in point. In addition and in accordance with the relational reading of legitimacy, which foregrounds the asymmetric relation between rulers and ruled, Beetham (1991, 77–89) points out that any normative justification of relations of rule has to include a normative account of a common interest, which recognises and encompasses the interests of rulers and ruled, and a principle of differentiation, which accounts for the difference between them. Buchanan's insistence on human rights norms serves as a notion of a common good. In contrast, charisma, tradition and bureaucratic hierarchy (see Weber), personal authority (see Easton) or meritocratic principles as expressed, e.g. by the institution of democratic elections (see Beetham 1991, 81–82) are examples of principles of difference. However, to be of value for a specific political order, abstract principles of difference and, even more so, notions of a general interest need to be specified.

This insight lies at the heart of procedural conceptions of legitimation. Prominently, Habermas conceptualises legitimacy as a political order's validity claim of being justifiable and worthy of recognition. It can be established if an order contributes to realising the fundamental moral and ethical beliefs of its society's members (Habermas 1976, 42–43). In order to be compatible with the idea of individual autonomy, this claim has to be specified and supported by good reasons in public discourses and to be recognised as valid by the members of a political order. 'At present, only those rules and conditions of communication which enable us to distinguish an agreement or accordance under free and equal agents from a contingent and forced consensus assume legitimating force.' (46, my translation) As a consequence, legitimacy is to be understood as only ever a temporarily valid result of these processes of legitimation, within which citizens examine, criticise or validate claims to legitimacy. In this sense, voiced consent (not a general belief in legitimacy) is indispensable because legitimacy as a quality of rule is in constant need of renewal or actualisation. At the same time, legitimate rule must provide for processes of legitimation, i.e. for opportunities to question and criticise it in order not to cut itself off from legitimation, but to allow for its renewal (Beetham 1991, 94–108).

These arguments would remain incomplete, however, without answers to the following questions: Who is bound by set norms and rules? Over whom is power wielded? Who is to have a share in the general interest? From whom are rulers different? And who actually is to participate in processes of legitimation? Answers are implied, but not specified above. While a political order may contribute to its own legitimacy insofar as it meets its ends and guarantees the existence and functioning of processes of legitimation conforming to the rule of law (e.g. Luhmann 1983), its legitimacy depends on the judgement of the subjects or subject of legitimacy. Thus, the subject of legitimacy forms not only the counterpart to political rule but also constitutes the foundation on which the construction of legitimate political rule relies.[4] Norms and processes of legitimation relate political rule to its subjects, or rather bind that rule to them. These subjects are meant to decide upon the legitimacy of the relationship themselves.[5] Thus, at present, it is mostly the people who constitute the internal but nonetheless authoritative source of political legitimacy. This position leaves room for different accounts of who 'the people' is meant to be. A nation, a homogeneous community or a heterogeneous, perhaps multicultural society (see e.g. Canovan 2008)? While already contested within the state, these questions pose major challenges beyond the state as they refer to the conditions of the possibility of legitimate relations of rule.

In sum, legitimacy designates a political order's validity claim of being justifiable and worthy of recognition in terms of socially shared norms (quality), which due to the underlying asymmetric relation between the object and the subject of legitimacy, between a system of rule competent to set binding norms on the one hand and the people or collective of individuals subject to it on the other, needs time and again to be scrutinised and temporarily to be re-approved or dismissed (process). It refers to norms and processes that express shared notions of a common interest or justify the difference between rulers and ruled, as well as to the processes of (re-)establishing or reforming these norms and this relationship time and again. Only legitimate rule allows for a constructive relationship between a people and a political system of rule in which the subjection of individual persons does not fundamentally contradict their equal autonomy. Legitimacy affects, as functional conceptions suggest, the stability and effectiveness of political rule, but legitimate rule can and must always provide for processes of reflection about and reform of decision-making processes. In other words, it has to allow for reflexive second-order decisions about itself (Habermas 1976, 43).

This conception of legitimacy is sufficiently abstract not to be bound to national or statist contexts. Norms and processes will remain points of contention in domestic discourses on legitimacy, which mostly take the subject and object of legitimacy for granted. Yet, once we take legitimacy to be a valid standard beyond the state as well, this perspective, which calls for a constructive relation between the different elements of legitimacy, between norms and processes as well as subjects and objects, raises further challenges to be faced academically as well as politically.

3. Legitimacy debates under transnational conditions

In order to recognise the contentious issues at stake in the varied debates on transnational legitimacy, to understand the interrelation of the different questions and to comprehend the underlying changes and challenges that we are to confront, I will now sketch how selected political as well as academic debates relate to the four elements of the relational conception of legitimacy. I argue that debates on norms and processes beyond the state imply uncertainties, if not struggles about the subject and its relation to the object of legitimacy. Making explicit and discussing who the subject of legitimacy is and how its relation to its object should be understood pose one of the main conceptual challenges we have to confront when debating legitimacy transnationally. In addition, we have to find ways to constitute subjects of legitimation legitimately. While both challenges call for broadening and deepening our understanding of legitimate political orders as well as legitimate second-order decisions, constituting subjects of legitimation, in particular, represent a structurally new and meta-jurisdictional task for thinking about the legitimacy of political orders under transnational conditions.

3.1. *Norms, processes and implicitly contested subjects of legitimacy*

Mass demonstrations worldwide as well as at G7, G20, WTO, UN or EU summits, often directed against free trade agreements, military interventions or refugee and migration politics as well as against the modes of decision-making pursued beyond the state, all subject inter-, trans- or supranational politics to political and academic scrutiny.[6] More precisely, both (1) norms and (2) processes of legitimacy are subject to debate. In the following paragraphs, each will be discussed in turn.

(1) Demonstrations against the UN-sanctioned intervention in Libya in the spring of 2011 show that humanitarian interventions and the developing norm of a 'Responsibility to Protect' (R2P) face public opposition. Protests against the situation of refugees in Europe and worldwide illustrate that the standards and norms of refugee and migration politics are subject to fierce political debate. Some of the most pertinent and pervasive conflicts arise when the protection or promotion of human rights clashes with norms of state sovereignty. Simultaneously, especially during the Eurozone crisis, which began in 2008, debates about the possibility of redistributive politics and, thus, of solidarity across different states and among their citizens tend to proliferate. In all of these cases, it is contested which norms we believe should transcend boundaries and are valuable and valid not only in but also beyond, the state. Theoretical debates reflect these disputes as discussions about the validity and scope of human rights are complemented by disputes about the relation between human and citizens' rights, or between human rights and national sovereignty. A prominent way of framing these debates is the opposition of cosmopolitan positions and communitarian or liberal nationalist arguments. While the former consider individual and border-transcending human rights as primary, the latter defend the integrity of cultural, social or political communities. Thus, communitarians find fault with cosmopolitans' renunciation of or disregard for (pre-)political communities or identities, while cosmopolitans complain about communitarians' tendency to essentialise political communities.[7] As a consequence, the disputes about guiding principles result from disagreements about which collectivity to consider as primary when norms are contested – the community of humankind or particular (pre-)political communities. As still others find fault with what they consider to be increasing depoliticisation of important political decisions, i.e. the fact that abstract norms tend to serve as guiding principles for reflexivising political orders without recourse to political decision-making (Mouffe 2005; Held and Patomäki 2006), the question for the relevant agents becomes even more pressing.

Translated into the logic of legitimacy developed above, several aspects are worth discussing. As important guiding principles of inter- and transnational politics are contested, political and academic contributions struggle to develop theoretical justifica-tions for different understandings of a 'general interest'. Against this background, critics ask who is to decide on the validity of norms and ends of international, transnational or global governance and call for political processes of will-formation and decision-making about precisely these general guiding principles. Defining a fundamental and abstract 'general interest' does not substitute for processes of political decision-making (see (2)). Moreover, the fundamental point of contention in disputes about different norms and their relationship are not the norms themselves, but who is to share the general interest and to constitute the relevant community: all human beings equally or members of a specific political community (as concerns human rights politics), European citizens in general or citizens of a member state (as concerns solidarity and redistribution in Europe)? These considerations point not only towards processes of decision-making but also pose the question of the subject of legitimacy as well as of the underlying asymmetric relations of rule.

(2) Protests against WTO, IMF or G7 negotiations and free trade agreements have persisted for a long time – not just since the violent demonstrations in Seattle in 1999. Protestors criticise not only the norms but also the rules and modes of decision-making within these organisations. Analyses of the relative standing of weak states figure prominently alongside debates on transparency and the role of NGOs. In the context of debates on the EU's democratic deficit, the rules of decision-making within the Council, the role of the Parliament and the influence of the so-called comitology, i.e. a series of committees influencing the making, adoption and implementation of EU laws, have been widely debated. In addition, academic contributions discuss the role of deliberation and the modes of arguing and bargaining in international and transnational negotiations (e.g. Risse 2000; Deitelhoff and Müller 2005).

At first glance, these debates about how questions are discussed and decisions made, i.e. about procedural aspects of legitimacy, highlight existing asymmetries of power. However, the focus on interstate compromise and consensus as well as on deliberative modes of will-formation correlates, again, with a focus on reflection and on developing generalizable interests. Asymmetries of power tend to be subject to debate insofar as they interfere with fair processes of decision-making. The question arises whether attempts to overcome asymmetries within decision-making processes are meant to overcome structures of rule beyond the state in general. If they do, the call for transna-tional legitimacy is misled. If, however, enduring institutional structures are perceived as structures of rule, asking for a general interest is only one part of the equation and additional questions impose themselves. As far as norms are concerned, defining a common general interest would need to be complemented by a principle of difference in order to explain the characteristics of the asymmetric relation between the rulers and ruled in question. In terms of processes, questions concern the assignment or election of officials and the consensual or majoritarian modes of decision-making. The difficulty of filling this void illustrates that, beyond the state, the relation between the subject and object of legitimacy is blurred. Who is to participate and to decide? Are states or individuals the relevant actors? Who forms the constituency of which structure of rule? Thus, who are the relevant subjects of legitimacy and in what relationship do the subject and object of legitimacy stand? Debates about norms and processes of legitimation beyond the state cannot answer these questions on their own. As, however, the different contributions always denote states, groups or individuals as relevant agents, they offer insights into the major cleavages in debates on the subjects of legitimacy (see 3.2.).

In sum, transnational debates on norms and processes of legitimacy exhibit major uncertainties or disagreements concerning the subject and its relation to the object of legitimacy. The fundamental importance of these issues needs to be further appreciated. Though convincing conceptions of legitimacy successfully relate all four elements to each other, questions for its subject and object are logically prior, i.e. conceptions of norms and processes contingent on what we take the subject–object relation to be. Thus, developing systematic approaches on these issues is the major conceptual challenge we have to face when debating legitimacy transnationally and a precondition for developing convincing conceptions of legitimacy under conditions of globalisation.

3.2. *The jurisdictional challenge: explicating subject and object of legitimacy*

Conflicts about who the legitimate actors are to decide beyond the state have arisen in different contexts. Civil society actors criticise not only structural discrimination against small or weak states in the WTO, IMF or G7 but also the exclusion of minority groups and other non-state actors, especially indigenous people.[8] Thus, they attack the underlying understanding of the relevant subject of legitimacy. At the same time, nationalist movements counter cosmopolitan pleas for a different political order by national or nationalist reassertions of the territorial state as the sole legitimate institution wielding power within as well as beyond the state. Lastly, as concerns the EU context more specifically, the interplay of state representatives in the EU Council and directly elected members of the European Parliament causes debates about their relation and comparative powers, and thereby about the relative standing of states and citizens of the EU. The relation between states and individual citizens is, then, one major focus of theoretical debates. As governance mechanisms assume more influence as well as independence from state consensus, potential asymmetries between institutions and ultimately individual actors expose the statist view – the idea that states are the legitimate representatives of their peoples beyond the state – to questions and ground calls for additional and different mechanisms of legitimation. The conceptual challenge of how to define the subject arises again (Habermas 2008, 2012; Scharpf 2012). Steffek's call not only to acknowledge the link between governments and international institutions but also to include citizens' beliefs into the equation is a case in point (2007, 186–190). Yet, the varied positions on possible subjects of legitimacy held domestically translate into a variety of different questions transnationally: What characteristics must a subject of legitimacy have? Should states act as legitimating subjects? Can NGOs or minority group representatives function as subject of legitimacy? How do individual and collective actors relate to each other?

The relational conception of legitimacy, however, makes us recognise that thinking about a subject of legitimation in isolation can only take us so far. Answers to the subject question always have to bear in mind the object and the asymmetric relation between the subject and the object of legitimacy as well. On one hand, a further look at what are considered to be the relevant systems of rule in need of legitimation becomes necessary. While a change in the objects of legitimacy through a proliferation of governance institutions, is often taken as a given point of departure in discussions about legitimacy beyond the state, the character of mechanisms of governance and the question of whether they should be considered as systems of rule in the classical sense is still contested (e.g. Nagel 2005). Thus, it is necessary to develop a better understanding of what causes different mechanisms of governance to be in need of particular kinds of legitimation. On the other hand, as our conceptions of subjects and objects of legitimacy are changing, it becomes more and more urgent to recognise how they are related to each other. Only based on systematic accounts of these asymmetric relations, i.e. on complete images of the jurisdiction, can we specify and judge which norms and processes we take as valid with regard to specific objects and subjects. Finally, we need to keep in mind the interrelation and respective dependence of subject and object, as well as norms and processes of legitimacy. While the discussions we witness start from any of the four elements of legitimacy discussed here, all of them, norms and processes, subject and object have to be rendered explicit if the legitimacy of a jurisdiction is to be evaluated.

In the case of the EU, e.g. it needs to be specified which institutions are to be considered as objects of legitimacy due to their asymmetric relationship with states and/or citizens and who is to assume the role of the relevant subjects. To date, the EU solution to combine a statist chain of legitimation of the EU Council with directly elected parliamentary representatives of the citizenry can be understood as the furthest developed, yet in no way uncontroversial attempt to recognise, value and balance the different potential subjects of legitimacy or the different roles citizens assume in a multi-level order (Habermas 2012). Norms and processes have to fit this frame. Against the background of the asymmetric subject–object relation of rule, it becomes possible to discuss, e.g. whether the principle of solidarity between individual citizens is valid not only on the state level but on the European level as well and whether it is to justify redistributive EU politics (norms), or which procedures of will-formation and decision-making are to apply in the Council or the Parliament, as well as in EU-wide decisions and European Parliament election (processes).

At the same time, the EU example illustrates that the continued importance of states and the simultaneous proliferation of mechanisms of governance beyond the state make it necessary to ask how a pluralisation and fragmentation of rule as well as the differentiation within and pluralisation of its subjects do affect the fundamental relations of legitimacy. How do the conceptions of legitimation of different jurisdictions, of possibly plural objects and their subjects, as well as the corresponding norms and processes, relate to and influence each other in a potentially multi-level system of governance (see e.g. Hurrelmann 2006)? Thus, we have to face the boundaries of and interrelations between different jurisdictions. At this point, a structurally different, meta-jurisdictional challenge ensues.

3.3. *The meta-jurisdictional challenge: determining the subject of legitimacy*

Parallel to the increased interdependence of states, the proliferation of governance mechanisms and the potential pluralisation of subject–object relations of legitimacy transnational migration have brought up questions of boundaries, more specifically about immigration and free movement, integration and naturalisation policies.

Thereby, it has triggered normative questions about who has legitimate claims to be or become member of a society or *demos* (Carens 2005; Bauböck 2005, 2007; Benhabib 2004, 2011; Owen 2011). Theoretical discussions about principles of affectedness or subjectedness reflect these questions (Goodin 2007; Owen 2012). These debates show that questions of how to determine the subject of legitimacy, or rather its boundaries, whom to include in the subject and whom to exclude from it constitute yet another challenge. Due to increasing migration and interdependence between jurisdictions, those affected by a decision might not be able to participate in it; those subjected to a political order might not be the ones to partake of its legitimation.

Against this background, Fraser (2008, 14–6, 85–92) questions the so-called Westphalian frame, i.e. the international system of sovereign territorial nation-states, and aims at (re-)introducing the frame of the political order into the academic and political debates:

> Today [...] arguments about justice assume a double guise. On the one hand, they concern first-order questions of substance, just as before. [...] But above and beyond such first-order questions, arguments about justice today also concern second-order, meta-level questions. What is the proper frame within which to consider first-order questions of justice? Who are the relevant subjects entitled to a just distribution or reciprocal recognition in the given case? (Fraser 2008, 15)

Any determination of the subject implies decisions about whom to include and whom to exclude from participation in processes of legitimation and thus causes asymmetric relations between citizens and non-citizens. Consequently, the subject of legitimacy, or more precisely its constitution and boundaries form the centre of another conceptual and normative challenge we have to face when debating legitimacy transnationally. The subject as well as the contingent subject–object relation do not only need to be re-introduced into the discourse but also – on a meta-level – to be considered as an object of legitimacy itself.

It is misleading to approach this normative challenge as one of a different dimension or kind of legitimacy, as conceptions of 'horizontal legitimacy' suggest. According to Schmelzle (2007, 173–179), horizontal legitimacy refers to the social basis of a political association, to the interrelations between the members of the ruled collectivity and to its boundaries and principles of integration. Chwaszcza (2012, 86–87) discusses which kinds of relations between citizens as members of a people let them accept majority rule and, thus, form preconditions of democratic rule beyond the state as well. Both of these accounts contribute to the discussion by explicitly introducing the question of the subject into the debate and by emphasising the importance of relations between citizens as a necessary complement to the relations between a system of political rule and the people or collective of citizens. At the same time, both focus on given political communities and on their internal structure without questioning their external boundaries. Only the external boundaries, however, constitute a potentially stable asymmetric relation between citizens and non-citizens. Additionally, the mere possibility of stable asymmetric relations, which lies at the heart of calls for legitimacy, is precluded by the very term 'horizontal legitimacy'. Conceptions of horizontal legitimacy therefore miss the challenge the subject's legitimacy poses.

In order to meet this challenge, it is necessary to introduce a change of perspective, which helps to systematically differentiate jurisdictional and meta-jurisdictional questions. Asking about the 'legitimacy of the people', as Näsström (2007) does, provides a more productive approach, in line with the insight that boundaries between orders constitute an asymmetric relation between inside and outside, included and excluded, in need of legitimation – if the latter is perceived and recognised as a mechanism of rule.[9] It is Fraser, again, who develops an approach to handle this challenge. In her terminology, the question of the frame, as a 'second-order, meta-level question' (2008, 15), needs to be answered on a third level of frame setting:

> [We] can discern a third-order species of political injustice, which corresponds to the question of the 'how.' Exemplified by undemocratic processes of frame-setting, this injustice consists in the failure to institutionalize parity of participation at the meta-political level, in deliberations and decisions concerning the 'who.' (2008, 26)

Fraser calls for the criticism of unjust boundaries and for debates on how to legitimately decide about the frame or subject of justice. In terms of the argument made here, discussing the legitimacy of the subject means to recognise the potentially profound asymmetry between citizens and non-citizens. In order to account for this, the legitimating subject itself is to be considered as the object to be legitimised. A higher order question ensues and the configuration of object and subject, norms and processes changes. This, I understand, is the basic insight provided by Fraser.

However, in line with the relational concept of legitimacy developed so far, which prohibits a sole focus on the subject but foregrounds the relation between subject and object (as the 'frame' of legitimacy) as well as norms and processes, I would like to propose a different denomination of the questions we face when debating legitimacy transnationally.[10] I suggest to understand traditional questions of legitimacy, which Schmelzle (2012, 420, 431–432) classified as second-order questions, as jurisdictional and the questions concerning the legitimacy of the frame as meta-jurisdictional[11] questions. On the meta level, Fraser's notion of the 'who' of justice (broadened to encompass the subject in its relation to the object of legitimacy) turns into the object to be legitimised. Fraser's question of the 'how', in turn, refers to processes necessary to develop a generalizable interest and to account for the asymmetric relation constituted by the boundaries under scrutiny. The principles of affectedness or subjectedness can be understood as propositions concerning the norms to be applied. Thus, the two-level distinction offers a structured account of the challenges we face.

Yet once more, one question remains open. Who is to decide? Who is the subject of legitimacy in case of meta-jurisdictional decisions? At this point, Fraser (2008, 40–43) acknowledges a potential circularity in the argument and proposes a critical-democratic approach, which envisions a continuing process of constituting and re-constituting the 'who' of justice over time. Thereby, she proceduralises the underlying paradox, which is known in democratic theory as the boundary problem: the paradox of legitimately determining the scope and boundaries of a *demos*. Democratic decisions on the *demos* are logically not possible prior to the constitution of a *demos* (Näsström 2007, 641). 'Democracy can be practiced for making collective decisions once the collectivity has been defined, but democratic methods themselves are inadequate to establish the bounds of the collectivity, whose existence democratic theory simply presupposes.'

(Whelan 1983, 22) What matters most, at this point, is pointed out by Näsström. She calls for recognizing the fundamental democratic contingency of boundaries and embraces the inevitable gap in the constitution of the people as 'productive, a generative device that helps to foster ever new claims for legitimacy' (Näsström 2007, 626, see also 632, 642–646). However, one approaches this democratic paradox, there will always continue to exist a gap in the legitimacy of any jurisdiction concerning its frame. It is this gap that causes the additional meta-jurisdictional challenges we face when debating legitimacy transnationally – because it is under transnational conditions that it is rendered remarkably visible.

4. Conclusion: debating legitimacy transnationally by means of the relational conception of legitimacy

Approaching the debates on transnational legitimacy from the point of view and with the help of an analytical conception of legitimacy, I have shown how the various debates we witness relate to all four elements constituting legitimate relations of rule, not only to norms and processes but also to the subject and object of legitimacy. Developing new and weaker understandings of legitimacy does not provide an adequate answer to these challenges. Instead, taking seriously a relational conception of legitimacy as the conceptual core of twentieth century theoretical thinking about legitimacy not only enables us to structure the debates we witness. It also allows us to better understand their interrelations as well as the additional challenges faced not only by international democratic theory but also by any attempts to debate legitimacy transnationally.

First, the subject and object of legitimacy, and most importantly their interrelation, need to be discussed explicitly in each case. Persuasive and context-sensitive accounts of legitimacy have to consider the asymmetric relation between subject and object *as well as* to develop normative and procedural conceptions of shared interests and explanations of the difference between rulers and ruled, which render this relationship productive. It makes a difference what we take the object and whom we take the subject of legitimacy to be – territorial states or functional governance mechanism, states, individuals or groups. The fact that the justification of asymmetric relations of rule often forms a void in debates about legitimacy beyond the state not only indicates that the necessity of the standard of legitimacy itself is contested. It also underlines that the awareness of asymmetric relations of rule as the core concern of the notion of legitimacy and its fundamentally relational character have yet to be explicated in many debates about legitimacy beyond the state.

Second, determining the frame of legitimate rule legitimately constitutes a meta-jurisdictional challenge, which is rendered visible under transnational conditions and imposes itself in theory and practice. Introducing alternative notions or dimensions of legitimacy into the discourse neither solves this problem nor does justice to the concept of legitimacy itself. Instead, reverting to the relational logic of legitimacy is advisable at the meta-level as well. Thus, the meta-jurisdictional challenge necessitates a change in perspective, a step back from or out of traditional debates, which enables us to perceive an additional, meta-jurisdictional, constellation of elements of legitimacy. It is still to be decided whether meta-jurisdictional questions call for the same or different norms and processes of legitimation as jurisdictional questions of legitimacy. However, whatever answers we hold to be valid to meta-jurisdictional questions, whatever we take to constitute the asymmetric relations we want to justify, the basic structure of accounts of legitimacy remains the same. The relational conception provides a theoretical grasp on both, the jurisdictional as well as the meta-jurisdictional challenge of debating legitimacy transnationally.

Both challenges call for deepening our understanding of legitimate political orders, not only of the validity of norms and possible processes beyond the state but also of the objects and above all subjects of legitimacy. Consequently, a series of questions come up which future research will have to answer: How do different contexts and conditions influence the standards of legitimacy that mechanisms of rule have to meet? Which kinds or degrees of legitimacy are relevant or necessary in different contexts? To which norms and processes do different relations of governance and rule correspond? Do the same norms and processes apply to higher order as well as to first-order questions? Who forms, or might form, legitimate subjects of legitimacy beyond the state? What consequences does a pluralisation of subject–object relations have and how do the standards of legitimacy of partial orders or different levels relate to each other as well as to the legitimacy of the political order in its entirety?

Finally, while the perspective offered in this article hopefully provides a theoretical perspective that proves fruitful when debating legitimacy transnationally and examples that resonate not only in the European context, it relies mainly on American and European contributions. However, a more genuinely transnational debate is necessary. Non-Western and extra-European perspectives and voices need to be part of the debates as indispensable interlocutors. This becomes even more urgent if we keep in mind that legitimacy is never only an analytical category. Within as well as beyond the state, it always also implies a political statement for or against a specific political order by means of which scientists, theorists or philosophers themselves actively participate in a political discourse about legitimacy (Mulligan 2007, 75).

Notes

1. See Zürn, Binder, and Ecker-Ehrhardt (2012) as well as De Wilde and Michael (2012) for processes of politicisation and Hurrelmann, Schneider, and Steffek (2007); Forst and Schmalz-Bruns (2011), or Meine (2012) for the upsurge of literature on legitimacy.
2. Fundamentally, Dahl (1999) and Miller (2010) contradict the possibility of democracy beyond the state, while e.g. Schmalz-Bruns and Forst (2011, 2–3) observe that the possibilities of democratic legitimation beyond the state are uncertain. According to Clark (2007), any analogy between domestic and inter- or transnational politics is precluded because the different logics of international and world society confront each other beyond the state without there being a clear hierarchy yet.
3. See e.g. Breitmeier (2008) on environmental governance, Huckel Schneider (2015) on global health governance and Steffek and Hahn (2010) on transnational NGOs.
4. This is one of the main reasons why a relational conception of legitimacy points towards conceptions of *democratic* legitimacy (see e.g. Beetham 1991, 89, 135; Buchanan 2002: 718–719). Other readings can be defended; weaker criteria like those of the acceptance of human rights, transparency or accountability can be integrated into the relational conception. For the sake of the argument presented here, I accept this broader perspective. Yet, as democratic legitimacy is unequivocally based on the assumption that source and end of

the political order is the people or group of individuals who collectively organise their lives according to a set of shared normative beliefs and processes of will-formation and decision-making, the influence of democratic theory on the conception of legitimacy, as well as on the argument presented here can and should not be denied.

5. Following this argument, Scharpf's distinction between input-oriented and output-oriented legitimacy, which is especially popular in the European context, and even more so, the increasing isolation of arguments of problem solving and efficacy as the basis of legitimacy have to be critically assessed (Scharpf 2010, 2012). Not only is output legitimacy to include notions of a common good (Steffek 2012) but also by itself, it cannot comply with a relational conception of legitimacy. It tends to reduce the constructive relationship between the subject and object of legitimacy to a pure provision of output by the object of legitimacy. A political order, however, is only legitimate if it provides for mechanisms, which relate its output to the input provided by the subjects themselves (Kraus 2004; Schmelzle 2007; Meine 2012, 62–66).

6. To a large extent, the following discussion focusses on examples from international organisations and in particular, the European Union. The latter is the institution which, to date, has developed more supranational features than any other trans- or supranational institution and which exhibits many of the issues under debate most explicitly. Thus, the discussion reflects the focal points of many of the major contributions to debates on transnational justice or democracy (e.g. Habermas 2012; Pogge 2008). Post-colonial contributions invigorate these critical discussions, but they also rightly disclose the limited character of this focus (Dhawan 2012).

7. See e.g. Habermas (1998); Pogge (2008); Held (2010); Benhabib (2011) and Miller (2012) on human rights and their relation to and national sovereignty or responsibility, and e.g. Brock (2013) on the debate between cosmopolitans and communitarians.

8. For a post-colonial and more far-reaching approach to the question of the subjects of legitimacy not only in but also beyond the state, see again e.g. Dhawan (2012).

9. Abizadeh (2008; 2010) and Miller (2010) disagree about whether boundary regimes are to be considered as systems of rule and whether the excluded are to be included in decisions on these boundaries.

10. In Fraser's terms, ordinary representation as well as redistribution and recognition constitute first-order issues of justice, while the question about the 'who' of justice forms a second-order (or meta-political) and the question about the 'how' a third-order (or meta-meta-political) question of justice (Fraser 2008, 15–21, 31–37). Unfortunately, this account blurs the distinction between orders. Firstly, even the question of ordinary representation already constitutes a higher order issue than questions of redistribution and recognition for which it sets the frame (Olson 2008). Secondly, the questions of 'how' and 'who' do not constitute questions of different orders, but together form one order of questions – just as any one constellation of subject, object, norms and processes does.

11. The notion of meta-jurisdictional issues is taken from the debate on territorial rights. Buchanan defines meta-jurisdictional authority as 'the right to create or alter jurisdictions' (2003, 233). Stilz pursues this idea further: 'Metajurisdictional powers are powers over powers: They confer authority on certain agents to decide who has powers to make primary rules over which pieces of territory' (2009, 196).

References

Abizadeh, A. 2008. "Democratic Theory and Border Coercion: No Right to Unilaterally Control Your Own Borders." *Political Theory* 36 (1): 37–65. doi:10.1177/0090591707310090.

Abizadeh, A. 2010. "Democratic Legitimacy and State Coercion: A Reply to David Miller." *Political Theory* 38 (1): 121–130. doi:10.1177/0090591709348192.

Bauböck, R. 2005. "Expansive Citizenship: Voting beyond Territory and Membership." *PS: Political Science and Politics* XXXVIII (4): 683–687.

Bauböck, R. 2007. "Stakeholder Citizenship and Transnational Political Participation: A Normative Evaluation of External Voting." *Fordham Law Review* 75 (5): 2393–2447.

Beetham, D. 1991. *The Legitimation of Power*. Basingstoke: Macmillan.

Benhabib, S. 2004. *The Rights of Others: Aliens, Residents and Citizens*. Cambridge: Cambridge University Press.

Benhabib, S. 2011. *Dignity in Adversity: Human Rights in Troubled Times*. Cambridge: Polity.

Breitmeier, H. 2008. *The Legitimacy of International Regimes*. Farnham: Ashgate.

Brock, G., ed. 2013. *Cosmopolitanism versus Non-Cosmopolitanism. Critiques, Defenses, Reconceptualizations*. Oxford: Oxford University Press.

Buchanan, A. 2002. "Political Legitimacy and Democracy." *Ethics* 112: 689–719. doi:10.1086/340313.

Buchanan, A. 2003. "The Making and Unmaking of Boundaries: What Liberalism Has to Say." In *States, Nations, and Borders: The Ethics of Making Boundaries*, edited by A. Buchanan and M. Margaret, 231–261. Cambridge: Cambridge University Press.

Buchanan, A., and R. O. Keohane. 2006. "The Legitimacy of Global Governance Institutions." *Ethics and International Affairs* 20 (4): 405–437.

Canovan, M. 2008. "The People." In *The Oxford Handbook of Political Theory*, edited by J. S. Dryzek, B. Honig, and P. Anne, 349–362. Oxford: Oxford University Press.

Carens, J. H. 2005. "The Integration of Immigrants." *Journal of Moral Philosophy* 2 (1): 29–46. doi:10.1177/1740468105052582.

Chwaszcza, C. 2012. "The Practical Conditions of the Sovereignty of the People: The Status of Citizens in Multilevel Political Organisations." In *Territories of Citizenship*, edited by L. Beckman and E. Erman, 81–100. Basingstoke: Palgrave Macmillan.

Clark, I. 2007. "Legitimacy in International or World Society?" In *Legitimacy in an Age of Global Politics*, edited by A. Hurrelmann, S. Schneider, and J. Steffek, 193–210. Basingstoke: Palgrave Macmillan.

Dahl, R. A. 1999. "Can International Organizations be Democratic: A Skeptic's View." In *Democracy's Edges*, edited by I. Shapiro and H.-C. Casiano, 19–40. London: Cambridge University Press.

De Wilde, P., and Z. Michael. 2012. "Can the Politicization of European Integration be Reversed?" *Journal of Common Market Studies* 50 (S1): 137–153. doi:10.1111/j.1468-5965.2011.02232.x.

Deitelhoff, N., and H. Müller. 2005. "Theoretical Paradise – Empirically Lost? Arguing with Habermas." *Review of International Studies* 31 (01): 167–179. doi:10.1017/S0260210505006364.

Dhawan, N. 2012. "Transnational Justice, Counterpublic Spheres and Alter-Globalization." *Localities* 2: 79–116.

Easton, D. 1965. *A Systems Analysis of Political Life*. New York: Wiley.

Forst, R., and R. Schmalz-Bruns, eds. 2011. *Political Legitimacy and Democracy in Transnational Perspective. ARENA Report Series 2/11*. Oslo.

Fraser, N. 2008. *Scales of Justice. Reimagining Political Space in a Globalizing World*. Cambridge: Polity.

Goodin, R. E. 2007. "Enfranchising All Affected Interests, and Its Alternatives." *Philosophy & Public Affairs* 35 (1): 40–68. doi:10.1111/j.1088-4963.2007.00098.x.

Habermas, J. 1976. "Legitimationsprobleme Im Modernen Staat." In *Legitimationsprobleme Politischer Systeme*, edited by P. G. Kielmansegg, 39–61. Opladen: Westdeutscher Verlag.

Habermas, J. 1998. "Remarks on Legitimation Through Human Rights." *Philosophy & Social Criticism* 24 (2–3): 157–171. doi:10.1177/019145379802400211.

Habermas, J. 2008. "The Constitutionalization of International Law and the Legitimation Problems of a Constitution for World Society." *Constellations* 15 (4): 444–455. doi:10.1111/cons.2008.15.issue-4.

Habermas, J. 2012. *The Crisis of the European Union: A Response*. Cambridge, UK: Polity.

Held, D. 2010. *Cosmopolitanism: Ideals and Realities*. Cambridge: Polity.

Held, D., and H. Patomäki. 2006. "Problems of Global Democracy: A Dialogue." *Theory, Culture & Society* 23 (5): 115–133. doi:10.1177/0263276406067102.

Huckel Schneider, C. 2015. *The Legitimacy of Global Health Governance: Forces and Receptions of Change.* London: Routledge.

Hurrelmann, A. 2006. "Multi-Level Legitimacy: Conceptualizing Legitimacy Relationships between the EU and National Democracies." TranState Working Papers 41. Accessed March 5. http://www.econstor.eu/bitstream/10419/24954/1/514659483.PDF

Hurrelmann, A., S. Schneider, and J. Steffek. 2007. "Introduction: Legitimacy in an Age of Global Politics." In *Legitimacy in an Age of Global Politics*, edited by A. Hurrelmann, S. Schneider, and J. Steffek, 1–16. Basingstoke: Palgrave Macmillan.

Kraus, P. A. 2004. "Die Begründung Demokratischer Politik in Europa: Zur Unterscheidung Von Input- Und Output-Legitimation Bei Fritz W. Scharpf." *Leviathan* 32 (4): 558–567. doi:10.1007/s11578-004-0036-2.

Luhmann, N. 1983. *Legitimation Durch Verfahren.* Frankfurt am Main: Suhrkamp.

Meine, A. 2012. *Legitimität Weiter Denken? Anschlussmöglichkeiten Und Herausforderungen Des Politikwissenschaftlichen Legitimitätsbegriffs Jenseits Des Staates.* Würzburg: Ergon.

Miller, D. 2012. *National Responsibility and Global Justice.* Oxford: Oxford University Press.

Miller, D. 2010. "Against Global Democracy." In *After the Nation? Critical Reflections on Nationalism and Postnationalism*, edited by K. Breen, and S. O'Neill, 141–160. Basingstoke: Palgrave Macmillan.

Mouffe, C. 2005. *On the Political.* London, New York: Routledge.

Mulligan, S. 2007. "Legitimacy and the Practice of Political Judgement." In *Legitimacy in an Age of Global Politics*, edited by A. Hurrelmann, S. Schneider, and J. Steffek, 75–89. Basingstoke: Palgrave Macmillan.

Nagel, T. 2005. "The Problem of Global Justice." *Philosophy & Public Affairs* 33 (2): 113–147. doi:10.1111/j.1088-4963.2005.00027.x.

Näsström, S. 2007. "The Legitimacy of the People." *Political Theory* 35 (5): 624–658. doi:10.1177/0090591707304951.

Olson, K. 2008. "Participatory Parity and Democratic Justice." In *Adding Insult to Injury. Nancy Fraser Debates her Critics*, edited by K. Olson, 246–272. London: Verso.

Owen, D. 2011. "Transnational Citizenship and the Democratic State. Modes of Membership and Voting Rights." *Critical Review of International Social and Political Philosophy* 14 (5): 641–663. doi:10.1080/13698230.2011.617123.

Owen, D. 2012. "Constituting the Polity, Constituting the *Demos*: On the Place of the All Affected Interests Principle in Democratic Theory and in Resolving the Democratic Boundary Problem." *Ethics & Global Politics* 5 (3): 120–152. doi:10.3402/egp.v5i3.18617.

Peter, F. 2014. "Political Legitimacy." In *The Stanford Encyclopedia of Philosophy*, edited by E. N. Zalta. Accessed March 5. http://plato.stanford.edu/archives/win2014/entries/legitimacy/

Pogge, T. W. M. 2008. *World Poverty and Human Rights.* Cambridge: Polity.

Risse, T. 2000. "'Let's Argue!': Communicative Action in World Politics." *International Organization* 54 (1): 1–39. doi:10.1162/002081800551109.

Scharpf, F. W. 2010. *Community and Autonomy. Institutions, Policies and Legitimacy in Multilevel Europe.* Frankfurt a.M.: Campus.

Scharpf, F. W. 2012. "Legitimacy Intermediation in the Multilevel European Polity and Its Collapse in the Euro Crisis." MPIfG Discussion Paper 12/6. Accessed March 5. http://www.econstor.eu/bitstream/10419/66580/1/729524698.pdf

Schmalz-Bruns, R., and R. Forst. 2011. "Introduction: The EU as a Legitimate Polity?" In *Political Legitimacy and Democracy in Transnational Perspective*, edited by R. Forst and R. Schmalz-Bruns, 1–10. Oslo: Arena.

Schmelzle, C. 2007. "Governance Und Legitimität." In *Transdisziplinäre Governanceforschung: Gemeinsam Hinter Den Staat Blicken*, edited by S. De La Rosa, U. Höppner, and K. Matthias, 162–186. Baden-Baden: Nomos.

Schmelzle, C. 2012. "Zum Begriff Politischer Legitimität." In *Der Aufstieg Der Legitimitätspolitik: Rechtfertigung Und Kritik Politisch-Ökonomischer Ordnungen*, edited by A. Geis, F. Nullmeier, and D. Christopher, 419–435. Baden-Baden: Nomos.

Steffek, J. 2007. "Legitimacy in International Relations: From State Compliance to Citizen Consensus." In *Legitimacy in an Age of Global Politics*, edited by A. Hurrelmann, S. Schneider, and J. Steffek, 175–192. Basingstoke: Palgrave Macmillan.

Steffek, J. 2012. "Accountability Und Politische Öffentlichkeit Im Zeitalter Des Globalen Regierens." In *Transnationale Gerechtigkeit Und Demokratie*, edited by P. Niesen, 279–310. Frankfurt am Main: Campus.

Steffek, J., and K. Hahn, eds. 2010. *Evaluating Transnational NGOs: Legitimacy, Accountability, Representation*. Basingstoke: Palgrave Macmillan.

Stilz, A. 2009. "Why do States Have Territorial Rights?" *International Theory* 1 (2): 185–213. doi:10.1017/S1752971909000104.

Weber, M. 2004. "The Three Pure Types of Legitimate Rule." In *The Essential Weber. A Reader*, edited by S. Whimster, 133–145. London, New York: Routledge.

Weber, M. 1978. *Economy and Society. An Outline of Interpretive Sociology*. eds. G. Roth and C. Wittich, Berkeley: University of California Press.

Whelan, F. G. 1983. "Prologue: Democratic Theory and the Boundary Problem." In *Liberal Democracy*, edited by J. R. Pennock and J. W. Chapman, 13–47. New York: New York University Press.

Zürn, M., M. Binder, and M. Ecker-Ehrhardt. 2012. "International Authority and Its Politicization." *International Theory* 4 (01): 69–106. doi:10.1017/S1752971912000012.

REPLY

Legitimacy and the shadows of universalism: a response to Meine's 'Debating legitimacy transnationally'

Jessica Whyte

This is a reply to:

Meine, Anna. 2016. "Debating legitimacy transnationally." *Global Discourse* 6 (3): 330–346. http://dx.doi.org/10.1080/23269995.2016.1175084.

In a recent article on the Universal Declaration of Human Rights, Lydia Liu uses the phrase 'shadows of universalism' to refer to the civilizational narratives that shadowed the politics of universalism in the 1940s. Attending to these shadows, Liu argues, may enable us to grasp the discursive structure of human rights in recent history, and to move that discourse in a less parochial direction (Liu 2014, 390). Liu's remarks have relevance not only for human rights but also for broader questions of transnational legitimacy, like those raised by Anna Meine in 'Debating Legitimacy Transnationally.'

Meine's paper seeks to contribute to theorizations of transnational legitimacy by rethinking a relational account of legitimacy beyond the nation-state. In this context, political legitimacy concerns the underlying asymmetries of power between authoritative institutions and those affected by them, and Meine foregrounds the asymmetrical relations between ruler and ruled, or between objects and subjects of legitimacy. While questions of the subjects and objects of national legitimacy are never as simple as the supposed unity of nation and state would imply, Meine suggests that at the transnational level, things become more complicated, as both the subjects and the objects of legitimacy are unstable and open to contestation. As Meine argues convincingly, it 'makes a difference what we take the object and whom we take the subject of legitimacy to be'. 'Who is to participate and to decide?,' she asks. 'Are states or individuals the relevant actors? Who forms the constituency of which structure of rule?' Whatever answers we provide, Meine argues, will be faced with a 'meta-jurisdictional challenge'; that is, the decision that certain subjects are the relevant actors will require legitimation in turn.

These considerations are important for any attempt to think through the questionable legitimacy of contemporary forms of transnational governance, whether that of International Financial Institutions, United Nations or European Union asylum regimes, or transnational military interventions, to borrow Meine's examples. Today, proliferating transnational institutions and organizations arguably make these concerns more urgent than ever. Nonetheless, transnational economic and political governance has a long history, central to which is the history of Western colonialism and the proliferation of trading companies, mandates and trust territories, which separated government from sovereignty.

Today, the self-image of global governance is one of technocratic efficiency, economic development, good governance and humanitarian benevolence, not rapacious exploitation and civilizational hierarchy. 'Every empire, however,' as Edward Said reminds us, 'tells itself and the world that it is unlike all other empires, that its mission is not to plunder and control but to educate and liberate' (Said 2003). Whether or not one views contemporary practices of transnational governance as consistent with a longer history of European colonialism is likely to shape one's views about the legitimacy of contemporary governance institutions – and indeed, one's views about legitimacy more broadly.

In any case, there is no doubt that colonial practices, however brutal, required legitimation. As the Algerian legal theorist Mohammed Bedjaoui stressed in 1979, international law was instrumental in producing 'justifications and excuses to create legitimacy for the subjugation and pillaging of the Third World' (Bedjaoui 1979, 50). Bedjaoui's project for a New International Economic Order was only one aspect of a broader postcolonial attempt to challenge those discourses and legal doctrines that had served to justify colonialism, from the standard of civilization to trusteeship, and to constitute a new form of legitimacy that would overcome inequalities inherited from colonialism. Today, the defeat of the projects advocated by figures like Bedjaoui has seen the revival of discourses of civilizational hierarchy and trusteeship. Moreover, as Mahmood Mamdani notes, those subjected to transnational interventions (by the new subject 'the international community') are reconceived not as political subjects but as passive beneficiaries of protection (Mamdani 2010, 1).

In such a context, defining the subjects of legitimacy goes beyond the question of the conflict between cosmopolitan and communitarian accounts of will formation, to the very constitution of the human as political subject. While the communitarian/cosmopolitan debate, as Meine suggests, generates a conflict about which collectivities should be considered primary, 'the community of humankind or particular (pre-)political communities', this conflict is accompanied by a deeper conflict within each of these discourses. Communitarian accounts of transnational legitimacy now operate in the context of a fading norm of sovereign equality, and the creation of what Mamdani calls a 'bifurcated' international system, split between sovereign states composed of citizens, and trusteeships inhabited by wards (Mamdani 2010, 56). Cosmopolitan accounts, similarly, are faced with the fact that the constitution of the 'community of humankind' is itself beset by deep conflicts. For all its proclaimed universality, neither the 'man' of the 'rights of man' nor the 'human' of UDHR has ever coincided neatly with the human species.

To note this is to go further than Meine's claim that disputes 'about the validity and scope of human rights are complemented by disputes about the relation between human and citizens' rights, or between human rights and national sovereignty.' Rather, it is to suggest that the very attempt to utilize the human to ground the legitimacy of political projects must confront the borders of that humanity. While modern rights declarations largely took for granted the exclusion of women, slaves and colonial subjects from the category 'man', in the late 1940s, delegates representing colonial powers struggled against explicitly extending the Universal Declaration of Human Rights to the inhabitants of 'non-self-governing territories'.

If we wish to detect Liu's 'shadows of universalism' in our own time, the public opposition to the 2011 intervention in Libya and resistance to the developing norm of the 'Responsibility to Protect', which Meine cites as one instance of conflict over transnational legitimacy, deserves further consideration. The R2P itself emerged as a response to a perceived crisis of legitimacy afflicting the discourse of 'humanitarian intervention' in the wake of the NATO intervention in Kosovo. Gareth Evans, who chaired the International Commission on Intervention and State Sovereignty (ICISS) which formulated the R2P norm, has noted that any attempt to gain consensus in the UN General Assembly was forced to face the resistance to 'humanitarian intervention' on the part of leaders of decolonized states who were protective of their sovereignty and 'saw the non-intervention norm as one of their few defenses against threats and pressures from more powerful international actors.' (Evans 2006, 102). In formulating the R2P, ICISS sought to reassure those leaders who had reason to believe that the weakening of the principle of sovereignty may leave them exposed to unwelcome military interventions by more powerful states. 'Intervening to protect human beings', the ICISS report reads, 'must not be tainted by any suspicion that is [sic] a form of neo-colonial imperialism' (ICISS 2001, 45).

In attempting to dispel this suspicion, ICISS moved away from the language of 'the right to intervene', adopting instead the language of the 'responsibility to protect'. If, as Giorgio Agamben has noted, 'terminological choices can never be neutral,' then this terminological shift was aimed at generating a political consensus that the bellicose interventionist tenor of the former term had made less likely (Agamben 2008, 4). In his own book on the R2P, Evans notes that in the North, the language of the 'right to intervene' worked to rally people, while 'in the rest of the world it enraged as many as it inspired' (Evans 2008, 33). The problem, Evans stresses, is that the concept was too one-sided to acknowledge the anxiety of those states who had already found themselves subjected to the civilizing missions of the great powers. By speaking not of a 'right to intervene' but of a 'responsibility to protect' ICISS members sought to reassure these anxious states that the concept would not be simply be a civilizing mission in another guise.

One of the four key objectives to be met by any new account of intervention, according to ICISS, was 'to establish the legitimacy of military intervention when necessary and after all other approaches have failed' (ICISS 2001a, 11). Central to perceptions of legitimacy, the report argues, is the agency that has authorized the intervention. ICISS upheld the role of the UN Security Council as 'the applicator of legitimacy', which its report depicts as the connection between the exercise of authority and the recourse to power. Yet it also provided a number of other possible responses in cases in which the Security Council cannot come to agreement, from seeking authorization from the General Assembly to enabling interventions by regional or subregional bodies (ICISS 2001a, 53).

Furthermore, the ICISS report outlines a number of criteria for legitimate interventions, 'right authority, just cause, right intention, last resort, proportional means and reasonable prospects' (ICISS 2001b, 32). As Evans notes, all of its criteria for the use of force have an 'explicit pedigree in Christian "just war" theory' (Evans 2006). This recourse to a Christian language, formulated in part by theologians who sought to justify the Crusades, raises questions about the broader legitimacy of such criteria. Without refuting the claim, the ICISS background report notes that for some critics: 'Human rights are the contemporary Western values being imposed in place of Christianity and the 'standard of civilization' in the 19th and early 20th century' (ICISS 2001a, 11). Indeed, this is a position articulated not only by critics of human rights but also by as prominent a defender of human rights universalism as Jack Donnelly, who celebrates the emergence of universal human rights as a new standard of civilization, which recasts 'the important idea that international legitimacy and full membership in international society must rest in part on standards of just, humane or civilized behaviour' (Donnelly 1998, 21).

Although Meine mentions the protests that greeted the NATO Intervention in Libya as evidence of the contested legitimacy of the R2P, there is no discussion of resistance to the norm emerging from outside Europe. That those whose societies have been subjected to so-called 'humanitarian interventions' may have a stake in determining the legitimacy of such interventions would seem to be an obvious consequence of the author's theoretical framework. And indeed, in the wake of what many critics saw as NATO's overreach of its UN mandate in Libya, parallels to earlier colonial forms of intervention were clear enough to draw the ire even of defenders of the R2P like South Africa's Thabo Mbeki, whose government had played an important role in garnering world support for the norm. 'This is the same attitude as Westerners displayed during colonial times when they presided over our continent,' Mbeki wrote in the wake of the bombing campaign (cited in Dembinski and Reinold 2011).

In this context, the reliance on European and American sources to develop the framework of an account of transnational legitimacy is problematic. Meine is not oblivious to this problem. While she suggests in conclusion that 'Non-Western and extra-European perspectives and voices need to be part of the debates as indispensable interlocutors' these voices are nonetheless called on to take part in a conversation whose terms have already been established in their absence. This is particularly significant given that, as Meine suggests, legitimacy is not merely an analytic category but also 'implies a political statement for or against a specific political order by means of which scientists, theorists or philosophers themselves actively participate in a political discourse about legitimacy.' Given this, to include non-Western voices only after the terms of the debate have been established risks appearing as a political statement in favor of a bifurcated world order, whose hierarchies too closely resemble those of European colonialism. An examination of what, following Liu, we could call 'the shadows of legitimacy' may help to establish a less parochial account of transnational legitimacy that takes seriously the enduring legacy of colonialism.

Reference

Agamben, G. 2008. *State of Exception*. Chicago, IL: University of Chicago Press.
Bedjaoui, M. 1979. *Towards a New International Economic Order*. Tranek, NJ: Holmes & Meier.
Donnelly, J. 1998. "Human Rights: A New Standard of Civilization?" *International Affairs* 74: 1.
Dembinski, M., and T. Reinold. 2011. "Libya and the Responsibility to Protect—African and European Perspectives." Peace Research Institute (PRIF). 24, note 29. http://www.peacepalaceli brary.nl/ebooks/files/369284305.pdf.

Evans, G. 2006. "From Humanitarian Intervention to the Responsibility to Protect." *Wisconsin International Law Journal* 24: 3.

Evans, G. 2008. *The Responsibility to Protect: Ending Mass Atrocity Crimes Once and for All.* Washington, DC: Brookings Institution Press.

ICISS (International Commission on Intervention and State Sovereignty). 2001a. *The Responsibility to Protect.* Ottawa: International Development Research Centre.

ICISS (International Commission on Intervention and State Sovereignty). 2001b. *The Responsibility to Protect: Research, Bibliography, Background.* Ottawa: International Development Research Centre.

Liu, L. H. 2014. "Shadows of Universalism: The Untold Story of Human Rights around 1948." *Critical Inquiry* 40 (4): 385–417.

Mamdani, M. 2010. "Responsibility to Protect or Right to Punish?" *Journal of Intervention and Statebuilding* 4: 1.

Said, E. "Blind Imperial Arrogance." *Los Angeles Times*, July 20 2003. Accessed 1 June 2016. http://articles.latimes.com/2003/jul/20/opinion/oe-said20.

The discursive (de)legitimisation of global governance: political contestation and the emergence of new actors in the WTO's Dispute Settlement Body

Michael Strange

The World Trade Organization's Dispute Settlement Body provides the teeth of the global trade regime – empowering it with substantial means to adjudicate in disagreements between Member-states over the implementation of WTO law. The WTO's teeth have, however, also helped make the organisation controversial. The Dispute Settlement Body has frequently found itself at the centre of a much wider societal critique of the broader WTO – as well as contemporary global trade governance – in which its legitimacy to operate has been fiercely questioned.

The political sensitivity of its work has been made most apparent in those cases where the principles of WTO law appear to run counter to environmental or consumer safety concerns, taking the system into the mass media and making it the subject of street protests. Yet, where rulings have given new access to non-state actors campaigning for these concerns (e.g. *amicus curiae* provisions), there has been further controversy amongst Member-states over whether the Dispute Settlement Body has acted outside its delegated authority by effectively rewriting 'who' or 'what' is an actor in the system.

The changing character of this specific institutional arrangement is approached in the article as part of a wider struggle over the terms of what is 'legitimate' in global governance. Where WTO Dispute Settlement has been re-politicised, both inside and outside the formal institution, a contradiction becomes visible – between its legal-technocratic identity and a world that is fundamentally political. The legal normalisation of new actor identities needs to be understood in this context, as an attempt to manage that tension and reinforce the claim that WTO Dispute Settlement is legitimate. How the institution has changed and new identities emerged since its birth in 1995 is enhanced if understood in the context of a struggle in which the terms of what is legitimate in global governance are ultimately unfixed.

Introduction

The World Trade Organization's (WTO) Dispute Settlement Body (DSB) is an unlikely entity in global politics, given that the panels and the appeals process through which it adjudicates disputes amongst WTO Member-states consist of only a small selection of individuals ruling on matters with huge economic and political consequences – challenging conventional norms of state sovereignty in the interests of global trade governance. It provides the 'teeth' of the WTO, a respectably high compliance rate enforcing WTO law (Leitner and Lester 2011; Elsig 2007). Yet, this apparent success has also exposed it to criticism – in particular, of lacking legitimacy to both the interests of developing country Member-states and the societies it affects. The political sensitivity of its work has been made most apparent in those cases where the principles of WTO law appear to run counter to environmental or consumer safety concerns, taking the system into the mass media and making it the subject of street protests. Yet, where rulings have given new access to non-state actors campaigning for these concerns (e.g. *amicus curiae* provisions), there has been further controversy amongst Member-states over whether the DSB has acted outside its delegated authority by effectively rewriting 'who' or 'what' is an actor in the system. Whilst WTO Dispute Settlement is intended to only follow WTO law and not add or rewrite rules that are formally the outcome of Member-state negotiations, in practice it functions according to the principle of *stare decisis*. That is, in writing WTO Dispute Settlement rulings the persons involved have come to justify their decisions sometimes in reference to earlier rulings taken by the body rather than rest their conclusions exclusively on the Member-state agreements and relevant technical information provided by the states party to a dispute, as will be discussed later. This was never meant to be and, where these rulings have given new powers to non-state parties, that apparent transference of agency has created significant levels of tensions amongst the Member-states as to whether the DSB has acted outside its delegated authority as an agent of the Member-states. This has led to questions over the legitimacy of the WTO's dispute settlement mechanism.

Contestation over the functioning of this specific institutional arrangement needs to be seen as part of a wider struggle over the terms of what is 'legitimate' in global governance. Here, the argument sides with those scholars who consider legitimacy to be a context-dependent concept only given meaning within a particular political community between governed and governor(s). Given the importance of relationality here, the (de)legitimation of WTO Dispute Settlement – that goes beyond debate, to include the emergence of new forms of agency (or political subjectivity) – is a discursive process. Questions of legitimacy in global governance should be treated as discursive battles in which alternate articulations compete to become hegemonic. Drawing upon existing findings and interviews with civil servants in the WTO Secretariat and other relevant bodies, the article traces how different actors have shaped the discursive battle over whether or not this key part of global governance is legitimate. For example, the apparent inclusion of new actors within the WTO's Dispute Settlement mechanism – to be discussed later in the article – is understood here as the emergence of new subject positions within a discursive shift between alternate paradigms of 'good' global governance.

The enquiry is structured as follows. First, drawing upon existing scholarship on legitimacy in global governance, the article outlines the discursive basis of this concept. Next, the discussion turns to the empirical case, first briefly introducing the WTO's mechanism for dispute settlement and then tracing its development with the emergence of new agents. Studying the WTO Dispute Settlement mechanism provides, as the analysis shows, rich material by which to understand the broader processes through which global governance is (de)legitimated, existing as it does at the intersection between the law and politics. There remains an ongoing struggle to, on the one hand, shift global trade governance to the sphere of the law and so erase the political, whilst on the other hand, re-politicise that mechanism and so reopen the space for alternative conceptualisations of 'good' governance in global trade. At the same time, there remains a controversy over whether giving non-state actors such as environmental groups increased access to WTO Dispute Settlement conversely enhances the system's legitimacy, by making it accountable to those groups, or weakens the system's legitimacy, by undermining the primacy of Member-states.

The WTO's DSB exists to not only resolve conflicts between Member-states over the interpretation of WTO agreements but, and more importantly, to also shift the supranational regulation of national policies deemed as relevant to transborder trade flows from the sphere of politics to law. Such a move is highly significant given the depoliticisation involved, isolating decision-making from normative concerns so as to be a largely technocratic affair in which liberalisation takes unquestioned precedence over wider societal projects. Tracing the ongoing discursive process over the terms of its legitimate function, conversely, exposes the 'return of the political' – that is, both the attempts of external actors to re-politicise this wide-encompassing policy field, and potentially also the limits of the law where new political actors have emerged within the system.

Legitimacy and political community in global governance

Although the International Monetary Fund and the World Bank have existed since 1946, it was only in the 1980s that public attention came to really notice their role along with that of the increasingly prominent General Agreement on Tariffs and Trade. New public fame for what had been rather technical bodies little discussed in the mainstream media reached new heights with the creation of the WTO on 1 January 1995. The spread of regionalism, exemplified in its most extensive form in the European Union (EU), only added to a growing awareness that domestic policy processes were increasingly subject to decisions made at higher levels. This led commentators to ask a common question: Do these new global forms of governance create a barrier between us and the policy mechanisms through which we are governed (e.g. Elsig 2007; Esty 2002)? In response, a debate emerged around the question of legitimacy within global governance (Bexell, Tallberg, and Uhlin 2010; Hurrelman, Scheider, and Steffek 2007; Buchanan and Keohane 2006; Hurd 1999), centred around two key questions: (a) what are the criteria for determining if global governance is legitimate? and (b) who/what should be responsible for deciding and enforcing this criteria? Given the commonality with which diverse parties debating the shape of global governance in general have used the term 'legitimacy', one might be forgiven for assuming there is a commonly assumed definition – that is, it has been operationalised in the sphere of how to organise the production of public goods at the global level.

In its simplest form, legitimacy means that the governed consider the governor/s to be the rightful holders of that authority – irrespective of acceptable disagreements over how to rule. What disagreement might be sufficiently unacceptable so as to break the bond between governed and governor/s is down to those respective actors. Harking back to a Weberian tradition, for most scholarship on legitimacy the substance of its central term is purely context-dependent. Whilst frustratingly unclear at a general level, 'legitimacy' becomes bounded and acquires its content through the political community formed between governed and governor/s – that is, in terms of the culture and available set of laws, norms and expectations by which the actors involved can make sense (Abromeit and Stoiber et al. 2007; Dingwerth 2007; Clark 2005, 2007).

The 'English School' of International Relations has had a particular influence in how legitimacy is thought of at the global level since the concept plays a pivotal role in much of how its subscribers theorise state-to-state relations. States are seen as interdependent, acting in concert as parts of an 'International Society' in which behaviour is structured by a series of shared norms (Clark 2005). In the case of international politics, of course, the same actors (states) play multiple roles – as both governed and governors (with the governance function performed via a series of state-created institutions). The norms framing the terms of 'legitimate' behaviour are not the exclusive product of states. Ian Clark (2007) added the term 'World Society' to acknowledge that, along with International Society, non-state actors play an active part seeking to shape global governance norms. Whilst the International Society of states remains dominant, key norms defining legitimate action in the global arena have their origins in World Society, including human rights; sustainable development; and, more historically, anti-slavery. World Society is the same as what Jens Steffek has termed 'citizen-led' legitimacy in global governance, where it identifies a societal effect on international norms (2007, 186–189). The point in mentioning this is to make clear some initial attempts within existing literature to mark out the field of relations through which the terms of 'legitimate global governance' are contested. Yet, clearly there are significant problems for those wishing to define these terms in any sense concrete.

Several scholars have argued that for authority to be considered legitimate those it affects need to feel a shared community identity with their governors (Beetham and Lord 1998, 33–34; Scharpf 1999, 8). Nationhood, for example, provides a clear community and demos.

Yet, nation state-based understandings of legitimacy cannot be directly transferred to the global level (Elsig 2007, 79; Clark 2007, 193). There is no transnational equivalent of the national demos, although there are those who argue the task to create one is not insurmountable (Bohman 2005; Rosenau 2000). For example, Michael Zürn has argued that no demos has substance outside of politics but must be constructed – a process made harder, but not necessarily impossible, at the global level (2000, 196–200). Indeed, Clark criticises any assumption that legitimacy hinges on the existence of a pre-existing pre-political demos (Clark 2007, 196). Rather, legitimacy emerges at the same time as the demos – with the former playing a constitutive role in defining the relationship between the latter and its ordering mechanism – the governor/s (e.g. the state).

Two things need to be re-emphasised at this point: first, that the political community of governed and governor/s provides the basis through which legitimacy is discursively articulated; and, second, that political community itself is a discursive construction. Whilst one might claim that, if we follow this logic, there is so little left that is not discursive that the term 'discourse' loses its value, this would be an over-reaction. Rather, what we see in the above argumentation is a two-stage process, each of which involves a different set of relations and social practices.

To help us better understand the discursive basis of legitimacy in global governance, it helps to consider what proposals have been made towards building a 'transnational demos'. For example, to build such an entity requires a transnational public discourse and transnational solidarity – or, what Steffek has termed, a 'normative consensus' (2007, 180; Zürn 2000, 203). Faced with the likelihood that few individuals would be sufficiently motivated to spend resources engaging in such a normative consensus, Zürn has suggested policy issues serve as the centrifuge of multiple transnational demoi (2000, 195). This mirrors the reality of global governance that is organised by the principle of functional differentiation as opposed to constituting a single entity (Held and McGrew 2002; Wolf 2002, 38).

Thus far, it has been argued that legitimacy in global governance necessitates the identification of political communities linking both governors and governed. However, rather than attempt to create one global demos, legitimate global governance is more feasible if we accept the existence of multiple demoi. Each demoi is differentiated not by geographical territories but functional or issue criteria, for example, trade, human rights, environment. Each demoi would, in this understanding, include a broad range of actors linked by a common engagement with a governance field like 'trade'. Clark argues that these communities cannot be predefined but are formed via a political process (2007, 208). With perhaps some exceptions (e.g. the World Social Forum), the world society of non-governmental organisations (NGOs) and other civil society groups interacting to contest the norms of legitimate global governance do so only when clustered around particular issues, for example, climate change, HIV medication, whaling. The respective issue provides the nodal point for their convergence and sense of political community (see Figure 1). However, the contours of the community only take shape through a negotiated process in which power relations inevitably play a significant part.

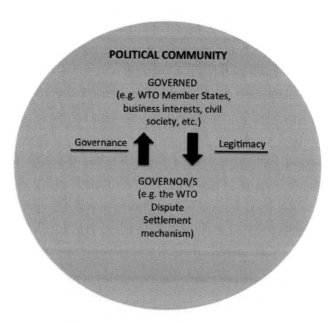

Figure 1. Legitimacy requires a political community between the governor/s and the governed, represented by the grey sphere. The governor/s and the governed provide each other with, respectively, governance and legitimacy.

There is substantial overlap between whether the focus on legitimacy in these above outlined debates is normative – that is, that global governance *should* for moral reasons be seen as legitimate by a particular community – and analytical, where legitimacy is treated as a fundamental basis of authority. This overlap is impossible to avoid, though, if we see global governance as something that is ultimately discursive. In the case of WTO Dispute Settlement, a first implication is that it requires legitimacy to function.

Yet, the argument needs further development if we are to understand the discursive character of legitimacy for an institution such as WTO Dispute Settlement that formally claims its legitimacy as a legalistic entity. Whilst that institution is the product of an earlier political contestation, surely its political community is defined by its constitutional basis? This question overlaps with the neighbouring debate on accountability, heavily influenced by Grant and Keohane's (2005) pivotal contribution in which they distinguished between relations based upon either delegation or participation. In that model, arguments over accountability – which can be read as 'legitimacy' for the purposes of this article – are structured along a divide, or misunderstanding, as to who/what the WTO should be accountable. Should they be accountable to their delegates – that is, usually the states who have legally delegated the organisation authority to fulfil its designated function – or a wider community (i.e. affected 'stakeholders') who demand participation in their operation? The first position states that a body like the WTO is accountable (again, read 'legitimate' here) if it is responsive to the demands of its delegates. The second position says this is insufficient and must include a level of responsiveness to a wider community (e.g. environmental NGOs, workers, etc.). The danger here is if research treats institutional decision-making rules and the criteria for defining legitimate global governance as the same thing, ignoring the discursive basis of legitimacy. This is clear when critically considering the institutional-based understanding of legitimacy developed by Fritz Scharpf (1999) and others, as discussed next.

The discursive foundations of legitimacy

Fritz Scharpf (1999) brought clarity to the concept of legitimacy by disaggregating it into the two sides of decision-making: the *input*, where information and interests are collected; and the *output* (the decision). A third category to add here concerns the legitimacy of the actual process through which policy decisions are produced – what has been called 'throughput' legitimacy (Risse and Kleine 2007; Schmidt 2010a, 2010b, 2013). Yet, what does this mean for a discursive reading of legitimacy?

Neatly phrased by Vivien Schmidt, the legitimacy crisis of governance beyond the nation state is 'policy without politics' and 'politics without policy' (2010b). Policies are decided without societal input – risking inappropriate policies; society cannot productively vent its politicisation via influencing policy – risking more extreme forms of politicisation. Scharpf's *input legitimacy* requires that those affected by governance feel able to influence – either directly or indirectly via representatives – what goes into the policy engine (1999, 7–13). Institutionally speaking, input legitimacy requires formalised mechanisms ensuring fair representation of those affected. National elections serve this function at the national level. European parliamentary elections partially serve this function at the EU level. Lacking a single governmental chamber at the global level, input legitimacy must look to the many international organisations in existence.

Input legitimacy is not just about institutions geared towards greater deliberation and pluralism. For deliberation to have substance, there must be societal actors with the ideas and discourse through which global governance can be contested. In the case of the EU, Schmidt sees a central problem for input legitimacy being the lack of a strong 'European' collective identity amongst citizens governed under the EU (2013, 15–17). Rather, individuals within the EU predominantly still speak in terms of policy as if it were a national affair without sufficient understanding of themselves as 'European citizens'. Without that discourse, it is not possible to reconnect politics and policy. This problem is even more acute in the case of global governance bodies such as the WTO where there is no formal 'world citizenship'.

The importance of identity to input legitimacy is stressed by Beetham and Lord (1998), as well as Scharpf (1999), and ties the discussion back to Zürn's (2000) call for a transnational demos outlined earlier. However, the difficulty of achieving a sufficiently strong identity connecting citizens into supranational political communities has led many to turn to *output legitimacy* (Scharpf 1999, 11). If the governed cannot influence the governors, then the basis of legitimate governance must instead rest on its ability to solve problems.

Problem-solving is what Beetham and Lord call the 'performance' side of governance and which they disaggregate into the delivery of security rights, economic and welfare rights, and civil or legal rights (1998, 94–122). For example, whilst few would claim that the WTO is a democratically representative organisation, there is a much more substantial debate concerning if it helps or hinders the economic and welfare rights of individuals. By putting aside participation and emphasising quantifiable goods produced by governance, output legitimacy appears apolitical. However, output legitimacy is complicated by the fact that it is not always clear what policy problems need to be solved for a community to view the solutions as 'right' (and legitimate). For example, calls for the WTO to accommodate greater concern for the negative societal and environmental effects of unfettered trade liberalisation – so-called 'embedded liberalism' – demonstrate the political side of output legitimacy (Elsig 2007, 84–85).

Indeed, as Schmidt writes, 'output policy legitimization for the most part occurs in the communicative discourse of the political sphere' (2013, 10). The output legitimacy of global governance cannot rest on just producing policy solutions, but requires that the governors are able to *tell* the governed that those solutions have been produced. This is particularly important when citizens lack understanding of global governance. For output legitimacy to function at the global level, then, requires that those affected by the governance can appreciate the 'good' it produces (Papadopoulos 2007, 485). It means that governors must justify their actions to the governed, stating how their policies have provided effective solutions (Føllesdal 2007, 216). Even if this does not mean convincing all of the governed that the governance is 'good', the task remains a significant challenge since there are frequently few if any direct communication channels between governor/s and governed at the global level. Furthermore, the criterion by which output legitimacy is to be assessed – the desired policy outcomes – is inherently a political process (Mügge 2011). Again, then, it requires some kind of common dialogue to determine outputs if actors are to measure to what extent those outputs have been met and, thus, whether the governance is legitimate.

Therefore, both *input* and *output* forms of legitimacy require that there exists a form of political community linking the governed and governor/s. For Scharpf, the sense of 'being involved' required for input legitimacy is simply impractical in supranational forms of governance where any political community is only thin (1999, 8–11). By comparison, output legitimacy requires only a 'perception of a range of *common interests* that is sufficiently broad and stable to justify institutional arrangements for collective action' (emphasis in original) (Scharpf 1999, 11). Notably, this does not need to be a 'thick' identity but, rather, may be one of many collective identities to which individual members of the constituency belong – whether defined by territory or problem-field, for example. However, as Schmidt (2013) makes clear, output legitimacy does demand a collective discourse in which actors can agree a shared narrative in which policy outputs are both attributed to global governance and deemed as desirable.

Likewise, *throughput legitimacy* necessitates some kind of political community for it to function. Risse and Kleine (2007) identify three components to throughput legitimacy: (1) legality, (2) transparency and (3) quality (2007, 73). For its legality, global governance is subject to a complex network of national and international law. Transparency requires that it is clear *who* takes *what* decision, something that is harder where global governance is complex (Urry 2005).

The 'quality' component of throughput legitimacy overlaps extensively with the deliberative democratic aspect of input legitimacy by demanding both pluralism (access by the governed) but also a public sphere fostering mutual learning between those involved (Risse and Kleine 2007, 73–74). For example, providing access for NGOs is not, as Schmidt points out, sufficient where many of those organisations are increasingly 'technocratic' and 'thus removed from actual citizens' (2010a, 27). To foster throughput legitimacy, the bond between governed and governor/s needs to be effectively built into the mechanisms of actual decision-making.

To summarise thus far, input, output and throughput approaches to legitimacy all require political community but to varying degrees. Output legitimacy may appear comparatively simple to achieve, but Schmidt shows that in the case of the EU it is often not an obvious (or apolitical) matter as to what constitutes 'European' policy solutions (2010a, 2014). At each stage of the policy process, the terms of 'legitimate governance' are formed discursively within a political community. To understand legitimacy within global governance – and in the case examined here, of the WTO's DSB – it is then necessary to look at similar discursive processes through which this is (de)contested. However, what are the boundaries of that political community in which legitimacy is constituted: do they rest exclusively on the institutional relationship between the WTO and its Member-states, or a wider set of actors as already suggested in the introduction to this article?

Researching legitimacy

The above discussion has argued that legitimacy is discursive, constituted relationally between the governor/s and the governed within a shared political community. Even where the policy process appears to provide a means to systematise how scholars conceptualise legitimacy, each stage remains subject to a discursive process. Legal institutional structures that include rules for decision-making and ensuring accountability claim to provide criteria for determining legitimate global governance. However, these claims have no basis outside of their constituent political communities. Given this, the analysis that follows approaches its subject – WTO Dispute Settlement – by first marking out how the institution states its own legitimating criteria. Drawing upon existing research and interviews with civil servants in the WTO Secretariat and other relevant bodies, the analysis then considers the practice of WTO Dispute Settlement, tracing its development to look for incidents where its legitimating criteria have been contested. The purpose of the analysis is not to determine whether or not such developments make the system more legitimate, but rather to help map the political terrain in which WTO Dispute Settlement is both possible and is subject to change.

The WTO's Dispute Settlement Body and its legitimacy 'crisis'

There is, apparently, a clear political community already existing to guide and develop the terms of what is 'legitimate' in the operation of the WTO's DSB, demarcated by the legal-institutional arrangement first formalised through the Uruguay Round of nation state negotiations that led to the overall creation of the WTO. The Dispute Settlement Understanding (DSU) – the legal text undergirding the institution – claims a set of criteria for determining its input (who can be involved), throughput (how the process works, including how decisions should be reported) and output (decisions and their implementation) legitimacy.

The WTO is a political organisation tasked with facilitating collective debate, negotiation, monitoring and adjudication towards the standardisation of domestic trade regulations. Everyday decision-making occurs via the General Council, which consists of delegates representing all the WTO Member-states. The General Council may convene as either the Trade Policy Review Body (TPRB) or the DSB. The TPRB provides the eyes and ears of the WTO to the extent that it collects data on new domestic trade regulations. However, there is no direct mechanism allowing the WTO to act on this data. Rather, it is in the DSB that the WTO serves an adjudication function between its Member-states.

Member-states possess the exclusive right to be parties within the WTO Dispute Settlement system and so police WTO law. To launch a dispute, a Member-state must lodge a formal complaint with the DSB, accusing a fellow Member-state of engaging in trade practices that run in violation of WTO agreements (Kim 1999; see also, Strange 2015). Each stage of the process follows a legally defined timetable, providing a degree of automaticity structuring how the actors interact with one another. The first stage is the *consultation*, at which the Legal Affairs division of the WTO Secretariat brings together the complainant and respondent, both Member-states. These consultation meetings include a mix of information-gathering and potential reconciliation, depending on the particular interests at play with respect to whether the parties are most concerned to produce an easy resolution or develop a stronger case to be carried onto the next stage of the process.

If the consultation stage fails to resolve the dispute, the complainant can request the establishment of an adjudicatory panel. The *panel* stage begins with the selection of three panellists to adjudicate the dispute (Shoyer 2003). The complainant and respondent are presented with a sample of five to seven individuals – suggested by the Legal Affairs division of the WTO Secretariat for their expertise in law or economics. A party is able to propose its own nominees for the panel, though these are usually vetoed by the opposing party, hence why the Secretariat is active at this stage. The Secretariat will continue providing additional samples of potential panellists until the parties accept the full table of three individuals. Once this occurs, the panel may start its work.

The role of the panel is to consider both written submissions and evidence given in oral hearings by the parties to the dispute. The oral hearings are closed and confidential to all but the parties to a dispute. The panel produces a report that first just describes the dispute. The parties may then respond with respect to, in particular, any potential factual inaccuracies. This then feeds into an interim report, with another chance for feedback from the parties, and then a final report that states whether or not a violation of WTO law has occurred.

The parties have the right to appeal the findings. Appeals are lodged with the Secretariat of the Appellate Body – the special appeals procedure designed to limit the powers of the panel process. As with the panels process, the Appellate Body involves a table of 'experts' to whom the parties must provide both written submissions and oral statements. Unlike the panels process, however, the Appellate Body draws its members from a pool of individuals selected by all WTO Member-states meeting as the DSB.

Unless every Member-state chooses to reject a report – which would include all parties to that dispute – it will be accepted on the basis that there is no negative consensus (McCall Smith 2003). The 'losing' respondent Member-state is then expected to comply with the ruling and its recommendations. It is the responsibility of the successful complainant to report any incidence of non-compliance – in which case, a new dispute is effectively launched. If non-compliance persists, the complainant may be granted the right to impose trade sanctions upon the non-complying party in accordance with the estimated cost of the ongoing violation. The comparatively high compliance rate enjoyed by the WTO Dispute Settlement rulings greatly enhances the institution's claim on output legitimacy (Leitner and Lester 2011).

To summarise, although WTO Dispute Settlement creates a formidable institutional mechanism designed to enforce WTO trade agreements upon the Member-states, the mechanism itself is not a police body. The policing function is carried out by the Member-states, who possess the exclusive right to bring cases as well as enforce compliance. If going by the DSU alone, the criteria for determining the institution's legitimacy are clear where there are formally agreed rules on determining who should influence proceedings, the terms of good conduct for proceedings and what the institution can be expected to produce. Yet, despite its formal intergovernmental character, ever since WTO Dispute Settlement first began functioning on 1 January 1995 research has increasingly identified the presence of additional agency – non-state actors – in the practice of WTO Dispute Settlement. The developing and, therefore, fluid character of agency is argued in this article to be symptomatic of a wider discursive process in which the basis of legitimate governance for WTO Dispute Settlement has been regularly re-contested that goes beyond its formal design.

The re-contestation of legitimacy in WTO Dispute Settlement

Member-states are the primary actors in WTO Dispute Settlement. Whilst new forms of agency have emerged, their direct contribution to shaping decisions by panellists or Appellate Body members is hard to measure. This section is not intended to question that, but rather to problematise 'Member-states' as a fixed category and so in the process underline a series of changes that can best be understood as part of a wider re-contestation over the terms of legitimacy in WTO Dispute Settlement. This re-contestation challenges the legalistic attempt to fix the institution's claim to legitimacy within the DSU.

This section presents WTO Dispute Settlement as subject to a continual process of re-contestation over the terms of its legitimate governance. In particular, this process has seen substantial criticism from actors external to the institution – most notably against rulings seen as detrimental to environmental issues – but, and importantly for the argument described above, a struggle amongst institutional actors – including Member-state delegations, individuals tasked with ruling on cases, private legal firms and others – re-articulating the purpose and identity of the system.

Politicisation and the emergence of new actors in WTO Dispute Settlement

One of the most controversial and publicly known cases ruled upon by the WTO DSB was *US-Shrimp* that featured prominently amongst the list of criticisms voiced by those protesting against the WTO's Seattle Ministerial Conference in December 1999. The case has particular salience in this article as the key point where WTO Dispute Settlement became subject to an increasingly wider political community. The case concerned whether US environmental rules restricting shrimp imports caught using practices that threatened turtle populations breached WTO rules. Environmentalists active in the Seattle protests branded themselves as 'turtles' – a term used extensively in placards stating an alliance with trade unions against the WTO: 'Turtles and Teamsters together at last!'

Environmental groups demanded a right to be heard by the panellists adjudicating the dispute, but were initially refused. As non-state actors, they could only formally submit materials for consideration if asked to do so by the Member-states party to the dispute. Whilst the United States Trade Representative included some materials, environmental groups complained publicly at the lack of direct representation. When the United States lost the case at the panel stage and sought appeal via the Appellate Body, the question of access for non-state actors was reconsidered. Whilst the Appellate Body ultimately ruled against the US ban on shrimps on the grounds of non-discrimination – that the same high standards were not demanded of the US fishing fleet – the right of Member-states to discriminate on environmental grounds was upheld, and those environmental groups gained the right to submit information to panels and the Appellate Body independently of Member-states – meaning free of state-censure. In Scharpf's terms, widening access to the submission process makes most sense in terms of input legitimacy, whereas acknowledging that Member-states can discriminate along environmental grounds would be more relevant to the institution's throughput legitimacy. However, the argument here is not that these developments make WTO Dispute Settlement necessarily more legitimate, since legitimacy is argued here to be discursive and not fixed upon any apolitical basis. The analysis here is therefore focused on the discursive battle at play in the re-contestation over what is (il)legitimate.

In *US-Shrimp*, the Appellate Body's ruling created a new legal identity within the WTO Dispute Settlement system whenever they may make submissions as *amicus curiae* ('friends of the court'). The identity was not contained within the DSU that Member-states had negotiated. Rather, it emerged only as a result of this ruling by the Appellate Body that was provoked by politicisation external to the formal institution (Steger 2002; Reinisch and Irgel. 2001, 136–143; Appleton 1999, 2000). Potentially the inclusion of *amicus curiae* is 'much ado about nothing', as some (e.g. Mavroidis 2001) have suggested, since there is no requirement that panels and the Appellate Body actually read these submissions.

Conversely, some practitioners engaged in WTO Dispute Settlement have argued that the impact of *amicus curiae* should not be simply dismissed since the submissions they provide sit amongst the pile of data considered by panel and Appellate Body members when ruling on a case.[1] Furthermore, the *amicus curiae* principle remains a point of significant contention amongst WTO Member-states. Support for its creation originally came from the United States, whilst developing country Member-states have been highly critical – criticising it as undermining the primacy of sovereign states. The reason it stands out as most significant in the context of this article, however, is that it evidences the rewriting of WTO law.

This is a body of law that, given its sensitivity to the norm of state sovereignty, is formally intended to do no more than codify the agreements negotiated amongst the WTO Member-states. It differs from domestic law, for example, which runs on the basis of *stare decisis* – where law develops depending upon how it is ruled upon in court decisions. The WTO Dispute Settlement was meant to resolve disagreements between states over the interpretation of WTO law, not to add anything as substantial as a new category of actor to the submission stage. The *amicus curiae* principle first emerged in the context of unprecedented public contestation around *US-Shrimp*, in the later 1990s where the wider legitimacy of the WTO as a body for regulating global trade was subject to high levels of critique with street protests and mass alliances created to contest its role in global governance (Wilkinson 2005).

There is a growing body of literature highlighting the importance of symbols and discourse in understanding the formation and operation of the global trade regime (Strange 2011, 2014; Eagleton-Pierce 2012; Ford 2003). As argued earlier, debates over legitimacy need too to be seen as part of a wider discursive struggle over the terms of good governance. This discursive process does not consist of competing political demands alone, but includes the emergence of new identities as the discourse shifts. Here, the emergence of the *amicus curiae* principle illustrates one such subject position that reflects a discourse over the meaning of legitimacy for the WTO's DSB.

The discursivity of what constitutes legitimacy in WTO Dispute Settlement is apparent too in the poorly defined but ever-present role played by business interests. For some working in that system, business actors are not only active but amongst the most significant actors pushing disputes.[2] In part this is due to legislation within several Member-states – most notably, the EU and United States – requiring that business actors are given a direct means to request their state trade representative properly consider any request they may make towards filing a dispute (Shaffer 2006a; Garrett and Smith 2002). Member-states are already deeply reliant on business interests due to the information often only they can provide, or at least give most cheaply, to fight and defend their interests in WTO Dispute Settlement (Bown and Hoekman 2005; Shaffer 2003). Whilst this is not a new phenomenon to trade negotiations overall, it does stretch the category of who or what is an actor in WTO Dispute Settlement where Member-states rely extensively upon business actors in writing their submissions to panels and the Appellate Body. Formally, business actors cannot attend the oral hearings of either stage but, in practice, Member-states can choose which individuals make up their delegations and sometimes business actors have been included.[3] Often business actors have an additional role through funding the private legal firms – *private counsel*, as will be discussed next.

As with the *amicus curiae* principle, the provision to allow *private counsel* in WTO Dispute Settlement was not included within the text that came out of the negotiations that created the WTO. Rather, there has been an often-heated debate between Member-state delegations over whether to allow representation by private legal firms. Developing country Member-states have been overwhelmingly in favour, seeing *private counsel* as a means to supplement their starkly under-resourced trade departments when engaging in WTO Dispute Settlement (Shaffer 2003; Layton and Miranda 2003; Garrett and Smith 2002). In contrast, developed country Member-states argued that any representation of Member-states by private legal firms risked putting those practices into a conflict of interest, faced with the potential difficulty of working for different Member-states. Since its creation, the *private counsel* provision has seen Member-states of all hues make regular use of international legal firms specialising in WTO law. A gradual shift has occurred, moving the terms of legitimacy away from a conventional understanding of state sovereignty to a more legalistic, technocratic approach in which states need no longer directly represent themselves but can purchase the services of external agents. These agents – the legal firms working as private counsel – are not passive service providers, but are active in advertising their work to Member-states. In many cases, they offer services to developing country Member-states on a *pro bono* basis. They also work closely with the range of actors that exist to enhance the capacity of those less-resourced Member-states to utilise WTO Dispute Settlement.

Engaging in WTO Dispute Settlement – whether as the complainant bringing a case or the plaintiff defending – requires that Member-state delegations are equipped with a high level of technical competence. When the system was first created in 1995, the only service existing to help the less-equipped Member-states to represent their interests was the Legal Affairs division of the WTO Secretariat. However, the higher-than-expected number of cases brought to the dispute system created an excessive burden on this assistance. Furthermore, WTO Secretariat staff experienced a conflict of interest between their duty of impartiality and the demands of less-resourced Member-states for help in enhancing their capability to represent themselves in the dispute settlement mechanism (Van der Borght 1999). One solution was the 2001 creation of the Advisory Centre on WTO Law (ACWL). Though an intergovernmental body, the ACWL is funded on a relatively *ad hoc* basis where a group of developed country WTO Member-states voluntarily donate funds which are, in turn, used to help finance a team of lawyers –

and, in some cases, private counsel – to assist developing country WTO Member-states in pursuing or defending a case in the WTO Dispute Settlement mechanism. Significantly, ACWL legal staff can be asked to represent a Member-state in oral hearings. The emergence of the ACWL underlines the discursive process through which WTO Dispute Settlement has been, and continues to be, made legitimate. That is, the legitimisation of WTO Dispute Settlement is not a fixed, apolitical project, but one that exhibits a regular and constant process of re-articulation in which competing ideas of 'good' governance appear, and in which new actors emerge.

Likewise, the operation of WTO Dispute Settlement has relied upon a wider range of actors that include NGOs that enhance the capacity of Member-states to use the system. Whilst much of this work falls under the topic of 'technical-capacity enhancement' – a topic frequently treated as a relatively straightforward task of strengthening the knowledge of particular Member-state delegations – the argument in this article is that it reflects a wider discursive struggle over the terms of legitimate WTO dispute settlement. In several cases, NGOs have tried to enter the system and so affect that struggle. This was apparent in *US-Shrimp*, as already stated, but also in less combative engagements. For example, in *EC-Sardines* – a case against EU attempts to ban Peruvian imports of a Sardine-like fish as 'sardines' – the UK Consumer's Association, which supported the case as a means of lowering the price of fish for consumers, provided a dossier that formed part of Peru's complaint submission (Shaffer 2006b). It is significant that a UK-based NGO chooses to formally side with the Peruvian delegation in order to advance its own interests against the EU's position. That is, a national NGO steps outside of domestic context to align itself with another Member-state. WTO Dispute Settlement, in this example, goes beyond a state-to-state entity to involve a more complex series of interactions in which national lines and levels become blurred. The NGO, here, plays with what is an intergovernmental body to engage in a supranational form of governance. The strength of Peru's winning case was in part built upon its being seen as on the side of the consumer's – or 'publics' – interest.

Since WTO Dispute Settlement began, one NGO has emerged as particularly central as a provider of analysis often intended to enhance the ability of developing country Member-states to use the system – that is, the International Centre on Trade and Sustainable Development (ICTSD). In addition to producing research papers, the ICTSD has sometimes been described as the ambassador of the ACWL – setting up regional dialogues in major cities within Africa, Asia and Latin America involving meetings between WTO delegations from developing countries with business interests, as well as lawyers from international trade law firms offering *pro bono* work.[4] These dialogues are intended to help developing country governments better understand how to use WTO Dispute Settlement, as well as establish closer working relations between legal firms offering private counsel, and local business with the potential to lobby governments to launch a case.

The work of NGOs like ICTSD, including its collaboration with the intergovernmental body the ACWL, might be easily dismissed as just a rationalistic response to the inevitable difficulties of implementing WTO law – that the WTO Secretariat and the WTO Member-state delegations alone are insufficient. Why, then, is it relevant to talk about the role of the ICTSD as demonstrating a wider discursive struggle over the terms of legitimacy in WTO dispute settlement? In the case of the *amicus curiae* or *private counsel* provision, the relevance of discourse is certainly clearer, in that they refer to a rewriting of the WTO's DSU text that goes against its original state-centric identity. In answer, the argument made here is that treating the role of ICTSD as purely an exercise in technical-capacity building misses the political process taking place.

Whilst the ICTSD does not have a formal role in the WTO system, it plays a major role in organising events at which WTO Member-state delegates and Secretariat staff debate both with one another and other actors including politicians, academics, lawyers and the media. In the case of WTO Dispute Settlement, it becomes apparent that the ICTSD is not an actor limited to contesting the system from outside – with, for example, political demands contained within its research documents – but has over time emerged effectively within the functioning of that system. That this is possible shows, again, how the terms of what is legitimate governance for WTO Dispute Settlement has changed and, treating this process as discursive, allows us to see the process not as finished but still subject to a continuing re-articulation.

Conclusion

The emergence of new identities in WTO Dispute Settlement has led to a debate over if, and how much, these apparently new forms of political agency challenge the system's formal state centrism. Yet, as with the example of the *amicus curiae* principle, it is debatable as to how much the creation of these new avenues of 'actorness' have altered the structure of agency in WTO Dispute Settlement. In response, the article has argued that the emergence of these new identities should be viewed as the product of a discursive struggle over the terms of what is legitimate in WTO Dispute Settlement. And, as seen in the external political battles that contextualised the emergence of the *amicus curiae* principle, that discursive struggle exceeds the formal institutional structure of the WTO and its Member-states.

Underlying this struggle has been a general concern with representation, including both how societal concerns (e.g. environmentalism) should be heard and how to ensure that the less-resourced Member-states are able to utilise the system to advance their own interests. The politics provoked by these discussions has been central to the constitution of the *amicus curiae* and *private counsel* principles. Likewise, it has provided the context in which it has become legitimate for Member-states to engage closely with civil society actors like the ICTSD in formulating their own 'interests'. Concurrently, the proliferation of subject positions in WTO Dispute Settlement has enabled individuals representing businesses a greater range of access points to the system.

Where new subject positions have been legally codified through Appellate Body rulings, what becomes apparent is a two-way process between de- and re-politicisation. That is, WTO Dispute Settlement exists to de-politicise the management of regulations governing cross-border trade flows by resolving disputes between Member-states over the interpretation of the agreements they have signed. As a mechanism, it reflects a wider shift towards legalism in global governance – a process that includes the technocratisation of other policy areas including trade. Yet, each time it is implemented, WTO Dispute Settlement potentially faces the destabilising contradiction – that between its legal-technocratic identity and a world that is fundamentally political. Within and without the formal institution, the system has been frequently re-politicised.

The WTO Dispute Settlement system is subjected to a continual discursive struggle over its legitimacy – whether expressed in terms of its efficacy, or degree of representation, what matters is that its identity as a purely legal-technocratic body is contested. To maintain that identity, however, a process of re-articulation can be seen that has led to the emergence of new actor identities – some codified within the internal workings of the system (e.g. *amicus curiae, private counsel*), and some formally external but nevertheless essential to its operation (e.g. ICTSD). None of these new identities is revolutionary in the sense that WTO Dispute Settlement has been radically altered, yet equally it is clear that the system has changed beyond how it was originally conceived within its founding charter. If those changes are seen simply as apolitical, technocratic decisions, then research misses out on the social processes driving what are political developments.

What is legitimate in WTO Dispute Settlement is not predetermined, but acquires its meaning or context within a particular political community. That community is not static and limited to Member-states alone but, as argued above, includes a much broader social context in which, in some cases, street protests and movements have become relevant. If the apparent inclusion of more actors makes WTO Dispute Settlement appear more democratic, this is only because the political community shaping that system sees the value 'democracy' as a condition for legitimate governance.

Acknowledgement

The author would like to thank the editors of this special issue, as well as the two anonymous reviewers for their invaluable comments.

Funding

This work was supported by the Danish Social Science Research Council.

Notes
1. Based on an interview with a practitioner.
2. Based on interviews with several practitioners.
3. Based on interviews with practitioners.
4. Based on interviews with personnel in both the ICTSD and ACWL.

References

Abromeit, H., and M. Stoiber. 2007. "Criteria of Democratic Legitimacy." In *Legitimacy in an Age of Global Politics*, edited by A. Hurrelman, S. Schneider, and J. Steffek, 35–56. Basingstoke: Palgrave.

Appleton, A. 1999. "Shrimp/Turtle: Untangling the Nets." *Journal of International Economic Law* 2 (3): 477–496. doi:10.1093/jiel/2.3.477.

Appleton, A. 2000. "Amicus Curiae Submissions in the Carbon Steel Case: Another Rabbit from the Appellate Body's Hat?" *Journal of International Economic Law* 3 (4): 691–699. doi:10.1093/jiel/3.4.691.

Beetham, D., and C. Lord. 1998. *Legitimacy and the European Union*. London: Longman.

Bexell, M., J. Tallberg, and A. Uhlin. 2010. "Democracy in Global Governance: The Promises and Pitfalls of Transnational Actors." *Global Governance* 16 (1): 81–101.

Bohman, J. 2005. "From *Demos* to *Demoi*: Democracy across Borders." *Ratio Juris* 18 (3): 293–314. doi:10.1111/raju.2005.18.issue-3.

Bown, C., and B. Hoekman. 2005. "WTO Dispute Settlement and the Missing Developing Country Cases: Engaging the Private Sector." *Journal of International Economic Law* 8 (4): 861–890. doi:10.1093/jiel/jgi049.

Buchanan, A., and R. Keohane. 2006. "The Legitimacy of Global Governance Institutions." *Ethics & International Affairs* 20 (4): 405–437. doi:10.1111/j.1747-7093.2006.00043.x.

Clark, I. 2005. *Legitimacy in International Society*. Oxford: Oxford University Press.

Clark, I. 2007. "Legitimacy in International Society or World Society?" In *Legitimacy in an Age of Global Politics*, edited by A. Hurrelman, S. Schneider, and J. Steffek, 193–210. Basingstoke: Palgrave.

Dingwerth, K. 2007. *The New Transnationalism – Transnational Governance and Democratic Legitimacy*. Basingstoke: Palgrave Macmillan.

Eagleton-Pierce, M. 2012. *Symbolic Power in the World Trade Organization*. Oxford: Oxford University Press.

Elsig, M. 2007. "The World Trade Organization's Legitimacy Crisis: What does the Beast Look Like?" *Journal of World Trade* 41 (1): 75–98.

Esty, D. C. 2002. "The World Trade Organization's Legitimacy Crisis." *World Trade Review* 1 (1): 7–22. doi:10.1017/S1474745601001021.

Føllesdal, A. 2007. "Legitimacy Deficits Beyond the State: Diagnoses and Cases." In *Legitimacy in an Age of Global Politics*, edited by A. Hurrelman, S. Schneider, and J. Steffek, 211–228. Basingstoke: Palgrave.

Ford, J. 2003. *A Social Theory of the WTO – Trading Cultures*. Basingstoke: Palgrave Macmillan.

Garrett, G., and J. M. Smith. 2002. "The Politics of WTO Dispute Settlement." *UCLA International Institute*. http://escholarship.org/uc/item/4t4952d7.

Grant, R. W., and R. O. Keohane. 2005. "Accountability and Abuses of Power in World Politics." *American Political Science Review* 99 (1): 29–43. doi:10.1017/S0003055405051476.

Held, D., and A. McGrew. 2002. *Governing Globalization*. Cambridge: Cambridge University Press.

Hurd, I. 1999. "Legitimacy and Authority in International Politics." *International Organization* 53 (2): 379–408. doi:10.1162/002081899550913.

Hurrelman, A., S. Scheider, and J. Steffek, eds. 2007. *Legitimacy in an Age of Global Politics*. Basingstoke: Palgrave.

Kim, H. C. 1999. "The WTO Dispute Settlement Process: A Primer." *Journal of International Economic Law* 2 (3): 457–476. doi:10.1093/jiel/2.3.457.

Layton, D., and J. Miranda. 2003. "Advocacy Before World Trade Organization Dispute Settlement Panels in Trade Remedy Cases." *Journal of World Trade* 37 (1): 69–103.

Leitner, K., and S. Lester. 2011. "WTO Dispute Settlement 1995–2010 – A Statistical Analysis." *Journal of International Economic Law* 14 (1): 191–201. doi:10.1093/jiel/jgr007.

Mavroidis, P. 2001. *Amicus Curiae Briefs before the WTO: Much Ado about Nothing*. Jean Monnet Working Paper 2/01. New York: NYU School of Law.

McCall Smith, J. 2003. "WTO Dispute Settlement: The Politics of Procedure in Appellate Body Rulings." *World Trade Review* 2 (1): 65–100. doi:10.1017/S1474745603001356.

Mügge, D. 2011. "Limits of Legitimacy and the Primacy of Politics in Financial Governance." *Review of International Political Economy* 18 (1): 52–74. doi:10.1080/09692290903025162.

Papadopoulos, Y. 2007. "Problems of Democratic Accountability in Network and Multilevel Governance." *European Law Journal* 13 (4): 469–486. doi:10.1111/eulj.2007.13.issue-4.

Reinisch, A., and C. Irgel. 2001. "The Participation of Non-Governmental Organisations (NGOs) in the WTO Dispute Settlement System." *Non-State Actors and International Law* 1: 127–151. doi:10.1163/15718070121003482.

Risse, T., and M. Kleine. 2007. "Assessing the Legitimacy of the EU's Treaty Revision Methods." *JCMS: Journal of Common Market Studies* 45 (1): 69–80. doi:10.1111/jcms.2007.45.issue-1.

Rosenau, J. 2000. "Change, Complexity, and Governance in Globalizing Space." In *Debating Governance*, edited by J. Pierre, 167–200. Oxford: Oxford University Press.

Scharpf, F. 1999. *Governing in Europe – Effective and Democratic?* Oxford: Oxford University Press.

Schmidt, V. 2010a. *The European Union in Search of Political Identity and Legitimacy: Is More Politics the Answer?* Institute for European Integration Research Working Paper Series (05/2010). Wien: Austrian Academy of Sciences.

Schmidt, V. 2010b. "Democracy and Legitimacy in the European Union Revisited: Input, Output and 'Throughput' Legitimacy." In *Working Paper for the Research College on the Transformation of Europe*. Berlin: Otto Suhr Institute, Freie Universität.

Schmidt, V. 2013. "Democracy and Legitimacy in the European Union Revisited: Input, Output and 'Throughput'." *Political Studies* 61: 2–22. doi:10.1111/post.2013.61.issue-1.

Shaffer, G. 2003. *Defending Interests: Public-Private Partnerships in WTO Litigation.* Washington, DC: The Brookings Institution.

Shaffer, G. 2006a. "What's New in EU Trade Dispute Settlement? Judicialization, Public – Private Networks and the WTO Legal Order." *Journal of European Public Policy* 13 (6): 832–850. doi:10.1080/13501760600837153.

Shaffer, G. 2006b. "The Challenges of WTO Law: Strategies for Developing Country Adaptation." *World Trade Review* 5 (2): 177–198.

Shoyer, A. 2003. "Panel Selection in WTO Dispute Settlement Proceedings." *Journal of International Economic Law* 6 (1): 203–209. doi:10.1093/jiel/6.1.203.

Steffek, J. 2007. "Legitimacy in International Relations: From State Compliance to Citizen Consensus." In *Legitimacy in an Age of Global Politics*, edited by A. Hurrelman, S. Schneider, and J. Steffek, 175–192. Basingtoke: Palgrave.

Steger, D. 2002. "The Rule of Law or the Rule of Lawyers?" *The Journal of World Investment & Trade* 3 (5): 769–792. doi:10.1163/221190002X00274.

Strange, M. 2011. "Discursivity of Global Governance: Vestiges of 'Democracy' in the World Trade Organization." *Alternatives: Global, Local, Political* 36 (3): 240–256. doi:10.1177/0304375411418601.

Strange, M. 2014. *Writing Global Trade Governance – Discourse and the WTO.* London: Routledge.

Strange, M. 2015. "Do Non-State Actors Enhance the Accountability of Global Governance? – the Case of WTO Dispute Settlement." *Global Policy and Governance* 3 (1): 95–112.

Urry, J. 2005. "The Complexities of the Global." *Theory, Culture & Society* 22 (5): 235–254. doi:10.1177/0263276405057201.

Van der Borght, K. 1999. "The Advisory Center on the WTO Law: Advancing Fairness and Equality." *Journal of International Economic Law* 2 (4): 723–728. doi:10.1093/jiel/2.4.723.

Wilkinson, R. 2005. "Managing Global Civil Society – The WTO's Engagement with NGOs." In *The Idea of Global Civil Society – Politics and Ethics in a Globalizing Era*, edited by R. Germain and M. Kenny, 156–199. London: Routledge.

Wolf, K. D. 2002. "Contextualizing Normative Standards for Legitimate Governance Beyond the State." In *Participatory Governance*, edited by J. R. Grote and B. Gbikpi, 35–50. Opladen: Leske.

Zürn, M. 2000. "Democratic Governance Beyond the Nation-State: The EU and Other International Institutions." *European Journal of International Relations* 6 (2): 183–221. doi:10.1177/1354066100006002002.

Political contestation and the emergence of new actors, but who governs? A response to Michael Strange

John Mikler

This is a reply to:

Strange, Michael. 2016. "The discursive (de)legitimisation of global governance: political contestation and the emergence of new actors in the WTO's Dispute Settlement Body." *Global Discourse* 6 (3): 352–369. http://dx.doi.org/10.1080/23269995.2015.1070019.

Since its creation, the World Trade Organization (WTO) has been the subject of heated debate as to its legitimacy, with particular focus on the operations of its quasi-judicial Dispute Settlement Mechanism (DSM). The debate has primarily revolved around the extent to which it undermines state sovereignty (e.g. see Krasner 2001; Bagwell and Staiger 2001), what room to move is left for states to act in the interests of their citizens (e.g. see Weiss 2005; Aggarwal and Evenett 2014), and whose interests are served in the process of its operations. Some authors have defended its legitimacy and the desirability of its agenda (e.g. Wolf 2004; Bhaghwati 2004), and the WTO itself has found it necessary to defend itself from the constant attacks it receives. Indeed, in WTO (2008), it declares that 'from the money in our pockets and the goods and services that we use, to a more peaceful world, the WTO and the trading system offer a range of benefits', before outlining the 'ten benefits' it confers on the world.[1] Therefore, Michael Strange's (2016) analysis builds on a rich tradition of attacking and re-conceiving the legitimacy of the WTO. Although possessing all the hallmarks of a profoundly democratic institution, with membership comprised of 161 states on the basis that membership affords them an equal voice, yet it is the case that who is heard/not heard, and how they are heard/not heard, matters a great deal. This is not just a matter of what we see on the procedural surface but a question of legitimacy: who has voice and who governs.

However, rather than considering a state-centric view of legitimacy, Strange focusses on the role of discourse and 'relationality' in considering the WTO's processes and the outcomes it delivers, particularly the '(de)legitimisation of global governance' through 'political contestation and the emergence of new actors'. What he seeks to do is demonstrate that the WTO's DSM has been 're-politicised' as a result of new actors that are discursively re-shaping its role. He seeks to consider the extent of the 'new avenues of "actorness"' opened in the process that have altered the DSM and impacted the legitimacy of the WTO itself. But at what stage could it be said that the WTO was not a subject for political contestation? How can we say it has been 're-politicised' as opposed to some state of existence or time when it was unproblematically simply performing a 'legal-technocratic' function, as he puts it? I doubt one can say that this was ever clearly the case in reality. Furthermore, the point that globalisation and global governance are characterised by a range of state and non-state actors and their inter-actions is widely accepted. Therefore, what is the 'actorness' he refers to? He seems to suggest that there are actors that are defined as such because they act like an actor, which is tautological, or have actor-like qualities because they resemble those of other actors, like states. Perhaps my lack of clarity on such points may not be a problem shared by others, but more importantly my confusion extends to the proof for the conclusions drawn as a result of the framework he establishes. I realise that for reasons of ontology and epistemology, 'proof' is by definition not possible in any analysis of discourse and discursive power, but even so on the basis of the evidence presented I feel that the point of his analysis is not as clearly demonstrated as might be desired. There are three reasons for this: (1) the outputs of the system as opposed to the inputs; (2) the legitimacy of the voices heard, or the inputs themselves; and (3) the absence of the discourse to demonstrate it.

It is approaching two decades since the excitement surrounding the protests in respect of 'US-Shrimp' and the 'Battle of Seattle', but I do not think it overly pessimistic to say that the WTO's core agenda and the results its DSM produces are virtually unchanged since then. That is to say, the outputs do not seem to reflect the concerns input by those contesting the system that produces them. The Doha Development Round has failed, and the neoliberal agenda underpinning the WTO and the World Bank and International Monetary Fund (IMF), the other two members of the 'Unholy Trinity' as Chang (2008) calls them, seems as firmly in place as ever. Despite declarations of fundamental changes in global governance in the wake of the 2008 global financial meltdown, the 'Globalisation Consensus', as Wade (2009) calls it, endures because those whose interests it serves are still 'in charge': powerful states and powerful private actors from them. Despite the protests, despite the involvement of new voices, despite supposedly new agendas to recognise concerns of those weaker than the WTO's most powerful member states and the corporations that hail from them, and despite the greatest challenge to neoliberal capitalism since the Great Depression of the 1930s, we seem to have a WTO that exists and operates to deliver the same outcomes as it did at its inception: a world of integrated markets characterised by free trade and investment flows. I cannot help but agree with authors such as Drezner (2007, 20) that while the existence of alternative discourses espoused by civil society is clear, it is much harder to demonstrate that these discourses are pervasive let alone 'too ideationally powerful for states to ignore'.[2]

The outputs produced by the DSM system therefore arguably appear little affected by the new actors involved in providing inputs to it and their attempts at discursive delegitimisation. If anything, it would seem that they have been co-opted by the system to relegitimise it. Therefore, in focussing on the inputs there seems to be some wishful thinking involved, which I am more than willing to admit I share, that political contestation should have produced change. However, there is also a question of who is doing the contestation, and thereby providing the inputs. This goes to the question of 'input legitimacy', that 'those affected by governance feel able to influence – either directly or indirectly via representatives – what goes into the policy engine'. This is treated too uncritically in the analysis. Authors such as Scholte (2002) and Dryzek (2012) point out that the role played by global civil society is a highly problematic terrain, while Chandhoke (2005) outright criticises the power relations underlying the discursive contestation of global governance by non-state actors, especially Non-Government Organisations (NGOs). Those whose voices are heard are largely drawn from the most powerful states, and the NGOs through which they act are similarly based there. Therefore, rather than speaking on behalf of those affected by the governance status quo, they risk speaking *instead* of them. This is not to say that what we have is a case of the new actors failing to influence the operations of the WTO, but there seems little critical weight given to the possibility that the NGOs themselves are reflections of geopolitical patterns of power rather than a response to them.

Finally, I hoped to see more of the discourse itself in an article about discursive delegitimisation. Certainly, the process of the DSM and arguments as to how the inclusion of new actors in it had transformed its operations and procedures were outlined. But the basis for these is given as 'interviews with practitioners' or with 'personnel'. Who were they that their views may be said to matter? What were they asked? What did they say? How has the discourse changed, and by implication how has discursive power of the WTO been contested or re-constituted? All we are told is that the conclusions drawn are the result of 'existing findings and interviews with civil servants in the WTO Secretariat and other relevant bodies'. Apart from good research being replicable on the basis that the method of its conduct should be transparent, the result is that while the conclusion reached that 'what is legitimate in WTO Dispute settlement is not pre-determined, but acquires its meaning or context within a political community' may be true, what this means in terms of both the inputs and outputs of the DSM is harder to discern.

Overall, as a conceptual piece on discourse, legitimacy and global governance I found the analysis interesting and enlightening. However, to demonstrate the impact of contestation on discursive legitimacy involves a more critical focus on the inputs and outputs, as well as evidence for a link between the two. We need to consider this as well as the process by which it may, or may not, occur. I cannot help but feel that based on the outputs of its processes, those who have input continue to be the WTO's most powerful member states and the voices of non-state actors drawn from them. In other words, state-centric under-standings of the operations of the WTO and the dominant voices whose interests are served by its agenda remain salient. They continue to be the key constructers of legitimacy, and as such those who govern, perhaps regrettably, have essentially not changed.

Notes

1. An earlier version of this document addressed '10 common misunderstandings', but it would seem that rather than attacking its critics as misunderstanding, there has been a decision that defending its *rasions dêtre* should now be cast in more positive terms.
2. On pages 21–22 he goes on to argue that while negotiations held under the auspices of the Organization for Economic Cooperation and Development (OECD) in the late 1990s to produce a Multilateral Agreement on Investment that would have extended the WTO agreements are claimed to have been scuppered by global civil society, in reality they may also be seen as failing due to the unwillingness of the states involved in the negotiations.

References

Aggarwal, V. K., and S. J. Evenett. 2014. "Do WTO Rules Preclude Industrial Policy? Evidence from the Global Economic Crisis." *Business and Politics* 16 (4): 481–509. doi:10.1515/bap-2014-0040.

Bagwell, K., and R. Staiger. 2001. "National Sovereignty in the World Trading System." *Harvard International Review* 22 (4): 54–59.

Bhagwati, J. 2004. *In Defense of Globalisation*. Oxford: Oxford University Press.

Chandhoke, N. 2005. "How Global is Global Civil Society?" *Journal of World-Systems Research* 11 (2): 356–370.

Chang, H. 2008. *Bad Samaritans: The Myth of Free Trade and the Secret History of Capitalism*. New York: Bloomsbury Press.

Drezner, D. W. 2007. *All Politics is Global: Explaining International Regulatory Regimes*. Princeton: Princeton University Press.

Dryzek, J. S. 2012. "Global Civil Society; The Progress of Post-Westphalian Politics." *Annual Review of Political Science* 15: 101–119. doi:10.1146/annurev-polisci-042010-164946.

Krasner, S. 2001. "Think Again: Sovereignty." *Foreign Policy* 122(Jan/Feb): 20–29. doi:10.2307/3183223.

Scholte, J. A. 2002. "Civil Society and Democracy in Global Governance." *Global Governance* 8 (3): 281–304.

Strange, M. 2016. "The Discursive (De)Legitimisation of Global Governance - Political Contestation and the Emergence of New Actors in the WTO's Dispute Settlement Body". *Global Discourse* 6 (3): 352–369. http://dx.doi.org/10.1080/23269995.2015.1070019.

Wade, R. 2009. "Is the Globalization Consensus Dead?" *Antipode* 41 (1): 141–165.

Weiss, L. 2005. "Global Governance, National Strategies: How Industrialized States Make Room to Move under the WTO." *Review of International Political Economy* 12 (5): 723–749. doi:10.1080/09692290500339768.

Wolf, M. 2004. *Why Globalisation Works*. New Haven and London: Yale University Press.

WTO. 2008. *10 Benefits of the WTO Trading System*. Lausanne: WTO Secretariat. Accessed 5 June 2015. https://www.wto.org/english/res_e/doload_e/10b_e.pdf.

Resisting legitimacy: Weber, Derrida, and the fallibility of sovereign power

Thomas Clément Mercier

ABSTRACT

In this article, I engage with Derrida's deconstructive reading of theories of performativity in order to analyse Max Weber's sovereignty–legitimacy paradigm. First, I highlight an essential articulation between legitimacy and sovereign ipseity (under-stood, beyond the sole example of State sovereignty, as the autopositioned power-to-be-oneself). Second, I identify a more originary force of legitimation, which remains foreign to the order of performative ipseity because it is the condition for both its position and its deconstruction. This suggests an essential *fallibility* of the performative, which implies a 'mystical' legitimacy and a paradoxical, divisible and self-differential representation of sovereignty. The structural differentiality of legitimacy and sover-eignty signifies an irreducible coloniality of law and language, but also suggests the possibility of an unconditional resistance located in the radical interpretability of the law, beyond determined repre-sentations of powers, dominations, sovereignties or resistances. This reflection is triggered by a reading of Cynthia Weber's theory of 'performative states', describing sovereignty under the form of an impossible ontology, which leads me to elaborate the notion of legitimation-to-come as a non-ontological 'concept': this notion of unconditional legitimacy, beyond sovereignty, binds beliefs and phantasms to the unpresentable force of the event. Pursuing the efforts of scholars such as Rob Walker and Cynthia Weber, I sketch the implications of this archi-performative legitimacy regarding the methodological protocols of International Relations and sociol-ogy, in view of elucidating the persistent ontological presupposi-tions of these disciplines.

> [S]overeignties are rarely as structurally, logically or topologically tight as their practices would have us believe. Sovereignties fall apart in the always potential contingency of everyday life. Even the most absolute sovereign authority has unintended consequences. What can go wrong often does. The unanticipated happens.
>
> (Walker 2010, 192)

Until recently, sovereignty was conceived as infallible. Etymologically, the name suggests a hyperbolic *superiority*, superiority itself[1]; it implies the automatic success of a self-legitimating, autonomous *arkhe*, instantiating power as commencement, originary authority and principle of command. Through the defining feature of self-determination, sovereignty supposedly excludes failure. This exclusion permeates all its philosophical and sociological definitions, even the most empirical or critical. Failure was certainly not an option for the triumphant State such as defined by Max Weber – to the extent that the term 'success' (*Erfolg*) was made part of its definition:

> The state is the human community that, within a defined territory – and the key word here is 'territory' – (successfully [*mit Erfolg*]) claims the *monopoly of legitimate force* for itself. (2008, 156, 2012, 397)[2]

It is impossible to overestimate the importance of this definition for subsequent works in sociology and international relations (IR). One could argue that the whole history of IR consisted in unfolding the theoretical implications of Weber's definition for the international, followed by its meticulous deconstruction in the hands of constructivists and poststructuralists. Schematically, the main objects of contention were: Weber's postulate that the State's monopoly of legitimate violence could be contrasted with international anarchy, and its influence on Morgenthau, Aron and subsequent 'Realism' (Ashley 1988; Walker 1993a, 1993b, 180; C. Weber 2010, 20–21); Weber's inscription of the State within a definite territory, thus essentialising structural categories of inside/outside (Walker 1993b, 126), and defining them according to sovereign 'ontopology' (Derrida 1994, 102; Campbell 1998, 80); Weber's reluctance to account for the State's foreign policy and its decisive role in defining the State's prerogatives as a systemic actor (Thomson 1994; C. Weber 1995, 106); the incapacity of the definition to encompass all forms of sovereign States (C. Weber and Biersteker 1996, 14), and its overall lack of historicity (Thomson 1994).

These studies have profoundly reshaped IR theory by challenging one of its most persistent presuppositions. Here, I offer a theoretical examination of Weber's definition by emphasising two terms, 'success' and 'present', which durably influenced our views of the State as a nexus of sovereignty and legitimacy, and our conception of political theory as an *ontology of domination*. The second term, 'present', immediately follows Weber's definition: his description reflects 'the specific characteristic of the present (*Gegenwart*)' (2008, 156). This appeal to contemporaneity, to the presence of the present, is constant in Weber's 'sociology of domination', explicitly positing the State as a finished product, achievement and *telos*: 'the concept of the state has only in modern times reached its full development' (1978, 56). The motifs of 'success' and 'presence' consolidate each other and orientate the whole of Weber's theory of politics *as* domination (*Herrschaft*) through its culmination in the State. But what are the presuppositions in defining legitimacy ontologically, from the perspective of *present success*?

In this article, I interrogate Weber's socio-ontology of success, by challenging the co-constitutionality of sovereignty and legitimacy and by emphasising their structural fallibility. First, I analyse Cynthia Weber's seminal critique of IR theory and her interpretation of State sovereignty as performative. Performativity theories de-naturalise legitimacy by exposing its discursive character: the State performs itself by successfully producing the conditions of its legitimacy and legibility. I extend this analysis, beyond the example of State domination, to the accreditation of 'ipseity', that is, the definition of the self-same, or self-presence. According to Jacques Derrida:

> Before any sovereignty of the state, of the nation-state, of the monarch, or, in democracy, of the people, ipseity names a principle of legitimate sovereignty, the accredited or recognized supremacy of a power or a force, a *kratos* or a *cracy*. (2005a, 12)

Performative interpretations of legitimacy run the risk to validate this recognition of ipseity, and to enact an ontology of political domination tacitly acknowledging State sovereignty *as* successful autoposition: what Derrida names 'ipsocentrism', or 'ipsocracy' (2005a, 17, 51). By contrast, I highlight, following Derrida, a principle of fallibility consubstantial with performativity. This leads me to emphasise the differential and phantasmatic structure of legitimacy, and to elaborate the non-ontological and post-performative notion of 'legitimacy-to-come'. It suggests an unconditional resistance beyond ipseity, exceeding discourses of successful self-presence and performative legitimacies.

1. Performativity, sovereignty and legitimacy

J.L. Austin inaugurated performativity studies by attempting to distinguish between performative and constative dimensions of language. He suggested that constatives are either true or false, while performatives instantiate their own event, and thus cannot be said to be true or false within admitted conditions of referentiality (1962, 4, 25). One of the most powerful gestures of critical IR was to de-naturalise State sovereignty by emphasising its performative dimension. This resulted in reframing IR theory. The notion of performativity questions the methodological foundations and the conceptual protocols of the discipline, notably by challenging the limit between theory and praxis. In her essay 'Performative States' (1998), Cynthia Weber argues that 'sovereign nation-states are not pre-given subjects but subjects in process and that all subjects in process (be they individual or collective) are the ontological effects of practices which are performatively enacted' (1998, 78). Drawing on the work of Judith Butler, she suggests that States are constructed discursively in ways that posit the State and its four components – authority, territory, population and recognition – as 'natural' and 'prediscursive' (1998, 92).

While performativity studies have always been concerned with questions of legitimation, these never quite came to the centre of the argument.[3] This might be due to a structural difficulty regarding the 'juridical power' of the performative (Butler 1997, 48), on which the articulation between performativity and legitimacy relies. Indeed, the performative finds itself on both 'sides' of the legitimation process: it must always be legitimated (this is the condition of its 'success' or 'felicity') *and* legitimating (because it produces an utterance with juridical value). Performativity is a principle of foundation *and* conservation (Derrida 2002b, 272–277), thus blurring the limit between foundational and procedural representations of legitimacy. This double-sidedness seems to imply a tautological circularity which disseminates the origin of legitimacy. The question of legitimation concerns: (1) the performative statement under scrutiny – for instance, such or such practice or discourse of State sovereignty; (2) the legitimacy of the performative conventions which have supposedly legitimated or enabled said practice or discourse; (3) the legitimacy of the interpretative models through which one appraises these matters of performativity-legitimacy. Each one of these analytical levels may, at once or in turn, be envisaged as performative or constative, as legitimating or legitimated device, which allows for all possible confusions, conflations, with the risk to validate, *qua* performative ontologisation or essentialisation, existing structures of legitimation. In isolating a performative in view of theoretical or critical appraisal, one must always presuppose (at least provisionally) the presence and legitimacy of contextual conventions that made the performative 'successful' or 'unsuccessful', and made the critical pondering of this 'success' possible in the first place. This interpretative effort involves a performative selection that cannot be entirely neutral, or can only pretend to be so by masquerading itself into a theoretical constative.

This problematisation of performative legitimacy directly concerns sovereignty, inasmuch as sovereign power presents itself as the unchallenged foundation of legitimacy and law. However, like performatives, singular sovereign decisions (characterised, at least in principle, as self-determined and autoposited) may be placed, depending on interpretations or appraisals, on either side of the legitimating–legitimated divide. In all rigour, the logic of performative sovereignty requires that performatives enclose themselves into a perfect, tautological circle of self-justified force and forceful self-justification. The notion of 'successful' performative would thus allow the closure of this circle in the fictional moment of its inauguration. In this moment, the performative *is* force, *is* legitimacy, *is* selfhood, *is* performative, etc. – 'performative tautology or a priori synthesis' (Derrida 2002b, 267). This tautological position suggests an absolute self-referentiality, the *sui generis* capacitating title of a performative power which would ultimately rely only on itself to produce the discourse of its self-legitimation, thus consolidating the phantasm of an ipsocratic *coup* de force:

> A 'successful' revolution, the 'successful' foundation of a state (in somewhat the same sense that one speaks of a 'felicitous performative speech act') will produce after the fact [*après coup*] what it was destined *in advance* to produce, namely, proper interpretative models to read in return, to give sense, necessity and above all legitimacy to the violence that has produced, among others, the interpretative model in question, that is, the discourse of its self-legitimation. (Derrida 2002b, 270)

The term 'success' thus carries the weight of the argument. The epistemic risk is to validate the phantasm of sovereign ipseity by confirming and closing this 'hermeneutic circle' through the authority of another performative (Derrida 2002b, 270). In accrediting this ontological circularity, one enacts, seemingly constatively, but always through some performative interpretation (with practical implications), the 'success' of the sovereign performative and of its self-legitimation. Sovereignties thrive on this a priori conflation of performative and constative, because it results in equating sovereignty with its 'own' performative power, as if it were indeed the product of its 'own' narrative.

If I emphasise the self-legitimating dimension of the performative, it is because self-legitimation or 'self-justification' (*Selbstrechtfertigung*) plays a decisive role in Max Weber's sociology of domination. Indeed, Weber defines politics and the State as structures of domination (*Herrschaftstrukturen*) inasmuch as they acquire and sustain legitimacy: 'the continued exercise of every domination (in our technical sense of the word) always has the strongest need of self-justification through appealing to the principles of its legitimation' (1978, 954). According to Weber, the need for legitimacy is a 'universal fact' concerning all displays of power or force (*Macht*). Legitimacy modifies power into domination (*Herrschaft*) by affecting its 'empirical structures' (1978, 953, 1980, 549). In this presentation, legitimation operates according to a logic of *supplementarity* (Derrida 1997, 163): self-legitimation contributes to power structures at an essential level by constructing the 'legend' of superiority, but is defined as a non-originary characteristic of the order since it only justifies already-existing 'superiorities' (Weber 1978, 953–954; 1980, 549–550). Power, as *dominant* power, superior mastery, superiority *itself*, is postulated as already-existing subject, a powerful ipseity which generates its own 'legend', the discourse of its self-legitimation. Power comes *first*, as the factual superiority of a 'real' ipseity (the dominant subject: an individual, or a group of individuals), which merely needs to justify this powerful position, and does so because it *can*. It has the power to do so because it has the power to *be itself* and thus to *justify* itself. Power is its own origin, self-present, a 'preddiscursive' selfness (as Cynthia Weber puts it), a site from which it can generate legitimacy as mere supplement.

2. Fallible performatives

Despite critical potentialities enabled by performativity theories, the risk is to essentialise sovereignty and legitimacy and to give *credit* to the performative gesture by conceiving it as successful – even when the intent is to criticise it.

However, Butler explained in *Excitable Speech*,[4] following Derrida, that 'the failure of the performative is the condition of its possibility': 'That performative utterances can go wrong, be misapplied or misinterpreted, is essential to their "proper" functioning' (1997, 151). This fallibility of the performative is necessary for a simple reason: if the performative were absolutely conform to pre-existing referents or norms, if it merely validated or enacted, without rupture or 'distance', the legitimating conventions which supposedly enabled it, then it could not be said to produce an event in any meaningful way (while this is the condition for performativity [Austin 1962, 56]). This performative would not even be identifiable as such: it would escape all possibility of representation, interpretation or appraisal. If it is to produce an event, a performative must involve a rupture of context, some interpretative gesture vis-à-vis existing norms, thus exposing itself, from the onset, to counter-interpretations: the conditions of its legitimacy are the conditions of its illegitimacy, because the performative can never thoroughly stabilise all protocols of legitimation as it opens itself to *other* interpretations, other protocols of legitimacies, legitimacies-to-come.

As such, the performative must always fail to be unmitigatedly legitimate and legitimated; the conditions of its 'success' or 'failure', the very conditions of its theoretical or empirical intelligibility, depend on future interpretations. These can never, for the same reasons, present themselves absolutely and without contradiction. Legitimating discourses aim to suture the contradictions inherent to the performative by fabricating a cohesive narrative; however, the self-differential character of such discourses cannot be absolutely contained, and is bound to surge under the form of an event, contradicting and altering self-legitimating narratives. The event is a 'force of *rupture*', otherly, excessively unpredictable because it disrupts the powers of anticipation consubstantial with performative ipseity (Derrida 1994, 37). Legitimacy can only stabilise, forcefully but imperfectly, the force of the event (Derrida 2002a, 235); its function is to provisionally repress the event, that is, its constitutive otherness. However, otherness precedes and challenges the position of self-legitimating narratives; as such, it is an immanent force of alteration. This force of *différance* affects the performative before and beyond its stabilisation into determined performative 'acts', 'subjectivities', 'powers', 'authorities' or 'dominations' – all of which we may call, following Cynthia Weber, 'performative *states*' (be they 'states' or 'States').

Since it depends on future interpretations, reconstructions and legitimations, the true 'success' of the performative remains to come: it does not *present* itself ontologically, and remains ultimately enclosed into a mystique. I emphasise this notion because the 'mystical' will return in my analysis of Max Weber's *verstehende Soziologie*:

> Even if the success of performatives that found a law (for example, and this is more than an example, of a state as guarantor of a law) presupposes earlier conditions and conventions (for example, in the national and international arena), the same 'mystical' limit will reemerge at the supposed origin of said conditions, rules or conventions, and at the origin of their dominant interpretation. (Derrida 2002b, 242)

Essentially secretive, self-differential, performatives involve an obligating force of law which remains irreducibly anchored in some fabulous of fictional power. Performative 'success' cannot present itself *as such*; it ultimately relies on belief, and this is what the concept of legitimacy comes to express: 'The performance of legitimacy is the credible production of the legitimate, the one that apparently closes the gap which makes it possible' (Butler 1997, 151). The performative thus capitalises on 'credibility' (to use Butler's term), on 'beliefs' (to use Max Weber's term), or on what Derrida calls, thus naming the paradoxical effectiveness of this 'make-believe' without opposite, the *phantasma*:

> *phantasma* also named for the Greeks the apparition of the specter, the vision of the phantom, or the phenomenon of the revenant. [...] No more than myth, fable and phantasm are doubtless not truths or true statements as such, but neither are they errors or deceptions, false witness or perjuries. (2002a, 28)

The notion of phantasmatic legitimacy would thus imply a *hauntological* (rather than ontological) understanding of performativity (Derrida 1994, 202). Etymologically, 'performativity' suggests an act which can fully accomplish the event that it instantiates: 'to perform' derives from Old French *parfornir* (to carry out, furnish completely). Such conception of performativity entails full self-presence. In contrast, phantasmaticity would signify an unfulfilled performance, incapacitated in its effort to instantiate the event that it strives to perform. By definition, a phantasm does not *present* itself: it exceeds categories of felicity or infelicity, veraciousness or falsity, being and nothingness. Phantasmaticity suggests a non-ontological relation to truth and legitimacy: it is neither representational (like the constative) nor (self-)presentational (like the traditional performative).

3. Deconstructing the sovereignty–legitimacy paradigm: coloniality and symbolic powers

Accounting for the fallibility of legitimation challenges Max Weber's co-implication between sovereign power and legitimacy. In several places in *Economy and Society*, Weber thematises legitimation as an instrumentalisation of 'cultural phenomena' in order to consolidate domination. Weber's conception of domination presupposes a spontaneous obedience, some irreducible 'will to obey' (1980, 122), which may be politically fostered through influencing cultural or psychological factors allowing obedience. This includes forms of 'mass domestication' through the efforts of religious authorities (1978, 477), the production and imposition of legends justifying the superiority of the dominant group (953–954), or specific politics of education and language, as demonstrated in the chapter 'The basis of legitimacy':

> The scope of determination of social relationships and cultural phenomena by virtue of domination is considerably broader than appears at first sight. For instance, the domination exercised in schools has much to do with the determination of the forms of speech and of written language which are regarded as orthodox. (1978, 215; 1980, 123)

This factoring of culture into practices of domination is one of the most noted aspects of Weberian sociology. Bourdieu, for instance, elaborated on the cultural implications of this paradigm of domination-legitimation, which he reconceived as symbolic capital, power or violence, also involving a politics of performativity (1991).

The interconnection between political and cultural-linguistic dimensions was approached differently by Derrida: in *The Monolingualism of the Other* (1998), he defined an essential 'coloniality' in 'the very language of the Law', in 'law as language' (39). This irreducible coloniality implies the violence of an 'originary "alienation" which institutes every language as a language of the other: the impossible property of a language' (63). I shall return to this structural 'otherness' (or heteronomy) of law in my concluding remarks, as it might suggest another representation of legitimacy, beyond socio-ontological categories and 'successful' performativities.

Before we get there, Derrida defines the tendency 'to reduce language to the One, that is, to the hegemony of the homogeneous' (1998, 40). This attempt at 'homo-hegemony' is at work in all culture, which implies some epistemic violence or 'domes-tication', alienation and expropriation, be it in their traditionally 'colonial' form or not. Max Weber's paradigm of legitimation-domination, notably through the guise of educa-tional politics and cultural domestication within the State, strangely resembles a form of 'domestic' coloniality. This recalls the oxymoronic notion of '"domestic" intervention', once hypothesised by Cynthia Weber (1995, 106); while this notion seems nonsensical according to the protocols of socio-ontology and IR theory, it also provides an alter-native model interrogating politics of sovereignty and their reliance on homo-hegemonic structures. This ipsocratic tendency, which might be translated, in Max Weber's terms, as an effort to monopolise legitimacy, belongs first and foremost to the structure of language itself, thus exceeding in its scope traditional concepts of governmental power, centralised sovereignty or political legitimation. This does not mean that this monopolising effort is not in itself 'legitimate': it *is* the very legitimacy of performative power at work, characterised, in its forceful effort of self-assertion and self-legitimation, by a tendency to conceal the heterogeneity of the event precisely because heterogeneity signifies the defeat of performativity.

A deconstructive approach to performativity strives to emphasise the fallibility of homo-hegemonic monopolisations and to do justice to the event before and beyond performa-tive ontologies. The very idea of monopolistic legitimacy supposes the concealment of differential legitimations implied by the logic of interpretability. Derrida, in a critique of Bourdieu, expressed his distrust vis-à-vis the sociological concept of legitimation for analogous reasons: all effort of institutionalisation implies a de- and re-contextualisation of legitimacies, that is, a differing legitimation or a differing interpretation of existing legitimacies (which are, in themselves, 'always heterogeneous and worked through by contradictions'). 'This simple fact is enough to threaten the very concept of legitimation to the core: it has no opposite. Nonlegitimacy can appear as such, be its signs ever so discreet, only in a process of prelegitimation' (2002d, 14). The notion that legitimacy is heterogeneous in and through the performed homo-hegemony of the dominant's 'legend' goes to complexify definitions of the State as monopolising legitimate violence. It also implies that there is no 'outside' of legitimacy. Every political situation and domination, even the most centralised in appearance, dissimulates conflicts in legitimacies and interpretations thereof. Incidentally, this very same conviction is what justified Max Weber's suspicion towards what he names the 'juristic' conception of 'sovereignty', which conceals, in the name of sovereign 'unity', the competitive character of transactions and negotiations between different organs *within* the State (1978, 670). The same doubts may be raised with regard to Weber's axiomatics: defining legitimacy as monopolistic operates a performative, forceful stabilisation of differential violences, within the State and beyond, and always in the name of some legendary homo-hegemony.

How does this affect the definition of the State as a strictly 'sociological' object? The expression of (legitimate) sovereignty, through its Weberian translation into the 'monopoly of the legitimate use of physical constraint', is put into question, *virtually*, with every performative interpretation of its legitimating principles (and of the violence enacted supposedly in the name of these principles). Each interpretative reading of practices, within or outside the State, already constitutes, potentially, a rupture of its monopoly by calling for other legitimations (and by anticipating, at least virtually, the violence of their enforcement). Similarly, each operation of law enforcement *attributed* to 'the State', even the least violent and most routinised in appearance, potentially betrays the monopoly of legitimate violence because it ultimately depends on interpretative-performative readings, which may always highlight the illegitimate character of such operations. The same can be said about anyone attempting to justify the 'conservation' or 'reproduction' of the so-called 'present' situation, as they must argue their case through invoking some nonpresent past or present, in the name of some ('better' or 'less bad') future. Every time one speaks for 'us', each time one says 'we', 'our present', 'our State', 'our people', they must speak in the name of an unpresentable performative event (Derrida 2002b, 269), and anticipate some other, undefinable 'success' beyond names and legitimacies. The success of this performance can never be fully justified in the presence of the present.

In 'Force of Law', Derrida argued that 'there is something of the [...] revolutionary situation [...] in every reading that founds something new' by providing a transformative, and therefore forceful, interpretation of the law and of its legitimating principles. This reading, because it is *already* performative, may only appear as illegitimate, unreadable and unintelligible with respect to so-called 'present' norms: its conditions of legitimacy remain 'unreadable in regard to established canons and norms of reading' (Derrida 2002b, 271). Whenever one criticises the present situation, the current 'state' of affairs, one may only do so in the name of different legitimating principles, according to a different enunciation of said principles; however, one must always partly play on something of the previous norm. Anyone calling for a transformation of institutions, be it against the State or 'within' the State, must justify her/his efforts by assuming different legitimating principles, differential interpretations of existing legitimacies. This effort of legitimation can only be somewhat violent and illegitimate because it implies delegitimating at least *some* aspects of the existing order, forecasting different laws (and their enforcement). Due to this constitutive interpretability-fallibility of performativity, what is enforced as legitimate violence may also appear, at least virtually, as illegitimate violence: in 'the "logic" of this readable unreadability' (Derrida 2002b, 271), legitimate violence may always be *read as* violent illegitimacy – both in turn and at once.

Consequently, the notion of 'self-legitimation' becomes nonsensical: legitimation always depends on differential interpretations, which will claim to validate (or invalidate) 'the State' before or beyond the ipseity of a self. There is no 'selfness' of the State. What *figures* the State in its spectral structure is a series of practices and legitimating conventions, already potentially illegitimate because fundamentally contradictory or incompatible, and phantasmatically gathered through the 'presence' without presence of the State. Beyond performative legitimacy, the State signifies the instantiation (or stabilisation) of this impossible cohabitation (co-haunting) of legitimacy and illegitimacy, legitimacy *as* illegitimacy, co-implicating the State *and* its other (the State *as* its other) in and through what Cynthia Weber may have called an 'impossible' ontology (1998, 92). This impossible contradiction is made *seemingly* possible through the spectral body of a phantasmatic sovereignty, and is re-instituted, each time anew and self-contradictorily, through forceful self-domestication and destructive violences, always physical *and* symbolic, both locally focused and spectrally disseminated.

Emphasising the phantasmatic dimension of the State's 'domination' is *not* to say that the phantasm does not have 'undeniable consequences', and often forceful, hurtful implications (Derrida 2011, 185). However, the phantasm escapes, by definition, conditions of performative ontology: self-instantiation, self-presence and sovereign ipseity. *If* there is 'the State', it involves structural divisibility, suicidal practices and self-betrayals, but also brutal reinventions and violent convulsions which, each time singular, put to question homo-hegemonic sovereignties and their conditions of legitimation: 'the state is both self-protecting and self-destroying, at once remedy and poison'. This constitutes its 'autoimmunitary logic' (Derrida, in Borradori 2003, 124).

We are thus far from defining the State as a homogeneous structure involving the presently, successfully claimed monopoly of legitimate violence. Postulating this 'success' already constitutes a performative, legitimating reading of what the State strives to perform in the form of homo-hegemonic domination. Actually, the term 'domination' (*Herrschaft*) remains attached to the phantasm of sovereign ipseity of the Lord (*Herr, dominus*). It is not certain that this concept, as it perpetuates a vision of politics dependent on the ipseity of the self-same, can account for the irreducibly disseminated and differential character of spectral violence.

4. Phantasmaticity and fictionality

What remains to be discussed is the 'logic' of the phantasm, beyond traditional limits of psychoanalysis and political theory. According to Derrida, psychoanalysis has not yet undertaken and thus still less succeeded in thinking, penetrating, and changing the axioms of the ethical, the juridical, and the political, notably in those seismic places where the theological phantasm of sovereignty quakes and where the most traumatic, [...] the most cruel events of our day are being produced. (2002a, 244)

Exceeding categories of socio-onto-phenomenology, the phantasm involves 'a symptomatology of the unconscious' (57). It implies some vision or visibility, appearance and disappearance of the phenomenal apparition, but escapes the fully visible presence of *theoria* (contemplation). The phantasm does not present itself: its existence may only be reconstructed, presumed, allegedly testified, and supposes an irreducible appeal to *belief* and faith, even to 'self-belief' – a notion which signifies a split within the identity of individual ipseity, thus affecting the Weberian motif of 'subjective signification' with irreducible self-division. No one has ever 'seen' a State, its sovereignty or legitimacy. Furthermore, no one can testify absolutely for one's interpretation of the State, and for the promise of ipseity that it supposes. One cannot demonstrate the reality of the phantasm, circumscribe its truth or draw its limits. However, the phantasm cannot be simply rejected as illusion through theoretical dissipation. The phantasmatic is precisely what allows what 'may' be to have some sort of operability: it upholds referentiality without referent. Its non-ontological character does not mean that the phantasm is ineffective; it might even be extremely powerful at other levels, through effects of haunting and 'unconscious beliefs', which suggests an uncanny force of performativity, under the 'amorphous' form of phantasmal eventness (Derrida 2011, 185–186). The phantasm may remain silent, invisible and secret, at once conscious and unconscious. This uncanniness is precisely what makes it most terrifying for ontological conceptualisation. 'Ontology opposes [hauntology] only in a movement of exorcism. Ontology is a conjuration' (Derrida 1994, 202).

However, it would *seem* that in the State, the phantasmatic should be at its most powerful: 'An omnipotent fantasy, of course, because it is a fantasy of omnipotence. [...] the word sovereignty has only ever translated the performative violence that institutes in law a fiction or a simulacrum' (Derrida 2005b, 106). As a phantasmatically centralised, monopolistic point of referentiality, as the locus of the greatest force and legitimacy, State sovereignty supposedly upholds all phantasmaticity through the attempted legitimation of its own phantasm. This is the very violence of its fabular power. But even so it preserves an irreducible fictionality affecting the conditions and structures of legitimate domination. As a 'subject' (a supposedly *sovereign* subject), I do *as if* I could grasp the event of the State as an all-powerful performative; *as if* it were possible to know once and for all if such a performative is successful or not; and *as if* I knew what success *is*. The phantasm signifies the irreducible possibility of fictionality in all language and experience (Derrida 2002c, 354), especially whenever and wherever some sovereign ipseity is concerned. In this spectral economy, the possibility of fiction contaminates all transactions and definitions, all ontologies, which implies that we must speak *as if* there were no phantasms, *as if* we knew exactly what we meant when we speak of 'the State', and, first and foremost, *as if* we knew what we meant when we say 'I', 'I believe', 'I believe I *can* say I' (etc.). For instance: '*I believe* in the legitimacy of the State', or '*I believe* that the State successfully claims the monopoly of legitimate violence'. The 'as if' of the phantasm forces us to abide by an originary fictionality, an irreducible substrate of belief, and this at the very moment when we claim that there *may* be something other than fictions, and that ontological categories *may* be more than *quasi*-ontological, phantas-matic categories. There is no other option than to believe that there be more than mere beliefs, more than legitimate beliefs or credible legitimacies: in this nexus of legitimacy and 'religiosity' (Derrida 2002b, 70), the believer's sovereign ipseity and that of the 'thing' believed (par excellence: the theologico-political phantasm of State sovereignty) are mutually fantasised and spectrally cemented. This process of reciprocal haunting makes it impossible to identify the source of legitimation and sovereignty (be it the individual's or the State's): their common origin is this originary belief without opposite, 'this fiduciary "link"' to the other as pure singularity (2002b, 55). Needless to say that, in this appeal, what one calls 'believing' may only appear as paradoxical, fragile and haunted.

5. Max Weber's 'as if': *Macht*, domination and legitimacy

If I insist on the fictionality of the 'as if', that is because it is explicitly and repeatedly mentioned by Max Weber. It constitutes the paradoxical foundation, admittedly 'awk-ward' (1978, 946), of his sociology of domination. According to Weber, the analogical structure of the 'as if' (*als ob*) remains absolutely 'unavoidable', simply because it allows him to account for domination *sociologically*, that is, faithfully to 'sociological concep-tuality' (1980, 544). What is at stake is the possibility of defining domination (*Herrschaft*) in opposition to the formless concept of *Macht*. This distinction is crucial, because the 'sociological concept of domination' (1978, 53) also determines those of 'politics' and 'the State' (as *Herrschaftsstrukturen*).

    Macht has usually been translated as 'power'. However, it could also be translated as 'force' or 'might', which might be more suitable in this context because the English notion of 'power' often designates legitimate, instituted force (such as State power, which could be rendered in German by the term *Gewalt*, and that Weber would certainly describe as *Herrschaft*). Weber clearly specifies that *Macht* is a very general, potentially pre-political concept, exceeding the scope of a pure sociology of domination: 'The concept of power [*Macht*] is sociologically amorphous. All conceivable qualities of a person and all conceivable combinations of circumstances may put him [*sic*] in a position to impose his will in a given situation' (1978, 53). Because *Macht* is not precise enough of a notion, Weber suggests that it be avoided, preferring the more 'technical' concept of domination: 'The sociological concept of domination must hence be more precise and can only mean the probability that a *command* will be obeyed' (1978, 53). Whatever the worth of this conceptual precision, it is of interest that the notion of *Macht* is from the onset considered as inapplicable in a sociological perspective, which means that political sociology can only concern itself, as sociology of domination, with *this* representation of domination, understood as the probability that an order will be followed. Weber thus conceives political sociology as a study of the conditions of possibility of compliance or submission, which shall indeed lead to a sociological enactment of the *successful* reproduction of domination. His theoretical exclusion of the concept of *Macht* is as much a recognition of epistemic limits (the *amorphousness* of power or force, unpredictable and escaping ontological *formalisation*), as it is a delimita-tion of the field of applicability and domain of competence of sociological methodology.

There cannot be any socio-ontology of *Macht*, and this is why one needs a 'precise' conceptualisation of domination.

Legitimacy is the most important, but also the most fragile element of this theoretical architecture. Legitimacy depends on an *analogical* reasoning which subordinates obedience to an irreducible 'as if'. In a situation of 'domination', everything happens *as if* the dominated were making the will of the dominant the maxim of their own action:

> As 'domination', we shall understand here the following state of affairs: that a manifest *will* (an 'order') of the 'dominant(s)' intends to affect, and effectively affects, the activity of others (the 'dominated', singular or plural), in such a way that such activity, to a socially relevant degree, occurs *as if* the dominated had made the content of the dominant's order the very maxim of their activity for its own sake. (This is what we call 'obedience'.)
>
> This formulation, with the '*as if*', sounds *awkward*, but it is *unavoidable* if one wants to take as basis the concept of domination that we have hypothesised. (M. Weber 1978, 946; 1980, 544; my emphasis)

Why is the 'as if' unavoidable? This is for two correlated and somewhat mutually exclusive reasons. First, it is a requirement of Weber's definition of sociology,

> a science concerning itself with the interpretative understanding of social action and thereby with a causal explanation of its course and consequences. We shall speak of 'action' insofar as the acting individual attaches a subjective meaning to his [*sic*] behaviour – be it overt or covert, omission or acquiescence. (1978, 4)

In accounting for the 'subjective' signification of obedience, interpretative sociology conceives the 'phenomenon of domination' (1978, 216; 1980, 124) through the validation of its legitimation. In doing so, it seeks to establish causal inferences, as well as typological and taxonomic classifications of domination-legitimation (more exactly: of different ideal types of dominations in function of their mode of legitimation). Without the assumption ('as if') of this subjective meaning (and thus of general criteria of validation for different types of dominations), there would be no way of dissociating domination from the amorphousness of *Macht*. Consequently, the conditions of possibility of legitimacy are also the conditions of legitimation of sociological methodology in its capacity to *interpret* power and domination and, subsequently, politics and the State.

Second, Weber is extremely cautious in determining the conditions of possibility of interpretative sociology – which must presuppose, following empirical cases, a methodological individualism, the recognition of an interplay between honesty and dishonesty, the postulate of self-consciousness, the pondering of irrational motives, and so on (1978, 4–22). The mitigating factors of 'probability', 'plausibility' or 'possibility' (7–20) are thus as much on the side of interpretative methodology as on that of domination itself (understood as the *probability* that an order will be obeyed). This implies a redoubling of the 'as if': not only the 'dominated' individual *seems* to act *as if* the content of the dominant's order determined the maxim of her/his activity for its own sake, but the sociologist-interpreter must proceed *as if* this 'as if' were sufficient to determine the *presence* of legitimacy, that is to say to determine the reality, effectiveness and influence of legitimacy *as such*, as *successful* – and of the State as such. Because legitimacy 'itself' escapes empiricity, while remaining 'unavoidable' in order to distinguish domination from purely amorphous *Macht*, the sociologist must proceed *as if* there were no 'as ifs', and *as if* interpretability were tantamount to socio-ontological description. This conflation supposes the reduction of the interpretative 'as if' (the assumed 'subjective signification' of an activity) into the ontological indication of the *presence* of legitimate domination *as such*. This ontological reduction is finally enacted when, despite all 'as ifs', sovereign domination is *defined* as 'success' – exemplarily through the definition of the State's claim to the monopoly of legitimate violence as essentially 'successful'. This decision suspends all the 'as ifs' so as to validate legitimate domination ontologically, as being-present *as such*.

6. Believing beyond ipseity: auto-heteronomic legitimacy

As a conclusion, I wish to thematise an overarching contradiction in the epistemic principles of Max Weber's interpretative sociology.

On the one hand, Weber strives to account sociologically for so-called 'irrational phenomena': 'sociological investigation attempts to include in its scope various irrational phenomena, such as prophetic, mystic, spiritual and affectual modes of action, formulated in terms of theoretical concepts which are adequate on the level of meaning' (1978, 20; 1980, 10). The consequence of this phenomenology (or phantasmatology) is an inflation of discourses concerned with 'subjective signification', be it rational or irrational. The appeal to 'beliefs in legitimacy' (1978, 31) is constant in *Economy and Society*, and conditions all matters of legitimation, not only in the 'technical', 'sociological' sense of the term, but in its irreducibly disseminal polysemy. The obligatory force of legitimation potentially assumes political, economic or religious dimensions – the three domains being brought together, notably, through the antanaclastic use of the term 'credit' (*Kredit*) (1978, 588; 1980, 355). The recourse to the *credo* of 'beliefs', and thus to a certain religiosity, concerns more particularly charismatic legitimacy, which is explicitly defined as secularising a Christian motif: 'The concept of "charisma" ("the gift of grace") is taken from the vocabulary of early Christianity' (1978, 216). However, Weber repeatedly emphasises the role of beliefs in relation to specifically 'rational' modes of legitimation, such as State domination (for instance: 1978, 903–904, where notions of 'prestige' and 'consecration' play a significant role). In the last instance, the legitimating power of narrative fiction ('self-legitimation', 'legend') must always find effectiveness through the belief, or 'acceptance' (953), of dominated *individuals*. Nothing can ultimately *prove* this acceptance, or, conversely, its 'problematisation' (953). The force of legitimacy remains dependent on the mystique of an 'as if' which, in itself, cannot be empirically observed 'as such', escaping phenomenologisation or ontologisation.

On the other hand, Weber attempts to stabilise the effects of this limitless phantasmaticity by maintaining socio-ontological categories. The main recourse of this ontology is his methodological individualism, anchoring Weber's phantasmatology into an ipsocentric representation of reality. In a fashion reminiscent of Marx and Engels' theory of ideology (such as exposed in *The German Ideology*), this gesture starts with an anthropological grounding of *phantasmata* 'in the heads of real men'. 'Collective constructs' are essentially defined as mere 'thoughts' or 'representations', although, as such, they affect 'tremendously' and even 'dominate' the activity of individuals (1978, 14; 1980, 7). Even so, this dominant power of beliefs, which supposedly determines structures of legitimate obedience, remains dependent on the analogical logic of the 'as if'. In many ways, Weber's definition of the domination-obedience structure functions as a parodic perversion of Kant's categorical imperative. For instance, from the *Groundwork*: 'The formal principle of these maxims is, act as if your maxims were to serve at the same time as a universal law (for all rational beings)' (Kant 1997, 45). But while Kant's categorical imperative is the transcendental condition of moral *autonomy*, Weber formalises, under the structure of legitimate domination, a radical *heteronomy*, since the dominated individual acts *as if* s/he were making the content of the dominant's will the maxim of her/his 'own' action. In and through legitimation, domination functions as a transfer of *will*, as if the dominant's 'will' ventriloquised the dominated, and expressed itself directly through the dominated's action. It happens as if the dominant's 'order' or 'will' did not even need to be enunciated as such, in a sort of machinistic automatism through which legitimate law is enacted without performative interpretation or transformative translation, and without remainder. Of course, Weber makes it perfectly clear that the resources of obedience may be diverse, contradictory and ultimately unknowable. The role of violent coercion, for this matter, is particularly ambiguous.[5] However, legitimate domination implies 'a minimum will to obey' (1980, 122), which supposes some abdication of personal will in the name of some other's law. What Weber fails to conceptualise is the paradoxical, unconscious mechanism of this wilful abdication in favour of *another* will. In this operation, Weber still sees the ipseic expression of 'subjective meaning', a *wilful* abandon. The logic of legitimacy and the underlying concept of beliefs ('rational' or not) substantiate the paradox of a 'spontaneous heteronomy', 'voluntary servitude', while maintaining intact the ontological category of ipseity – however phantasmatic and self-contradictory it might be.

The notion of 'belief' carries the weight of the argument. Everything is laid out by Weber as if it were possible to *theorise* beliefs, to take 'subjective meaning' as ontological object through and beyond sociological interpretability. This is due to the fact that Weber binds the presence of 'beliefs' to what he believes to be the only scale of signification accessible to sociological interpretation: 'subjective understanding' and methodological individualism (1978, 13). Weber justifies this by the notion that sociology should be free of value judgements (*Wertfreiheit*), so that the sociologist may describe actors' beliefs and thus define (through axiological neutrality) the subjective signification of activity. But what does *believing* mean, 'this strange and troubling, *unheimlich* [uncanny] concept of belief or credit, of the act of faith, of trusting'? (Derrida 2014, 153) 'What difference is there between *believing* and *not believing* for the unconscious' – and for the phantasm? (Derrida 2011, 157)

'Believing' does not stand for anything simple at all. Derrida (2014) notes that believing does not have an opposite. Believing involves cognitive uncertainty and the phantasmatic 'as if' – that is, a form of representationality foreign to theoretical knowledge, before full presence of consciousness. If I believe in something (for instance, in the legitimacy of the State), it signifies that I *only* believe in it, and whatever the strength of my faith, believing also implies the seduction of its own simulacrum, self-simulation, self-convincing and make-believe, and therefore 'nonbelief' (*incroyance*). I can only let 'myself' believe in something that must *also* be, in all rigour, somehow *unbelievable*, quite simply because it cannot be demonstrated beyond the phantasmatic. Spectral possession is already haunted by its opposite. Believing signifies *not* believing, both at once and in turn:

> To believe is this strange divided state or this strange divided movement, quasi-hypnotic, in which I am not myself, in which I do not know what I know, in which I do not do what I do, in which I doubt the very thing I believe or in which I believe. Believing, in sum, is not believing; to believe is not to believe. And the whole origin of religion, like that of society, culture, the contract in general, has to do with this nonbelief at the heart of believing. (Derrida 2014, 154)

Therefore, Weber's positing of the existence of beliefs *as such* is already an interpretative gesture, and so are attempts to construct 'believing' as a sociological object. The theoretical positing of beliefs, their description as present and localised signifiers, and their ascription to determinate individuals, already imply a stabilisation of conditions of legitimation, notably through a masking of the essential self-division consubstantial with believing. This self-separation of the believing subject affects all ipseity: 'this internal division, this properly analytic dissociation, this cleavage, this split [*schize*] of believing haunted by nonbelief is almost quasi-hypnotic, one might say spectral, quasi-hallucinatory, or unconscious' (2014, 154). Such hallucinatory spectacle signifies an irreducible alienation, a dissociative experience in and through which beliefs uncannily escape from the personal control of subjectivity *as* ipseity: beliefs exceed identity and property, they do not *belong*. However, Weber's anthropology persists in attaching believing to a logic of ipseity, to an individual 'power-to-be-oneself', notably through the paradoxical *possession* of one's 'own' beliefs. Even so, the subject's actions are determined heteronomically, as the other's law. The subject is her/himself, but also, and at once, *not* her/himself.

Through the formulation of the 'as if' consubstantial with his hermeneutics of domination, Weber touches upon something of the paradoxical essence of law and legitimation in relation to ipseity. The paradox is as follows: I have no other choice than, performatively, enacting the law, through my obedience, my beliefs, my interpretations, my practices, and so on, be it in order to 'accept' it or to contest it – but law 'itself' remains fundamentally heterogeneous and inappropriable. This double structure determines our relation to 'Law as Language':

> Its experience would be ostensibly *autonomous*, because I have to speak this law and appropriate it in order to understand it *as if* I was giving it to myself, but it remains necessarily heteronomous, for such is, at bottom, the essence of any law. (Derrida 1998, 39)

The movement of this inevitable, though ultimately impossible, appropriation is what Derrida names the 'auto-heteronomic' structure of Language as Law. As such, this double structure *both* allows the peformative position of ipseity *and* forbids the closure of its performative power into tautological self-legitimation.

This double movement is not without violence. First, it permits the performative positing of law, legitimacy, power, domination, colonialisms, sovereignties, ipseities and all violences which go with these ontological categories. Second, however, it *also* signifies the essential inappropriability and inappropriateness of such categories, always-already deconstructible, disjointed by the othering violence of the event. This second 'concept' of violence is thus an 'originary alienation', implying a constitutive heterogeneity. It also makes future ameliorations and progress possible: it is an archi-performative promise, whose performance is structurally undecidable and fundamentally pervertible. This promise addresses itself to the *im-possible* other (possible inasmuch as it is impossible), beyond determined conventions, performative self-legitimations and sovereign ipseities.

*

In his lecture 'Politics as a Vocation', first given in 1919, Max Weber already approached this structural im-possibility of the event, within the State and perhaps beyond, through what I would call the self-excessive character of politics:

> It is completely true, and all historical experience confirms it, that what is possible could never have been achieved if one had not constantly reached for the impossible in the world. (2008, 207)

If we disconnect Weber's political theory from its socio-ontological presuppositions (starting with its methodological individualism and its ipsocratic concept of domination), we have here a definition of the event as fundamentally im-possible and nonlegitimate. The event must exceed conditions of possibility and legitimation attached to traditional performatives. In its im-possibility, the event suspends phantasms of 'successful' sovereignties and legitimacies, performative conventions and beliefs, in order to *make* law.

As such, the im-possibility of the event is not an accidental characteristic of politics, which would remain localised, for instance, in its revolutionary 'moments' – inseparable, according to Weber, from the 'extra-ordinary' and irrational character of charisma: this 'specifically revolutionary force' (1978, 244). On the contrary, the radical a-legitimacy of the event is what makes it possible for politics (and the State) to have a history: 'it is the whole history of law' (Derrida 2002b, 270), a self-differential history. The event signifies the fallibility of historical legitimacies because the conditions of its success and/or failure remain to come.

Why insist on 'fallibility' rather than 'failure'? Simply because, in order to determine an undeniable failure, one that would be absolutely certain and decidable as 'non-success', we would still have to rely on some performative power or transcendental agency, under the form of some sovereign decision based on conditions of legitimacy-illegitimacy. By contrast, the fallibility of the performative (fallible in the face of the event) maintains the conditionality of the 'as if' and suggests the coming of the other beyond ontological success or failure. Legitimation-to-come destabilises homo-hegemonies and their legitimating criteria; it is essentially rebellious to the order of presence and success. It resists performative conventions by materialising an internal excess 'within' the State and already beyond, an 'impower' preceding power and affecting it unconditionally (Derrida 2002a, 98).

The legitimation-to-come signifies the unconditionality of deconstructive interpretability, which disrupts legitimacies by pointing to their structural divisibility and differentiality, forcing them to mutate and to adapt. It is an autoimmune force of transformation, a becoming-other. This force implies an 'unconditional resistance' (Derrida 2002a, 204), first because it is a principle of self-resistance. It resists ipsocentric categories in the name of the other, of *another* performativity which remains to come, stronger and more legitimate, despite its fallibility, than ontological ipseity. As such, it cannot be ontologised; it cannot give rise to new ontologies. The force of the event does not constitute a 'super- or hyper-sovereignty' (Derrida 2011, 290). Rather, it signifies an infinite process of deposition: a sovereignty *in différance*.

Notes

1. The term 'sovereign' derives from '*superanus*', the power above, higher, *superior* (Derrida 2005a, 168; Bennington 2006).
2. I have modified most translations of Weber's writings. Every time I did, I specified the reference to the existing English translation, followed by the reference to the German text.
3. An analysis of legitimacy in relation to performativity can be found in Lyotard's *The Postmodern Condition* (1984), which defined performative power as strictly self-legitimating (47). In *Excitable Speech* (1997), Judith Butler staged a conversation between Bourdieu and Derrida articulating performativity and legitimacy, and highlighting modes of performative resistance to dominant powers.
4. Butler's approach to performativity then diverges from Derrida's, notably by introducing the notion of 'dominant discourse'. Unfortunately, I cannot discuss her argument in the limits of this essay.
5. Max Weber's definition of State authority entertains a perplexing ambiguity concerning the legitimating power of violence itself. In his account of rational-legal domination, State violence is legitimated (that is the 'normal' or normative articulation between violence and legitimacy), but it is also said to be *legitimating*: centralised political violence (and especially the power 'over life and death') 'guarantees' legitimacy, and provides a surplus of 'prestige', even 'consecration' to the modern institution of State sovereignty (1978, 904). This articulation between violence and legitimation is precarious and somewhat self-contradictory: *on the one hand*, legitimate domination implies that obedience must be spontaneous, and cannot exclusively result from violence, threat, intimidation or fear (37) (because, in this case, domination would conflate with 'amorphous' forms of *Macht* as coercion, whatever its resources); *on the other hand*, political domination (for instance, the State's) is explicitly defined as the type of domination whose 'specific' characteristic is the use of 'physical force (*Gewaltsamkeit*)', or the threat of its use, as the 'last resort' of its domination (54). Between the actual exercise of violence, the threat of using force (inducing fear or intimidation), and 'spontaneous', legitimate obedience per se (which supposedly *excludes* violence *and* threat), it becomes difficult to delineate legitimacy and nonlegitimacy, *Herrschaft* or *Macht*, and to decide if obedience is actually based on fear or on legitimacy-beliefs. On these premises, how does one define and circumscribe 'fear' as opposed to 'beliefs'? And how could this difficulty not contaminate conceptualisations of legitimate domination as consensual?

Funding

Open access for this article was funded by King's College London.

References

Ashley, R. K. 1988. "Untying the Sovereign State: A Double Reading of the Anarchy Problematique." *Millennium – Journal of International Studies* 17 (2): 227–262. doi:10.1177/03058298880170020901.

Austin, J. L. 1962. *How to Do Things with Words. The William James Lectures Delivered at Harvard University in 1955*. London: Oxford University Press.

Bennington, G. 2006. "The Fall of Sovereignty." *Epoché* 10 (2): 395–406. doi:10.5840/epoche20061027.

Borradori, G. 2003. *Philosophy in a Time of terror. Dialogues with Jürgen Habermas and Jacques Derrida*. Chicago: The University of Chicago Press.

Bourdieu, P. 1991. *Language and Symbolic Power*. Cambridge: Polity Press.

Butler, J. 1997. *Excitable Speech. A Politics of the Performative.* New York: Routledge.

Campbell, D. 1998. *National Deconstruction. Violence, Identity, and Justice in Bosnia.* Minneapolis & London: University of Minnesota Press.

Derrida, J. 1994. *Specters of Marx.* Translated by Peggy Kamuf. New York: Routledge.

Derrida, J. 1997. *Of Grammatology.* Corrected edition, Translated by Gayatri Chakravorty Spivak. Baltimore: Johns Hopkins University Press.

Derrida, J. 1998. *Monolingualism of the Other; or, The Prosthesis of Origin.* Translated by Patrick Mensah. Stanford: Stanford University Press.

Derrida, J. 2002a. *Without Alibi.* Translated and edited by Peggy Kamuf. Stanford: Stanford University Press.

Derrida, J. 2002b. *Acts of Religion.* Edited by Gil Anidjar. London: Routledge.

Derrida, J. 2002c. *Negotiations.* Translated and edited by Elizabeth Rottenberg. Stanford: Stanford University Press.

Derrida, J. 2002d. *Who's Afraid of Philosophy? Right to Philosophy 1.* Translated by Jan Plug. Stanford: Stanford University Press.

Derrida, J. 2005a. *Rogues. Two Essays on Reason.* Translated by Pascale-Anne Brault, and Michael Naas. Stanford: Stanford University Press.

Derrida, J. 2005b. *Paper Machine.* Translated by Rachel Bowlby. Stanford: Stanford University Press.

Derrida, J. 2011. *The Beast and the Sovereign Vol. II.* Translated by Geoffrey Bennington. Chicago: The University of Chicago Press.

Derrida, J. 2014. *The Death Penalty Vol. I.* Translated by Peggy Kamuf. Chicago: The University of Chicago Press.

Kant, I. 1997. *Groundwork of the Metaphysics of Morals.* Translated and edited by Mary Gregor. Cambridge: Cambridge University press.

Lyotard, J.-F. 1984. *The Postmodern Condition: A Report on Knowledge.* Translated by Geoff Bennington, and Brian Massumi. Manchester: Manchester University Press.

Thomson, J. 1994. *Mercenaries, Pirates, and Sovereigns. State-building and Extraterritorial Violence in Early Modern Europe.* Princeton: Princeton University Press.

Walker, R. B. J. 1993a. "Violence, Modernity, Silence: From Max Weber to International Relations." In *The Political Subject of Violence,* edited by D. Campbell, and M. Dillon, 137–160. Manchester: Manchester University Press.

Walker, R. B. J. 1993b. *Inside/Outside: International Relations as Political Theory.* Cambridge: Cambridge University Press.

Walker, R. B. J. 2010. *After the Globe, Before the World.* New York: Routledge.

Weber, C. 1995. *Simulating Sovereignty.* Cambridge: Cambridge University press.

Weber, C. 1998. "Performative States." *Millennium – Journal of International Studies* 27 (1): 77–95. doi:10.1177/03058298980270011101.

Weber, C. 2010. *International Relations Theory. A Critical Introduction.* 3rd ed. London: Routledge.

Weber, C., and T. J. Biersteker, eds. 1996. *State Sovereignty as Social Construct.* Cambridge: Cambridge University Press.

Weber, M. 1978. *Economy and Society. An Outline of Interpretive Sociology.* London: University of California Press.

Weber, M. 1980. *Wirtschaft und Gesellschaft. Grundriss der Verstehenden Soziologie.* Tübingen: J.C.B. Mohr (Paul Siebeck).

Weber, M. 2008. *Complete Writings on Academic and Political Vocations.* Edited by J. Dreijmanis, Translated by G. C. Wells. New York: Algora Publishing.

Weber, M. 2012. *Gesammelte Politische Schriften.* Paderhorn: Salzwasser-Verlag.

The sovereignty of sovereignty and the restricted object of critical IR

Paul Rekret

This is a reply to:

Mercier, Thomas Clément. 2016. "Resisting legitimacy: Weber, Derrida, and the fallibility of sovereign power." *Global Discourse* 6 (3): 374–391. http://dx.doi.org/10.1080/23269995.2016. 1151729.

In his article 'Resisting Legitimacy' (2016), Thomas Clément Mercier's aim is to challenge what he calls 'the ontology of domination' that he takes to be definitive of much of International Relations (IR) theorising. I take this to refer to a will to order, the assumption that juridical foundations are somehow inherent to politics.[1] In particular, Mercier lends a searching eye to what he frames as 'critical IR', personified here in the figure of the constructivist scholar Cynthia Weber. Weber is made to stand in for theories of IR which, in exposing the discursive character of any claim to state sovereignty, seek to expose and undermine claims to its necessity.[2] In what follows I want to challenge what I see as a restricted picture of 'critical IR' offered here.

Mercier's intervention hinges upon what he worries is the way in which the 'critical IR' literature assumes what I would call the 'sovereignty of sovereignty'. That is, while asserting the contingent conditions for the emergence of the modern state, 'critical' theorists are said to nonetheless implicitly presume the success of claims to sovereignty. In doing so, they reproduce the very 'ontology of domination' definitive of modern politics, and thus, while not viewing any particular political order as necessary, nonetheless presume the necessity of order.

In response, Mercier seeks, by drawing on the work of French philosopher Jacques Derrida, to locate a more essential 'fallibility' to *any* claim to sovereignty through a deconstructive account of the aporetic logic of 'presence' at work in such claims. Political order, it will turn out, is not nearly as successful as even its critics presume. Mercier locates this aporetic logic across a range of Derrida's texts; one could arguably even push the claim further and see it as the fundamental (for lack of a better word) insight of Derrida's oeuvre as a whole.[3] In either case, despite the infamous density of Derrida's prose, the argument is in fact relatively straightforward.

Take for instance, Derrida's engagement with the concept of 'invention' (Derrida 2007). Inventions, Derrida claims, begin 'by being susceptible to repetition, exploitation, reinscription' (Derrida 2007, 16). The status of an invention is only recognisable *qua* invention by its insertion into a system or economy of conventions. Without such an inscription of the singular event (of invention) into a more general context, we would not be able to confer the status of invention upon it at all. But this re-inscription also entails a loss of the absolute singularity of the invention itself. By definition, inventions can never be present.

Perhaps my favourite exemplar of this logic though is Derrida's reading of Francois Ponge's poem 'Fable'. Ponge (quoted in Derrida 2007, 8) writes: 'with the word *with* begins then this text, of which the first line says the truth'. Ponge's phrase is contained in the first word of the poem but only in its repetition does its meaning appear. The implication is that only through repetition can one confirm that what is new appears, but this necessary repetition simultaneously destabilises, undermines and contaminates the new. The poem eludes us, it can't be pinned down.

The point of this deconstructive repartee is that the presence of the event of invention and indeed, *presence* itself, is thus indeterminable. Disjointure, repetition and the constant retro-activity of presence entails ceaseless deferral of the invention or of Ponge's phrase. Another way to look at this is to say that any sense of *presence* is the effect of a metaphysical gesture or habit, one whose conditions are the deferral or play anterior to it. With this aporetic logic in mind, we are now in a position to locate its work in the concept of sovereignty.

In my view, the clearest expression of the deconstructive account of sovereignty comes in Derrida's (2005) late book *Rogues*.[4] In that text, as in others cited by Mercier, Derrida argues that sovereignty always generates its own autoimmune process. Any justification, claim to legitimacy, or reference to rule or law necessarily undermines the sovereignty of sovereignty since it makes authority in some way conditional. Conversely, any foundational or constitutional act cannot but be illegitimate since no precedent could justify it. Sovereignty could only remain as such by evading any extension into time and space at all, and so by a total absence of sovereignty. Not unlike the meaning of Ponge's poem, sovereignty cannot be made present.

The point Mercier draws from this (im)possibility of sovereignty is to go beyond the constructivist's implicit presupposition that sovereignty is successful. Or, in Mercier's decidedly more Derridean phrasing, the point is 'to emphasise the fallibility of homo-hegemonic monopolisations and to do justice to the event before and beyond performative ontologies'. Yet the chief merit of Mercier's article is that he does not simply reiterate Derrida. Indeed, the bulk of the text entails a nuanced and sophisticated extrapolation of this aporetic logic in the political tradition's most important theorisation of sovereignty and legitimacy: Max Weber's.

Summarising very briefly, Mercier argues Weber arrives at his account of legitimacy through an 'analogical' reasoning whereby the subject acts 'as if' her will is identical to that of the state. As such, Weber's version of legitimate power calls for an interpretative wager on behalf of the sociologist who, after all, is incapable of reading minds. Yet as Mercier convincingly demonstrates, Weber makes the *illegitimate* leap from this interpretive gesture to treating subjective belief as an empirical object. The sociologist does after all have to pretend that he can read minds if he is to give an account of legitimacy. The point is that through the analysis of legitimacy – grounded as it is on making *present* identical wills – it becomes apparent that Weber's object, as with sovereignty more broadly, is inherently 'fallible', always incomplete.

The upshot for Mercier is that in noting this inherent fallibility we imply that any 'will to obey' is only a product of the conceptual architecture of sovereignty. If legitimacy amounts to an identity between sovereign and popular will, then it posits the sovereign as autonomous from dissent. Our very concept of sovereignty conditions obedience and presumes order and hierarchy as necessary. Accordingly, noting its fallibility moves us beyond its implicit 'ontology of domination' to an 'unconditional resistance' which the sovereign by definition cannot extinguish.

Despite its erudition, it seems to me this Derridean approach employed by Mercier severely curtails how a critical IR might proceed and limits what its object might be. The 'unconditional resistance' attended to here preserves the sovereignty of sovereignty since it takes for granted the very concepts it sets out to deconstruct. For instance, insofar as this approach locates the problem of political power in terms of the formal question of its juridical or sovereign foundations, it reproduces the modern political move of effacing what for example, Michel Foucault famously showed to be a range of disciplinary practices by which the body of a productive and obedient modern subject was produced and social role and function internalised (Foucault 1995). Foucault's genealogical approach to modern political power is of relevance here because it asks us to move our frame of reference to a different terrain, premised as it is upon the notion that juridical or contractual and so sovereign order is conditioned by the production of the *presence* of the body to a range of carceral institutions responsible for producing normal, obedient and productive subjects. From the perspective of Foucault's history of disciplinary power, the analysis of sovereignty advanced by Derrida/Mercier has not yet 'cut off the king's head' (Foucault 1995, 89). It still seeks to understand power from the perspective of domination rather than production.

One could derive a commensurable argument from Marx who, like Foucault, relates the emergence of an abstract modern conception of the state to the co-emergence of an abstract individual. As Marx writes in the *Contribution to the Critique of Hegel's Philosophy of Right*, 'the political constitution as such is perfected for the first time when the private spheres have attained independent existence' (Marx 1970). Whereas pre-modern society was defined by the indistinction between politics and social life, modernity is defined by 'the abstraction of the state *as such*', independent from the particularities of social life. This abstraction of the state is of course illusory since it is grounded upon the ideal of a community of free and equal citizens whose mutual relations depend on law. But it is also a *real abstraction* insofar as it takes on a specific reality for modern life.[5] Like Foucault, Marx situates the political concept of the state within a broader set of historical conditions and as inseparable from the emergence of a society of 'free', 'independent' and productive individuals.

My claim is that Mercier's critique of sovereignty remains at the level of the formal conditions of the concept and therefore merely reproduces the very abstraction or autonomy of the political from material inequalities of social life upon which, as both Marx and Foucault show, the modern 'ontology of domination' (to borrow Mercier's term) is based. To locate an 'unconditional resistance' in conceptual and methodological slippages and aporias of power's foundations reproduces the very abstractions upon which that power is founded. In other words, resistance is *conditioned* and restricted by the philosophical move which inaugurates it.

Now of course the Derridean response here would be the one Derrida actually makes against Foucault in *Rogues*. The claim to displace the formal question of sovereignty, Derrida maintains, itself amounts to an implicit claim to sovereignty (Derrida 2005, 148). That is, Foucault's historical account (and presumably Marx's) implies a sovereign claim to have determined the *presence* of sovereignty in history. In fact, the historian might be said to be twice guilty of a sovereign gesture: first, by determining and so reducing the *presence* of sovereignty to some fixed points in history and second, by claiming to transcend sovereignty, he repeats the sovereign act over history itself. But this retort merely launches us into a theoretical game of nesting dolls where we're caught between competing formulations of sovereignty: one privileging the formal conditions of its concept, the other the material conditions of its historical context.[6]

Yet without starting with the historical conditions of the modern state, we reproduce that state's very claim to necessity that Mercier wanted to overcome. The gesture towards 'unconditional resistance' here is thus politically disabling insofar as it inscribes finitude into the emancipatory collective act in advance. The affect at work here is one of resignation: resistance is unconditional because it is ceaseless, yet it is only ceaseless because it takes the institution it resists on its own terms.

Notes

1. See, for instance, Schürmann (1987) and Marchart (2007).
2. One wonders to what extent this inaugural gesture framing the object of inquiry offers a rather partial if not reductive picture of what critical literature in international relations might be.
3. I make this claim in Rekret (2016).
4. For a more extensive assessment, see Rekret (2012).
5. On this point, see Sayer (1987), chapter 4.
6. I develop this argument in Rekret (2012).

References

Derrida, J. 2005. *Rogues: Two Essays on Reason*. Stanford, CA: Stanford University Press.

Derrida, J. 2007. *Inventions of the Other*. Stanford, CA: Stanford University Press.

Foucault, M. 1995. *Discipline and Punish: The Birth of the Prison*. Translated by A. Sheridan. New York: Vintage Books.

Marchart, O. 2007. *Post-Foundational Political Thought: Political Difference in Nancy, Lefort, Badiou & Laclau*. Edinburgh: Edinburgh University Press.

Marx, K. 1970. *Critique of Hegel's Philosophy of Right*. Translated by J. O'Malley. Cambridge: Cambridge University Press.

Mercier, T. C. 2016. "Resisting Legitimacy: Weber, Derrida, and the Fallibility of Sovereign Power." *Global Discourse* 6 (3): 374–391. doi:10.1080/23269995.2016.1151729.

Rekret, P. 2012. "The Impasse of Post-Metaphysical Political Theory: On Derrida and Foucault." *Telos* 2012: 79–98. doi:10.3817/1212161079.

Rekret, P. forthcoming. "The Aporia and the Problem." In *Between Foucault and Derrida*, edited by Y. Aryal, V. Cisney, and N. Morar. Edinburgh: Edinburgh University Press.

Sayer, D. 1987. *The Violence of Abstraction: Analytical Foundations of Historical Materialism*. Oxford: Basil Blackwell.

Schürmann, R. 1987. *Heidegger on Being and Acting. From Principles to Anarchy*. Translated by C.-M. Gros. Bloomington: Indiana University Press.

The evolving and interacting bases of EU environmental policy legitimacy

M. Leann Brown

ABSTRACT

Some recent scholarship has focused on concerns that implementation and compliance difficulties are undermining the legitimacy of European Union environmental policies and even the EU itself. Other officials and analysts, however, contend that environmental policy is one of the EU's most successful policy areas. While most discuss 'legitimacy' in unspecified or dichotomous terms, it is instead a more nuanced and contested concept. This study investigates several evolving and interacting bases of legitimacies associated with 'permissive acceptance' (based upon functional need, scientific and technical authority, and policy effectiveness), 'appropriateness' (based upon normative consensus, legalization, and adjudication), democracy (based upon representation, participation, and deliberation), and identity (based upon global leadership and 'othering'). These legitimacies vary in terms of their strength, stability, and durability among the multiple European actors and institutions.

Recent scholarship has expressed concern that implementation and compliance difficulties are undermining the legitimacy of European Union (EU) environmental policies and even the EU itself (Grant, Matthews, and Newell 2000; Jordan and Schout 2006: ix; Livanis 2010). Other officials and analysts contend, however, that environmental policy is one of the EU's most successful policy areas, pointing to the promulgation of hundreds of pieces of legislation and regulations covering a host of environmental concerns ranging from the quality of drinking water to migratory birds (Johnson and Corcelle 1989; Kramer 1995; Collier 1999, 81). They insist that environmental protection enjoys widespread public support capable of generating and increasing support for the entire integration project. These concerns and assertions invite a consideration of the evolving and interacting bases of EU environmental policy legitimacy.

While most discuss 'legitimacy' in unspecified and/or dichotomous terms (i.e. institutions, policies, and/or behavior are or are not legitimate), it is instead a more nuanced and contested concept. Backstrand et al. (2008, 38) embrace this definition: 'the acceptance of a particular social order, rule, norm, or institution by set of actors or by a specific community'. March and Olsen (2009, 2) discuss legitimacy in terms of 'appropriateness':

> The logic of appropriateness is a perspective that sees human action as driven by **rules** of appropriate or exemplary behavior, organized into institutions. Rules are followed because they are seen as **natural, rightful, expected**, and legitimate. Actors seek to fulfill the obligations encapsulated in a **role, an identity**, a membership in a political community or group, and the ethos, practices and expectations of its institutions (emphasis added).

Banchoff and Smith (1999, 4) contend that the concept of legitimacy has become almost synonymous with democratic governance, and Baber and Bartlett (2005, 92) go a step further to designate commitment to participation and compliance as the strongest indicator of environmental policy legitimacy. Ultimately, most scholars concur that identity, defined as trust and 'mutual sympathies', 'a sense of community' and/or a 'we-feeling' (Deutsch et al. 1957, 36) is the strongest and most stable and durable basis for legitimacy. So, rather than a dichotomy of complete legitimacy or a lack therefore, it is more useful to think of various legitimacies occupying places along a continuum in terms of strength, stability, and durability. This contribution posits that the various legitimacies and different actors' perceptions of legitimacy derive from the phenomena's several interacting sources and bases. While the sources and levels of legitimacy clearly defy strict categorization, several potential interacting bases of legitimacies are permissive acceptance (based upon functionalist criteria, expert and technical authority, and policy effectiveness), appropriateness (based upon normative consensus and legalization), democratic processes and active commitment, and identity (based upon global leadership and 'othering'), among other factors. To summarize:

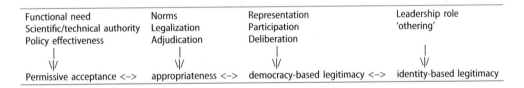

Functional need	Norms	Representation	Leadership role
Scientific/technical authority	Legalization	Participation	'othering'
Policy effectiveness	Adjudication	Deliberation	
|/	|/	|/	|/
Permissive acceptance <–>	appropriateness <–>	democracy-based legitimacy <–>	identity-based legitimacy

These legitimacies derive from diverse sources and logics, thus defying a single theoretical orientation. They may be thought of, however, as gaining strength, stability, and durability from their interactive and cumulative processes and the extent to which the sources derive from increasingly *active* and *internalized* incentives, authority, and motivations culminating with EU actors' according environmental policy legitimacy as a reflection of the 'Self'. These legitimacies have interacted and evolved across time and among European actors and institutions, from the general to the attentive public, to the EU bodies and officials associated with various policy areas, to legal actors, to scientific experts and academic analysts, and to environmental groups and green parties, among others. These multiple bases and forms of legitimacy help explain why scholars disagree over whether and the extent to which polity and policy effectiveness are related to legitimacy, how legitimacy in one policy area is related to legitimacy in others, and how legitimacy in one sector affects the legitimacy of the entire body and *vice versa*.

Legitimacy as permissive acceptance

Permissive acceptance of EU environmental policies may proceed from functionalist, instrumental/utilitarian, and/or consequentialist logics (Eriksen and Fossum 2004, 437). Over time, the requisites for creation of the Single Market, the transnational scope of many environmental problems, expert and technical authority, and policy effectiveness ('output legitimacy', see Scharpf 1999), have provided foundations for a permissive acceptance of EU environmental policies.

The original mission of the European Community (EC) was to create a Single Market fostering freedom of movement of goods, services, capital, and people across Member States' (MSs) frontiers. Environmental protection was not mentioned in the 1957 Treaties of Rome that established the organization. The desperate need for economic recovery from war-time devastation and to provide an alternative to communism as the Cold War loomed prompted former enemies to undertake these cooperative ventures. EC Member States acknowledged that divergent environmental legislation can distort economic competition, and during the 1960s, they promulgated several environmental directives in support of Single Market objectives. Lodge (1989, 321) confirms that initially EC interest in environmental policy was 'spurred not so much by an upsurge of post-industrial values ... or to give the EC a "human face" as by the realization that widely differing national rules on industrial pollution could distort competition'. Thus, EC environmental policies initially represented 'spillover' (Haas 1958) from Single Market objectives rather than values and normative consensus or treaty-based legalization of environmental protection. Over subsequent decades, other functional imperatives have driven EU policies such as environmental problems like acid rain and pollution of rivers that transverse several MSs, which cannot be addressed autonomously and require regional cooperation. These two functional/utilitarian bases for permissive acceptance of EU environmental policies have only increased over time as it has become clear that completing the Single Market and dealing with increasingly complex and harmful environmental problems require regional cooperation.

Permissive acceptance of environmental policies has also been fostered and rein-forced by the need for and the authority of scientific and technical information and experts. From the early 1970s, the EC sought to martial information and expertise in support of environmental objectives. Particularly during these early years, Orhan (1999, 38) informs that 'Policies were based on an unshakeable faith in the capacity of science and technology to solve environmental problems'. Scientific research and scientists were assumed to be 'fact-based' and value-neutral, respectively, and policymaking was under-stood as a rational and technical exercise in the service of the public interest rather than serving the values and interests of decision makers.

Article 130r(3) of the 1987 Single European Act requires that the Community consider available scientific data in its policy-making (Hildebrand 2005). At every stage of policy-making, the EU by law avails itself of scientific input. Committees, working groups, and networks include scientific and technical experts among their membership, and confer-ences and hearings are convened to engage in agenda-setting, issue framing, policy alternative deliberations, and policy implementation and evaluation. The Commission, as drafter of legislation and regulations, 'steerer' of policy networks, and monitor of policy compliance, also brings a great deal of expertise to the policy processes. Martens (2008,

645) quotes a Commission official as saying, 'we are perceived as a repository of knowledge and experience'. The Commission often uses resolutions and White and Green papers to inform and persuade.

Input from scientific and technical communities extends to the level of individual projects. The 1985 Environmental Impact Assessment Directive[1] requires evaluations of environmental costs of projects at the regional level, and Directive 2001/42/EC[2] implements the global 1991 Convention on Environmental Impact Assessment in a Transboundary Context and the 2001 Protocol on Strategic Environmental Assessment. Overtime there has been a democratizing of input on the planning level. The 2003 Public Participation Directive provides for public involvement in the drawing up plans and programs relating to the environment[3] guaranteeing input from a variety of societal sources (Marsden 2011, 267–269).

During the 1980s and 1990s, the EU also created a number of semi-autonomous agencies to serve as 'apolitical' sources of scientific data and policy expertise. The European Environment Agency (EEA) was founded in 1990 and began operations in Copenhagen in 1994. Its primary mission is to collect, analyze, and disseminate information to support its member countries' environmental decision-making, assessment, and public participation on all levels from the local to the global. In 2002, a European Food Safety Authority began operations in Parma, Italy and a European Chemicals Agency was established in Helsinki in 2007. The Commission also draws upon the expertise of independent sources such as the Institute for European Environmental Policy and European Academies' Science Advisory Council (Hildebrand 2005, 99, Martens 2008, 637).

Since the 1990s, a more skeptical attitude has emerged with regard to the role scientific information and experts play in the policy process. Early EU policies dealt with the most pressing and best-understood environmental problems, and more recent problems (such as climate change) are characterized by novelty, complexity, and scientific uncertainty. Highly contentious policy challenges, such as the BSE ('mad cow') crisis and questions surrounding genetically-modified foodstuffs have raised questions about science as an objective mode of inquiry governed by universally understood and accepted criteria. Scientific information and experts were rallied to support all sides of these policy debates and it became clear that the scientific community and individual scientists may represent their own values and objectives. Orhan (1999, 47) explains that 'Science, like all human knowledge, is grounded in and shaped by the normative suppositions and social meaning of the world it explores'.

Even as political leaders were increasingly required to rely upon scientific expertise to understand environmental problems and to serve as a basis of legitimacy for the policy process and outcomes, decision-making processes and policies were increasingly challenged by opposing scientists, environmental advocacy groups, and the general public. The EU turned to two solutions to shore up legitimacy based on scientific input, use of the precautionary principle and the democratization of scientific analysis and input. Together these responses were referred to as 'civic' or 'negotiated' science. O'Riordan and Cameron (1994, 66) explain:

> [Science-democracy partnerships raise] the issue of civic science, or a negotiated science in which participation becomes a means of brokering knowledge and valuation between

scientific processes and public opinion. Precaution opens up the scope for this, because precaution encourages thoughtful and creative dialogue between an activated citizenry and the wider scientific community.

The precautionary principle is usually ascribed to German legal tradition. The EU embraces the 1992 Rio Declaration formulation of principle 15 which provides that 'Where there are threats of serious or irreversible damage, lack of full scientific certainty shall not be used as a reason for postponing cost-effective measures to prevent environmental degradation'.[4] When faced with inadequately understood environmental problems,[5] the precautionary principle allows time for scientific knowledge to increase and gives officials time to gather more information, include a wider range of participants in policy deliberations, and undertake implementation in a step-by-step manner. Public input can supplement scientific expertise by providing locally relevant information and social value insights. Critics charge that employing the precautionary approach undermines effectiveness by restricting research and innovation and that public participation in policymaking complicates and delays decision-making. However, continuing with traditional approaches to scientific uncertainties undermines permissive acceptance by leaving policies open to further protest and delayed implementation and compliance. By acknowledging the inherent uncertainties of science, EU scientific-public advisory groups work together to reach consensus, increase accountability, and gain public trust rather than use scientific information and experts as weapons in policy debates (Hunt 1994, 123–124, Carr and Levidow 1999, 161–172).

While functionalist spillover, the necessity of addressing transfrontier environmental problems, and expert authority and negotiated science are potential sources of permissive acceptance, many scholars regard policy effectiveness as the most important source of permissive acceptance-based legitimacy. Analysts with a policy output-orientation tend to define effectiveness as the ability to achieve policy objectives in a cost-effective, efficient way with minimum undesired side effects (Scharpf 1999; Grant, Matthews, and Newell 2000, 1), but this definition conveys a limited conceptualization of the effectiveness of EU environmental efforts. The EU has faced divergent environmental challenges along its evolutionary path, so assessing policy effectiveness is a moving target in terms of the polity's objectives and indicators of success. During 1970s through the mid-1980s, the primary challenges were to place environmental protection on the agenda of the economic organization, to articulate and legalize environmental objectives and principles to a status comparable to economic integration and growth goals, and to address the most health-threatening environmental concerns such as water quality. Once those goals were achieved culminating with the 1987 Single European Act, the organization devoted itself to promulgating hundreds of pieces of legislation and regulations and bringing its MSs' legislation in line with these obligations. After the 1992 Maastricht Treaty, the relatively less difficult environmental objectives had been achieved by legislation and regulation, and the polity was confronted with increasingly novel and scientifically uncertain issues, within increasingly complex political processes, including increasing numbers of MSs, many of whom assigned environmental issues relatively low priority and lacked the administrative capacity to vigorously pursue environmental objectives.

Scholars' different definitions, criteria, and indicators of effectiveness yields disagreement over whether the EU has been, is, and will be environmentally effective. Collier (1997, 1) contends that 'Environmental policy is considered to be one of the European Union's most successful policies'. It has established a treaty foundation for undertaking environmental objectives and allocated powers comparable to economic ones to EU environmental bodies. It has promulgated hundreds of pieces of legislation and regulations undertaking comprehensive and complex environmental policies. And, along the way, it has articulated and constitutionalized innovative norms and principles that shape global discourses and negotiations around environmental issues.

If the criteria for success is the degree to which EU efforts change MSs' behavior, there is some evidence that the EU has produced a 'ratcheting up' of environmental standards, particularly among MSs with previously nonexistent or ineffective environmental institutions and policies (Grant, Matthews, and Newell 2000, 66). And, positive policy outcomes for the environment have been noted in some specific issue-areas such as water quality and restoration of the ozone layer.

However, with the rash of new legislation and regulations as well as member enlargement in the decade after the Single European Act, a maelstrom of criticism regarding EC environmental policy effectiveness emerged. In 1995, the European Environment Agency (1995, 1) concluded that:

> The European Union is making progress in reducing certain pressures on the environment, though this is not enough to improve the general quality of the environment and even less to progress towards sustainability. Without accelerated policies, pressure on the environment will continue to exceed human health standards and the often limited carrying capacity of the environment.

Grant, Matthews, and Newell (2000, 66–67) assessment is similarly negative: 'the overall impact of EU environment policies through the legislative route has not been a notable success'. Policy implementation and enforcement have been weak, many policies have not achieved their intended outcomes, and there has been a slow and unrelenting deterioration of environmental quality. Often EU environmental effectiveness is undermined by other policy initiatives such as in those of the Common Agricultural Policy and Single Market. Grant *et al.* derive these conclusions by focusing mostly on rates of delayed, incomplete, or inadequate MS transposition of directives; the annual numbers of complaints and alleged breaches of EU law deriving from the public and Parliamentary questions and/or petitions; and the number of environmental infringements cases handled by the Commission and/or heard by the European Court of Justice. Livanis (2010, 84) informs that between 1998 and 2007, 25% of all infringement proceedings brought before the European Court of Justice (ECJ) were related to the environment compared to 21% that pertained to the Single Market.

The usefulness of these indicators to assessing and comparing effectiveness is debatable. Over the years, the quantity and types of environmental obligations have proliferated and changed and EU citizens, nongovernmental organizations, and EU bodies have increased knowledge of and procedures whereby complaints might be lodged. With stronger norms, principles, and legal embeddedness of environmental goals, the EU and its citizens have a greater expectations and commitment with regard to

environmental protection. Increasing numbers of complaints and infringements proceedings may indicate increased effectiveness and legitimacy of EU environmental
governance. More environmental problems are being addressed by EU governance
and EU citizens and bodies participate more actively in insuring implementation and
compliance.

Acknowledging implementation and compliance challenges and their consequences
for legitimacy, the EU has promulgated several communications and directives to
improve policy effectiveness. Some like the Directive on Strategic Environmental
Assessment[6] require certain plans and programs to undergo environmental assessment
even before they are adopted with the view to improving effectiveness and integrating
environmental and other EU policy objectives. The Commission has proposed strategies
such as providing more environmental information online; enhanced inspection and
surveillance mechanisms; a more consistent structure for citizens to present environmental grievances and concerns; a framework for environmental challenges in MS courts
that is more predictable for citizens, authorities and firms; better European networking
for MS bodies and institutions; and clearly-structured implementation plans to help MSs
make resources available to address environmental problems requiring elaborate, well-
orchestrated solutions.[7]

To facilitate implementation and compliance (including employing naming, faming,
shaming strategies), the Commission publicizes annual data regarding MSs' transposition and compliance rates. Since most EU environmental legislation assumes the form of
directives which specify the policy objectives to be achieved but leave to MSs the means
to accomplish those objectives, directives must be transposed into state law. The
Commission calculates each MSs' transposition deficit by considering directives for
which no transposition measures have been communicated to the Commission, those
considered partially transposed by the MSs after they have communicated some transposition measures, directives considered partially transposed by the MSs but for which
the Commission has initiated an infringement procures for non-communication and the
MS has not notified new transposition measures after the latest procedural step taken by
the Commission. The transposition deficit does not include directives considered as
completely transposed by the MS but which measures are still being examined by the
Commission (i.e. no steps have been taken after the latest notification).[8] The
Commission also annually issues information on MSs' compliance deficits, i.e. MSs who
have incorrectly transposed directives. In May 2015, compliance difficulties regarding
environmental directives were comparable to those in other sectors:

> Environment: 8 out of 111 directives in force incorrectly transposed (7.2%)
> Employment and social policy: 5 out of 73 directives incorrectly transposed (6.8%)
> Financial services: 8 out of 74 directives incorrectly transposed (10.8%)
> Transport: 8 out of 123 directives incorrectly transposed (6.5%)[9]

The Commission ultimately may bring infringement proceedings against non-com-
pliant MSs to the European Court of Justice which will adjudicate and possibly impose
fines.[10] It can be summarized that while the EU has encountered difficulties with
implementation and compliance records (particularly during the 1990s), environmental
policy performance indicated by implementation and compliance rates is comparable to
other policy areas.

Legitimacy in the form of permissive acceptance is derived via rational choice; policy choices are motivated by needs, interests, preferences, cost–benefit analysis, and expected consequences; i.e. a 'narrow view of economic citizenship' (Eriksen and Fossum 2004, 436). This is a relatively unstable basis for legitimacy in that citizens' and elites' acceptance of environmental policies is conditional and their priorities subject to change as they confront various policy challenges, as predicted by Inglehart's (2008) materialist values. Eriksen and Fossum (2004, 440–441) contend that to achieve long-term, effectiveness-based legitimacy, a common set of values and/or more formal institutions are needed. They explain that 'the consequentialist mode of legitimation is ... insufficient. Indirect and performance-based legitimation does not suffice to account for the present-day EU in democratic terms'.

Many scholars contend that a 'permissive consensus' persisted with regard to the EC until the early 1990s. Hooghe and Marks (2008, 118, 123–125) write that after the 1992 Maastricht Treaty, support for integration 'essentially disappeared'. Proliferating European legislation and regulations reached deeper into society, affecting citizens' daily lives and creating winners and losers in ways that made EU policies salient and contested. Politicization was only heightened by sustained debates and referenda over successive treaties and the EU constitution.

By the mid-2000s, many judged overall EU legitimacy among the public at an all-time low, and the organization's capacity to govern was increasingly called into question (Jordan and Schout 2006, ix). However, EU officials' and the general publics' 'permissive acceptance' of the EU's pursuit of environmental objectives has remained strong over the decades.[11] One must conclude that acceptance of EU environmental policies derives from bases more essential and integral than functionalist spillover, cost–benefit analysis, the authority of scientists and experts, and/or the policy's performance record.

Legitimacy as 'appropriateness'

As was noted, March and Olsen inform that a stronger, and more stable and enduring legitimacy derives from the conceptualization of a behavior as natural, customary, expected, and rightful. Important bases of this legitimacy are value and norm consensus; the articulation of supporting principles; the embedding of these values, norms, and principles into treaties, policies, laws, and regulations; and rulings by the ECJ in support of these values, norms, and principles.[12] Embedding values, norms, and principles within treaties, policies, legislation and regulations shapes and educates society across generations 'through the language of law' (Baber and Bartlett 2005, 91).

While environmental awareness and prioritization are not uniform among European citizens, environmental values are deeply entrenched within European publics and national institutions and there has been no demonstrated willingness to roll back environmental regulations since the late 1970s, despite neoliberal economic tendencies to reduce the role of governments and promote market-based policy instruments and voluntarism (Orhan 1999, 53). Eurobarometer surveys have consistently demonstrated European citizens' support for addressing environmental problems at the regional level (see footnote 12).

Over time, EU environmental values and norms have been articulated into principles[13] that guide policymaking and the promulgation of legislation and regulations and have been constitutionalized into successive EU treaties. At the October 1972 Paris Summit, the European Council confirmed that 'economic expansion is not an end in itself', laid down several environmental principles, and agreed to adopt an environmental policy. In the concluding communication, summit participants elaborated that economic expansion 'should result in an improvement in the quality of life as well as in the standards of living ... [and] particular attention will be given to intangible values and to protecting the environment' (quoted in McCormick 2001, 47). Since 1973, the EU has enacted seven multi-year Environmental Action Programmes (EAPs) establishing principles and priorities and outlining measures to be undertaken in various policy areas. These programs demonstrate MSs' growing value commitment to coordinate and harmonize environmental regulations to level the economic playing field and to protect the environment. EAPs mostly represent contemporary thinking regarding the environment and medium-term planning rather than treaty-based law. However, by the end of the 1970s, the ECJ had ruled that environmental policy fell within the EEC's competence as an implied power.

The first two EAPs (1973–1977 and 1977–1981) mostly provided for remediation of past environmental damage rather than proactively pursuing environmental protection. However, a new conceptualization of environmental resources as constituting the basis for and imposing limits to economic and social development was discernible in the Third EAP (1982–1986). Environmental goals were no longer to be regarded as separate and subordinate to Single Market ones, and were to be integrated into other policy areas such as agriculture, energy, industry, and transportation (CEC 1983). Hildebrand (2005, 25) informs that the Third EAP was the first EEC effort to end the subordination of environmental objectives to economic ones.

In 1985, the European Council meeting in Brussels upgraded environmental protection to be regarded as a fundamental part of agricultural, economic, industrial, and social policies (Johnson and Corcelle 1989, 3). In a preliminary ruling that same year concerning the Directive on the Disposal of Waste Oils, the ECJ opined that:

> The principle of freedom of trade is not to be viewed in absolute terms but is subject to certain limits justified by the objectives of general interest pursued by the Community... The Directive must be seen in the perspective of *environmental protection, which is one of the Community's essential objectives* (emphasis added; Case 240/83, *Procureur de la Republique v. l'Association de Defense des Bruleurs d'Huiles* quoted in Koppen 2005, 74–75).

Koppen contends that this ruling is an example of judicial activism – environmental protection was not yet an 'essential objective' because it had not been enshrined in the treaties. Instead, this ruling demonstrated ECJ support for treaty changes being discussed. The ruling placed environmental protection on a more equal footing with Single Market objectives as long as environmental measures were not discriminatory or disproportionate (Koppen 2005, 75).

Between 1972 and 1986, in addition to the three EAPs, the EC enacted more than 100 environmental measures. Likely in reaction to the lack of treaty basis and the EAP and the directive format of many environmental decisions, Rehbinder and Stewart (1985, 33) describe the pre-Single European Act EAPs and other environmental measures as 'Soft law [which] consists of programs and declarations of a non-binding nature ...' representing 'a new type of policy developed through *political consensus* of the member states'. [emphasis added]

The 1987 Single European Act (SEA) provided the first explicit treaty basis to address environmental issues. Articles 130r, s, and t lay out several principles of environmental protection: preventing environmental damage is preferred to remediation, environmental problems should be addressed at their source, and the 'polluter pays'. Articles 100a and 130t allow MSs to introduce more stringent environmental standards than those agreed to in the EU as long as they are 'not a means of arbitrary discrimination or a disguised restriction on trade between Member States'. In slight overstatement, Hildebrand (2005, 36) writes: 'The protection of the environment is now formally of equal or even superior status to all other Community objectives'. In many ways, environmental policy had come of age. Almost immediately, the ECJ confirmed the new environmental provisions when in 1988 it supported Danish legislation requiring that beer and soft drinks be marketed in reusable containers despite potential negative consequences for the single market.[14] In a July 1991 ruling associated with 'the titanium dioxide case',[15] the ECJ registered its preference that the EC deal with environmental matters under Article 100a which made it more difficult for a few MSs to block environmental proposals (Haigh and Baldock 1989, 15).

The late 1980s also brought a major shift in EC understandings associated with this policy area to include sustainable development (SD). In 1987, the United Nations-initiated World Commission on Environment and Development published *Our Common Future* (hereafter the *Brundtland Report*), and ideas associated with SD gradually infiltrated the Single Market-oriented EC discourse. The *Brundtland Report* explains that 'Humanity has the ability to make development sustainable – to ensure that it meets the needs of the present without compromising the ability of future generations to meet their own needs'. It continues:

> In essence, sustainable development is a process of change in which the exploitation of resources, the direction of investments, the orientation of technological development, and institutional change are all in harmony and enhance both current and future potential to meet human needs and aspirations (WCED 1987, 16, 43).

The 1992 Maastricht Treaty committed the EU to promote harmonious and balanced expansion of economic activities and 'sustainable non-inflationary growth respecting the environment ...' (Article 2), and gave the ECJ power to impose fines for non-implementation of environmental legislation. The subsidiarity principle became applicable to all policy areas where the EU doesn't have exclusive competence, and the EU is to ensure that environmental objectives are applied consistently across policy areas. Additional environmental prerogatives were conferred on the European Parliament, and the EU is empowered to make binding international environmental agreements on behalf of the MSs. The Fifth EAP was entitled *Towards Sustainability* (CEC 1992; Gottweis 1999, 65).

The Preamble and Article 2 of the 1997 Amsterdam Treaty confirm SD as a fundamental objective of the EU, and MSs' rights to maintain higher environmental standards than those established by the EU if they so choose. It also extended co-decision procedures to directives adopted on the basis of the environmental paragraph 130 s, increasing the powers of the EP (Skjaerseth and Wettestad 2002, 102). Jordan and Fairbrass (2005, 45) write that with the ratification of the Amsterdam Treaty, creating a legal foundation for providing environmental protection and SD was completed; environmental policy was now a 'mature' policy area.

The European Council adopted its first Sustainable Development Strategy at a meeting in Goteborg in 2001 which serves as a foundation for mainstreaming SD to reduce negative policy externalities, benefit from synergies, and provide a more integrated approach to problem solving based on better instruments such as environmental impact assessments (CEC 2002; Geyer and Lightfoot 2010, 348). In 2006, the EU renewed its commitment to SD in its articulation of a SD strategy for the enlarged EU by laying out principles to guide policy, key objectives, and identifying its most serious challenges. Article 3(3) of the 2008 Lisbon Treaty arguably broadens the EU definition of sustainable development – the EU shall 'contribute to peace, security, [and] the sustainable development of the Earth'. Lisbon states that '[e]nvironmental protection requirements must be integrated into the definition and implementation of the Union's policies and activities, in particular with a view to promoting sustainable development' (Council of the EU 2008, 21, 68; Benson and Jordan 2010, 469).

Few would dispute that environmental values, norms, principles, policies, laws, regulations, constitutionalization, and judicial affirmation constitute a firm foundation for labeling EU environmental policies as appropriate, 'rightful', customary, and expected. Functional needs, cost–benefit analyses, and scientific authority and advocacy laid the foundation for value and normative consensus among Europeans except the most doctrinaire free market advocates and Eurosceptics; these norms were then articulated into principles and legalized in treaties, laws, and regulations. Rulings by the ECJ reaffirmed the appropriateness and 'rightfulness' of EU policies in support of the environment in some cases even at the expense of Single Market objectives. Normative and legal bases of legitimacy are also clearly more stable than permissive acceptance based on functional needs and cost–benefit analysis relative to other policy objectives and outcomes. Yet particularly since the end of the Cold War, the legitimacy of EU environmental policy and the EU itself has been called into question on the grounds that it suffers from a 'democratic deficit'. This suggests that citizen representation, participation, and deliberation (what some refer to as 'active commitment') constitute the basis for another legitimacy.

Democracy-based legitimacy

At the outset, the EC was an elite-driven project committed to the creation of a Single Market, however, democratic government is a requirement for EU membership.[16] Early in the polity's development, democracy-based legitimacy relied upon the MSs' representative democratic credentials. In 1978, the European Parliament (EP) became the first and remains the only directly-elected body. Before the 1990s, debates regarding democracy among politicians and academics mostly operated out of state-centric models and focused on strengthening the powers of the EP. Most agree that the EP is the 'greenest' EU bodies,[17] Green parties achieved representation among EP party groups in 1984,[18] and the Environment Committee is recognized as among the most influential, as illustrated by its heavy workload and the fact that it deals with more co-decision legislation than any other committee (Burns 2005, 89). However, even as the EP gained in strength, particularly via co-decision powers conferred in the Maastricht and Amsterdam treaties, some deemed this level of representative democracy insufficient to address the democratic deficit.[19] Detractors point out the low turnout in EP elections and the fact that voters tend to cast their ballots on the basis of national issues rather than European ones.

Early in the 1990s, a new norm emerged insisting on the necessity of 'civil society' participation in decision-making, transferring the conversation from representative democracy to participatory democracy. The Fifth EAP (CEC 1992, 49) informs that:

> [T]he basic strategy therefore is to achieve full integration of environmental and other relevant policies *through the active participation of all the main actors in society (administrations, enterprises, general public)...* [emphasis added].

Adherence to and increasing expert and technical input, subsidiarity,[20] sustainable development, policy integration, and market-oriented principles increase participation from all levels including nongovernmental, grassroots, and transnational actors, making decision-making more inclusive, equitable, transparent, and accountable. Nagpal (1995; cited in Conca and Dabelko 1998, 263); writes:

> [T]here is a remarkable consensus that a sustainable society must be democratic, with multiple fora for negotiation and decision making. Democracy is not exclusively about the creation of formal institutions and processes but it is also about improving the collective capacity to resolve common problems in an effective and peaceful manner.

Inclusive and transparent processes reduce the risk that decisions will be based on inadequate information, not take into account the needs of all stakeholders, will favor the interests of the powerful, will not be effectively implemented, and thus enhance effectiveness- and democracy-based legitimacy. For stakeholders to participate effectively, they must possess the rights, the freedom, and the capacity to participate including having access to adequate resources including complete and timely information (Lélé 1991, Woods 2010).

The Commission has been at the forefront of the movement to increase participation in the EU (Smismans 2003, Saurugger 2010, 472). As was discussed, the legal and procedural changes wrought by the SEA and the subsequent rash of new environmental legislation and regulations exacerbated ongoing implementation and compliance problems and concerns that environmental challenges were going unmet. Policymakers interpreted these problems as signaling a needed for expanded participation via partnerships and networks. Seeking to create horizontal connections between and among various sectors and to increase vertical interaction with societal actors, the Commission created three categories of dialogue groups:

(1) a consultative forum to serve as a sounding board for EU environmental policymaking in relation to its economic agenda[21];
(2) an implementation network comprised of MSs' officials; and,
(3) a policy review group composed of MSs and DG Environment officials.

A number of additional transparency measures were announced by the Commission, including earlier publication of its annual work plan and the delineation of a code of conduct on access to information supported by technological innovations (Lenschow 1999, 46).

DG Environment's efforts to become more inclusive and participatory was to be achieved by creating networks; Ward and Williams (1997, 439) confirm that 'networking provides the non-tangible infrastructure for this process'. They identify the 1990 *Green Paper on the Urban Environment* as the first sustained discussion and effort by DG Environment to include subnational governments (SNGs, i.e. cities, regions, etc.) in policy-making processes. Prior to the 1990s, interactions between DG Environment and SNGs had been limited and sporadic. Increasing SNGs', interest groups', and experts' input into environmental policy was seen as a way to improve the practicality of policies and to enhance implementation and compliance. SNGs' participation in networks was envisioned as a means to increase awareness and understanding of the EU across the various levels of government. Transnational networks also represented a mechanism whereby the Commission could gain access to representative European expertise and opinion while simultaneously coordinating and controlling interactions with lobbyists, avoiding lobbying overload. Networks were also regarded as a way to improve policy effectiveness.

At the outset, the net consequences of these legal and procedural changes were mixed. The thrust of the network concept was to change the roles of SNGs from implementers of hierarchically-mandated policy into innovators, leaders, partners, and facilitators. Throughout the 1990s, however, SNGs' abilities to participate effectively in network governance were limited due to the lack of resources, lack of knowledge of participatory opportunities on the regional level, and a lack of political will.

Questions persisted as to how the networks would be structured and managed, how the 'new governance' related to old forms of governance (i.e. legislation and regulations), and how their effectiveness and legitimacy could be guaranteed. The Commission had significant experience working with networks in relation to lobbying and policy-making activities, but seemed less certain how networks could be used to govern, implement policies, and achieve compliance. Policymakers realized that new coordination capacities would have to be created and managed to address the increasingly interconnected policy processes, but few had the time or political incentives to identify and create bureaucratic procedures, provide staff training, or manage the networks (Jordan and Schout 2006, xi–xiii). However, by the end of the decade, the responses of environmental networks were changing from reactive efforts to improve access to funding and to enhance their economic performance via lobbying to proactive partnership in policymaking. Ward and Williams (1997, 460) expressed optimism that SNGs-Commission networks also were becoming more formal and stable, and that 'a process of incorporation ...[was] occurring'.

Beginning in the late 1990s, the EU sought to achieve its environmental objectives via 'new modes of governance', particularly the Open Method of Coordination (OMC, articulated in 1998) with regard to policymaking and Cardiff Process (codified in 2000) which aims to incorporate environmental objectives into other policy areas. The OMC and the Cardiff Process involves creating networks of regional, state, and subnational partners, both public and private, within and across sectors to engage in environmental target-setting and benchmarking, performance reporting, identifying 'best practices' via peer review, and 'naming, faming, and shaming'. The multiple actors involved are encouraged to develop a sense of ownership of environmental problems. The EU hoped that the new modes of governance will encourage the multiple sectors to 'design out' potential negative environmental externalities from policies at early stages of the policy process (Jordan and Schout 2006, x), and that the heightened level of participation would improve the effectiveness- and democracy-based legitimacy of environmental policies.[22]

The case may be made that the changes in governance wrought during this period represented progress in participatory and deliberative democracy in that many more participants were brought into the decision-making, implementation, and evaluation stages of environmental policymaking. Access to both context-specific and scientific/technical expertise was enhanced through the introduction of new participants including semi-autonomous specialized agencies. The introduction of network governance also portended benefits in effectiveness-based legitimacy in terms of flexibility, efficiency, and democracy-based legitimacy derived from expanded participation, consensus and understanding building, and policy commitment.

In 2004 and 2007, twelve new states joined the EU introducing formidable challenges to the achievement of regional environmental objectives and to the effectiveness and legitimacy of governance. Environmental problems of increasing scale, complexity, and scientific uncertainty proliferated.[23] EU governance, in general, has become more deeply and widely involved in European citizens' lives increasing politicization and decreasing effectiveness-based legitimacy in all policy areas (Jordan and Schout 2006, 20). However, civil society participation in decision-making is formalized in Article 8b of the 2009 Lisbon Treaty and is regarded as essential to what is regarded as a legitimate legal order (Fligstein and Stone Sweet 2002, Saurugger 2010).

Some scholars, particularly those informed by communitarianism and/or communicative logics, contend that deliberative democracy rather than representative and participatory democracy is the most stable and enduring source of democratic legitimacy. 'Deliberation' refers to interactions by actors who are open to persuasion by force of superior arguments. Deliberative democracy creates a public space wherein citizens can contemplate and debate what constitutes the 'common good', and establish trust, solidarity, and eventually a common identity. Participants recognize each other as fellow-citizens, and deliberation helps shape their preferences, and allows citizens to accept the results of deliberation as 'right' and worthy of respect, enhancing commitment and policy compliance and effectiveness (Sandel 1982; Eriksen and Fossum 2004, 443). Eriksen and Fossum (2004, 445–446) elaborate:

> Public deliberation is the way to find out what is good, right, and just in the political sphere of action. It is only possible to test the quality of arguments in debate in which all affected parties are involved. This is the task of the public sphere, the realm outside of state administration and the market and in which people gather and become a public and hold the decision-makers accountable.

The only requirement for deliberative democracy is free and open debate in terms of the public good. Eriksen and Fossum (2004, 446–452) explain: 'The demos is to be shaped by political means; hence, there can be no European demos without a European democracy'.[24]

Identity-based legitimacy

Significant debate centers on whether the EU has a common identity, and if so, what constitutes this identity. Eriksen and Fossum (2000, 42) ask:

> What is the European Union...? It is not a state based on a common identity, a fixed territory and an established demos, nor is it a loosely coupled system of allies who co-operate on the basis of mutual interest. The EU involves a lot more than international co-operation, meaning co-operation among states but it is not a new state.

Most scholars focus on common values and norms, some conceptualization of a shared European history and culture, and even geography as bases for an EU identity but, as was noted above, a common identity may also derive from deliberative democracy and consensus regarding what constitutes the 'good life'. Human beings possess a primordial need for belonging, and participation and deliberation allow them to clarify who they are, who they are not, and who they wish to become. Habermas (2000, 40) explains the need for a common identity:

> Pluralist culture gets involved in hermeneutic conflicts on the constant revision of the traditions it can choose; existing institutions find themselves confronted with the need to provide rational justifications, so that legitimate orders increasingly become dependent on deliberate politics and democratic legislation; and the individual persons who are exposed to the pressure to decide between even more alternatives, are compelled to stabilize themselves by creating a highly abstract Ego identity.

In addition to the universal political values outlined in the Copenhagen Criteria (i.e. the rule of law, human rights, respect for and protection of minorities), environmental protection is an ontological and cosmopolitan norm recognized globally as necessary for the good life. Thus, the EU identity as protector of the environment is affirmed externally global norms, by the United Nations and, to a lesser degree, other regional organizations (i.e. 'Partial Others') (Eriksen and Fossum 2004, 436–446).

Beyond the EU green identity's being affirmed by universal values and global organizations, the EU has sought to identity itself as a global environmental leader. The 1971 ERTA case[25] granted implied powers to the Commission to enter into agreements with external parties in all areas where it enjoyed internal competence in its ruling that 'No separation must be created ... between the system of internal Community measures and external relations' (quoted in Koppen 2005, 72). Each EAP has included international dimensions in EU planning, and Article 130r of the 1987 SEA called for cooperation with third countries and international organizations on environmental matters (Hildebrand 2005, 34). Europeans and the EU have pioneered in creating and disseminating principles and discourses like the subsidiarity and precautionary principles and SD, and devised innovative policy instruments such as eco labels and carbon emissions trading schemes. In signing the 1997 Kyoto Protocol to the UN Framework Convention on Climate Change, EU MSs committed individually and as a bloc to reduce greenhouse gases 8% over the 2008–2012 period relative to 1990 levels, compared to 6% and 7% commitments made by Japan and the United States, respectively. Globally, the EU also links environmental objectives to other policy issues such as trade, development assistance, and promoting democratic governance in fora such as the World Trade Organization and bilateral and regional negotiations. Eckersley (2004, 80–81) writes that Europeans have made the transition 'from environmental exploiter and facilitator of private environmental exploitation to public environmental trustee ...'.

Much constructivist literature contends that an actor's identity is shaped by who she is not relative to Partial and Radical Others as well as who she is (Lebow 2008). As the United States declined to provide global leadership in protecting the environment, particularly during in the George W. Bush administration (2001–2009), Collier writes that 'the US emerged as the global villain, while the EU's negotiating position was welcomed by all but the most radical environmentalists'. Acting as a bloc, the EU exerts pressure on other states, facilitating the concluding of global environmental agreements (Collier 1999, 81, 99).

Some scholarship discusses EU global leadership in various policy areas in terms of its representing a civilian, normative, and/or ethical power (Duchene 1972). Conceptualizations of the EC as a 'civilian power' reflected aspirations to escape Europe's militaristic past and the constraints of the Cold War. The idea of 'normative power Europe' (Manners 2002) grew out of the idealism and 'constructivist turn' that characterized International Relations at the end of the Cold War. Diez (2005, 614) writes that:

> The discourse of the EU as a normative power constructs a particular self of the EU (and it is indeed perhaps the only form of identity that most of the diverse set of actors within the EU can agree on), while it attempts to change others through the spread of particular norms.

EC Commission Olli Rehn concurs that Europe is defined by values rather than geography: 'Certainly, geographical borders set out the framework but values define the borders' (quoted in Zielonka 2013, 44). In a 2009 speech at the Konrad-Adenauer-Stiftung in Berlin, then European Parliament President Jerzy Buzek explained:

> Europe has become a role model. The universal appeal of our values can be seen in our Southern and Eastern neighbourhoods. Unlike in the past, these values are integrated not through conquest or domination, but through free and voluntary acceptance. This is not only a chance for peace, justice and a better life for these people – this is also our chance to make Europe shine in the world (quoted in Zielonka 2013, 43).

Maull (2005, 788) concludes that conceptualizations of the EU as a civilian and/or normative power connote that the 'EU exercises influence and shapes its environment through what it is, rather than through what it does'. However, 'ethical power Europe' depicts the increasing strategic role the EU wishes to play globally by acquiring a broader range of power capabilities. The concept of ethical power Europe encompasses civilian and military power as well as social and material power. The conceptualization of ethical power Europe suggests that the EU has the capacity and willingness to act to shape what is 'normal' and 'appropriate' in international relations, domesticating international relations to coincide with its own identity. And, this international normative transformation elicits a reciprocal influence, enabling and legitimating the EU to assume a more assertive role in international affairs (Aggestam 2008, 2–4). Europe's aspirations to exercise and *be* a normative/ethical power includes being a global environmental leader. Commission efforts to enhance EU legitimacy via identity strategies including environmental ones have been steadily more manifest over the past two decades (Eriksen and Fossum 2004, 455). And, again, identity-based legitimacy is the most stable, durable, and strongest form of legitimacy.

Conclusion

Scholarly literature critical of EU environmental policies has focused on its ineffectiveness, defined as problems with implementation and compliance, and the broader EU literature expresses concern over the polity's 'democratic deficit'. These two concerns lead many to conclude that the EU lacks legitimacy. These conversations often fail to define 'legitimacy', but most seem to operate out of a dichotomous understanding of 'legitimacy' – the actor or action is or is not legitimate. This study unpacks and problematizes the concept of legitimacy by positing that there are various definitions, logics, and forms of legitimacy deriving from various interacting and evolving bases. These legitimacies may be associated with different actors in different time periods, and they vary in terms of their stability, durability, and strength. Legitimacy as 'permissive acceptance' may derive from a functionalist, instrumental, or consequentialist logics. This form of legitimacy may derive from the environmental policy's functional necessity or usefulness to achieving other organizational goals such as completing the Single Market, or the necessity of collectively addressing transnational and global issues like aid rain, riverine pollution, or climate change. Permissive acceptance may also derive from the authority of scientific and technical experts and scientific data's role in the policy-making process (a source of 'input legitimacy'). Finally, permissive acceptance may derive from the perception that the policy is effective, variously defined as achieving implementation and compliance or policy goals, among other indicators. Actors according EU environmental policies permissive acceptance are not necessarily committed to environmental values, and their permissive acceptance may wax and wane as priorities change, as attitudes toward scientific and technical information change, and as perceptions of the effectiveness of environmental policies change. However, permissive acceptance based on these factors may lay the foundation for normative commitment, the articulation of principles, and the legalization of these principles and goals.

A stronger, more stable, and more durable legitimacy derives from the 'logic of appropriateness'. Based on value and norm consensus, policies enjoying this form of legitimacy are deemed natural, rightful (e.g. fair, legal), customary and expected. The strength and durability of this legitimacy are enhanced by the norms being articulated as principles that serve as a basis for policies, action programs, regulations, legislation, treaties, measuring compliance, and adjudication. Environmental policies embedded in treaties and affirmed by rulings of the European Court of Justice have strong claims to appropriateness, rightfulness, and expectedness. As a matter of fact, in some instances both EU law and rulings by the ECJ accord greater priority to EU environmental objectives than those associated with creating the Single Market. Many actors afford environmental policies legitimacy on the basis of legalization alone, and this form of legitimacy is very stable and durable over time.

Legitimacies defined as permissive acceptance and appropriateness derive from relatively passive bases, however, democracy-based legitimacy relies on active participation by the governed. Overtime, the literature focusing on the democratization of the EU has evolved from a state-centric understanding of democracy as electoral and representative in nature, to democracy as widening and deepening participation, to democracy as deliberation associated with a communicative logic. At present, a global consensus obtains that all polities' legitimacy derives from democratic processes ('input legitimacy'), however defined. The EU has responded to this imperative by increasing the power of the EP, deepening and widening participation (e.g. via increasing input from committees and working groups and creating the Committee of the Regions), and discussing and/or moving through a series of governance reforms including the Cardiff Plan, Open Methods of Coordination, new modes of governance, and multilateral and network governance. Deliberative democracy-based legitimacy is particularly useful in increasing knowledge and per-missive acceptance among new participants, increasing policy effectiveness via context-specific input from multiple actors and increasing participants' commitment to implementation and compliance. Moreover, deliberative interactions are essential to creating trust, solidarity, and a sense of community, the foundations for identity-based legitimacy.

While some lament that the EU has yet to solidify an identity or to constitute a public sphere, the polity has worked to present itself as a leader in environmental institution building and to distinguish itself from the United States (a 'Partial Other') in the global environmental negotiations like those associated with climate change. The EU has also sought to integrate environmental objectives within other global regimes such as trade and foreign assistance. This basis of legitimacy is clearly the most stable and durable, and over time the Commission has sought increase its identity-oriented strategies. As might be expected, some European actors such as Green Parties, environmental non-governmental organizations, and officials most directly responsible for promoting the environmental agenda such as DG Environment, the Environment Committee of the EP, and the European Environment Agency accord EU environmental policy identity-based legitimacy. The EU has moved well beyond utilitarian bases of permissive acceptance of environmental policies; the creation and legalization of environmental norms and principles provide a foundation for general acceptance of the appropriateness of these policies. Over time, participatory and deliberative democracy and the EU's assuming global leadership in environmental protection will translate into the EU environmental policy's enjoying more identity-based legitimacy.

Notes

1. Council Directive 85/337/EEC of 27 June 1985. *Official Journal* L 175/40.
2. Directive 2001/42/EC of the European Parliament and of the Council of June 2001 on the Assessment of the Effects of Certain Public and Private Projects on the Environment, *Official Journal* L 197/30.
3. Directive 2003/35/EC, *Official Journal* L 156/17.
4. Eckersley (2004, 135–136) considers constitutionally embedding the precautionary princi-ple a parsimonious and effective way to require a systematic consideration of all potential environmental impacts, including on nonhuman species and future generations. Constitutionalization of the precautionary principle is justifiable on grounds of fairness and its helpfulness to managing risk and avoiding displacement of environmental pro-blems across time and space. She concludes: 'No single decision rule is likely to do more to protect environmental victims'.
5. Wynne (1992) identifies four categories of scientific 'unknowns': risk, when the odds of danger are known; uncertainty, when the odds of danger are currently unknown but the data necessary for assessment may eventually be available; ignorance, when scientists are unaware of what they do not know; and indeterminacy, when the phenomenon is

unpredictable and outcomes open-ended or when the validity of present knowledge is contingent.

6. Report from the Commission to the Council, the European Parliament, the European Economic and Social Committee and the Committee of the Regions on the application and effectiveness of the Directive on Strategic Environmental Assessment (Directive 2001/ 42/EC) /* COM/2009/0469 final */

7. In 2012, the Commission estimated that the cost of non-implementing current legislation was approximately E50 billion a year in health costs and direct costs to the environment (http://ec.europa.eu/environment/legal/law/com_improving.htm).

8. In May 2016, examples of directives two years or more overdue in terms of their transposition included Directive 2009/31/EC Geological storage of carbon dioxide, Directive 201031/ UE Energy performance of buildings, and Directive 2010/75/UE Industrial emissions (integrated pollution prevention and control). http://ec.europa.eu/internal_market/scoreboard/ performance_by_governance_tool/transposition/index_en.htm

9. The Commission warns that only the European Court of Justice can definitively determine whether a directive has been correctly transposed, and advises that this be kept in mind when interpreting compliance deficit data. http://ec.europa.eu/internal_market/score board/performance_by_governance_tool/transposition/index_en.htm

10. Some specifics regarding environmental infringements 2007–2014 are provided here:

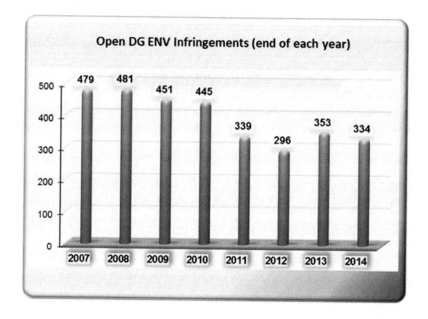

Source: http://ec.europa.eu/atwork/applying-eu-law/index_en.htm

11. A 2011 Eurobarometer poll of EU citizens' attitudes toward the environment reveals that 95% of citizens feel that protecting the environment is important to them personally, 64% believe that action to protect the environment should be undertaken at the European level, and 89% think that more funding should be allocated to protect the environment (http://ec.europa.eu/environment/pdf/ebs_365_en.pdf).

12. While these concepts overlap somewhat and are contested, this study discusses 'values' as salient and stable beliefs regarding what is important and what is good or bad. 'Norms' are standards of acceptable and preferred behavior regarded as customary and expected. Norms prescribe and proscribe actions serving to guide and regulate behavior (see Legro

1997; Finnemore and Sikkink 1998). 'Principles' are fundamental assumptions that serve as a basis for rules, codes of conduct, laws, regulations, and measuring policy compliance.

13. McCormick (2001, 48–85) provides a summary of the principles that have evolved to guide EU environmental policies (in no particular order): the precautionary principle, the polluter pays, prevention over remediation, subsidiarity, the safeguard principle (which allows MSs to adopt more stringent environmental standards than those in EU law), environmental impacts should be considered at the earliest possible stage of decision making, sustainable development, the proximity principle (i.e. environmental damage should be addressed at the source), the integration principle, scientific and technical data are to be taken into account, the international principle, market-oriented solutions, and the proportionality principle.

14. In this case, the ECJ held that environmental protection (along with protection of public health, the fairness of commercial transactions, and the protection of the consumer) constitutes one of the acceptable 'mandatory requirements' under which MSs could restrict goods from other MSs. It should be noted however, that the Court ruled that the portion of the Danish legislative prescribing the types of containers to be used was disproportionate (Case 302/86 *Commission v. Denmark* discussed in Jacobs 2006, 188).

15. This is Case C-300/89, Commission v. Council.

16. In June 1993, the European Council reaffirmed membership requirements that became known as the Copenhagen Criteria:

> Membership requires that candidate country has achieved stability of institutions guaranteeing democracy, the rule of law, human rights, respect for and protection of minorities, the existence of a functioning market economy as well as the capacity to cope with competitive pressure and market forces within the Union. Membership presupposes the candidate's ability to take on the obligations of membership including adherence to the aims of political, economic and monetary union (Council of the European Union 1993).

17. The EP has been referred to as a 'champion of the environment' (Burns 2005: 89).

18. The European Green Party (EGP) first contested European Parliament elections in 1979 achieving representation in 1984 as part of the Rainbow Alliance. Following the 1989 elections, the Green Party formed a separate group in the EP. Reduced in numbers in the 1994 elections, the Greens formed part of the European Radical Alliance, but a successful outcome in 1999 allowed them to combine with the European Free Alliance. In the 2004, 2009, and 2014 elections, 35 (4.8% of EP members), 48 (6.2% of EP members), and 50 (6.7% of EP members) Green Party members, respectively, were elected to the EP. The EGP ran the first election campaign featuring common motifs and slogans in all EU countries (Bomberg 1998, http://europeangreens.eu/front).

19. A minority of scholars argue that the democratic deficit is a myth based on assertions that the EU remains an intergovernmental body that takes its decisions via democratically-elected governments and/or that EU policies are predominantly regulatory and are best developed by technical experts (Majone 1996; Saurugger 2010, 474).

20. The subsidiarity principle requires that:

> In areas which do not fall within its exclusive competence, the Community shall take action ... only if and in so far as the objectives of the proposed action cannot be sufficiently achieved by the Member States and can therefore, by reason of the scale or effects of the proposed action, be better achieved by the Community (Article 5, formerly Article 3b, of the TEC, CEC 1992).

The subsidiarity principle may increase the number of participants in environmental decision-making, bring in additional and alternative sources of knowledge, make environmental policy more context specific, and increase opportunities for deliberation and normative and policy consensus building, however, at the same time it introduced more ambiguity and uncertainty in policymaking and implementation, undermining another basis of legitimacy – policy effectiveness.

21. Forum membership included four representatives from regional and local authorities, five representatives from consumer and environmental groups, two representatives from trade unions, nine industrial representatives, two representatives from agricultural and agri-food organizations, and nine individuals acting in a personal capacity (Lenschow 1999, 46). Between 1998 and 2010, the EU created 37 social dialogue committees who generated more than 300 documents such as guidelines and codes of conduct (Pop 2010).

22. These transitions in governance are not without problems. No MS completely made the transition to new modes of governance, and the EP generally failed to join the networks. In 2003, the European Environment Agency (p. 277) wrote with regard to the Cardiff Process, 'the process ... lacked urgency and has yet to have a significant impact on sectoral policy making, let alone on improvements on the ground'. And, the following year, the Commission conceded that 'the [Cardiff] process has failed to deliver fully on expectations'. A reviewer to this article succinctly concludes that the Cardiff Process 'has been buried quietly without an official funeral'.

23. Two salient examples: The 'Mad Cow Crisis', which began in Britain in 1986 and persisted for more than a decade, was compared to the 1965–1966 'Empty Chair Crisis' in its undermining confidence in European integration, and MSs often blatantly refused to comply with EU decisions regarding genetically modified organisms.

24. There have been some efforts to add direct democracy to the EU democratic repertoire. Major treaty changes are subject to referenda in several MSs. There have been multiple efforts to increase citizen access to information. And, web-based technologies have been applied to perceived legitimacy concerns.

25. This is Case 22/70, Commission v. Council.

References

Aggestam, L. 2008. "Introduction: Ethical Power Europe?" *International Affairs* 84 (1): 1–11. doi:10.1111/inta.2008.84.issue-1.

Baber, W. F., and R. V. Bartlett. 2005. *Deliberative Environmental Politics, Democracy and Ecological Rationality*. Cambridge: The MIT Press.

Backstrand, K., J. Khan, A. Kronsell, and E. Lovrand, eds. 2008. *Environmental Politics and Deliberative Democracy, Examining the Promise of New Modes of Governance*. Cheltenham: Edward Elgar.

Banchoff, T., and M. P. Smith. 1999. *Legitimacy and the European Union, The Contested Polity*. London: Routledge.

Benson, D., and A. Jordan. 2010. "European Union Environmental Policy after the Lisbon Treaty: plus ça change, plus c'est la même chose?" *Environmental Politics* 19 (3): 468–474. doi:10.1080/09644011003690948.

Bomberg, E. 1998. *Green Parties and Politics in the European Union*. London: Routledge.

Burns, C. 2005. "European Parliament: The European Union's Environmental Champion?" In *Environmental Policy in the European Union: Actors, Institutions andProcesses*, edited by A. Jordan and C. Adelle, 87–105. London: Earthscan.

Carr, S., and L. Levidow. 1999. "Negotiated Science—The Case of Agricultural Biotechnology Regulation in Europe." In *European Discourses on Environmental Policy*, edited by M. Wissenburg, G. Orhan, and U. Collier, 159–173. Aldershot: Ashgate.

Commission of the European Communities (hereafter CEC). 1983. "Council Resolution adopting the Third Environmental Action Programme." *Official Journal of the European Communities* C46, 17.2.1983: 1–16.

CEC. 1992. *Towards sustainability: a European Community Programme of policy and action in relation to the environment and sustainable development*. COM (1992) 23 final, volume 2. Luxembourg: Office for Official Publications of the European Community.

CEC. 2002. *A European Union Strategy for Sustainable Development*. Luxembourg: Office for Official Publications of the European Communities.

Collier, U. 1997. "Sustainability, Subsidiarity and Deregulation: New Directions in EU Environmental Policy." *Environmental Politics* 6 (2): 1–23. doi:10.1080/09644019708414325.

Collier, U. 1999. "Towards Sustainability in the European Union—Beyond the Rhetoric." In *European Discourses on Environmental Policy*, edited by M. Wissenburg, G. Orhan, and U. Collier, 81–101. Aldershot: Ashgate.

Conca, K., and G. D. Dabelko, eds. 1998. *Green Planet Blues*. Boulder: Westview Press.

Council of the European Union. 1993. "Presidential Conclusions, Copenhagen European Council." 7.A.iii. http://www.europarl.europa.eu/enlargement/ec/pdf/cop_en.pdf

Council of the European Union. 2008. *Consolidated versions of the Treaty on European Union and the Treaty on the Functioning of the European Union*. Brussels: Council of the European Union.

Deutsch, K. W., S. A. Burrell, R. A. Kann, M. Lee Jr, M. Lichtermann, R. E. Lindgren, F. L. Loewenheim, and R. W. Van Wagenen. 1957. *Political Community and the North Atlantic Area, International Organization in the Light of Historical Experience*. Princeton: Princeton University Press.

Diez, T. 2005. "Constructing the Self and Changing Others: Reconsidering 'Normative Power Europe'." *Millennium - Journal of International Studies* 33: 613–636. doi:10.1177/03058298050330031701.

Duchene, F. 1972. "Europe's Role in World Peace." In *Europe Tomorrow. Sixteen Europeans Look Ahead*, edited by R. Mayne, 32–47. London: Collins.

Eckersley, R. 2004. *The Green State*. Cambridge: MIT Press.

Eriksen, E. O., and J. E. Fossum, eds. 2000. *Democracy in the European Union: Integration Through Deliberation?* London: Routledge.

Eriksen, E. O., and J. E. Fossum. 2004. "Europe in Search of Legitimacy: Strategies of Legitimation Assessed." *International Political Science Review* 25 (4): 435–459. doi:10.1177/0192512104045089.

European Environment Agency. 1995. *Environment in the European Union*. Copenhagen: European Environment Agency.

European Environment Agency. 2003. *Europe's Environment: The Third Assessment*. Copenhagen: European Environment Agency.

Finnemore, M., and K. Sikkink. 1998. "International Norm Dynamics and Political Change." *International Organization* 52 (4): 887–917. doi:10.1162/002081898550789.

Fligstein, N., and A. Stone Sweet. 2002. "Constructing Politics and Markets: A Institutionalist Account of European Integration." *American Journal of Sociology* 107 (5): 1206–1243. doi:10.1086/341907.

Geyer, R., and S. Lightfoot. 2010. "The Strengths and Limits of New Forms of EU Governance: The Cases of Mainstreaming and Impact Assessment in EU Public Health and Sustainable Development Policy." *Journal of European Integration* 32 (4): 339–356. doi:10.1080/07036331003797547.

Gottweis, H. 1999. "Regulating Genetic Engineering in the European Union." In *Transformation of Governance in the European Union*, edited by B. Kohler-Koch and R. Eisling, 59–80. London: Routledge.

Grant, W., D. Matthews, and P. Newell. 2000. *The Effectiveness of European Union Environmental Policy*. Houndmills: Macmillan Press.

Haas, E. B. 1958. *The Uniting of Europe*. Stanford: Stanford University Press.

Habermas, J. 2000. "Beyond the Nation-State? On Some Consequences of Economic Globalization." In *Democracy in The European Union, Integration through Deliberation?*, edited by E. O. Eriksen and J. E. Fossum, 29–42. London: Routledge.

Haigh, N., and D. Baldock. 1989. *Environmental Policy and 1992*. London: British Department of the Environment.

Hildebrand, P. M. 2005. "The European Community's Environmental Policy, 1957 to '1992'." In *Environmental Policy in the European Union: Actors, Institutions and Processes*, edited by A. Jordan and C. Adelle, 19–41. London: Earthscan.

Hooghe, L., and G. Marks. 2008. "European Union?" *West European Politics* 31 (1–2): 108–129. doi:10.1080/01402380701834739.

Hunt, J. 1994. "The Social Construction of Precaution." In *Interpreting the Precautionary Principle*, edited by T. O'Riordan and J. Cameron, 117–125. London: Earthscan.

Inglehart, R. F. 2008. "Changing Values among Western Publics from 1970 to 2006." West European Politics 31 (1–2): 130–146. doi:10.1080/01402380701834747.

Jacobs, F. 2006. "The Role of the European Court of Justice in the Protection of the Environment." *Journal of Environmental Law* 18 (2): 185–205. doi:10.1093/jel/eql012.

Johnson, S. P., and G. Corcelle. 1989. *The Environmental Policy of the European Communities*. London: Graham and Trotman.

Jordan, A., and J. Fairbrass. 2005. "European Union Environmental Policy after the Nice Summit." In *Environmental Policy in the European Union: Actors, Institutions and Processes*, edited by A. Jordan and C. Adelle, 42–46. London: Earthscan.

Jordan, A., and A. Schout. 2006. *The Coordination of the European Union, Exploring the Capacities of Networked Governance*. Oxford: Oxford University Press.

Koppen, I. J. 2005. "The Role of the European Court of Justice." In *Environmental Policy in the European Union: Actors, Institutions and Processes*, edited by A. Jordan and C. Adelle, 67–86. London: Earthscan.

Kramer, L. 1995. *EC Treaty and Environmental Law*. Sweet & Maxwell: London.

Lebow, R. N. 2008. "Identity and International Relations." *International Relations* 22 (4): 473–492. doi:10.1177/0047117808097312.

Legro, J. 1997. "Which Norms Matter? Revisiting the "Failure" of Internationalism." *International Organization* 51 (1): 31–63. doi:10.1162/002081897550294.

Lélé, S. M. 1991. "Sustainable Development: A Critical Review." *World Development* 19 (6): 607–621. doi:10.1016/0305-750X(91)90197-P.

Lenschow, A. 1999. "Transformation in European Union Environmental Governance." In *Transformation of Governance in the European Union*, edited by B. Kohler-Koch and R. Eisling, 37–58. London: Routledge.

Livanis, I. 2010. "Conforming or Muddling Through: Explaining Variations in Compliance with European Union Environmental Policy." PhD dissertation, University of Florida.

Lodge, J., ed. 1989. *The European Community and the Challenge of the Future*. New York: St. Martin's Press.

Majone, G. 1996. *Regulating Europe*. London: Routledge.

Manners, I. 2002. "Normative Power Europe: A Contradiction in Terms?" *JCMS: Journal of Common Market Studies* 40 (2): 235–258. doi:10.1111/jcms.2002.40.issue-2.

March, J. G., and J. P. Olsen. 2009. *The Logic of Appropriateness*. ARENA Working Paper WP04/09. Oslo: Center for European Studies.

Marsden, S. 2011. "The Espoo Convention and Strategic Environmental Assessment Protocol in the European Union: Implementation, Compliance, Enforcement and Reform." *Review of European Community & International Environmental Law* 20 (3): 267–276. doi:10.1111/reel.2011.20.issue-3.

Martens, M. 2008. "Administrative Integration through the Back Door? The Role and Influence of the European Commission in Transgovernmental Networks within the Environmental Policy Field." *Journal of European Integration* 30 (5): 635–651. doi:10.1080/07036330802439608.

Maull, H. W. 2005. "Europe and the New Balance of Global Order." *International Affairs* 81 (4): 775–799. doi:10.1111/inta.2005.81.issue-4.

McCormick, J. 2001. *Environmental Policy in the European Union*. Houndsmill: Palgrave.

Nagpal, T. 1995. "Voices from the Developing World: Progress Toward Sustainable." *Environment: Science and Policy for Sustainable Development* 37 (8): 10–35. doi:10.1080/00139157.1995.9930952.

O'Riordan, T., and J. Cameron, eds. 1994. *Interpreting the Precautionary Principle*. London: Earthscan.

Orhan, G. 1999. "European Environmental Policy at the Intersection of Institutions and Ideas." In *European Discourses on Environmental Policy*, edited by M. Wissenburg, G. Orhan, and U. Collier, 35–57. Aldershot: Ashgate.

Pop, V. 2010. "This WEEK in the European Union." *EUObserver/Weekly Agenda*, January 8.

Rehbinder, E., and R. Stewart. 1985. "Legal Integration in Federal Systems: European Community Environmental Law." *The American Journal of Comparative Law* 33: 371–446. doi:10.2307/840235.

Sandel, M. 1982. *Liberalism and the Limits of Justice*. Cambridge: Cambridge University Press.

Saurugger, S. 2010. "The Social Construction of the Participatory Turn: The Emergence of a Norm in the European Union." *European Journal of Political Research* 49: 471–495. doi:10.1111/ejpr.2010.49.issue-4.

Scharpf, F. W. 1999. *Governing in Europe: Effective and Democratic?* Oxford: Oxford University Press.

Skjaerseth, J. B., and J. Wettestad. 2002. "Understanding the Effectiveness of EU Environmental Policy: How Can Regime Analysis Contribute?" *Environmental Politics* 11 (3): 99–120. doi:10.1080/714000635.

Smismans, S. 2003. "European Civil Society: Shaped by Discourses and Institutional Interests." *European Law Journal* 9 (4): 473–495. doi:10.1111/eulj.2003.9.issue-4.

Ward, S., and R. Williams. 1997. "From Hierarchy to Networks? Sub-central Government and EU Urban Environment Policy." *JCMS: Journal of Common Market Studies* 35 (3): 439–464. doi:10.1111/jcms.1997.35.issue-3.

Woods, K. 2010. *Human Rights and Environmental Sustainability*. Cheltenham: Edward Elgar Publishing.

World Commission on Environment and Development (WCED, *The Brundtland Report*). 1987. *Our Common Future*. London: Oxford University Press.

Wynne, B. 1992. "Uncertainty and Environmental Learning 1, 2 reconceiving Science and Policy in the Preventive Paradigm." *Global Environmental Change* 2 (2): 111–127. doi:10.1016/0959-3780(92)90017-2.

Zielonka, J. 2013. "Europe's New Civilizing Missions: The EU's Normative Power Discourse." *Journal of Political Ideologies* 18 (1): 35–55. doi:10.1080/13569317.2013.750172.

The evolving and interacting bases of EU environmental policy legitimacy: a reply to Brown

Rüdiger Wurzel

This is a reply to:

Brown, M. Leann. 2016. 'The evolving and interacting bases of EU environmental policy legitimacy.' *Global Discourse* 6 (3): 396–419. http://dx.doi.org/10.1080/23269995.2016.1153826

This is a very welcome and highly topical article especially when considering that not only have legitimacy issues been raised about the EU's environmental policy but about the very existence of the EU in the 2010s (as can be seen from, for example, the referendum on the UK's membership in the EU and the rise in support for Eurosceptic parties in once pro-European countries such as the Netherlands). As Brown (2016) rightly points out, EU environmental policy is one of the most popular common policy areas among European citizens (e.g. Eurobarometer 2014). One could therefore conclude that EU citizens' consistently high support for a common environmental policy should help to reduce the EU's 'legitimacy deficit'. However, as Brown's article shows the issue is more complex than appears at first sight.

Brown's article puts forward a nuanced, insightful analysis which differentiates between (1) legitimacy as permissive acceptance, (2) legitimacy as 'appropriateness', (3) democracy-based legitimacy, and (4) identity-based legitimacy. She rejects a 'dichotomous' understanding of legitimacy (i.e. that the actions of an actor are either legitimate or not) while arguing that the four different types of 'legitimacies may be associated with different actors in different time periods, and they vary in terms of their stability, durability, and strength' (Brown 2016, 412). This constitutes an innovative conceptual approach which leads to very interesting ideas and arguments about the evolution of the EU's environmental policy and its changing legitimacy base over time.

Brown is cautious when stating that different types of legitimacy 'may be associated with …. different time periods [italics added]' (Brown 2016, 412). However, the empirical data provided for the different types of legitimacy gives the (albeit largely implicit) impression that a sequential development of the above-mentioned four different types of legitimacy can be observed in the evolution of EU environmental policy. Such a sequential timeline is, however, a problematic one.

Most environmental policy observers will probably agree that policymakers relied strongly on legitimacy as permissive acceptance when adopting early EU environmental policy measures. Brown rightly flags up the importance of the Single European Market (SEM), which was then still called Common Market, for the justification of what in essence often amounted to the harmonisation of different environmental national standards on the EU level. Albert Weale (1999, 40) has argued that early EU environmental policy constitutes 'a textbook illustration of the [Monnet] method at work' (Weale 1999, 40) which was driven by the logic of 'integration by stealth' (Hayward 1996). Jean Monnet, who was one of the founding fathers – there were very few female politicians in EU politics in the 1950s something which has fortunately long since changed – had envisaged that functional spill-over, issue-linkage pressures, and engrenage would become major driving forces for the adoption of new common policies which in turn would foster deeper political integration. In accordance with the Monnet method, the Commission used its initiative monopoly to propose the harmonisation of nationally different environmental standards in order both to ensure the functioning of the internal market and to expand the EU's (and thus also its own) institutional powers. Member governments and the pro-integrationist European Court of Justice (ECJ) went along with this approach. However, Weale (1999, 40) also warns that '[p]atterns of environmental policy are not explained by the pure logic of spillover'. For example, the EU 1976 bathing water directive (76/440/EEC), 1979 drinking water directive (79/869/EEC) and some of the 1970s' ambient air quality directives clearly cannot be explained (solely) with reference to the SEM. These measures largely tackled local collective action problems at the subnational member state level and, at best, had only a very tenuous link to the SEM. They were primarily justified with reference to the Preamble of the 1957 European Economic Community (EEC) Treaty which mentioned the importance of the raising of living standards for the EEC. Although the Preamble provided only a very weak legal basis, member governments largely did not challenge these measures largely because they were popular among environmental NGOs and the general public (e.g. Wurzel 2008).

Brown's assessment of democracy-based legitimacy is generally a very good and insightful one. However, the conclusions drawn from it are arguably overly optimistic. The EU's Open Method of Coordination (OMC), which relies on the identification of 'best practices' through peer review, benchmarking and naming and shaming never really took off in the environmental policy field. Similarly, the so-called Cardiff Process, which had been championed by the 1998 UK EU Presidency with the aim of integrating environmental requirements into all of the different Council formations and thus also into all EU policy areas, soon ran its course without any tangible results. In fact, the OMC has arguably made worse the democratic deficit because it sidelined the only directly elected EU institution, namely the EP which Brown rightly calls the 'greenest' of all EU institutions, although its green credentials have waned in recent years (e.g. Burns et al. 2013). Brown is correct in arguing that 'deliberative interactions are essential to creating trust, solidarity, and a sense of community, the foundations for identity-based legitimacy' (Brown 2016, 413). However, whether the OMC and Cardiff Strategy (as well as the other initiatives which Brown identifies) can really produce identity-based legitimacy on the EU level is doubtful. Trying to increase participatory and deliberative democracy at the EU level constitutes a huge challenge, partly because the EU resembles still largely only a 'would-be polity' (Lindberg and Scheingold 1970) rather than a state-like polity.

Brown rightly mentions that the EU has 'sought to integrate environmental objectives with other global regimes such as trade and foreign assistance' (Brown 2016, 413).

However, the EU's legitimacy has not only been questioned by internal actors (such as Eurosceptic member governments and parties) but also from outside the EU. As Vogler (1999, 2016) has observed, especially in the early years of the international climate change negotiations, the EU's 'actorness' was repeatedly questioned by, in particular, developing countries who were concerned about sovereignty issues. Because the EU has only a relatively weak legal base for signing international environmental treaties, such treaties have been so-called mixed agreements which have to be signed by both the EU and member governments.

Considering the initially relatively weak legal basis for EU environmental policy, the marked national differences in geography (e.g. island states vs. densely populated continental states), economic development (e.g. affluent Northern European vs. relatively poor Southern and Central and Eastern European states), levels of environmental awareness (e.g. high levels of postmaterialism vs. low levels of environmental awareness), different environmental regulatory traditions (e.g. precautionary principle vs. scientific proof) and differences in levels of support for European integration (pro-European vs. Eurosceptic governments/member states), it is no small achievement for the EU to have adopted a fairly comprehensive common environmental policy which enjoys strong support among EU citizens from across a wide range of member states (Wurzel 2012).

References

Brown, M. L. 2016. "The Evolving and Interacting Bases of EU Environmental Policy Legitimacy." *Global Discourse* 6 (3): 396–419. doi:10.1080/23269995.2016.1153826.

Burns, C., N. Carter, G. A. M. Davies, and N. Worsfold. 2013. "Still Saving the Earth?: The European Parliament's Environmental Record." *Environmental Politics* 22 (6): 935–954. doi:10.1080/09644016.2012.698880.

Eurobarometer. 2014. *Attitudes of European Citizens Towards the Environment.* Special Eurobarometer 416. Brussels: Commission of the European Union.

Hayward, J. 1996. "Conclusion: Has European Unification by Stealth a Future?" In *Elitism, Populism, and European Politics,* edited by J. Hayward, 252–258. Oxford: Clarendon Press Oxford.

Lindberg, L., and S. A. Scheingold. 1970. *Europe's Would-Be Polity: Patterns of Change in the European Community.* Eaglewood Cliffs, New Jersey: Prentice-Hall.

Vogler, J. 1999. "The European Union1 as an Actor in International Environmental Politics." *Environmental Politics* 8 (3): 24–48. doi:10.1080/09644019908414478.

Vogler, J. 2016. "Global Climate Politics: Can the EU be an Actor?" In *Still Taking a Lead? The European Union in International Climate Change Politics,* edited by R. K. W. Wurzel, J. Connelly, and D. Liefferink. London: Routledge.

Weale, A. 1999. "European Environmental Policy by Stealth: The Dysfunctionality of Functionalism?" *Environment and Planning C: Government and Policy* 17 (1): 37–51. doi:10.1068/c170037.

Wurzel, R. K. W. 2008. "Environmental Policy: EU Actors, Leader and Laggard States." In *Leaderless Europe,* edited by J. Hayward, 66–88. Oxford: Oxford University Press.

Wurzel, R. K. W. 2012. "From Environmental Disunion Towards Environmental Union?" In *European Disunion. Between Sovereignty and Solidarity,* edited by J. Hayward and R. K. W. Wurzel, 215–232. Basingstoke: Palgrave/Macmillan.

Do Catalans have 'the right to decide'? Secession, legitimacy and democracy in twenty-first century Europe

Kathryn Crameri

ABSTRACT

Secession is normally viewed as legitimate only as a last resort for oppressed peoples, but contemporary independence movements in Europe are working hard to shift perceptions of the legitimacy of secession as a democratic phenomenon. In this context, the recent growth of the independence movement in Catalonia has given rise to a direct confrontation between two opposing conceptions of the legitimacy of secession in democratic nation-states. On one hand, pro-referendum Catalans claim that a vote on the matter would be entirely consistent with the basic principles of democracy. On the other, the Spanish government rests its denial of a referendum on the legal authority of the Spanish Constitution, which states that Spain must remain united. This article traces the two competing discourses of democratic and legal legitimacy (what we might call the 'right to decide' vs. the 'duty to abide') through an examination of the rhetoric of key political actors. It concludes that the Catalan government's attempt to prove that Catalonia could constitute a politically legitimate independent state, and should therefore be allowed to ask its residents whether they wish it to do so, is particularly significant as a challenge to generally accepted 'remedial right' theories of secession.

The twenty-first century has so far witnessed an unprecedented number of democratic challenges from separatist movements to the established nation-states at the core of the European Union. The failure of the 2003 'Ibarretxe Plan' for the Basque Country to achieve a vote on free association with the Spanish state did not deter others from pursuing similar agendas (Keating and Bray 2006). This included Scotland, whose success in holding a referendum on independence with minimal opposition from the rest of the United Kingdom has spurred on others, including Veneto and Flanders, and given added weight to the demands of Catalonia, where pressure for a binding vote has been building since a string of makeshift local consultations were held in 2009–2010. The Scottish example proves that calls for secession can be managed democratically through standard processes of political negotiation and consultation, as indeed they have been previously in Canada (Evans 2013, 9). Nevertheless, the concept of secession itself remains highly problematic, and it is often viewed as a 'last resort' that will receive international approval only under the most extreme circumstances (Buchanan 2003, 331).

Given its reluctance to do anything other than affirm the sanctity of existing state boundaries, the international political community has generally tried to characterise secession as an internal matter for the nation-states concerned (Buchanan 2003, 340–341). Despite attempts to elicit support from figures as diverse as Barack Obama, Julian Assange and Lady Gaga,[1] Catalan calls for a Scottish-style referendum therefore remain entirely dependent on the approval of the Spanish government, since the power to hold a referendum of any kind is reserved to the state under the terms laid out in the Spanish Constitution.[2] In fact, a binding referendum would not technically be possible without prior constitutional reform, since it would contradict key clauses that guarantee the territorial unity of Spain (Ferreres Comella 2014, 586–588). Whether a purely consultative vote could be authorised has been the subject of great debate, with legal opinion on the matter as divided as public opinion; the legal problem here revolves around whether a consultation could be used to prompt constitutional reform or would have to take place as part of a process that was already underway (588).

In any case, the current right-wing government led by Mariano Rajoy has made it clear that it has no intention of sanctioning any form of referendum on secession, nor will it enter into any negotiations whose aim would be to give Catalonia more powers within the Spanish state. This has given rise to a war of words and gestures which has included a purely symbolic 'public consultation' held in Catalonia on 9 November 2014. As a result, charges of disobedience and misuse of public funds have been brought against the president of the Catalan Autonomous Government, Artur Mas.[3] Rajoy has characterised the vote itself as 'illegal' and the concept of Catalan secession as 'uncon-stitutional' and – therefore – illegitimate (Rajoy 2014).

As the contemporary heir to historic forms of Spanish nationalism, Rajoy's *Partido Popular* (People's Party, PP) has a particularly centralist conception of the Spanish state which also surfaced during the party's first term of majority government, under José María Aznar, from 2000 to 2004. However, it is not alone in its opposition to Catalan independence, since most Spanish leftists also stress the concept of 'national solidarity', even when they are more than just pragmatic proponents of regional devolution (Balfour and Quiroga 2007, 72). Catalonia is a key driver of Spain's economy (as is the Basque Country), and a net contributor to the interregional fiscal transfers that support its poorer regions (Bel 2013, 190–192). This economic centrality partly explains the pragmatic approach to territorial accommodation taken during Spain's transition to democracy, which resulted (through a rather haphazard evolution) in the 'State of Autonomies' that exists today. However, the system has come under increasing strain, both from the 'competitive federalism' emanating from all 17 regions as they jostle for improved competencies (Balfour and Quiroga 2007, 60), and from Basque and Catalan demands for self-determination. The current government's hard-line stance against Catalonia's 'right to decide' therefore needs to be seen in this context.

The discourse surrounding the legitimacy or otherwise of the Catalan independence movement has become increasingly polarised ever since the Catalan parliament approved a 'Declaration of Sovereignty and the Right to Decide' in January 2013, as the precursor to demanding a referendum.[4] The majority of the text was declared unconstitutional by Spain's Constitutional Court in March 2014, in a judgement that affirmed that Spain itself was the only sovereign nation, and the 'right to decide' could only be exercised within the limits prescribed by the Spanish Constitution of 1978.[5] The Spanish government's refusal to negotiate other options has effectively stymied the development of any 'third way' between these two poles, with the result that this term itself remains incredibly vague, denoting anything from enhanced autonomy for Catalonia within the present system to federal and even confederal re-arrangements of the Spanish state. At the time of writing, the only two positions that have been clearly articulated are (1) that the Catalans are a sovereign people who have the democratic right to decide their own relationship with the Spanish state, or (2) that Catalonia forms part of a sovereign Spanish nation-state that remains 'indivisible' until such time as the people of Spain see fit to amend – through the proper legal process – the Constitution that prescribes this indivisibility.[6]

Given the extensive coverage of this dispute in the Spanish media (by which I mean traditional, new and social media), it is not surprising that questions regarding the legitimacy of Catalonia's claims and the Spanish government's right to ignore them have become a matter of fierce public debate. Manuel Arias Maldonado goes as far as to say the following:

> Spanish society is currently embroiled in a permanent debate about matters that are fundamental to philosophy and political theory. This is the only way to describe the problem of the legitimacy of power, the relationship between legitimacy and legality, the definition of what is just, and the defensibility of civil disobedience in a democratic context. (Arias Maldonado 2014)[7]

The aim of this article is to examine the character and evolution of this debate during a 2-year period from the passing of the 'Declaration of Sovereignty' in January 2013 to the calling of 'plebiscitary' Catalan elections in January 2015. The discussion draws mainly on political speeches, written statements from political parties and institutions, and press articles. After a brief introduction to the ways in which the legitimacy of secession may be conceptualised, the article places the Catalan independence movement in the context of Spain's ongoing crisis of both economic stability and institutional legitimacy. It then turns to examine the rhetoric used by the current Spanish government to dismiss Catalan claims, and the Catalan autonomous government's attempts to counteract this.

The significance of these competing discourses for Spain and Catalonia is clear: together, they describe a political conflict that has reached an impasse so serious that Spain's entire future as a nation-state depends on how it is eventually resolved. However, they also shed light on a much broader context: the apparently growing attraction of the concept of 'independence in Europe', and the attempts of members of various territorial minorities to make a convincing case for the desirability and democratic legitimacy of this option. The idea of secession as a legitimate political choice regardless of the circumstances has been given a significant boost by the Scottish referendum, implying that the idea of secession as a 'remedial' right is outdated, at least within the context of the 'unity in diversity' promulgated by the European Union. Catalonia's struggles with a Spanish state that will not accept this view will no doubt further shape the evolution of this discourse on a European, and possibly a global, scale.

Legitimising secession

The second half of the twenty-first century saw an increasing acceptance of regional government, or at least administration, within Western European nation-states (Keating 2000; Loughlin 2009). While it has been argued that devolution has generally been a force for stability in Western countries that encompass national minorities (Guibernau 2006), for some of these the question of secession has now become urgent. Indeed, many of these secession movements are led by nationalist parties in power in elected regional institutions. They therefore enjoy political legitimacy within the particular democratic sphere of regional government, but does this political legitimacy extend to a democratic right to secession?

We should of course draw a distinction between democratic legitimacy and political legitimacy, even though the two concepts are clearly related. Without going into the details of the extensive debates on this relationship in political philosophy (for a summary of which see Peter 2014), a major question is the extent to which political legitimacy is in itself derived from democratic legitimacy, and vice versa. If the two are separable, then even a non-democratic government may enjoy political legitimacy in certain circumstances (Peter 2014, 13). In contrast to these 'instrumentalist' positions that see outcomes as more important than the process by which these are arrived at, Allen Buchanan's view is that political legitimacy derives from 'a Robust Natural Duty of Justice' at whose core we find 'the protection of basic individual rights' (Buchanan 2002, 718). Since democratic institutions are the best guarantor of these rights and of the 'fundamental equality of persons', democracy is 'necessary if the exercise of political power is to be morally justifiable' (Buchanan 2002, 715, 719).

Frederick Barnard raises a broader point relating to morality by asking 'whether or not norms sanctioning processes intended to authenticate democratic governance demand the convergence of political rightness with universal moral rightness' (Barnard 2001, 12). According to Jaime Lluch, questions of morality are in fact central to the concerns of secessionist and autonomist groups and will tend to dictate the extent to which territorial accommodation is seen as an acceptable compromise. Lluch argues that 'sub-state nationalists inhabit a "moral polity" in which reciprocities are expected and notions of the common weal and mutual accommodation are essential' (Lluch 2012, 435). If this moral contract is perceived to be broken, the sub-state nationalist will adopt a particular federalist, autonomist or separatist position depending on the extent to which s/he believes that the nation-state has a genuine will to fix the problem (Lluch 2012, 440). While this is a rather limited conception of morality compared with that which informs Buchanan's normative concept of political legitimacy, the idea of the moral polity still rests on Buchanan's fundamental premise of 'genuine political community among equal persons' (Buchanan 2002, 719). Sub-state nationalists who are unhappy with the amount of reciprocal recognition they get in return for their loyalty to the democratic nation-state are therefore likely to question its authority over them, if not its legitimacy, partly on the basis that this undermines the equality that is seen to be a fundamental characteristic of democracy.

As we will see, the debate on Catalan independence revolves squarely around the concept of democracy and involves two competing and contradictory definitions of how the term applies to this particular context. For most Catalans, whether or not they are in favour of independence, the idea that they should be able to vote on their status vis-à-vis Spain has become the embodiment of the meaning of democracy in the current crisis.[8] This is expressed in the popular slogan 'votar és democràcia' – 'voting is democracy' – which has become, for example, a handy twitter hashtag for those posting messages in support of a binding referendum or of those who organised the unofficial vote on 9 November 2014. On the other hand, the Spanish government and most of the Spanish media equate democracy firmly with legality: specifically, in the form of the inviolability of the Spanish Constitution of 1978 which prohibits the secession of any part of the nation-state. They therefore deny the legitimacy of all actions taken by the Catalan Autonomous Government – the *Generalitat* – to claim sovereignty for the Catalan nation and hold a referendum or plebiscitary elections on independence.[9] Catalan politicians and pro-independence groups have attempted to counter this argument by pointing out that the law is not an absolute but a product of democratic processes, and it therefore needs to be flexible enough to respond to changing political circumstances (Forcadell Lluís 2013, 17). They deplore the failure of the Spanish government to accept the need for negotiations towards a political settlement.

One of the main areas of debate in theories of secession concerns the extent to which its legitimacy depends on some kind of injustice having been perpetrated on the group that is attempting to secede. Indeed, some theories are based on the premise that unilateral secession can only really be justified in such terms; these have come to be known as 'remedial right only' theories (Buchanan 1998, 227–228). Allen Buchanan argues that 'from the standpoint of international law, the unilateral right to secede – the right to secede without consent or constitutional authorization – should be understood as a remedial right only, a last-resort response to serious injustices' (Buchanan 2003, 331). Furthermore, he states that 'in affirming a remedial understanding of the right to secede, international law should unambiguously repudiate the nationalist principle that all nations (or "peoples") are entitled to their own states' (331). Nevertheless he qualifies this, first by supporting the premise that the international community should strongly support attempts to guarantee the human rights of minorities and to find alternatives to secession (such as autonomy), putting pressure on the nation-state if necessary. Second, he provides for a relatively broad definition of the kind of injustice that might legitimise secession (Buchanan 2003, 331, 351–352). This includes 'the state's persistence in violations of intrastate autonomy agreements' as well as more standard justifications such as the violation of basic human rights or 'unjust annexation' (352).

In contrast, Christopher Heath Wellman argues that 'many groups have a primary right to secede even in the absence of past injustices' (Wellman 2013, 118). Wellman's argument rests on a very different premise from Buchanan's, which is that a large group may decide to secede as long as this does not cause undue harm to the political entity from which it breaks. He explains that 'because the liberal cannot justifiably restrict political liberty which is not sufficiently harmful, a secessionist party has the right to secede when its independence will not jeopardize political stability' (118). A split from a stable first-world democracy – Wellman uses the example of Quebec and Canada – should not produce any long-term adverse effects that the original nation-state would not be able to overcome. The idea of political legitimacy is key to Wellman's argument, since the main issue is whether both of the resulting states are in a position to retain that legitimacy vis-à-vis their own people (113). International recognition of each state's legitimacy would naturally follow on from this. Spain and Catalonia ought to fall into the same category as Canada and Quebec in terms of their ability to form separate legitimate states. However, as we will see in the next section, the Spanish state is in fact undergoing a crisis of political legitimacy, only part of which is related to the question of its relationship with Catalonia.

A crisis of political legitimacy in Spain

As a relatively young democracy, forged in the wake of the dictatorship of Francisco Franco which ended only with his death in 1975, Spain has been rightly proud of its rapid political transformation. However, the global economic crisis that struck Spain in 2008 exposed a number of existing cracks in its political and economic foundations, which have now become gaping holes. The depth of Spain's crisis was an indicator of fundamental problems that had been successfully hidden by factors such as Spain's enhanced international standing and a construction boom (Royo 2014). Sebastián Royo argues that these pre-existing flaws could be found in virtually all of Spain's institutions, including the monarchy, the judiciary, banks and their regulators, and the education system. These combined with failings in the country's political institutions to the effect that 'economic success spurred by the country's modernization and EU membership was not sustained because the governments (at all levels: local, regional and national) became less accountable and responsive to citizens' (Royo 2014, 1570). This lack of accountability and responsiveness has been exacerbated by the economic crisis, to the point that perceptions of the legitimacy of virtually all of Spain's institutions have fallen dramatically in the last few years (Royo 2014, 1576–1577).

A few brief examples will help to explain why the general public has become so disillusioned. Corruption and clientelism among the political elites have been a perennial problem for Spain even in democracy, but recent scandals have revealed the full extent of its reach into the highest levels of government. For example, the government bailout of failed banking conglomerate Bankia in 2012 was followed by revelations that its board members had been issued undeclared credit cards drawing on a hidden fund (Schaefer Muñoz, Enrich, and Bjork 2012; De Barrón and Pérez 2015). Meanwhile, those who had bought preference shares in the bank only to see them plummet in value are still waiting for a verdict on whether the sale itself was fraudulent (EFE 2013). As for the monarchy, the behaviour of King Juan Carlos during the crisis, which included a luxury trip to Botswana to shoot elephants (possibly accompanied by a mistress), sent his popularity rating plummeting and eventually resulted in him abdicating in favour of his less controversial son, Felipe. Even this has not removed the monarchy from the public gaze, with King Felipe's brother-in-law Iñaki Urdangarin on trial for embezzlement, and his sister Cristina accused of complicity in the resulting tax fraud.

Spain's devolved system of government as a whole has come under increasing scrutiny because of the duplication of administrative structures it is perceived to entail, as well as the creation of regional political elites that are also highly susceptible to corruption and clientelism (Royo 2014, 1574). It is certainly the case that Spain's autonomous communities have in no way been immune to these diseases, with numerous regional politicians arrested – for example – in an anti-corruption raid in October

2014 (Kassam 2014). Catalonia's major scandals in recent years have centred around the illustrious Pujol family, directly implicating the former president of the *Generalitat* Jordi Pujol, who confessed to having substantial undeclared funds in a bank account in Andorra. His claim that this was an inheritance is still to be tested. Meanwhile, one of his sons, Oriol, a high-ranking member of his father's party who was in many ways the heir to his political legacy, has been accused of influence peddling. The Spanish courts are so overwhelmed by the number of recent corruption cases that these are taking years to come to trial, further eroding public confidence in the justice system.

Public frustration with Spain's governing elites, caused mainly by these scandals and their ineptitude in the handling of the economic crisis, has led voters to embark on a somewhat desperate search for alternatives. The sweeping victory of the PP in the 2011 general elections was one symptom of this, but the party has been no more adept at handling the crisis than the left-wing government before them. Civil movements and protests have therefore flourished, and these have included an increase in visibility of the Republican movement, small- and large-scale protests to try to prevent evictions that are the result of repossessions for mortgage arrears and the *Indignados* anti-austerity movement.

While it would be simplistic to say that the increase in support for Catalan independence is solely attributable to this same search for alternatives, it is clear that some of its newer supporters have indeed responded to it in this way (Serrano 2013b, 19). The independence 'project' was already well formulated by the time the full extent of the crisis became apparent, unlike other alternatives such as the *Indignados* and the eventual birth of anti-establishment party *Podemos*. Nevertheless, *Podemos* is rising in popularity in Catalonia as well as the rest of Spain and may present a significant challenge to the pro-independence vote (Duarte 2015). Catalan politics is therefore very much replicating the current pattern in the rest of Spain, with the historically dominant forces losing substantial support to newer and/or previously more minor parties.

Given this context, it is not surprising that much Catalan pro-independence rhetoric now revolves around the idea that Spain suffers from an acute democratic deficit (or 'shortage') of which the Catalans are prime victims (Bosch 2013, 115). The Catalan reaction, according to the pro-independence politician Alfred Bosch, has been to oppose this shortage 'with an extra dose of democracy', ensuring that the independence movement is as respectful of democratic processes as possible (Bosch 2013, 118). Antonio Elorza, on the other hand, argues that this respect is a myth because the Catalan institutions that promulgate this approach are themselves breaking a cardinal democratic rule: institutional neutrality (Elorza 2014). Writing in the newspaper *El País*, he says:

> Democracy is not a manipulable framework that can be adapted to suit whoever is in government, so that they can arrive at a result that is consistent with their own aims. Democracy is a procedure that facilitates political decision-making, based on the participation of all citizens on an equal footing. This is the principle of isonomy, which dates back to Ancient Greece. But it's clear that this has not existed in Mas's Catalonia.

Elorza's attempt to tell us what democracy 'really means' is typical of the debate as a whole, in which everyone claims to have the 'true' definition of the term, in opposition to the false conceptions held by others. It is on the basis of their own definition of democracy that the commentator then goes on to assess the legitimacy of the other's position. No one will admit that such terms are in fact slippery and open to interpretation (Sadurski 2009, 22).

The 'Spanish' view

As has already been noted, arguments against Catalan sovereignty have come to coalesce around a legalistic definition of democratic rights based on the Spanish Constitution. The powers of the Autonomous Communities derive from this constitution, although the document is deliberately ambiguous about the nature and pre-existing rights of the 'collective subjects' (denominated 'nationalities and regions') that make up the Spanish state (Martínez-Herrera and Miley 2010, 8–10). On the other hand, it clearly states that sovereignty rests with the people of Spain as a whole, that Spain is 'indivisible', and that the Spanish government may suspend the powers of an Autonomous Community if it 'acts in a way that is seriously prejudicial to the general interest of Spain'.[10] It is on this basis that the PP have rejected any notion of the Catalans' 'right to decide', a right that it claims can only be exercised by the entire Spanish people (Rajoy 2014, 12, 13).

Furthermore, the PP's own concept of Spanish nationality has come to be fundamentally based on the idea of constitutional patriotism, despite this originally having been the preserve of the Spanish left (Balfour and Quiroga 2007, 90–91, 114–117). Constitutional patriotism has provided a new way of framing a discourse of national identity that avoids some of the pitfalls associated with the way the concept had been traditionally employed by the Spanish right. Nevertheless, as Balfour and Quiroga put it, calling for loyalty to the constitution above all else also has the effect of stressing its 'incontrovertibility', giving the PP a reason to 'deny any reform of the Constitution that would reflect changing identities' (Balfour and Quiroga 2007, 117). This obsession with 'the need to preserve societal oneness' flies in the face of liberal democratic principles that stress the need to protect 'plurality and the right to be different' (Barnard 2001, 4–5).

Spain's constitution allows for laws passed either by the central or autonomous governments to be challenged on grounds of unconstitutionality. The Constitutional Court that hears these challenges is also the body specifically charged with resolving conflicts of jurisdiction between the state government and autonomous communities.[11] Whereas it might have been assumed that the role of the court would diminish over time as the State of Autonomies became more embedded, in fact it has increased in importance. Two of its decisions are particularly pertinent to the discussion here. In 2008, it ruled on an act that had been passed by the Basque government that would have allowed it to hold a 'plebiscite' asking the Basque people for its support in negotiating with ETA and preparing the ground for further discussions on the Basque Country's 'right to decide' (Mees 2015, 54). In ruling against the act, the court also clarified that any consultation not sanctioned by the state that in any way resembled a referendum, even if it went by a different name and was not binding, would still be unconstitutional (Ferreres Comella 2014, 586; Serrano 2013a, 50–51).

Its second crucial ruling concerned the updated Catalan statute of autonomy that came into force in 2006. Despite having been through a long process of approval by the Catalan and Spanish parliaments and a referendum in Catalonia, several challenges were then received by the court, the most comprehensive of which came from the PP (Orte and Wilson 2009, 424–430; Ferreres Comella 2014, 573–574). The Constitutional Court took until 2010 to produce its verdict, which in fact left much of the text untouched, although it did invalidate certain key provisions (Ferreres Comella 2014, 574–575; Dowling 2013, 155–156). It also 'reinterpreted' a statement in the Preamble that referred to Catalonia as a nation, stating that while this could be accurate from a social, historical or cultural perspective, it could not be a legal definition since Spain is the only nation recognised in the constitution (Ferreres Comella 2014, 575).

The discourse of unconstitutionality as applied to matters related to Catalan autonomy was therefore well established by 2010, and it is no surprise that this was the primary term used by the PP to describe the 'Declaration of Sovereignty' of 2013 and Mas's plans for a consultation on independence announced several months later (Cué 2013). However, as the consultation itself drew nearer, 'unconstitutional' gave way to 'illegal' as the preferred term. Even though it was clear that this accusation of illegality was still predicated on the constitution, the word 'illegal' appeared now to be preferred for its greater clarity and impact.

This change of rhetoric was no doubt aimed particularly at the Catalans, whose attitude towards the constitution has become increasingly hostile despite having been one of the regions that voted strongly in favour of it at the time it was devised (Martínez-Herrera and Miley 2010, 11–12). The challenge to the 2006 statute through the Constitutional Court was certainly one factor in this, but it was also a symptom of a general feeling that, far from fulfilling the apparent promise of special treatment and recognition for Catalonia that had prompted high levels of support in 1978, the constitution was actually a brake on Catalan ambitions and was being used as an excuse to limit and even cut back its autonomy (López Tena 2007, 98–99). Calling the *Generalitat*'s actions 'unconstitutional', then, would be unlikely to have much impact on those Catalans who now dismiss the constitution as just another failed attempt to force them to conform to a centralising conception of the Spanish state. As Víctor Ferreres Comella puts it, 'the political forces that are pushing the process of "national transition" in Catalonia consider the Constitution to be a dead document as far as they are concerned' (Ferreres Comella 2014, 584). The term 'illegal' therefore carries greater force, and also an implied threat of legal action, which has of course been carried out in the charges laid against Artur Mas and two of his ministers after the vote on 9 November 2014.

In a speech given in Barcelona three weeks after the unofficial consultation on independence, Mariano Rajoy made a series of observations about the vote and its consequences as he saw them. First, he described it as a 'simulacrum of a consultation' – a phrase that had already been circulating for several weeks following its use in a speech by the leader of the PP in Catalonia, Alicia Sánchez Camacho, on 14 October (Rajoy 2014, 8; Europa Press 2014). The vote was such a 'farce', according to Rajoy, that two-thirds of the eligible voters declined to take part, resisting the 'pressure' put on them by the *Generalitat* to do so (Rajoy 2014, 8). The *Generalitat* had 'flouted the law' and divided Catalan society, and all for nothing, since its own figures after the vote showed that a majority of Catalans did not want independence (9). The planned process in Catalonia will now pass through the stages of 'so-called' plebiscitary elections, followed by the drafting of an 'illegal' constitution to be ratified in an 'illegal' referendum (13). Rajoy, however, pledges the following:

> Now, just to be clear, I am not going to let the unity of Spain be called into question, or the right of all Spaniards to decide what they want their country to be – in other words, national sovereignty –, or the equality of Spaniards and their fundamental rights. I won't let anyone call these into question. (13)

Approaching these matters through political dialogue is one thing, but 'politics cannot be an excuse to flout either the law or the will of the people' (14). 'If politics is an alternative to the application of the law, we are proposing something that is not very democratic at all' (14). Rajoy's speech very much represents a mature version of the discourse of legality which, by that stage, had come to dominate not just within the PP and its sympathisers but more broadly in sectors of the media and public opinion.

The PP's arguments draw on a liberal democratic perspective that prescribes a necessary 'trade-off' in which citizens forego direct participation in government 'for the functionality and accountability of representative democracy' (Isakhan and Slaughter 2014, 4). Thus, having accepted the Spanish Constitution and democratically elected their political representatives, Spaniards – Catalans included – are bound by the laws and policies those representatives put into place. The problem with this position is that Spain's economic crisis and continuous corruption scandals have critically damaged the perceived accountability of Spain's politicians. It is not surprising, then, that Catalan rhetoric is moving ever closer to 'civic republican' conceptions of democracy, 'in which democracy is thought of as a participatory, inclusive and deliberative form of government' (Isakhan and Slaughter 2014, 4). This is especially the case within the civil movement, which now has a very broad membership and a significant amount of influence on party-political actors (Crameri 2015; Dowling 2014, 222–223). However, this presents something of a paradox for the party currently in power in the *Generalitat*, whose political roots lie firmly in the same liberal democratic tradition espoused by Mariano Rajoy.

The 'Catalan' view

The two political parties that have had the most influence over the independence movement during the 2 years that concern us here are Artur Mas's *Convergència Democràtica de Catalunya* (Democratic Convergence of Catalonia, CDC), and *Esquerra Republicana de Catalunya* (Republican Left of Catalonia, ERC), led by Oriol Junqueras. ERC was the first of the two parties to move towards an explicitly pro-independence position, in the 1990s, whereas CDC's sudden conversion only occurred in 2012 (Dowling 2013, 153; 2014, 224). The change eventually resulted, in June 2015, in the end of a previously successful federation with *Unió Democràtica de Catalunya* (Democratic Union of Catalonia), which remains committed to trying to find some kind of 'third way' between independence and the status quo. CDC and ERC have now agreed to hold 'plebiscitary' elections in September 2015 at which they will present a joint candidate list including key members of civil pro-independence associations.

Despite their political differences in terms of their position on the left–right spectrum, CDC and ERC now have much in common when it comes to the arguments they use to justify independence, sharing in a coherent narrative that has been forged in the period since the debates over Catalonia's new statute (Dowling 2014, 227–228). Catalan identity has become a difficult basis on which to build a sense of common purpose because of the diverse origins of the community's population, although the Catalan language still plays a strong role in creating a sense of groupness (Brubaker 2004, 12–13; Serrano 2013a, 146). Much of the current political rhetoric therefore stresses factors to do with the economy, citing – among other things – Catalan taxpayers' 'unreasonable' contribution to propping up the poorer regions of Spain and the lack of state investment in Catalan infrastructure (Bel 2013, 165–252; Pons i Novell and Tremosa i Balcells 2005). Austerity measures following Spain's descent into economic crisis in 2008, and the perception that the two different Spanish governments in power since then have both been incompetent at managing the crisis, have heightened an already-existing feeling that Catalans would be better off running their own affairs. In this sense their claims mirror Christopher Wellman's description of the 'teleological approach' to secession (based on the function the state serves rather than the consensual process by which it is created), which 'allows secessionist parties to claim a right to secede grounded in *efficiency*' (Wellman 2013, 109–110).

Despite this stress on contemporary economic and political factors, claims of historical injustice visited by the Castilian-led Spanish state on Catalonia surface regularly in pro-independence discourse. Historical factors therefore appear as one in a long list of legitimising arguments for Catalan secession in the *White Paper on Catalonia's National Transition* that has been produced by a team of 'experts' recruited by the Catalan government (Generalitat de Catalunya 2014). The brief historical argument here concentrates on the fact that Catalonia was a differentiated entity for many centuries, with its own institutions (Generalitat de Catalunya 2014, 24). It is made clear that these institutions were lost in 1714 through military intervention (the defeat of Barcelona by Bourbon troops at the end of the War of the Spanish Succession), and that there was no possibility of recuperating a similar – and therefore sufficient – level of autonomy in the three centuries that followed.

However, the White Paper's suggested reasoning in support of claims to self-determination does not prioritise these historical factors. Instead, after a brief review of the main justifications permitted by 'remedial right only' theories of secession, it develops its case around the specific issue of the failure of three decades of attempts to achieve an acceptable level of autonomy within the Spanish state constituted in 1978 (Generalitat de Catalunya 2014, 20–23). It therefore attempts to invoke Allen Buchanan's category of 'violations of intrastate autonomy agreements' as Catalonia's primary justification for secession (Buchanan 2003, 352). These violations include the Spanish government's interference in the drafting of Catalonia's Statute of Autonomy of 2006 and the subsequent ruling of the Constitutional Court, which are labelled the most 'convincing' evidence (Generalitat de Catalunya 2014, 22).

As far as liberal democratic arguments based on the rights of the individual are concerned, these are certainly apparent in the White Paper. So, for example, the writers argue that the general right to self-determination is not just predicated on the collective consensus that confers legitimate political authority on a territory's elected representatives but also on the 'moral autonomy' of each individual member of that collective, to the effect that the right to constitute an independent state is a primary right of the individuals that make up the collective (Generalitat de Catalunya 2014, 19). This is of course reflective of the classic liberal position that puts individual liberty at the heart of all aspects of political thinking (Wellman 2013, 99). Interestingly, a stress on the rights of the individual also appears in some of the slogans of the civil pro-independence movement that circulate on social media: 'I want to decide', 'I want to be free'.

The liberal focus in this kind of rhetoric has the specific benefit of countering accusations that the Catalan independence movement is born out of a traditional ethnic nationalism. It does so by drawing attention away from questions about who constitutes the Catalan 'in-group' (Miley 2007, 195; García 2010; Serrano 2013a). Phrasing the desire for independence as a matter of the 'moral autonomy' of the individual plays down groupness and reinforces the argument that each Catalan should have the democratic right to vote on the way forward. It also gives rise to a dual discourse of legitimation, since if claims of injustice are rejected, an argument can be made that independence is the will of the people and their wishes should therefore be heeded regardless of whether there was injustice or not. Nevertheless, as the head of the institution trying to make this argument, Artur Mas is caught in a double bind: the Spanish government rejects the idea that his position represents the will of the majority of Catalans, and yet it denies him access to the tools – such as a binding referendum – that would allow him to prove that it does (Rajoy 2014, 7).

An important characteristic of Catalan nationalism in the context of this insistence on democratic rights is its commitment to non-violent forms of action. The peaceful nature of the mass demonstrations organised by the civil independence movement plays an important part here, with each event 'proving' Catalonia's commitment to non-violent protest, and therefore the legitimacy of the movement itself. This concern with proving legitimacy is also partly responsible for the scrupulous way in which all possible democratic avenues have been explored by the Catalan government. One example of this was the formal request to the Madrid parliament in January 2014 to be able to hold a consultative referendum, even though the petition was known to be futile from the start. By exhausting all possible steps, the Catalan government is reassuring the international community of its commitment to the democratic process, while at the same time calling into question the democratic credentials of a Spanish government that has consistently refused Catalan offers to negotiate. This also bolsters the case for secession as a remedial right.

Nevertheless, there is an internal danger inherent in this strategy. While Mas seems happy to prolong the journey towards independence in this way, members of the civil independence movement are getting increasingly frustrated with the lack of progress despite what they see as a clear mandate from the people to secede (Anon 2014). As a result, talk of a unilateral declaration following the planned elections in September 2015 is growing, even though still only a fifth of the Catalan people appear to support such a move (8TV 2015). Mas is understandably cautious about this option given the uncertain international reaction to a sudden unilateral declaration, even now that the Catalan government has shown that it would understand this very much as a last resort. Furthermore, the White Paper warns that a unilateral declaration might be followed by a 'conflict between the two orders [Spanish and Catalan], in which the authorities and directives of each of them would fight to get the upper hand and take control' (Generalitat de Catalunya 2014, 34–35). It goes on to say that

For this reason, the effectiveness of a unilateral proclamation of independence is largely conditioned by the existence of state structures with the capacity to exercise the functions of government over the territory and obtain social acceptance of their mandate.

One of Mas's pre-occupations is precisely to have in place these 'state structures' – including a tax office, energy infrastructure and security – before any declaration is made (Garcia Pagan 2015). Not only will this satisfy the concerns raised in the White Paper, it also addresses Wellman's condition that a seceding government must enjoy political legitimacy in the eyes of its own people if the secession itself is to be legitimate (Wellman 2013, 113).

Conclusion

When David Cameron was asked to justify granting a referendum on Scottish indepen-dence, he responded that he had viewed the request from the newly installed SNP government as legitimate because the party had been democratically elected on an unambiguous platform. Therefore, 'I did what I thought was the right thing, which was to say "you voted for a party that wants independence, you should have a referendum that is legal, that is decisive and that is fair"' (Watt 2014). His reasons were also pragmatic:

> I felt, as the prime minister of the UK, I had a choice. I could either say to them 'well you can't have your referendum, it is for us to decide whether you should have one.' I think that would have led to an almighty and disastrous battle between the Westminster parliament and the UK government and the Scottish government and the Scottish first minister.
>
> (Watt 2014)

Even though Cameron's reaction to the referendum request was no doubt predicated on an assumption that the 'no' vote would easily prevail, his explanation for the decision suggested that he had a moral responsibility both to accept the will of the Scottish people and to avoid a conflict that would be detrimental to both sides.

In contrast, the discourse employed in Spain by the PP and its allies in the media has sought to characterise the *Generalitat*'s request for a binding referendum as completely illegitimate, despite numerous indications of majority support among Catalans for such a vote. Furthermore, it is argued that the proposal originates from an exclusive and manipulative form of nationalism that is pitching itself malevolently against the legal authority of the Spanish government and the democratic validity of the Spanish Constitution. This approach attempts to paint the conflict as a case of a politically legitimate government facing an illegitimate separatist movement (Arias Maldonado 2014). However, both sides are represented by elected political parties with a democratic mandate, and therefore both enjoy political legitimacy, even if this operates in different spheres. Nor is the Spanish government a 'neutral' representative of the people, in contrast with a Catalan government that has forgotten this obligation. The current conflict therefore represents a battle between two opposing nationalisms, each of which is institutionally represented by legitimate political entities.

Frederick Barnard reminds us that liberal democratic governments are forced to operate in the context of 'the ideas of limited power and contingent authority in and through which they are definitionally identified and upheld' (Barnard 2001, 5). The PP's insistence on the infallibility of the Spanish Constitution seems to function as a way of trying to counteract or even deny this contingency, lending an authority to Rajoy's pronouncements on Catalan independence that they would not otherwise have. In contrast, for the Catalans the authority of the constitution is contingent on continued support from the citizens whose lives it regulates, rather in the manner of Renan's 'daily plebiscite'. The result is a 'clash of normative systems' (Ferreres Comella 2014, 584), in which no resolution seems to be possible since each side simply tries to invalidate the claims to normativity of the other.

Barnard also suggests that democratic norms are best derived from political activity, not from 'some antecedently self-validating authority or dogma' (Barnard 2001, 71). The Spanish government claims that since Catalan nationalism conditions the Catalan concept of democratic secession, the latter is therefore invalid. This disguises the fact that the concept of the nation that conditioned the constitution was substantially a product of a traditional form of Spanish nationalism of which the PP is a direct descendent (Balfour and Quiroga 2007, 46–47, 100–107). Equally, the PP's insistence on the Spanish Constitution as the ultimate source of authority means that its view of 'the rule of law' is also predicated on 'some pre-existing rightness' (Barnard 2001, 71). Furthermore, by equating the rule of law directly with democracy as if they were the same thing, the PP appears to make Spanish democracy itself contingent on the inviolable 'rightness' of the constitution. In its ruling on the possible secession of Quebec, the Canadian Supreme Court referred to the 'interaction between the rule of law and the democratic principle' as a requirement for generating political legitimacy and therefore a reason for the flexible interpretation of constitutional norms in a secession crisis (Supreme Court of Canada 1998, para 67). However, in the PP's view there can be no interaction between the two concepts – and therefore no conflict between them that requires political negotiation – because they are one and the same thing (Rajoy 2014, 15).

As we have seen, in the face of this national stalemate the preferred tactic of the *Generalitat* has been to hedge its bets over the arguments that might provide international recognition of the Catalan people's 'right to decide'. Even while fundamentally disagreeing with the 'remedial right only' approach that predominates internationally, the Catalans have found a possible route here in highlighting the state's persistent breaking of the reciprocal 'contract' on autonomy supposedly forged in the late 1970s. International precedents based on other premises are also invoked, including the UK and Canadian governments' pragmatic/democratic approaches to Scotland and Quebec, respectively (Evans 2013, 9–11; Supreme Court of Canada 1998). These are used to reinforce the argument that the democratically expressed will of the Catalan people trumps the preservation of the existing nation-state, and morally requires a negotiated political solution based on the acceptance of secession as a legitimate political goal. On top of this, we also see the Catalan government actively working towards the establishment of 'state structures' that will prove an independent Catalonia's capacity to create a new state that will have immediate political legitimacy in the eyes of its own people (Wellman 2013, 113) – perhaps even more so than the ailing Spanish rump state it would leave behind.

It is the last of these approaches that perhaps has the greatest potential for opening up new chinks in the international community's attitude towards secession. The granting of the 2014 referendum to Scotland implied that the duties of citizenship conferred upon the members of minority nations within democratic nation-states can be offset by a moral right to have the government attend to these citizens' desires. The Catalans are now demanding recognition of this right from the Spanish state. However, since such recognition is unlikely to be forthcoming, their leaders are also attempting to man-oeuvre themselves into a situation in which they have so many of the necessary institutions in place that international acceptance of their right to secede would seem a small and relatively insignificant step, at least in terms of its effects on the daily lives of people within the borders of the new Catalan state. Without a change in Spain's position on negotiation, this process can only drive a deeper wedge between the two sides and is likely to entail further damage to the Spanish government's own precarious political legitimacy.

Notes

1. See, for example, the list of 14,513 international figures who in 2013 were sent a copy of the book *Catalonia Calling: What the World Has to Know*; http://www.sapiens.cat/ca/personatges.php.
2. Spanish Constitution of 1978, Section 149.1.32.
3. His deputy and education minister were also charged.
4. 'Resolució 5/X del Parlament de Catalunya, per la qual s'aprova la Declaració de sobirania i el dret a decidir del poble de Catalunya', 23 January 2013.
5. Sentence 42/2014 of 25 March 2014, published in *Boletín Oficial del Estado* number 87, 10 April 2014, 77–99.
6. See the Spanish Constitution of 1978: Articles 1(2) and 2.
7. All translations from Spanish and Catalan sources are my own.
8. Surveys consistently show that around 80% of Catalans back a binding referendum, which is much higher than the figures for those who support independence (which varies greatly depending on the exact parameters of the question) (RAC1 2012).
9. The question of what constitutes the Catalan nation is a complex one, since cultural and in some cases political identification with Catalonia extends outside the borders of the Autonomous Community of Catalonia as it is currently constituted. This is one of the factors that complicates the perceived legitimacy of the president of the Catalan Government to speak for all Catalans.
10. Spanish Constitution of 1978, Sections 1, 2 and 155.
11. See Part IX Section 161 of the Spanish Constitution of 1978.

References

8TV. 2015. "Els catalans prefereixen un referèndum per ratificar la independència que una declaració unilateral si el 27-S hi ha majoria independentista." *8TV*, February 5. Accessed 20 Feburary 2015. http://www.8tv.cat/8aldia/videos/els-catalans-prefereixen-un-referendum-per-ratificar-que-una-declaracio-unilateral-si-el-27-s-hi-ha-majoria-independentista/.

Anon. 2014. "La ANC entrega 750.000 firmas al Parlament en favor de una declaración unilateral de independencia." *La Vanguardia*, September 15. Accessed 20 February 2015. http://www.lavanguardia.com/politica/20140915/54415983627/anc-entrega-750-000-firmas-parlament-declaracion-unilateral-independencia.html.

Arias Maldonado, M. 2014. "Legitimidad y legalidad en Cataluña." *El Diario*, September 27. Accessed 12 December 2014. http://www.eldiario.es/agendapublica/reforma-constitucional/Legitimidad-legalidad-Cataluna_0_307619574.html.

Balfour, S., and A. Quiroga. 2007. *The Reinvention of Spain: Nation and Identity since Democracy.* Oxford: Oxford University Press.

Barnard, F. M. 2001. *Democratic Legitimacy: Plural Values and Political Power.* Montreal: McGill-Queen's University Press.

Bel, G. 2013. *Anatomia d'un desengany.* Barcelona: Destino.

Bosch, A. 2013. "Judo in Madrid." In *What's Up with Catalonia?*, edited by L. Castro. Ashfield, MA: Catalonia Press.

Brubaker, R. 2004. *Ethnicity without Groups.* Cambridge, MA: Harvard University Press.

Buchanan, A. 1998. "The International Institutional Dimension of Secession." In *Theories of Secession*, edited by P. B. Lehning. London: Routledge.

Buchanan, A. 2002. "Political Legitimacy and Democracy." *Ethics* 112: 689–719. doi:10.1086/et.2002.112.issue-4.

Buchanan, A. 2003. *Justice, Legitimacy, and Self-Determination: Moral Foundations for International Law.* Oxford: Oxford University Press.

Crameri, K. 2015. "Political Power and Civil Counterpower: The Complex Dynamics of the Catalan Independence Movement." *Nationalism and Ethnic Politics* 21: 104–120. doi:10.1080/13537113.2015.1003491.

Cué, C. 2013. "Rajoy: 'Esa consulta es inconstitucional y no se va a celebrar'." *El País*, December 12. Accessed 6 February 2015. http://politica.elpais.com/politica/2013/12/12/actualidad/1386874919_926329.html.

De Barrón, I., and F. J. Pérez. 2015. "Caja Madrid Execs Were 'Encouraged' to Use Their Undeclared Credit Cards." *El País* (English), February 17. Accessed 6 March 2015. http://elpais.com/elpais/2015/02/16/inenglish/1424106983_175497.html.

Dowling, A. 2013. *Catalonia Since the Spanish Civil War: Reconstructing the Nation.* Brighton: Sussex Academic Press.

Dowling, A. 2014. "Accounting for the Turn Towards Secession in Catalonia." *International Journal of Iberian Studies* 27: 219–234. doi:10.1386/ijis.27.2-3.219_1.

Duarte, E. 2015. "Mas Times Catalan Election to Limit the Impact of Podemos." *Bloomberg*, January 14. Accessed 6 March 2015. http://www.bloomberg.com/news/articles/2015-01-14/catalan-leader-calls-early-vote-in-push-for-independence.

EFE. 2013. "Judge Cites Former Caja Madrid Chief, Other Officials Over Sale of Preferred Shares." *El País* (English), June 12. Accessed 6 March 2015. http://elpais.com/m/elpais/2013/06/12/inenglish/1371042400_211611.html.

Elorza, A. 2014. "Cataluña: la secesión." *El País*, October 13. Accessed 6 March 2015. http://elpais.com/elpais/2014/09/29/opinion/1411979766_939212.html.

Europa Press. 2014. "El PP da por 'acabado' el 'proceso independentista' y pide a Mas que no engañe con 'simulacros'." *Europa Press*, October 14. Accessed 30 January 2015. http://www.europapress.es/nacional/noticia-consulta-pp-da-acabado-proceso-independentista-pide-mas-no-engane-simulacros-20141014124704.html.

Evans, H. 2013. *Law and Legitimacy: The Denial of the Catalan Voice.* Brussels: Centre Maurice Coppieters.

Ferreres Comella, V. 2014. "The Spanish Constitutional Court Confronts Catalonia's 'Right to Decide' (Comment on the Judgment 42/2014)." *European Constitutional Law Review* 10: 571–590. doi:10.1017/S1574019614001369.

Forcadell Lluís, C. 2013. "Catalonia, a New State in Europe." In *What's up with Catalonia?*, edited by L. Castro. Ashfield, MA: Catalonia Press.

García, C. 2010. "Nationalism and Public Opinion in Contemporary Spain: The Demobilization of the Working Class in Catalonia." *Global Media Journal (American Edition)* 10. http://lass.purduecal.edu/cca/gmj/fa10/gmj-fa10-article3-garcia.htm.

Garcia Pagan, I. 2015. "La hoja de ruta del proceso detalla 18 meses de 'actos de soberanía'." *La Vanguardia*, January 16. Accessed 20 February 2015. http://www.lavanguardia.com/politica/20150116/54423677352/hoja-ruta-proceso-detalla-meses-actos-soberania.html.

Generalitat de Catalunya. 2014. *Llibre blanc. La transició nacional de Catalunya: Síntesi.* Barcelona: Generalitat de Catalunya.

Guibernau, M. 2006. "National Identity, Devolution and Secession in Canada, Britain and Spain." *Nations and Nationalism* 12: 51–76. doi:10.1111/(ISSN)1469-8129.

Isakhan, B., and S. Slaughter. 2014. *Democracy and Crisis: Democratising Governance in the Twenty-First Century*. Basingstoke: Palgrave Macmillan.

Kassam, A. 2014. "Spanish Authorities Arrest 51 Top Figures in Anti-Corruption Sweep." *The Guardian*, October 27. Accessed 6 March 2015. http://www.theguardian.com/world/2014/oct/27/spanish-authorities-arrest-51-anti-corruption-sweep.

Keating, M., and Z. Bray. 2006. "Renegotiating Sovereignty: Basque Nationalism and the Rise and Fall of the Ibarretxe Plan." *Ethnopolitics* 5: 347–364. doi:10.1080/17449050600865503.

Keating, M. 2000. *The New Regionalism in Western Europe*. Cheltenham: Edward Elgar.

Lluch, J. 2012. "Internal Variation in Substate National Movements and the Moral Polity of the Nationalist." *European Political Science Review* 4: 433–460. doi:10.1017/S1755773911000269.

López Tena, A. 2007. *Catalunya sota Espanya: L'opressió nacional en democràcia*. Barcelona: Magrana/Dèria.

Loughlin, J. 2009. "The 'Hybrid' State: Reconfiguring Territorial Governance in Western Europe." *Perspectives on European Politics and Society* 10: 51–68. doi:10.1080/15705850802700009.

Martínez-Herrera, E., and T. J. Miley. 2010. "The Constitution and the Politics of National Identity in Spain." *Nations and Nationalism* 16: 6–30. doi:10.1111/nana.2010.16.issue-1.

Mees, L. 2015. "Nationalist Politics at the Crossroads: The Basque Nationalist Party and the Challenge of Sovereignty (1998–2014)." *Nationalism and Ethnic Politics* 21: 44–62. doi:10.1080/13537113.2015.1003487.

Miley, T. J. 2007. "Against the Thesis of the 'Civic Nation': The Case of Catalonia in Contemporary Spain." *Nationalism and Ethnic Politics* 13: 1–37. doi:10.1080/13537110601155734.

Orte, A., and A. Wilson. 2009. "Multi-level Coalitions and Statute Reform in Spain." *Regional & Federal Studies* 19: 415–436. doi:10.1080/13597560902957500.

Peter, F. 2014. "Political Legitimacy." In *Stanford Encyclopedia of Philosophy*, edited by E. N. Zalta. Stanford University. http://plato.stanford.edu/archives/win2014/entries/legitimacy/.

Pons i Novell, J., and R. Tremosa i Balcells. 2005. "Macroeconomic Effects of Catalan Fiscal Deficit with the Spanish State (2002-2010)." *Applied Economics* 37 (13): 1455–1463. doi:10.1080/00036840500109134.

RAC1. 2012. "El ràcometre: l'opinió dels catalans." October 23. Accessed 9 January 2015. http://www.racalacarta.com/audio/audios_elmon/20121023_racometre.pdf.

Rajoy, M. 2014. "Intervención de Mariano Rajoy: Clausura de las Jornadas Estabilidad y Buen Gobierno en Corporaciones Locales." In *Jornadas Estabilidad y Buen Gobierno en Corporaciones Locales*. Barcelona: Partido Popular, Oficina de Información. http://www.pp.es/sites/default/files/documentos/14.11.29_discurso_mariano_rajoy_en_barcelona.pdf.

Royo, S. 2014. "Institutional Degeneration and the Economic Crisis in Spain." *American Behavioral Scientist* 58: 1568–1591. doi:10.1177/0002764214534664.

Sadurski, W. 2009. *Equality and Legitimacy*. Oxford: Oxford University Press (Oxford Scholarship Online).

Schaefer Muñoz, S., D. Enrich, and C. Bjork. 2012. "Spain's Handling of Bankia Repeats a Pattern of Denial." *The Wall Street Journal*, June 11. Accessed 6 March 2015. http://www.wsj.com/articles/SB10001424052702303444204577458553768029114.

Serrano, I. 2013a. *De la nació a l'estat*. Barcelona: Angle Editorial.

Serrano, I. 2013b. "Just a Matter of Identity? Support for Independence in Catalonia." *Regional & Federal Studies* 23: 523–545. doi:10.1080/13597566.2013.775945.

Supreme Court of Canada. 1998. *Reference re Secession of Quebec*. Report number [1998] 2 SCR 217. Ottawa, ON: Supreme Court of Canada.

Watt, N. 2014. "David Cameron Defends Decision to Allow Scottish Independence Vote." *The Guardian*, May 8. Accessed 13 March 2015. http://www.theguardian.com/politics/2014/may/08/david-cameron-defends-decision-scottish-independence-referendum.

Wellman, C. H. 2013. *Liberal Rights and Responsibilities: Essays on Citizenship and Sovereignty*. Oxford: Oxford University Press (Oxford Scholarship Online).

Scotland, Catalonia and the 'right' to self-determination: a comment suggested by Kathryn Crameri's 'Do Catalans Have the "right to decide"?'

Neil Davidson

This is a reply to:

Crameri, Kathryn. 2016. 'Do Catalans have "the right to decide"? Secession, legitimacy and democracy in twenty-first century Europe.' *Global Discourse* 6 (3): 423–439. http://dx.doi.org/10.1080/23269995.2015.1083326.

Introduction

Kathryn Crameri's article on the dilemmas of the Catalan movement for statehood is illuminating, particularly for those of us who have recently undergone the independence referendum experience in Scotland (Crameri 2016). At several points in her article, she contrasts the treatment of these two stateless nations at the hands of their central governments and finds the attitude of David Cameron's Conservative-led Coalition to be preferable, on democratic grounds, to that of Mariano Rajoy's comparably right-wing Partido Popular. It is understandable why supporters of Catalan independence would wish to use the British government's approach as a means of criticizing the Spanish government and Constitutional Court's blank refusal to concede a referendum, but this also gives Cameron too much credit.

Crameri does note that Cameron was 'no doubt' more inclined to recognise the Scottish National Party's mandate to hold a referendum because he expected the margin of victory for the No camp to be considerably greater than it ultimately was. Given the Conservative Party's general attitude to democracy, most recently demonstrated by its increasing reliance on statutory instruments to introduce new laws rather than attempt to pass legislation through Parliament, we can probably assume that this expectation carried greater weight than the democratic wishes of the Scots. Crucially, Cameron made a condition of holding the referendum that it included only two options, Yes or No to independence, and not – as the then Scottish National Party (SNP) leader Alex Salmond wanted – a third option for Maximum Devolution ('Devo Max'), which was probably the outcome desired by most Scots when the referendum was announced early in 2012. Support for independence had remained relatively stable at around 30% since the establishment of the Scottish Parliament in 1999, but was low on the priorities of even these supporters. Since Salmond was as aware of the polling figures as Cameron, there must be some doubt as to whether the SNP actually believed that an independence referendum could be won, hence the attempt to include Devo Max on the ballot. It is easy to forget this now, given the relative closeness of the actual result.

The main difference between Spain and Britain, at least in relation to their internal stateless nations, is not the respective attitudes of the current governing politicians, but rather their constitutions, and what these permit or forbid. Neither, however, recognizes any 'right' on the part of the Catalans or the Scots (or the Basques or the Welsh) to exercise self-determination to point of secession. Self-determination does not of course necessarily *mean* secession, it simply means being able to *decide* whether or not to secede. When a majority of Scots voted to remain part of the UK in 2014 they were exercising self-determination, but they were only granted permission to do so as the result of a miscalculation on the part of the governing coalition, not because they had possession of a right.

Crameri's expertise in the Catalan situation is clearly much greater than mine, so this comment will seek to explore two more general issues which her discussion brings into focus. One – an immediate one for the Scots, the Catalans, and any other national group seeking self-determination – is whether any right to it does, or *can* exist outside of the constitutional form of the states from which they hope to secede. Before turning to this theme, however, it may be worth reviewing the prior issue of what exactly is meant by 'nation' and 'nationalism', and whether the Scottish and Catalan variants are sufficiently similar to bear comparison with each other in the first place.

National consciousness, nationalism, independence

Scottish analysts of nationalism have divided on the question of whether Catalonia and Scotland are comparable at all. Keating, probably representing the majority, writes that they (and Quebec) need to be considered together as they 'are the places where the process of "stateless nation building" has been taken furthest' (Keating 2001, xv). MacInnes rejects this, partly because of the difference between the historical experiences of Catalonia and Scotland, but partly because what he regards as the inability of academics to offer a generally applicable definition of a nations or, consequently, to establish where their boundaries lie. As for the main factor which they are widely supposed to have in common, their 'statelessness': 'It is clear that the only sense in which these nations are stateless is that they are not independent states in their own right' (MacInnes 2004, 143). MacInnes' use of the word 'only' in this sentence is sufficiently audacious as to inspire a certain degree of admiration. It is true, of course, that the autonomous or devolved governments of Scotland, Catalonia and Quebec all exercise some of the functions of central states, including aspects of its repressive apparatus like Police Scotland. But local authorities in Britain have also exercised substantial state powers (although this is has been increasingly curtailed throughout the neoliberal period) and no one suggested that, for example, the former Strathclyde Regional Council was a state in its own right. It was rather a territorially defined component of the British state responsible for certain of its key functions, as are the Scottish Government and the Welsh assembly today. (Indeed, one of the least discussed aspects of the progress of neoliberalism in Britain is the way in which decrease of power at the local authority level has occurred in virtually inverse proportion with its increase at the level of the devolved national administrations.) The ability to participate as an actor in the international states-system is not an optional add-on to a list of domestic powers; it is definitional of *being* a capitalist nation-state (Davidson 2016, 220–235).

MacInnes is on far stronger ground when he points out that the reason why neither Scotland nor Catalonia have achieved statehood is not, for the most part, because of opposition from the existing nation-states, but because the majority of Scots and Catalans have not wanted to secede from them, even though both groups have a highly developed sense of their own nation-ness. This has puzzled many commentators. 'The most interesting commonality between Scotland and Catalonia', writes Greer, 'is that neither is a state despite credentials as nations second to none' (Greer 2007, 182). To explain this anomaly we need to make a number of definitions and distinctions.

First, what is a nation? There are both objective and subjective criteria for answering this question. The former, which usually involves a checklist of factors like language or territory, certainly presents an appearance of scientific rigour. Unfortunately, nations have a tendency to emerge in groups who do not tick all the factorial boxes, inconvenient though this undoubtedly is for social and political scientists; but telling the Swiss that they are not a nation because they lack a common language, or the Kurds that they are not a nation because the lack a contiguous territory is, however, unlikely to convince either of these (otherwise very different) groups. In fact, the only conceivable definition of a nation which does not immediately lead to anomalies and exceptions is a subjective one: a group of people feel themselves to be collectively distinct from other groups, usually for accumulated historico-cultural reasons, but they need not be. The reasons may be different from case-to-case, but this subjective feeling of identification is the only attribute which they all have in common. Hobsbawm has, however, identified two problems with a subjective definition of nationhood.

One is that it is 'open to the objection that defining a nation by its members' consciousness of belonging to it is tautological and provides only an a posteriori guide to what a nation is' (Hobsbawm 1990, 7–8). A subjective definition would, however, only be tautological *if group members did not already know what a nation was*. The only group of which this would not have been true was the first to consider itself a nation, since it would have had nothing to measure itself against. Following Smith, we can identify three basic positions on the historical emergence of nations. The first is 'primordialism', which is less a theory than the common sense assumption that nations have always existed throughout history. The second is 'perennialism', where modern nations are simply larger and more complex versions of earlier types of human community. The third position is 'modernism', which places their emergence much more recently in time (Smith 1986, 7–13, 1998, 1–24, 145–169). For our purposes the divisions within the modernist position, between the Classical sociological tradition (which emphasises the need for societies to achieve cohesion during the process of industrialisation) and the Marxist tradition (which emphasises the emergence of the capitalist system within which industrialisation takes place) are less important than their shared refusal of all ahistorical attempts to claim that nations are an inescapable part of the human condition. Of course, 'national consciousness' took as many centuries to become the dominant form of consciousness as the capitalist mode of production did to become the dominant mode of production, and it did so as a *consequence* of the latter. But once the former did emerge, above all in England during the sixteenth and seventeenth centuries, other groups could then identify it in themselves. In that sense it is irrelevant that Scotland was one of the most backward areas in Europe and Catalonia one of the most advanced at the time of their respective incorporations into Britain and Spain during the War of the Spanish Succession: national consciousness is an inescapable aspect of capitalist development (Davidson 2016, 67–76, 235–243).

Hobsbawm's other objection is that subjectivism 'can lead the incautious into extremes of voluntarism which suggest that all that is needed to be or recreate a nation is the will to be one: if enough inhabitants of the Isle of Wight wanted to be a Wightian nation, there would be one' (Hobsbawm 1990, 7–8). But this is a question of state viability, not national existence, and is one reason why national groups do *not* all seek statehood. One can put the point more strongly: given that there are a greater number of national groups (or potential national groups) than there are nation-states, there have to be reasons why a majority of people among any of the former should wish to achieve the latter and why many have not done so.

We therefore need to make a first distinction, between the sense of mutual recognition implied by the term 'national consciousness' on the one hand and 'nationalism' on the other. It is perfectly possible for people – including, until recently, the majority of modern Scots and Catalans – to develop the former without subsequently adopting the latter. National *consciousness* is a more-or-less passive expression of collective identification among a social group; national*ism* is a more-or-less active participation in the political mobilisation of a social group for the construction *or* defence of a state. The latter aspect is particularly important since defenders of the British or Spanish states have a propensity to act as if British or Spanish nationalism did not exist.

Smith has argued against the kind of political definition of nationalism offered here on the grounds that 'not all nationalisms have in practice opted for independent statehood: most Scots and Catalans, for example, have not to date supported their movements and parties which sought outright independence, and have settled instead for a large measure of social, cultural and economic autonomy within their borders'. He asserts that a consequence of defining nations politically is that they can only then be said to exist when embodied in a state, leading to a situation where 'Scotland cannot become a "nation" until the majority of Scottish voters agree with the SNP's platform and vote for an independent Scottish "nation-state"' (Smith 1998, 73, 75). This is a classic example of confusion between nationhood (consciousness of an identity) and nationalism (embedding that identity in a territorial state). The former has to exist before the latter is possible.

The second distinction concerns the reasons for desiring a nation-state, since there can be both nationalist reasons and non-nationalist (socialist, environmentalist) reasons for secession. One legal theorist (and Scottish Nationalist) the late Neil MacCormick argued that nationalism could take either an 'existential' form in which attaining statehood is an end in itself or a 'pragmatic' means to achieving social and political ends *through* statehood (MacCormick 1981, 247–265). MacCormick himself noted that the latter was a very 'weak' form of nationalism, but in certain contexts it need not be nationalism at all. As a political ideology, nationalism – *any* nationalism, relatively progressive or absolutely reactionary – involves two inescapable principles: that the national group should have its own state, regardless of the social consequences; and that what unites the national group is more significant than what divides it, above all the class divide. It is clear from the Scottish experience at least, however, that non-nationalist arguments for supporting independence were widely used by many Yes activists, particularly around the Radical Independence Campaign (Davidson 2014a; Davidson 2014b).

Legality and democracy

What have these definitions and distinctions to do with whether or not the Scots, the Catalans or any other national group have the right to decide on their future? In relation to the Catalan case, Crameri points out that they are subject to two conflicting principles. One is 'the right to decide', a democratic principle according to which they should be able to choose their own constitutional arrangements. The other is 'the duty to abide', a legal principle under which they should respect a Spanish constitution that excludes any threats to the territorial integrity of the nation-state. Supporters of the latter position could of course argue that it too involves a democratic principle, particularly given that the Catalans gave majority support to the constitution when it was adopted in 1978. Following Comella, Crameri notes that there are two normative systems in play here: how to choose between them? For the Catalans, the outcome is likely to be decided in the manner outlined in Marx's aphorism: 'Between equal rights, force decides' (Marx 1976, 344). In relation to political philosophy, however, a more theoretical position is perhaps required.

No nation-state recognizes a constitutional right to secede from it. Some, like the UK, do not refer to the issue at all, leaving politicians and state managers to deal with national issues on an ad hoc basis as they emerge, rather than tying their hands in advance with legal constraints. Others, among which the Spanish state is preeminent, explicitly exclude the possibility. There are strong continuities here with the Franco dictatorship – unsurprisingly, since the Spanish state was not overthrown or fundamentally transformed with the introduction of democracy after 1975. Instead a new *regime* was installed – in other words, there was a shift to a different form of capitalist rule which has since then been maintained continuously over a series of governments involving several parties or coalitions. One aspect of the new regime was the turn – more or less in line with the rest of the developed world – towards neoliberalism; but another, much rarer feature, was a new settlement involving the devolution of governance to what the constitution describes as the 'autonomous communities', while simultaneously maintaining the former dictatorship's obsession with 'indissoluble unity'. It is not surprising that the majority of Catalans supported the 1978 constitution, seeing it as finally guaranteeing recognition and protection of their 'nationality' after it being suppressed throughout the Franco era. However, as China Mieville writes, in general, 'it is very likely that the powerful will be able to accommodate or co-opt whatever progressive intentions are imbedded in a particular law', since 'it is usually the representatives of the powerful who actually make the laws, who force particular political contexts into the abstract legal form' (Mieville 2006, 120). Specifically, the constitution involves two long-term difficulties for the Catalans.

One was is that it effectively treats Catalonia – a stateless nation – on the same basis as the other 16 component parts of Spain, variously classified as communities, nationalities or regions. But most of the other nationalities, with the obvious exception of the Basque Country, have no history of national movements, and some of the communities were simply geographical constructs. The effect was to downplay the distinctiveness of the Catalan situation, by placing it on the same level as the Canary Islands. This was not simply a matter of status. During the 1980s just under 40% of the cases heard by the Constitutional Court involved Catalonia (Keating 2001 [1996], 150). But behind this apparent equality between entities with quite different histories and size, lay a deeper inequality. Castile, the territorial heart of the Spanish state, does not even exist as a nationality or as an autonomous community of any sort, but is divided into several regions, but the Castilian-speaking majority 'receives no appellation distinct from the nation as a whole': 'It is the nation's core – the national "default option"' (Gat 2013, 354).

The other and more serious difficulty is that the current regime can claim to be upholding the will of the majority in denying Catalonia, not only the possibility of independence, but even that of "statehood" within a new federal structure. And this is where the clash of normative values begins. For those who support the Catalans aspirations to statehood, defending their right to decide, to exercise self-determination, may seem unquestionable – particularly when so many voices are seeking to deny them it. As Erica Benner wrote in the 1990s, in her undervalued reconstruction of Marx' and Engels' views on nationalism: 'Today liberals and democrats of all shades are busy laying down conditions for the exercise of this right. Some have even begun to doubt whether the principle of self-determination should be interpreted as a right at all, since a variety of other considerations – including "strategic" ones – might in many cases have to trump it' (Benner 1995, 253). This conditionality applies even where groups clearly require not only self-determination but also actual secession as a 'remedial right in cases of last resort', as in the case of the Kurds.

Several of the liberal thinkers whom Crameri quotes display this hostility to secession: Buchanan argues that international law should repudiate the right of all nations or peoples to secede; Wellman, more generously, is prepared to countenance secession in the developed world providing it does no harm (or at least irrecoverable harm) to the existing nation-state. But even those accounts which appear to be more supportive of the right to self-determination also do so by emphasising *individual* rights to a personal identity which, in the words of one account, 'can be satisfied through a variety of political arrangements – the establishment of national institutions, the formation of autonomous communities, or the establishment of federal or confederal states – able to ensure individuals the opportunity to participate in the national life of their community'. There can be no 'overall guiding principle'; costs have to be weighed against benefits; and so on (Tamir 1993, 75).

The problem here, however, is not an insufficient commitment to this particular right, but whether it has any ontological reality in the first place. 'Rights talk' has not of course been confined to liberals. The 1896 London Congress of the Second International passed a resolution declaring that it stood 'for the complete right of all nations to self-determination' (Lenin 1964, 430–431; Luxemburg 1976 [1908], 107). As was quite often the case with the Second International, the adoption of a position did not mean that constituent parties or individual members regarded themselves as bound by it. As was also quite often the case with the Second International, however, revolutionaries in that body tried to both upheld Congress policy and clarify what it would mean in concrete terms if consistently applied. The clearest expression of their position was given by Lenin who explained what it meant in practice: 'the proletariat confines itself, so to speak, to the negative demand for recognition of the *right* to self-determination, without giving guarantees to any nation' (Lenin 1964 [1914], 410). In other words, socialists support the democratic demand of national groups (peoples) to be able to make an unimpeded decision about their constitutional status (self-determination) without necessarily supporting the particular decision which they make – and indeed, possibly arguing against it.

This is certainly a more consistent position than the liberal one and does not pretend that nations are simply the sum of individual subjects. It does, however, introduce new difficulties. One need not accept Rosa Luxemburg's belief in the ultimate pointlessness of national self-determination under capitalism to recognize the truth of her assessment: 'A "right of nations" which is valid for all countries and all times is nothing more than a metaphysical cliché of the type of "rights of man" and "rights of the citizen"' (Luxemburg 1976, 110–111). Who or what, for example, is supposed to confer such a right? Assuming these are not unalienable rights granted by the Creator, such as those listed in the American Declaration of Independence, they could perhaps be recognized in international law; but as Mieville writes: 'That law is made actual in the power-political wrangling of states, ultimately at the logic of capital, in the context of an imperialist system' (Mieville 2006, 316). The Palestinians have long since had reason to be aware that motions passed by the United Nations do not have the force of law, at least so long as they are not supported by the US and its allies. It is not, of course, that all rights are completely intangible; they can and have been won, including, most obviously, the right to vote; but these are outcomes of class and other social struggles within the territories of individual nation-states, subsequently enshrined in their laws, but 'at an international level, the struggle over the legal form is far more mediated' (Mieville 2006, 317).

But even discounting the metaphysical aspects of a right to self-determination, there is a more practical issue concerning its status as a right at all. For one thing, it clearly does not mean all nations, but something more like 'those minority nations which currently are not nation-states but in which a majority of the population wish to become a nation-state'. Lenin made this explicit in his famous distinction between 'oppressed' and 'oppressor' nations. A hundred years ago this distinction was relatively clear and provided a basis for deciding which national movements should be supported and which opposed by socialists The oppressed were those nationalities held against their collective will within the remaining absolutist or tributary empires of the Hapsburgs, Romanovs and Ottomans, or the colonies and semi-colonies of the Great Powers in Africa, Asia, Latin America and, of course, Ireland. These national movements had to be supported, whatever the exact nature of their politics, which were in most cases uninformed by socialist aspirations. (The oppressed approximate to those nations which require 'remedial right in cases of last resort' in liberal discourse.) On the other hand, there were the 'oppressor' nations (or in the case of the absolutist and tributary empires, states) which prevented the oppressed from achieving independent statehood. The nationalisms of these oppressor states had to be opposed, above all by working class within them. It was in this context that Lenin drew his famous analogy with the right to divorce: people should have the right to divorce, but this does not mean that every couple should necessarily do so. The assumption being that a situation of national oppression was analogous to an unhappy or abusive marriage, in which the abused or oppressed could be expected to exercise their 'right' to divorce or secession (Lenin 1964 [1914], 413).

The distinction between oppressor and oppressed was never an entirely adequate device for establishing the attitude of Marxists towards national movements. It had nothing to say about the attitude of socialists to nations which may have had legitimate grounds for claiming that they were oppressed – as Serbia did in 1914, for example – but which were part of a wider inter-imperialist struggle in which their situation was manipulated by one side. Nor did it provide guidance in a situation in which a socialist revolution in a multi-national empire – like Russia in 1917 – might result in some of the formerly oppressed nations seeking to secede *from* a worker's state, as for example, Ukraine attempted to do during the early stages of the Russian Revolution. My argument here is not that the positions adopted by Lenin and the Bolsheviks in these cases were necessarily wrong from a socialist perspective (although I believe they were in the case of Ukraine); it is rather that they were based on a wider set of political considerations than simply the oppressor/oppressed distinction. It could nevertheless be legitimately argued that these were exceptional cases and that as a broad distinction the categories of oppressor and oppressed generally allowed socialists to arrive at correct operational conclusions.

In the context of our present discussion, however, the central problem with the 'oppressor/oppressed' distinction is that it completely undermines the 'right to self-determination', even if we leave aside the 'oppressor' nations, since their position of power meant they were already more than capable of defending their interests, without any need to rely on 'rights'. In the case of those groups which remained loyal to, or identified themselves with the oppressors, the situation is more complex. The Ulster Loyalists in the North of Ireland were a manufactured majority in the Six Counties, but a minority in Ireland as a whole. Do they have the right to decide whether or not to remain British? There have been more recent cases where right-wing politicians have attempted to mobilise regional identities against social reforms, as in 2007 when the four *media luna* departments in the east of Bolivia voted for regional autonomy against the government of Evo Morales. Did they too have the right to decide whether or not to comply with Bolivian national legislation? In these examples, socialists could legitimately argue that respective adherence to British or regional identities was directed towards reactionary ends, but implicitly means abandoning the notion of a 'right to decide', since a right by definition has to be universal and cannot be restricted to those with whom we politically agree. An alternative strategy would be to deny that groups with which we disagree are nations at all, but this involves returning to the some variant of the discredited 'checklist' method of definition, in which one sets the criteria to get the result one desires: in this case the notion of a 'right to decide' can be retained, but only by denying the existence of certain nations.

Conclusion

The 'oppressed/oppressor' distinction is, in any case, of deceasing relevance. There are certainly still oppressed national groups. I have already referred to the Kurds and the Palestinians, and to these could be added the Tibetans and Chechens; but the colonial aspects of imperialism which provided the context in which it was originally formulated have mostly gone, never to return. More to the point, it is of little relevance in relation the cases we have been discussing, those 'stateless nations' seeking autonomy in or independence from long-established Western capitalist states. In some cases these had an earlier history of oppression, in others not; but by the 1980s differences between Catalonia and Quebec on the one hand and Scotland on the other were marginal. Today, the former are no more 'oppressed' than the latter, and pretending otherwise is simply to insult those who are suffering under genuine oppression. But simply rejecting their demands on that basis is to embrace a stultifying formalism which takes no account of the exigencies of the class struggle or the dangers of inadvertently supporting the existing constitutional structures of the leading capitalist nation-states. The preceding discussion suggests that there is, however, no secure ground from which to argue for a 'right to decide'. There needs to be a means of deciding which national movements to support in both making their decision and in the decision itself.

From a left perspective, it possible to argue, for example, that the secession is a means of resisting the neoliberal strategy of devolving responsibility for implementing austerity down from governing parties and central state apparatuses to elected bodies whose policy options are severely restricted both by statute and partial reliance on the central state for most of their funding. In the case of the devolved nations the assumption is that the people most likely to participate in local decision-making will be members of the middle-class, who can be expected to behave, *en masse*, in ways which will impose restrictions on local taxation and public spending, and thus maintain the neoliberal order with a supposedly popular mandate: atomised citizens voting for which services they want to close. In these circumstances, without any illusions in the ability of small states to resist the pressures of the world capitalist system, deciding to secede can be seen as both a progressive and democratic option which need not involve nationalism at all. In each case, however, constructing an argument for why a particular group should determine their own future has to be done on the basis of a political argument, and not by circumventing it through reliance on the notion of a 'right'.

References

Benner, E. 1995. *Really Existing Nationalisms: A Post-Communist View from Marx and Engels*. Oxford: Clarendon Press.

Crameri, K. 2016. "Do Catalans have 'the Right to Decide?': Secession, Legitimacy and Democracy in Twenty-first Century Europe." *Global Discourse* 6 (3): 423–439. doi:10.1080/23269995.2015.1083326.

Davidson, N. 2014a. "'Yes': A Non-nationalist Argument for Scottish Independence." *Radical Philosophy* 185 (May/June): 2–7.

Davidson, N. 2014b. "A Scottish Watershed." *New Left Review* II/89 (September/October): 5–26.

Davidson, N. 2016. *Nation-States: Consciousness and Competition*. Chicago, IL: Haymarket Books.

Gat, A. 2013. *Nations: The Long History and Deep Roots of Political Ethnicity and Nationalism*. Cambridge: Cambridge University Press.

Greer, S. L. 2007. *Nationalism and Self-Government: The Politics of Autonomy in Scotland and Catalonia*. Albany: State University of New York Press.

Hobsbawm, E. J. 1990. *Nations and Nationalism Since 1780: Program, Myth, Reality*. Cambridge: Cambridge University Press.

Keating, M. 2001 [1996]. *Nations against the State: The New Politics of Nationalism in Quebec, Catalonia and Scotland*. 2nd ed. Houndmills: Palgrave.

Lenin, V. I. 1964 [1914]. "The Right of Nations to Self-Determination." In *Collected Works, Vol. 20, December 1913-August 1914*, 393–454. Moscow: Progress Publishers.

Luxemburg, R. 1976 [1908]. "The National Question and Autonomy: 1. The Right of Nations to Self-Determination." In *The National Question: Selected Writings by Rosa Luxemburg*, edited by H. B. Davis, 101–156. New York, NY: Monthly Review Press.

MacCormick, N. 1981. *Legal Right and Social Democracy*. Oxford: Clarendon Press.

MacInnes, J. 2004. "Catalonia is not Scotland." *Scottish Affairs* 47 (May): 135–155. doi:10.3366/scot.2004.0031.

Marx, K. 1976 [1867]. *Capital: A Critique of Political Economy*. Vol. 1. Harmondsworth: Penguin Books.

Mieville, C. 2006. *Between Equal Rights: A Marxist Theory of International Law*. London: Pluto Press.

Smith, A. D. 1986. *The Ethnic Origins of Nations*. Oxford: Blackwell.

Smith, A. D. 1998. *Nationalism and Modernism: A Critical Survey of Recent Theories of Nations and Nationalism*. London: Routledge.

Tamir, Y. 1993. *Liberal Nationalism*. Princeton, NJ: Princeton University Press.

Building authoritarian 'legitimacy': domestic compliance and international standing of Bashar al-Asad's Syria

Aurora Sottimano

ABSTRACT

This paper will cast a closer look at the alleged 'legitimacy' of the Syrian regime and will show that the two main legitimating credentials of Bashar al-Asad – namely, his nationalist and reformist missions – carry with them an array of implicit norms and commitments, which shape the Syrian state–society relationship in such a way as to draw non-state actors into the spheres of power. Moreover this paper will examine various regional and international framings of legitimacy in relation to the Syrian war, charting the transition between diplomatic narratives of negotiation and intervention, humanitarian and security imperatives, religious conflict and war on terror. In so doing, the paper will question the common understanding of legitimacy as an evaluative concept embracing a variety of issues which play a role in justifying and maintaining effective political authority. Rather than exploring the legal validity or the moral justification for existing political institutions – as the notion of legitimacy suggests – my focus is on the persistent grip of power mechanisms and strategies of government which elicit discipline and compliance with the dicta of authoritarian rulers, and on how patterns of authoritarian state–society relations are established, justified and adapted to changing circumstances. An analysis of the imbrications of legitimacy and domination, I believe, will help us to understand the magnitude of current events in Syria and will contribute to a reflection about how we can achieve and sustain the movement away from authoritarianism.

1. Introduction

Few concepts seem to be as important to our understandings of the Syrian conflict as 'legitimacy' in the light of the claims of the various actors involved. First come the assertions of Syrian leaders themselves that it is they alone who possess the mandate to defend both population and state against the chaos allegedly engendered by radical Islamic groups supported by foreign elements. Throughout the conflict, a Syrian 'silent majority' has seemed to send the message that the regime continues to enjoy a certain 'legitimacy'. Second is the remarkable caution displayed by Western powers in withdrawing the accolade of legitimacy credit from a corrupt Syrian elite, e.g. the dissemination of contradictory statements by US officials about the 'loss of legitimacy' of the Asad regime. Third is the ambiguity of international diplomatic efforts, which have oscillated between 'the imperative' of promoting a democratic transition and 'the necessity' of recognising the regime as a legitimate interlocutor. Fourth is the appropriation of the 'war on terror' narrative on the part of almost all actors – international, regional and domestic – to legitimise their use of violence. Part and parcel of this is the international debate about the legitimacy of an international military intervention which has been sparked by the US-led aerial campaign against Islamic State (IS) targets in Iraq and Syria and more recently the Russian bombing campaign whilst over four years of turmoil has brought in its wake both a humanitarian catastrophe and the destruction of most of the country's infrastructures.

In the Syrian context, competing narratives suggest that the notion of 'legitimacy' is a catch-all concept that can be conveniently bent to support opposing power strategies. Nevertheless, the discrepancy between different notions of legitimacy can tells us something significant about modern political practices. Some preliminary thoughts about the limitations of the concept of legitimacy will clear the ground for an alternative approach centred on discursive power mechanisms. Part two identifies distinctive features of Syrian political discourse under Hafiz al-Asad (1970–2000) and how some of those practices have persisted under his son, Bashar. My aim is to understand how these discursive conditions have affected political mobilisation in these times of tumult. Part three analyses the Syrian regime's claims to legitimacy in the regional arena, and specifically its role in the axis of resistance. The last section discusses legitimation narratives in the context of the international relations of the Syrian uprising. Drawing on the theoretical contributions of Michel Foucault and Achille Mbembe, I argue that legitimation narratives and processes need to be examined within the context of power practices of discipline and normalisation that elicit acquiescence and complicity.

2. The concept of legitimacy and the political process

The literature of the notion of legitimacy suggests that it is a multidimensional and multilevel concept related with the justification and acceptance of political authority (Beetham 1991). There are at least three general understandings of legitimacy, which focus on legal, moral and social aspects of 'the right to govern' (Coicaud 2002). Political and legal philosophers consider legitimacy in relation with rules, laws and legal rights and focus on mandatory norms and binding values coupled with an open decision-making process and successful outcomes.[1] If understood as an absolute or a static set of attributes of an ideal-type government, the notion of legitimacy is of scarce use for a political analysis of realities that do not share with the West a history of democratic institution building. Indeed scholars who deploy the concept of legitimacy in connection with democracy often produce complacent claims about Western democracies, which impoverish both concepts. A moral understanding of legitimacy raises two general kinds of objections. First, in speaking of a progressive 'erosion' of legitimacy which parallels the growing use of violence in conflict situations, analysts implicitly endorse a dualist analytical framework that opposes legitimacy to violence. Yet legitimacy is invoked by political actors to justify their use of violence, rather than exclude it. Second, moral values are historical and context specific: a plurality of worldviews reflects social and geographical variations and people's historical experience with political and social institutions. Since principles of legitimacy evolve in relation with human experience, legitimacy is inherently social and socially constructed (Clark 2005; Rapkin and Braaten 2009). Yet social legitimacy remains an empty concept without an account of the moral or legal framework to which political actors subscribe (Habermas 1979). Hence we are left with a 'fuzzy' concept that reflects the complexity of social life too much to be a useful analytical criterion.

My concern here is less with conceptual problems per se than with the lines of enquiry which the mainstream understanding of legitimacy forecloses: namely the ability of authorities – including those who frequently violate the normative justification of their legitimacy – to prompt obedience even from those who are consistently disadvantaged by the political system. Failing to disentangle 'legitimacy' from other motivations for obedience to authorities, scholars merely equate legitimacy with acceptance and acquiescence. The conceptual muddle created by 'legitimacy' obscures subtle mechanisms of control that are central to the dynamics of social and political reproduction and thus impoverishes our thinking about power and social control. A pioneer work in this respect is Lisa Wedeen's study of Syrian political practices under Hafiz al-Asad, where she convincingly shows that a personality cult and the dissemination of ideology enforced citizens' obedience at the level of outward behaviour without necessarily producing value-laden legitimacy for the regime.[2] Moving from a similar broadly Foucaultian perspective – one in which political actors, concepts and policies do not evolve independently of discourses that enable and constrain them within specific configurations of power – I propose to problematise actors' claims to legitimacy on the Syrian scene and to focus on how such claims operate through discursive processes that elicit discipline, public dissimulation and compliance rather than the belief or emotional commitment that 'legitimacy' presupposes. My aim is to bring to the fore those mechanisms of control and political domination that specific discourses of legitimacy carry with them as a better way to grasp the complexity of the Syrian conflict.

3. The discursive underpinning of the Syrian regime's 'legitimacy'

A few weeks before the beginning of the Syrian uprising, President Bashar al-Asad famously predicted that Syria would avoid the popular unrest seen elsewhere in the Arab world, due to the fact that its foreign policy was more aligned with the popular will than were the pro-American stances of Tunisia and Egypt.[3] Indeed most scholarly work on Syrian politics points to the ideological legacy of the Ba'ath party – a mixture of nationalism and populism – as the legitimating backbone of the regime.[4] The Ba'athist capture of state power in 1963 marked the birth of an authoritarian populist regime that pursued a self-styled socialist strategy based on statism and autarchy. Its revolutionary discourse also marked the beginning of new modes of popular involvement in political struggles. Ba'athist leaders carved for themselves the role of a political 'vanguard' and pursued a vigorous institution building project in a declared effort to inculcate a 'socialist morality' across the social spectrum. 'Socialist' policies of nationalisation, agrarian and administrative reform, mass employment in the public sector and widespread education were significant in allying the support of workers and peasants to the Ba'sth.

From 1970, the selective open-door policy launched by Hafez al-Asad enlarged the regime social basis to include part of the commercial bourgeoisie without rolling back the subsidisation of household expenses and state employment – key elements of popular support and Ba'athist 'revolutionary legitimacy' – whilst deepening, rather than correcting, the social engineering practices of the Ba'ath. Semi-mandatory participation in mass organisations linked to the Ba'ath party embedded the whole population – students, women, workers, peasants and professionals – in army-like bodies called 'popular organisations' that were devoid of any autonomous power. Collectively these made it possible for the Ba'ath to impose itself heavily on Syrian society, even among those who regarded it with cynicism.[5]

Ba'athist efforts at state building and social reconstruction were never separated from the nationalist struggle to withstand foreign enemies. The strategies of 'steadfastness' pursued by Hafez al-Asad in order to withstand the 'permanent aggression' of the 'Zionist enemy' and regain the pride and territory lost in the 1967 war (Khalidi and Agha 1991) acted as a framework for total war, an epic narrative of heroic gestures and grand passions in the name of an endangered nation which always teetered on the brink of invasion and destruction. This nationalist discourse framed Syrian leaders' claim to legitimacy in many ways. First, the regime posed as an 'enlightened' vanguard at the helm of the state as well as a guarantor of internal cohesion and national independence. Fierce nationalism overshadowed the primary role played by the Asad family and fellow Alawis (the minority group to which the Asads belong) at the top echelons of state power and masked the growing divide between the authoritarian state and society. Second, the burden of Syria's historical mission required the exploitation of all national and human resource and legitimated a model of socialisation based on the unity of a 'compact front' behind Asad's leadership against the 'forces of reaction'.[6] Hence unanimity and social homogeneity further diluted the class content of Ba'athist socialism. Citizens 'efforts, fatigue and sacrifices'[7] took priority over social demands and eventually justified the reversal of the 'social gains' achieved by the Ba'athist 'socialist' revolution. Third, this political discourse centred on the 'perennial struggle' to counter Israeli military dominance in the region-defused criticism of Syria's sluggish development. Fourth, the new political correctness legitimised the crushing presence of the Ba'ath party and its security apparatus on all aspects of Syrian society, the militarisation of everyday life, exceptionalism in law and order, and strict obedience to a supreme authority in the name of a superior national interest.

Rather than opening up a genuine public space, Hafez's *infitah* policies resonated with the imperatives of cohesion, order and an obsession with control. Indoctrination, discipline, censorship and the personality cult of 'the immortal leader' President Asad worked to set strict guidelines for public speech and behaviour (Wedeen 1999). The political mythology propounded by the regime colonised all discursive space whilst popular participation had been reduced to the marches routinely orchestrated by the authorities to symbolise popular identification with the regime, its mission and its leader. Any deviance from the norm was tantamount to disloyalty, a sabotage of the country's mission, an attack on the moral foundations of the nation and ultimately a de-legitimation of the values of the political system – which inevitably plays into the hands of the enemy (Kitus 2014).

In order to understand the resilience of authoritarianism and the dynamics of mobilisation in Syria, it is imperative to consider the 'cultivation of authoritarian civilities' (Mbembe 1992) that accompanied the ossification of Syrian political life. People's familiarity with the disciplinary practices that have seeped into their social fabric – rather than a belief in regime narrative or in any legal or moral legitimacy of the authorities – is one of the crucial mechanisms which ensure obedience (Žižek 1989; Ismail 2006). The new Syrian political correctness cultivated an atmosphere of mistrust combined with self-censorship, mutual surveillance, dissimulation and unreflective compliance (Wedeen 1999, 2013). The regime set up a capillary system of espionage with several intelligence agencies controlling individual private lives, monitoring any 'deviant' behaviour and enrolling parts of the populace to spy on the rest and enforce obedience. Fear of those in power and of everyone else cancelled the possibility of any autonomous form of public collective action. Politics become a space that was open for identification and loyalty, but closed to discussion and negotiation between legitimate interlocutors. As a result, even those Syrian citizens who had no faith in its rhetoric continued to rally behind the regime whenever a threat of whatever magnitude came from outside the country, whether this be foreign criticism, diplomatic pressure or threatened military strike. Thus fear of change gradually started replacing hope for change and Syrians became silent supporters of 'the devil they know'.[8] These were the building blocks of the national identity and the 'legitimacy' of 'Asad's Syria'.

This is not to say that Syrian society had been totally fragmented and change was impossible: to acknowledge the strategies of control which are intrinsic in Syrian legitimating practices help us to understand the magnitude of the current developments. It can also explain the stalemate in diplomatic negotiations between actors – both the regime and the opposition – who are locked in mutually de-legitimising antagonistic logics that make of politics a zero-sum game. The reduction of the whole issue of change to the removal of the ruling groups from power merely reflects the binary construction of regime discourse with little understanding of the subtlety of such power (Wedeen n.d.). Mistrust and the lack of experience of any genuine political dialogue explain the difficulty for most actors on the Syrian scene to negotiate a common stance and devise a compelling vision for Syria's future.

3.1. Bashar's reforms

The instrumentality of the Syrian political discourse as a reservoir of norms and strategies for social control was not lost to the heir of the Syrian 'presidential monarchy'. The alleged legitimacy of Bashar al-Asad as expressed in his nationalist foreign policy and his economic reformist agenda shows a disquieting continuity with his father's rule.

President Bashar portrayed himself as a progressive moderniser whilst Syrian media marketed the young president and the glamorous first lady as new role models and cultivated the now 'politically correct' taste for commodities and the ambitions of social mobility associated with the official turn to a 'social market economy' (SME), which was announced with grand fanfare in 2005. Nevertheless, the regime did not create the institutional and legal framing that is necessary to govern the transition from planned to market economy. Instead of ensuring rule of law, institutional capacity and administrative accountability, Bashar's regime centralised power and patronage in the clan around the president at the expenses of the 'old guard' of Sunni barons – allegedly hostile to reforms (Hinnebusch 291). As a result, state monopolies were replaced by family cartels whilst businessmen close to the Asad clan captured the opportunities for enrichment opened up by the reform (Haddad 2012). Corruption and foreign imports drove productive industries and small manufactures into bankruptcy. In the new economic narrative, workers and peasants were replaced by civil society and the private sector, but the latter proved incapable to compensate for public sector job losses (Hinnebusch and Zintl 2015). The socio-political consequences were rising unemployment, lower life standards, a contraction of social security and a growing social polarisation between rich and poor, cities and the neglected rural periphery (Ababsa 2011).

It has been argued that the limits of Bashar's reforms coincided with the limits of state-business collusion (Haddad 2012) or institutional development (Hinnebusch 2014). Crucially, Bashar's reforms failed to question the modus operandi of the regime.[9] Rather than an economic strategy, the SME formula worked as an umbrella for a variety of demands, signalling green light to the market as well as sending assurances to those sections of Syrian society that had a stake in the maintenance of subsidies and public services. In such discourse, the state remained the sole arbiter of market correctness as well as the only interlocutor and the patron of all social actors. Rather than adapting to market laws, economic actors are bound to capture the benevolence of the authorities, thus implicitly recognising their own subordination. Hence the limit of economic reform was the logic of Syrian political discourse, which posits the autonomous and unchecked power of the authorities as the only guarantee of the morality and cohesion of the social body.

4. Syria in the regional axis of resistance

Bashar al-Asad also presented himself as a guarantor of the stability and regional status that his father had given to Syria – the two achievements that even opponents acknowledge. By 2005, Bashar's popularity was already in question. Syria's regional position suffered a blow after the possibly Syrian-inspired assassination of Lebanese Prime Minister Hariri and the withdrawal of its troops from Lebanon. Internationally isolated, embattled Syrian leaders portrayed international pressure as part of a conspiracy against their country and cast it as a choice between the stability that Syria enjoyed in the Asad years and regional chaos. This hampered efforts to open a dialogue on domestic political reforms and justified a clampdown on pro-democracy activists.

In summer 2006, the victory of the Lebanese Hezbollah against Israel's attack stunned Arab public opinion and marked a turning point in regional and Syrian politics. Against the background of a radicalisation of public opinion and the rise of non-state actors, Asad presented the prospect of 'a new Middle East whose essence is resistance'[10] composed of Hezbollah – the strongest Arab non-state actor – the Palestinian faction Hamas, the Islamic Republic of Iran and Syria. This axis constituted neither a military nor a sectarian Shia alliance, but rather a political coalition based on common enemies (the archenemy Israel and pro-Western Arab powers), a common rejection of Western policies in the Middle East and realpolitik gains.[5] For Iran, the alignment between Damascus and Tehran meant a significant foothold in the otherwise largely hostile Arab Levant and a line to supply its Hezbollah ally. Syria's support for Hamas and

Hezbollah served the Syrian regime's strategy to embody the Arab (state) voice against Israel. Hezbollah remained the strongest common interest between Syria and Iran and the cornerstone of the resistance axis.

Bashar's self-legitimation by association with Hezbollah started as early as he succeeded his father as president in July 2000. In the aftermath of the Israeli withdrawal from south Lebanon, the association between the 'victorious' Hezbollah and the young Syrian leader, who had no military or anti-Israel records of his own, provided Bashar with the credentials he needed to rule the 'country of steadfastness' (Hokayem 2010). Increasingly dependent on Damascus for arms supply, Hezbollah became the protector of Syria's interests in Lebanon and a staunch supporter of President Bashar, the 'young leader who has his finger on the pulse of the Arab street'.[11] Hezbollah saved the Syrian image after the Syrian humiliating withdrawal from Lebanon in 2005 and Hezbollah's victory in 2006 won popular support in the Arab world to the 'resistance axis', at a time when Syria was internationally isolated.

There is little dispute about the resonance of the resistance discourse with Syrians and the wider Arab public, as evidenced by Bashar's own admission that 'conspiring against the resistance would spell political suicide for me'.[12] Syria's militant foreign policy and its open-door policy towards more than a million Iraqi refugees since 2003 and thousands of Lebanese after the July 2006 war strengthened the political credibility of Syrian leaders.

4.1. *Defying the hegemons and pre-empting dissent*

In Hezbollah political narrative, the notion of al-*muqawama* or resistance (literally meaning the act of 'standing up to' injustice) is linked to a Shia political culture of rebellion against oppression and martyrdom. In Syrian political discourse, the victories of the Lebanese resistance became a vindication of the steadfastness policies of the Syrian regime and popular support for Hezbollah became a celebration of the 'national consensus on the centrality of the role of resistance'.[13] In this way, the resistance slogan refashioned the historical role of Syria as a confrontational state thus bringing the resistance under the umbrella of the Syrian leadership. The close relations with Hezbollah and its 'glorious' anti-Israeli record became the key achievement of Asad's resistance posture.

Since the 2006 war, the concept of *muqawama* was complemented by the notion of *mumana'a* (rejectionism or blocking). The Blocking Front (*Jabhat al-mumana'a*) was designed to thwart the American military, political and economic influence in the Middle East. In the normative imaginary of Hamas and Hezbollah, this reconceptualisation of 'resistance' implied a redefinition of their hierarchy of enmity: although Israel remained 'the greatest injustice' because of its very existence, the paramount conflict was now with the US and its efforts to reshape the Middle East (Saad-Ghorayeb 2011). This strategy tied Hamas, Hezbollah, Iran and Syria in a common effort at defying the regional (Israel) and global (US) hegemons through armed and diplomatic resistance to imperialist penetration and a common counter-hegemonic discourse. Far from indicating a passive posture (Cobban 2008), al-*mumana'a* involves a militant practice of rejection of the unjust world order imposed by the US as well as political and logistic support for the armed resistance. The notion of al-*mumana'a* also served to counter detractors of the Syrian regime, who denounced its inability to liberate the Golan Heights – the quietest front in the Arab–Israeli conflict. Hezbollah's leader Hasan Nasrallah outspokenly praised Asad's steadfast refusal to submit to US–Israel hegemonic plans in the region and his support of the armed resistance in Lebanon, Palestine and Iraq (Nasrallah 2009).

The Syrian embrace of the resistance axis can be seen as a strategy to relaunch the role of Syria as the backbone of a geopolitical reorganisation and the pivotal interlocutor in any regional settlement. The Syrian posture sent international actors the message that, unless they considered Syria's interests, 'this is what you get'[14] and signalled that only a strong regime in Damascus will be able to deliver peace in the face of the radicalisation of Arab public opinion. Domestically, Syria's strong connection with resistance groups is a strategy to channel domestic anger whilst depriving resistance slogans of their latent anti-regime potential (Hroub 2009). The resistance ethos – the celebration of the heroic guerrilla fighter, a close relationship with 'the street' and a contempt for inept state institutions – could turn into a model of mobilisation for the embittered masses: its appropriation allowed Syrian leaders to give voice as well as representation to the Arab masses, to defuse public anger for the regime's own political and economic failures and to brandish the banner of legitimate violence thus pre-empting any popular initiative and weakening potential opposition to the regime.

Furthermore, Syria's alignment with the 'resistance front' enabled the regime to accommodate its rhetoric with a resurgent Islam – which was not as yet fundamentalist nor militant (Landis and Pace 2006) – thus reinforcing its control on its own 'street' that was increasingly populated by veiled women and bearded men, who challenged the dominance of the 'secular' Alawi establishment (Hroub 2004). Although unable to control the Syrian religious establishments, the regime co-opted various religious figures into marketing to Syrians and to the broader Muslim world its brand of Arab-Islamic resistance (Pierret 2013). Syrian media portrayed Hezbollah's victory as an Arab Muslim achievement and routinely talked about Arabism and Islam as twin pillars of strength.[15] Meanwhile the promotion of Syrian Shia holy sites as pilgrim destination gave a religious dimension to the alliance between Syria and Iran.

By the end of Bashar's first decade in power, Syria re-emerged on the international stage without compromising its most significant national interests and its role in the resistance front. At a regional level, Syria established good relations with Turkey and Iraq whilst maintaining its alignment with Iran; Lebanese leaders moved back within the Syrian orbit whilst Hezbollah held on to its guns. Indirect negotiations with Israel and a détente with Saudi Arabia helped to end European ostracism whilst the international community recognised Damascus as a privileged interlocutor for regional stability (Wieland 2015). Domestically, Bashar's regime managed to redirect Syria's economy whilst maintaining the Syrian authoritarian paradigm, its security culture and the minoritarian character of its core (the army, security services and the top economic tycoons). Yet the exploitative face of Syria's reform hardened the lack of negotiating avenues with important forces of the Syrian population, soon exposed to the contagion of the Arab spring.

4.2. *The resistance front in the Syrian conflict*

Syrian leaders who hitherto had believed themselves adept at meshing their 'regime maintenance' with popular legitimacy reacted with intransigence to the sudden uprising against them. The regime opted for a 'military option' to crush the opposition, thus directly leading to the transformation of a peaceful movement into an armed conflict, whilst pointing to orchestrated machinations by foreign governments. Throughout the Syrian conflict, the discourse of resistance remained a key element that shaped its trajectory, reinforced by a renewed anti-imperialist stance against foreign interference and re-articulated to address the new jihadist threat.

There is little question that the rebellion stemmed from popular frustration with enduring despotic rule and growing social injustice (Corm 2013) rather than the sectarian and ethnic divisions that have become the dominant narrative frame of the conflict. Moreover, Islamic movements – let alone jihadist – were largely absent from the Syrian streets and only re-emerged within the framework of the competition to seize control of the new National Council – the organ representing the Syrian opposition abroad – and in the absence of credible, secular opposition parties. Yet President Bashar portrayed his regime as a victim of Islamist forces, conveniently grouping together Syrian activists and foreign fighters as 'terrorists'. By rallying the support of Syrian minorities and recruiting Alawis militias (shabbiha), the regime has infused the conflict with a sectarian dimension, which the Sunni opposition sought to exploit as a legitimation argument (Sunnis are roughly the 70% of the population) as well as to attract the support of Sunni regional backers (mainly Saudi Arabia and Qatar).

This twist in the regime discourse is a clear attempt to de-legitimise the uprising by reducing it to a radical and imported threat to Syria's stability, to cast aspersions on people's 'legitimate' political demands and to divide the alliance of regime opponents. The presidential election in 2014 was a part of the war campaign, with the sole rival candidate declaring that the electoral contest was between Syria and its enemies and that the president-to-be-elected would win against the US, the Arab monarchies and Turkey, which continue to back the terrorists. Meanwhile, domestic legitimacy has boiled down to a threat: the status quo or the *promise* of chaos – 'Bashar or we burn the country' – with little ambition for any collective national achievement (Khouri 2014).

The intransigence of the Syrian leadership and their decision to crush the uprising triggered another revolution in Syrian foreign relations. The participation of regional and international supporters, who gave political, financial and military backing to competing factions and foreign fighters, turned Syria into a battlefield for regional proxy wars as well as for American and Russian competition. Regionally, Syria fell 'victim to a mix of Iranian hubris, Saudi adventurism, and Qatari ambition' (Harling 2014) not to mention Turkey regional ambitions in a regional escalation that is costly to and unwinnable for all.[16]

The struggle for regional supremacy between Shia Iran and Sunni Saudi Arabia provoked deep intra-Sunni conflicts as Saudi Arabia, Qatar and Turkey competed for leadership of the uprising and of the Sunni world more broadly. Within the resistance front, the uprising undermined Hamas' partnership with the Asad regime thus leaving the anti-Israeli 'resistance front' detached from any major Palestinian faction.[17] Yet the uprising strengthened the cohesion of the remaining actors, united by the perception that the conflict poses an existential threat to them. Foreign interference in the uprising vindicated the front's anti-imperialist stance and led to a further re-articulation of their discourse. For Hezbollah, Iran and Syria, the conflict is a specific site in the broader regional struggle between the resistance and a US–Israeli orchestrated plot backed by pro-Western Arab states.[18] Iran's Supreme Leader Ayatollah Ali Khamenei identified Syria's support for the resistance movements as the main cause of America's hostile policies against the country and offered President Asad unconditional support.[19] Tehran interpreted regional backing for the Syrian opposition as a direct assault on Iran's regional position and soon intervened militarily with its Revolutionary Guards Quds Force to restore what it calls 'alignment' and resist the foreign plot to crush the axis and restructure the Middle East (Wege 2015).

4.3. *From resistance to transnational counter-insurgency*

With the development of the conflict, the resistance front discourse has further evolved. In a bid to break away from the accusation of participating in a Shia invasion of Syria orchestrated by Iran, the Hezbollah leadership has invested time and effort in explaining the strategic significance of its Syrian intervention: ISIS and other jihadist groups are viewed as a mere tool serving a US–Israeli project to overthrow the only openly anti-Israel and anti-American Arab government in the region; therefore these groups are legitimate targets. Moreover Hezbollah claims responsibility to protect what it calls the 'resistance backbone': this is not a mere buffer zone securing its supply lines through the Syrian hinterland, but rather the geopolitical and strategic environment that Hezbollah requires for its continued operational integrity. In this perspective, the war against the IS becomes an extension of the resistance campaign and Hezbollah assumes responsibility for wresting Syrian, Lebanese and Iraqi territories from jihadist control.

As the US launched its air strikes against jihadist positions in Syrian territories, the traditional 'enemies' of the Front (the US and Israel) are now discursively constructed as located in Syria, thus further supporting the conceptual development of the original resistance paradigm into a model of transnational counter-insurgency grouping Hezbollah's Resistance Army, the Islamic Revolutionary Guards Corps, Syrian armed forces and Iraqi militias – in spite of their different priorities – against transnational jihadist networks and international conspiracies. Legitimacy in the region has thus become externalised, a function of outside support and regional rivalries rather than stemming from domestic dynamics (Harling and Birke 2015).

Four years after the uprising began, the country has become 'an egregious example of a failed state' (Hinnebusch 2014) in which competing legitimacy claims can no longer be composed by the central authority. What remains of the Syrian people within the country itself – after more than 250,000 citizens have died and some four million (out of more than 22 million) have sought refuge into neighbouring countries – are now subject to different authorities: the Asad regime, which controls most of the main Syrian cities and less than two-thirds of the population left inside Syria; opposition forces in charge of 'liberated areas' scattered within the provinces of Idlib, Aleppo, Deraa and Latakia; and the IS, which has captured the city of Raqqa and vast territories in the eastern part of the country (Balanche 2015). Each of these entities asserts a legitimate right to rule over areas under its (precarious) control and to continue to fight enemies who, they proclaim, lack political legitimacy since they are either a criminal regime, a horde of terrorists, or a mass of infidels. Each parties brandish the de-legitimation of the enemy as an imperative for its annihilation in a zero-sum game that can only bring further escalation of the violence in a conflict which is already a humanitarian disaster of unprecedented proportions.

5. International framings of legitimacy in the Syrian conflict

Since the beginning of the armed conflict, Western powers have intervened through multilateral and unilateral diplomacy. Peace conferences (Geneva I and II, Moscow I and II) and UN Security Council resolutions have failed to produce solutions to the war but have provided an arena for the clash of preferences of the states involved, which ranged from support for a political transition that includes President al-Asad, to sanctions and military intervention to achieve regime change. Three debates revolving around legitimacy have animated the international scene: the assessment of Asad's legitimacy, the legitimacy of an international military intervention and the new 'war on terror'.

Western powers displayed a remarkable caution in withdrawing their legitimacy credit from the corrupt Syrian elite, even after the fanfare given to the American declaration, in mid-July 2011, that 'Asad has lost his legitimacy in the eyes of his people'.[20] The dissemination of contradictory statements on part of US officials reflected the ambiguity of international diplomatic efforts, which oscillated between 'the imperative' of promoting a democratic transition and the increasing 'necessity' to engage with the regime as an interlocutor in international talks. By the end of 2013, the chemical weapon agreement did nothing to end the Syrian tragedy but gave the regime de facto legitimacy as a partner in the international diplomatic process and as a guarantor of the deal. The unfolding of the war, which saw Syria's 'resistance axis' successfully fighting alongside regime forces whilst increasingly radicalised opposition groups were fighting each other, helped the regime to regain recognition among Western chancelleries as an acceptable option insofar as uncontrollable jihadists dominate the battleground. This confirmed the view that external factors are crucial for maintaining 'legitimacy' in Middle East politics (Hudson 1977; Hinnebusch 2003) although such de facto 'legitimacy' fits uneasily into the conventional definition of the concept.

The international debate about the legitimacy of an external intervention to end the Syrian conflict has largely been framed within the issues of international legality and public support. The opposition of Russia and China to a military action in breach of Syria's state sovereignty, on the ground that it would violate international law and lead to regime change, blocked the UN Security Council from giving legal legitimacy to any Western intervention (Putin 2013). Since American public opinion gave clear indications of 'war fatigue' and in August 2013, the British parliament blocked the interventionist fervour of its own government, Western governments continued in their diplomatic and public relations strategy of asserting their common moral standards as a substitute for exerting those robust diplomatic efforts needed to engage Syria and its allies into negotiation.

By 2013, the fighting had already reached levels of violence and destruction unprecedented in the region with no solution of the conflict in sight. However, it was not the scale of the Syrian humanitarian catastrophe but the rise of the IS and the spectre of international terrorism which eventually prompted an international intervention.

The rise of the IS marked a turning point in the Syrian conflict in a number of ways. The international approach to the war shifted dramatically: from a concern over the fate of Syria to a fight against IS; from weighting the legitimacy of the Syrian regime to questioning the legitimacy of the Syrian state and its 'fragile boundaries'; from assessing new Syrian political actors to mapping geopolitical interests. The aerial campaign launched by the US in September 2014 to contain the expansion of the IS in Iraq and Syria saw the participation of five regional authoritarian monarchies (Bahrain, Jordan, Qatar, Saudi Arabia and the United Arab Emirates) who are worried about the boomerang effect of their proxy war and paved the way for the rehabilitation of President Asad, who now joined in the fight against the IS. This shows that the Western initiative was result of realpolitik considerations – including the threat to the viability of the Iraqi state in which the US has so much invested and the preservation of the regional authoritarian status quo.

Despite lacking the imprimatur of the UN Security Council, Western observers have widely recognised the US-led aerial campaign as legitimate whilst criticising the initiative on operational grounds – given its meagre probabilities of success. The focus on the bombing campaign overshadowed a number of other questions, including the inability of the Security Council to take further action after the destruction of the Syrian 'declared' chemical weapon arsenal and the failure of international agencies, Western chancelleries and diplomatic processes in addressing one of the greatest catastrophes of our time – questions that could point to another 'loss of legitimacy'. These concerns quietly faded away from the international framing of the Syrian war when the 'war on terror' became the overarching legitimating narrative of the intervention.

5.1. *The (Arab) war on Islamic terrorism*

Since President Bush launched the 'war on terror' following the 11 September 2001 attacks on the US, Western public opinion has accepted as a hard reality the view that the preservation of international security means the mastery of violence, not its absence (Butler 2004), and that there are no limits on the use of violence in the name of morally bound justice (Heristchi 2005). Part of the 'war on terror' discourse is a strategy of political de-legitimation based on the practice of labelling opponents as a radical 'other', who can only be crushed, thus barring the possibility of assessing the validity of the enemy's claims. Soon a series of normative associations are attached to the named subject and the (arbitrary) process by which the subject was selected for denigration disappears. Also the suffering of civilians who are caught in the middle of such war becomes invisible: violence against them is merely the price of their liberation. In the West, the 'war on terror' is ultimately a discourse of simplification designed to ignore the complexity of political issues which would require addressing the opponents' claims and goals. A year into the bombing campaign, the West is still following a crisis management approach and relying on the time-tested formulae of identity politics and containment – of the axis of resistance, of Islamists and of terrorism – as a substitute for a clear political vision regarding the future of Syria (Harling and Birke 2015).

In the Arab world, the 'war on terror' is a new tool of authoritarian self-preservation, an attempt to scrub from history the mass uprisings which have swept the region. The way in which the 'war on terror' discourse has construed architectures of enmity explains how easily Arab leaders have adopted sets of slogans which mirror Western attitudes towards terrorism. For the resistance front, enemies include *takfiri* terrorists such as the

IS as well as 'enemy states', which are constructed as supporters of terrorism (Saudi Arabia and Turkey) or the very 'mother of terrorism' (the US and Israel).[21] The most atrocious acts of regional governments have become immune from criticism whilst they lead their countries into the abyss of the 'Arab war on terrorism', 'a surreal place, in which Hasan Nasrallah echoes George Bush' (al.Saadi 2013).[22] Without distinguishing between the various ideologies, goals and means of different opposition movements, the 'war on terror' creates self-fulfilling prophesies of enmity and produces the fundamentalism which it claims to fight (Gregory 2004). The real paradox about the sectarian narrative that has embroiled the region is that it marks a stunning victory for an inherently orientalist and Islamophobic cultural imperialism. In today's Arab world, the caricature of the terrorist is the bearded bogeyman who frightens Western audiences (al. Saadi 2013).

As a catchphrase for administering order on a global scale whilst capitalising on a culture of fear of the other, 'terrorism' has provided Syrian leaders with a fresh opportunity to re-articulate Syrian political discourse and to deploy its authoritarian mechanism at the regional level. The adoption of the 'war on Islamic terror' rhetoric allows the regime to gain 'legitimacy' among domestic minorities who fear the advent of Islamic rule and among international actors whilst justifying the brutality of its war on armed and civilian opposition. Hence the war on terror works as an endorsement and extension of the regime's own repression. What is paradoxical about this twist in political discourse is not the transformation of Bashar al-Asad's public image – from one of the benevolent presidents of a secular society to the militant hero of anti-Islamist terror. The Syrian regime has a long history of deflecting anti-regime struggle away from the authorities to a fight among confessional communities. In 1982, the military offensive launched by Hafez al-Asad on the rebellious town of Hama – which killed some 20,000 people and created a long-time memory of fear – was accompanied by an ideological offensive that reduced a political rebellion to a clash between government and armed Islamist. Over the decades of Asadian rule, the regime never ceased to cultivate social divides through the sectarianisation of the security apparatus and the manipulation of jihadist groups in Iraq and Lebanon. With this latest twist, Syrian political discourse has gone full circle: from a revolutionary discourse of emancipation and state building to a counter-revolutionary discourse with 'nothing else to offer than more Bashar al-Asad' (Harling 2014) and the fragmentation of the state. As the Syrian war enters into its fifth year, Syria has virtually disappeared whilst the aspirations of what is left of the Syrian people 'scattered now among tombs, jails, exiles' are absent from narratives of 'terror', 'proxy war', religious conflict and 'civil war' (Saleh 2014b). Concerns over another jihadist backlash against Western interests drive Western decision making – oblivious of their own divide-and-rule strategies which have cultivated radical antagonism in the region – whilst regional powers are fighting their own wars for hegemony on Syrian soil. Reduced to a geopolitical arena, Syria is now 'a country with no interior' (Saleh 2014a).

The launching of the Russian bombing campaign on 30 September 2015 has further exposed the expediency of claims to legitimacy in the Syrian war context. After having successfully pre-empted Western interventionism, Moscow has legitimised its own in terms of national interest and support of the 'legitimate' Syrian government in its fight against terrorists. International commentators have focused on Moscow's cold war with the US (Harling and Birke 2015) and its tacit competition with Iran (Hamidi 2015) as ways for Russia to regain a prominent place on the international scene and establish its influence on the future Middle East. In this context, the Asad regime is now re-legitimised owing to its position on the side of the emerging regional hegemon – Russia, which is establishing fait accompli on the battleground to secure the position of Bashar al-Asad and Iran, and its own regional interests, in the forthcoming diplomatic negotiations.

6. Conclusion: reproducing power and legitimacy claims

This essay has focused primarily on the ways in which claims to legitimacy act to uphold the domestic and regional political agendas of the Syrian regime, helping to maintain its authority and to guarantee its survival. This argument hints at the persistent grip on Syrian citizens of discursive power mechanisms which operate to curb their ability to imagine different solutions, even when legality, representation and morality have shown themselves to be a mere veneer. This paper has charted the trajectory of Syrian political discourse from a narrative of change to one of preservation of the status quo whilst arguing that the notion of legitimacy is misleading as an analytical criterion because it downplays the play of discipline and normalisation which is the backbone of Asad's governmental authority. Moreover, this paper has examined the regional and international framings of legitimacy in relation with the Syrian war, charting the shifts between diplomatic narratives of negotiation and intervention, security imperatives, religious conflict and war on terror.

The Syrian case shows the inadequacy of the mainstream notion of legitimacy as an analytical tool for understanding modern politics. The assumed correlation between legitimacy and belief and inverse correlation between legitimacy and violence both conceal the arbitrariness and violence embedded in legitimation processes and deflect attention from subtle mechanisms of control, such as the continual reinvention of legitimation strategies and the production of compliance, which are central to the dynamic of social and political reproduction. Hence the mainstream notion of legitimacy impoverishes our thinking about power and social control. What we need is a radical reframing of our conceptual categories away from the political docility of 'legitimacy' and towards a consideration of the discursive aspects of power and domination.

The political discourses of antagonism, resistance and terrorism that we have examined in this paper point to compelling architectures of power and imaginative geographies of violence, orders of worth and self-fulfilling prophesies of enmity. Legitimation claims are framed in – and constitutive of – such discursive constructions which underpin both governmental and social practices. The Syrian case shows that legitimations processes are performative or constructive processes of political imagination – of the self, of the other and of the space for action – as well as mechanisms for curbing the discursive space which challenges the status quo of power distribution. Only if we understand legitimation processes as forceful operations both in theoretical and practical terms, can we see that the political processes which shape consensus and conflict in the Middle East are not separate – as assumed by conventional analysis.

Notes

1. Among studies that have advanced general normative conceptions of legitimacy see Buchanan (2003); Buchanan and Keohane (2006).
2. Wedeen (1999). See also O'Kane (1993).
3. Asad interview with the *Wall Street Journal*, 31 January 2011.
4. The legitimacy of Hafiz al Asad's regime was largely based on the relative success of the 1973 war. See Hinnebusch (2001), chapter 7.
5. On the role of party and corporatist institutions in forming a middle-class peasant and urban constituency see Hinnebusch (2001) and Batatu (1999).
6. The 12th Ba'ath National Congress (6th Regional Congress) coined the slogan of the double battle, namely of 'development and liberation'.
7. Asad address to the Syrian Peasant Federation, 14 December 1972.
8. Author interview with Yassin al-Hajj Saleh, Istanbul, August 2014.
9. See for instance the newly opened unaccredited private schools and universities that coexisted with the broken education system and obsolete curricula of public schools.
10. Speech of President Asad, Syrian Journalists Union, August 2006.
11. See Hasan, Nasrallah speech, 13 March 2003, in Noe (2007).
12. Bashar al-Assad, quoted in SANA, 30 March 2011.
13. Al-Thawra, 5 April 2010. See also Rubin (2010).
14. Author's interviews, Damascus, March 2010 and Beirut 2012. See also al-Thawra, 16 August 2006, 'Syrians will fight Israel in every part of the Golan just as Lebanese resistance fought you'.
15. See 'The Conscience of the Arab Resistance', al-Thawra, 5 April 2010 and President Asad interview with al-Manar Television, 24 March 2010.
16. See Wieland (2015) among others.
17. In December 2011, Hamas transferred its political bureau from Damascus to Qatar. The PFLP-General Command of Ahmed Jibril, who supported the Syrian regime, was expelled by the PLO for involving Palestinians in the Syrian conflict.
18. Nasrallah's speech, delivered on the commemoration of the Prophet's birthday in early February 2012.
19. See: http://www.english.alahednews.com.lb/essaydetails.php?eid=16559&cid=504#. ViGFhX4rLIU
20. 'Clinton says Syria's Assad has lost legitimacy', Reuters 12 July 2011.
21. See 'Nasrallah: America is the mother of terrorism' in al-Akhbar, 23 September 2014: English.al-akhbar.com/node/21665
22. Examples of this are the lack of outrage over the killing of Muslim Brotherhood supporters in Egypt in 2013 and the silence regarding escalating repression in Gulf countries.

References

Ababsa, M. 2011. "Agrarian Counter –Reform in Syria." In *Agriculture and Reform in Syria*, edited by R. Hinnebusch, et al. Lynne Rienner for the University of St Andrews Centre for Syrian studies.

al.Saadi, Y. 2013. "The Rise of the Arab 'War on Terror' Discourse". *Muftah*.

Balanche, F. 2015. *The Political Geography of Syria's War: An Interview with Fabrice Balanche*, by Aron Lund, January 3. Washington, DC: Carnegie Endowment for International Peace.

Bar, S. 2006. "Bashar's Syria: The Regime and Its Strategic Worldview." *Comparative Strategy* 25: 353–445. doi:10.1080/01495930601105412.

Batatu, H. 1999. *Syria's Peasantry, the Descendants of Its Lesser Rural Notables, and Their Politics*. Princeton, NJ: Princeton University Press.

Beetham, D. 1991. *The Legitimation of Power*. Basingstoke: Macmillan.

Buchanan, A. 2003. *Justice, Legitimacy and Self-determination: Moral Foundations of International Law*. Oxford: Oxford University Press.

Buchanan, A., and R. O. Keohane. 2006. "The Legitimacy of Global Governance Institutions." *Ethics & International Affairs* 20 (4): 405–437. doi:10.1111/j.1747-7093.2006.00043.x.

Butler, J. 2004. *Precarious Life*. London: Verso.

Clark, I. 2005. *Legitimacy in International Society*. Oxford: Oxford University Press.

Cobban, H. 2008. "Hamas and the End of the Two State Solution." Boston Review, 1 May.

Coicaud, J.-M. 2002. *Legitimacy and Politics: A Contribution to the Study of Political Right and Political Responsibility*. Cambridge: Cambridge University Press.

Corm, G. 2013. "The Socio-Economic Factors behind the Revolutions of the Arab Spring." In *The Arab Spring Critical Analyses*, edited by K. E.-D. Haseeb. London: Routledge.

Gregory, D. 2004. *The Colonial Present*. Malden, MA: Wiley-Blackwell.

Habermas, J. 1979. "Legitimation Problems in the Modern State." In *Communication and the Evolution of Society* edited by T. McCarthy . Boston: Beacon Press.

Haddad, B. 2012. *Business Networks in Syria: The Political Economy of Authoritarian Resilience*. Stanford, CA: Stanford University Press.

Hamidi, I. 2015. "La présence militaire russe en Syrie ne se limitera pas à quelque mois ". *Al-Ahram hebdo*, 14 October.

Harling, P. 2014. "The Arab World into the Unknown". *The Arabist*, 14 January.

Harling, P., and S. Birke. 2015. "The Islamic State though the Looking-Glass." *The Arabist*, March 3. http://arabist.net/blog/2015/3/3/the-islamic-state-through-the-looking-glass

Heristchi, C. 2005. "Imaginative Geographies of the War on Terror." Paper presented at the 2005 CMES workshop, Exeter University, UK.

Heydemann, S., ed. 2004. *Networks of Privilege: The Politics of Economic Reform in the Middle East Revisited*. New York: Palgrave Press.

Hinnebusch, R. 2001. *Syria: Revolution from Above*. London: Routledge.

Hinnebusch, R. 2003. *International Politics of the Middle East*. Manchester: Manchester University Press.

Hinnebusch, R. 2014. "The Multiple Layers of the Syrian Crisis." *Political Insight*, 17 March.

Hinnebusch, R., and T. Zintl, ed. 2015. *Syria from Reform to Revolt*. Syracuse: Syracuse University Press.

Hokayem, E. 2010. "The Evolving State/Non State Nexus." *IISS Global Strategic Review*.

Hroub, K. 2004. "Triggering a Discourse of Resistance". *IP Journal*, 1 August.

Hroub, K. 2009. "The Arab System after Gaza." *Open Democracy*, 27 January.

Hudson, M. 1977. *Arab Politics: The Search for Legitimacy*. New Haven, CT: Yale University Press.

Ismail, S. 2006. "Authoritarian Civilities and Syria's stalled Political Transition." Paper presented at the American Political Science Association annual Meeting, Philadelphia, US.

Khalidi, A., and H. Agha. 1991. "The Syrian Doctrine of Strategic Parity." In *The Middle East in Global Perspective*, edited by J. Kipper and H. Saunders, 186–218. Boulder: Westview Press.

Khouri, E. 2014. "Assad and the Post-Eternity Era." *Qantara*.de 4 June.

Kitus, A. 2014. *A Post-structuralist 'Concept' of Legitimacy*. Tartu: University of Tartu Press.

Landis, J., and J. Pace. 2006. "The Syrian Opposition." *The Washington Quarterly*, winter 2006-07.

Mbembe, A. 1992. "Provisional Notes on the Postcolony." *Africa: Journal of the International African Institute* 62 (1): 3. doi:10.2307/1160062.

Nasrallah, H. 2009. "Nasrallah Commemorates Al-Quds Day" *speech*, 18 September 2009. Alahednews.com.lb.

Noe, N., ed. 2007. *Voice of Hezbollah*. London: Verso.

O'Kane, R. 1993. "Against Legitimacy." *Political Studies* 41: 471–487. doi:10.1111/post.1993.41. issue-3.

Pierret, T. 2013. "Angry Arab Interviews: Thomas Pierret on Syria." 25 April.

Putin, V. 2013. "'A Plea for Caution from Russia'. What Putin Has to Say to Americans about Syria." *The New York Times*, 11 September.

Rapkin, D. P., and D. Braaten. 2009. "Conceptualising Hegemonic Legitimacy." *Review of International Studies* 35 (1): 113–149. doi:10.1017/S0260210509008353.

Rubin, B. 2010. *The Resistance Strategy*. Herzliya: Global Research in International Affairs (GLORIA).

Saad-Ghorayeb, A. 2011. *Understanding Hizbullah's Support for the Asad Regime*. Beirut-London: Conflicts Forum.

Saleh, Y. A.-H. 2014a. "'Forty-four Months and Forty-four Years: 1- Two Blindfolds." *L'Internationale*, 16 November.

Saleh, Y. A.-H. 2014b. "Freedom, Social Change, and Syria". *Al-Jumhuriya*, 28 June.

Wedeen, L. 1999. *Ambiguities of Domination*. Chicago: Chicago University Press.

Wedeen, L. 2013. "Ideology and Humor in Dark Times: Notes from Syria." *Critical Inquiry* 39: 841–873. doi:10.1086/671358.

Wedeen, L. n.d. "Abandoning 'Legitimacy'? Order, the State, and Neoliberal Ideology". Unpublished paper, The University of Chicago.

Wege, C. 2015. "Iran and Assad Are Not Winning." *Fair Observer*, 1 April.

Wieland, C. 2015. "The ancient regime policy paradox." In Syria from Reform to Revolt, edited by R. Hinnebusch and T. Zintl. Syracuse: Syracuse University Press.

Žižek, S. 1989. *The Sublime Object of Ideology*. London: Verso.

Reply to 'Building authoritarian "legitimacy": domestic compliance and international standing of Bashar al-Asad's Syria' by Aurora Sottimano

Matthieu Rey

This is a reply to:

Sottimano, Aurora. 2016. 'Building authoritarian "legitimacy": domestic compliance and international standing of Bashar al-Asad's Syria.' *Global Discourse* 6 (3): 450–466. http://dx.doi.org/10.1080/23269995.2016.1152790

Aurora Sottimano's (2016) article correctly tackles the issue of legitimacy. It intends to show how an ordinary concept of political sciences could not fit with a specific context such as Syria as it has been previously framed. It is not to say that the author states that the rulers and governments have not built discourses which brought them this political tool. On the contrary, using Mbembé's category, 'cultivation of authoritarian civilities' and deploying a long historical investigation on the political-baathi stage, the author reframes this concept in order to highlight concrete technologies of power.

Lisa Weeden (1999) has suggested some insightful arguments to understand the Syrian case. Rather than enquiring about a totalitarian or an authoritarian regime, she proves how personality cult and 'acting as if' the citizen agreed on the political order were enough. From this perspective, the coercive apparatus had slowly curbed protest and opposition, and 'cultivated an atmosphere of mistrust combined with self-censorship, mutual surveillance, dissimulation and unreflective compliance' (6). Sottimano correctly argues that the regime enlarged its social base by curbing socialist rhetoric, and the bourgeoisie helped the Hafez al-Assad regime to survive. Unfortunately, Sottimano does not pinpoint differences inside the country and she often relies on general categories. Some details could have been added on the different points of view in the country: for instance, Aleppo clearly stood against the regime, whereas other localities were in favour of the regime. Introducing geographical differences allows the reader to understand how different parts of the country (Aleppo areas, Damascus, Alawite mountains, etc.) took different stances towards the regime.

Then the author discusses the underpinnings of the anti-imperialist stance of the Assad regime, which constitutes the main line of defence from 1970 to 2015, but she describes it as belonging to the 'resistance'. It would be better from my perspective to talk about anti-imperialism rather than resistance. Certainly, local actors used the word 'resistance'. But it does not reveal, to a general audience, the political and discursive mechanisms that legitimate its use. By claiming to be part of the resistance, the Assad regime denounced Israel as a colonial actor rather than tackling the nature of its state. It is part of a broader strategy to disqualify the opponent on the regional and internal stages.

Then the author describes how foreign affairs were used by the regime in order to build a wide consensus in society. These different steps built the key elements that allowed the president to argue that any opponent belonged to an external plot. For the author, the turning point was 2006, when Israel launched a new military campaign against Lebanon. During this war, Arab public opinion massively supported Hezbollah, as a 'resistant' group. It reversed Syria's isolation in Bush's Middle East. The author pinpointed how Iranian, Lebanese and Syrian authorities pulled together. This grouping symbolically formalised an international alliance, which claimed to be the front of refusal (*mumana'a*). Surprisingly, the author does not mention the common threat and the trauma that these actors shared: the Iraqi invasion. It would be interesting to investigate more fully how the American invasion reshaped the regional links. The 'refusal' front – those states that refused Israel and claimed to be acting against imperialist encroachment – denounced the American move in Iraq as an encroachment on Arab sovereignty and they feared to be the next target. At the same time, this war erased their main regional enemy: Saddam Hussein. From this perspective, the 2006 Israeli war created a common factor to bring together separate powers. The author avoided correctly speaking about a 'Shia axis'; on the contrary, she emphasises the strategic and discursive logics. This demonstration is brilliant as it escapes cultural determinism, which often fails to explain the regional combination precisely. Consequently, during the 2000s, the Syrian regime renewed its base of legitimacy thanks to the regional disturbances.

Quite convincingly, the author reduces the 'regime' to the figure of the president. She proves that he gathered power after his father's death. He played on a range of images: a 'young' and 'modern' president who is trained in Western academia; someone who tried to promote a new policy. This is well known and well documented (Lesch 2005). Surprisingly, the author does not investigate further how different components interacted: how the presidency co-opted new leaders in the security apparatus and how Assad built up a true network of power that reproduced similar mechanism to those used by his father. Several memoirs could be used to highlight this change: Khaddam's, Tlas' and, more recently, Chari's autobiographies pointed out the reconfiguration of tools of power (Tlass 2005). Moreover, this research could be further enriched by ethnographic investigation, especially as in the last years interviews have become more feasible since the uprising as many leaders fled in exile.

The author then turned to post-2011 evolutions. She perfectly proves how the debate on legitimacy shifted from domestic to international issues. From 2011 to 2012, massive demonstrations broke out in several cities. The regime lost control over the population and the national territory and it deployed massive repression to curb the protests. Then, it managed to block the internal situation on international debates: Assad argued that regional powers such as Saudi Arabia and Qatar fuelled the conflict. After the rise of Islamic State, he then presented his regime as the main defence of Western values against extremism. These twin discursive dynamics allowed the regime to reinforce its legitimacy as a state on the external stage. This point is very interesting and must be emphasised. It can lead to further inquiries on other case studies that investigate how connections between foreign partners and internal actors pave the way for the latter to increase their legitimacy on the internal stage. From this perspective, as Mbembé has recently claimed in an interview (Mbembé 2016), foreign discursive support can be better understood.

However, it is surprising that in the conclusion, the author never uses the notion of sovereignty. She departs from the assumption that legitimacy and sovereignty (or tools to be sovereign) are linked. This is very interesting but it could have been more clearly spelled out. Apart from these very few missing points, which do not undermine the quality of the paper, all the previous reasons explain why this article makes a compelling contribution to the current debate on political legitimacy in Syria.

References

Lesch, D. 2005. *The New Lion of Damascus: Bashar al-Asad and Modern Syria*. New Haven: Yale University Press.

Mbembé, A. 2016. "La France a peine à rentrer dans le monde qui vient." *Libération*, June 1.

Sottimano, A. 2016. "Building Authoritarian 'Legitimacy': Domestic Compliance and International Standing of Bashar al-Asad's Syria." *Global Discourse* 6 (3): 450–466. doi:10.1080/23269995.2016.1152790.

Tlass, M. 2005. *Mirat Hayati*. Damascus: Dar al-Tlas.

Weeden, L. 1999. *Ambiguities of Domination: Politics, Rhetoric, and Symbols in Contemporary Syria*. Chicago: University of Chicago Press.

Looking for a new legitimacy: internal challenges within the Israeli Left

Giulia Daniele

ABSTRACT

Considering current Israeli society in terms of the asymmetric power relations and privileges experienced by its heterogeneous population, this paper aims at questioning the role played by Israeli left-wing parties and grassroots organizations since the failure of the Oslo 'peace process', with a focus on the aftermath of the legislative elections of 2015. In general, most of the political initiatives led by the Zionist Left can be seen to have lost the internal legitimacy they need in order to challenge the assumptions underpinning the power asymmetries. By taking account of those narrative identities excluded from the mainstream Zionist Left discourse, among which are the Palestinian citizens of Israel, Mizrahi Jews, women's feminist activists and African asylum seekers, I attempt to problematize the ethnic, national, class and gender cleavages emerging in a situation which includes some complex instances of dispossession and marginalization. In a settler colonial context such as the one prevailing in Israel, I question whether the left-wing has been able to represent and to support the rights of the most marginalized communities and to face up to the neo-liberal and ethno-nationalist drift which is gathering increasing momentum inside the country. Deploying an approach that is contrary to the predominant narrative, which addresses the parties and the grassroots groups of the Israeli Left as types of activism based on a single and homogeneous platform, I draw attention to alternative socio-political initiatives that have often been silenced by the mainstream, such as those initiated by radical left-wingers, '48 Palestinians, Mizrahim, feminist activists, and also more recently by African migrants and asylum seekers. In this way, the paper also deals with the necessity of providing a means of expression for the critical points of view emerging from the most marginalized backgrounds of Israeli society, a need which is underlined by a good number of my interviewees, and a need which, if fulfilled, could enable the building up of a new and broader legitimacy within the Israeli leftist political arena.

Note: This article has been updated slightly since original publication. For more information, see Addendum http://dx.doi.org/10.1080/23269995.2016.1167456

1. Introduction

Just as the January 2013 Israeli elections, which resulted in the formation of a new coalition led by Benjamin Netanyahu, came after a military operation called 'Pillar of Cloud' which took place in 2012 in the Gaza Strip, the most recent Israeli elections in March 2015 occurred a few months after another military operation in the Gaza Strip named 'Protective Edge', which was pursued during the summer of 2014, when more than 2,200 Palestinians were killed (B'Tselem 2015, 5). The elections of 2015 have been characterized by the varied background of the right-wing parties, and especially by the political strategy of Netanyahu, which produced another election victory, albeit in a rather last minute and unexpected way. The Zionist left-wing leadership, on the other hand, failed to meet expectations and to be perceived by its electorate as having legitimacy, and the 'Zionist Union' (the coalition between the Labor Party, led by Isaac Herzog, and Hatnuah, founded by the former leader of Kadima Party's Tzipi Livni) produced a disappointing performance in a final neck and neck situation with Likud.[1]

Within the settler colonial framework (Piterberg 2008; Veracini 2006, 2010; Wolfe 1999) and as analysed by a growing literature dealing with Israeli internal politics (Ghanem 2010; Grinberg 2010; Filc 2010; Pedahzur 2012), since the failure of the Oslo Accords the Israeli political panorama has moved from a ruling conservative coalition led by Likud to a more extreme right-wing scenario in which Netanyahu's party has continued to keep a hold on power. In such a context, although the mainstream Israeli Zionist Left, namely the Labor Party along with what has been called the 'peace camp' (Bar-On 1996; Hermann 2009; Kaminer 1996), has announced its support for Palestinian statehood and its will to resume negotiations, it has not taken a clear position against the construction of settlements in the West Bank and the most recent rounds of military aggression in the Gaza Strip.

Looking at this situation, and with the outcome of the most recent legislative elections in 2015 in mind, this paper focuses on the contemporary nuances existing within Israeli leftist politics, in terms of both political parties and grassroots movements, and on the decline in importance of the role of the left and of its legitimacy, especially when viewed from the most marginalized communities and groups[2] within Israeli society. This leads to a detailed examination of the asymmetries of power and privileges that have grown up between Jews themselves and between Jews and non-Jews, and I will attempt to connect this reality with the internal debate that is going on inside the Israeli Left, and more specifically among those political activists who have been named as being of the 'radical Left'. This will allow me to shed light on the most critical and significant perspectives, strategies and initiatives that have emerged from the experiences of several activists I met and interviewed during my latest fieldwork in Israel in November and December 2014,[3] along with their analyses related to the results of the recent elections.

In order to examine issues of marginalization and inequality experienced from diverse components and backgrounds inside Israel,[4] I argue that it is necessary to consider the relationship between the Israeli Left's legitimacy and some further political alternatives that have called into question the Zionist hegemonic structure of Israeli society. In detail, I aim at contextualizing the weakening of this political legitimacy and the reasons why this decline, as described in diverse ways since the early 2000s (Levy 2009; Pappé 2001), has been possible. This analytical pathway also directs attention towards the fact that Israel has become an increasingly fragmented society shaped by the growing ethno-national and class conflicts (Kemp et al. 2004; Kimmerling 2008; Pappé and Hilal 2010; Ram 2011; Shafir and Peled 2002; Yiftachel 2006).

Building on this theoretical framework, the study I elaborate in the following pages aims to critically interrogate the legitimacy and the role of the Israeli Left in its wider sense, as seen through the eyes of those opposing the Zionist hegemonic mainstream. In this direction, and going along the lines set out by some academic debates dealing with the Israeli Left and its internal criticism (Greenstein 2014; Honig-Parnass 2011; Karpf et al. 2008; Leon 2004), this paper discusses the reasons why interlinking a series of grassroots struggles that have involved different marginalized actors with the political legitimacy of the Israeli Left still remains a challenging task, both within academia and in the context of recent Israeli politics. In doing this, in addition to examining the current discussion among radical leftists, I also focus on the most marginalized communities and groups, including the Palestinian citizens of Israel, the Mizrahim, and women and feminist activists, African migrants and asylum seekers in an attempt to uncover some examples of politics that have been at the margins of Israeli society and excluded from the Zionist hegemony. In spite of their position on the margins, these examples play key role in expressing internal critical positions and addressing the lack of credibility of the traditional Zionist Left.

2. The declining legitimacy of the Zionist Left

The Israeli context emerging in the aftermath of the 2015 legislative elections reveals a country that is undergoing very deep socio-economic fragmentation and is exposed to the increasing volume of ethno-nationalist discourses. On the one hand, the far right-wing scene seems to have invested in a discourse aiming at reinforcing its political legitimacy, whilst on the other hand, the Zionist Left has lost its role in the Israeli political panorama and left aside its primary principles. Referring specifically to the latter bloc and to the most recent creation of the 'Zionist Union', the situation which has resulted from the latest elections has represented something that was already predicted by the majority of leftist activists who have been protagonists in several political struggles since the early 1990s. In general terms, and according to several political activists I met throughout my field research, during the whole electoral debate the Labor Party has been viewed as rather elitist and disconnected from the everyday reality of the Israeli population, while the right-wing has played its cards explicitly by denouncing the risk of recognizing an independent Palestinian state and by advocating the disqualification of any Palestinian citizen present in Israel from participation in the political system.

Looking at the Israeli Zionist Left, after the Oslo Accords in 1993 and the assassination of Yitzhak Rabin 2 years later they have passed through a prolonged and ongoing decline, failing to counter the view of a wide section of the public who supported the narrative that what failed to materialize during the 'peace process' has been due to the political decisions made by the Left. On this, it has been said, with some justification, that the three bullets that assassinated Rabin also determined the end of the Israeli Left, since they prevented Palestinian citizens of Israel from becoming part of the political space and working together with the Jews (Grinberg 2015). Moreover, that period was the last one in which a left-wing bloc existed, consisting of Labor, Meretz and the Arab parties.

Accordingly, it is necessary to contextualize the declining political course of the Zionist Left, which means going back to the way through which the Zionist Left contributed to the failure of the Oslo Accords. In fact, if it is true that the 'peace process' broke down because of the Likud leadership's rejection of the deal, it is critical to underline how 'the more fundamental cause behind the loss of trust and the loss of momentum was the Israeli policy of expanding settlements on the West Bank which carried on under Labor as well as Likud (Shlaim 2005, 283), with this activity precluding the end of the conflict and, consequently, the establishment of any viable Palestinian state. Because of this, the Zionist Left has gradually lost its legitimacy among its political activists, who have either abandoned their active political roles or joined in more radical leftist groups and initiatives. Many of my interviewees have experienced similar political transformations, and one of them, Ofer Neiman, co-founder of Boycott from Within,[5] has described this to me thus:

> when I was a teenager I was a liberal Zionist, according to Meretz and B'tselem. During the Oslo years I was supporting the process, but I was sort of more supportive of Gush Shalom, another disillusionment I had. When the second Intifadah broke up, I joined a group for military refusers, Yesh Gvul, and also in Peace Now. First, I had no idea, I thought we could be together as a broad coalition and work together, but after I became more critical. In a way, it was a very gradual process, I came to the conclusion I do not want to justify the foundation of Israel and I see the connection between the problems of the occupation as an extension of the Israeli political system, an extension of Zionism, by taking more land and moving Palestinians out is much broader than going back to 1967. [...] Here, in Israel, even the Jewish working class is in a way a master race in comparison with the Palestinians. For instance, I used to be also active in Hadash,[6] I am not longer active in it because I came to the conclusion that the socialist approach does not work here in an apartheid society. (Neiman 2014)

Moreover, the Israeli socio-economic situation has been worsening and entering a stagnation that has amplified the gap between the richest and the poorest. The most demanding aspect has been the dramatic increase in the number of people below the poverty line, while a restricted financial elite has been gaining greater control over political and economic power (OECD 2014). Although the aim of this article is more focused on the current reality of the Israeli Left, of its forms of activism and of its internal challenges, it is not possible to overlook what happened in the summer of 2011, when protest activity was led mainly by what has become known as the 'Tent Movement'.

In spite of the wide media coverage of what has been perceived by some as a crucial moment of hope among Israelis (Reider and Abu Sarah 2011; Sherwood 2011), pleading for social justice has not been sufficient to achieve greater fairness within Israeli society. By underlining its apolitical nature, the Tent Movement leadership decided to ignore the ways through which the military occupation, along with the expansion of illegal settlements in the Palestinian territories, have led to deterioration of the Israeli welfare state (Hever 2010, Who Profits[7] 2015). The main reasons why the 2011 protests did not tackle such issues can be associated with both the fear of losing their widespread support from common people and the fact that the majority of Israelis is still more interested in maintaining the military occupation and, thus, in maintaining the security discourse, rather than caring about the creation of a more affordable welfare state (Gordon 2012; Leibner 2012; Levy 2011; Ohayon 2011). In particular, the unfeasibility of interrelating political and social struggles has deepened the internal fragmentation founded on class, ethnic, national, gender and political discriminations within Israeli society. As underlined by most of my interviewees, the majority of activists from the radical Left have not joined in such a wave of protests, while, on the other hand, they have criticized the Tent Movement as the expression of the mainstream and as serving to hide the ongoing military occupation.

In relation to the factors discussed above and to those historical trajectories that have transformed the Israeli left-wing arena, it is also important to mention the process of 'NGO-ization' as something which characterizes several peace-oriented organizations associated with the Zionist Left. This concept refers to the way in which diverse forms of grassroots activism have moved towards more professionalized and institutionalized structures without considering the peculiarity of each context in which the political initiatives take place, and particularly the increasing influence of foreign donors and, as a result, the organizations have mostly become depoliticized. The concept of 'NGO-ization' is cropping up in debates within academia from different disciplines and areas of study (Choudry and Kapoor 2013; Grewal and Bernal 2014; Lang 2013), and it has also been used in the Israeli-Palestinian context and with specific regard to women's activism both in the West Bank (Jad 2004) and inside Israel (Herzog 2008). Despite the growing relevance of this political pattern in Israeli leftist politics, the Zionist Left has not openly taken on board the notion that the effects generated by such a process have significantly modified the policies, practices and tools of several leftist grassroots organizations.

3. Radical left-wing activists and their position inside Israel

At present, a general sense of 'no alternative' has spread across Israeli citizens, which can also be defined in terms of 'the silent majority of complacency' (Derfner 2015) and is immobilizing any kind of feasible societal change. One of the resultant consequences has been the stigmatization of the radical Left, as being one of the major actors struggling against the hegemonic structure of Israeli society. This stigmatization has taken place using means which have even included violence, something which has become a regularly occurring symptom of the current political stagnation, and through the launch of intimidating attacks with the intention of intensifying the level of the pressure silencing dissent inside Israel, with these being directed firstly against the Palestinians, the non-Jews par excellence, and also against the most radical Israeli Jewish left-wingers. In most recent times, such a reality occurred during the military operation 'Protective Edge' in summer 2014, when the level of intra-Jewish hatred reached a frightening peak, although similar episodes of denigration towards leftist activists were not new in Israeli contemporary history (Filc 2010).

In a parallel way, in spite of the escalation in the number of Palestinian civilian casualties in Gaza throughout July and August 2014, the mainstream Zionist Left did not, with a few exceptions from some members of Meretz, join in the street protests organized in opposition to this military operation, which was also defined as an 'incremental genocide in the Gaza ghetto' (Pappé 2014). These mobilizations against the attack on Gaza were mostly led by radical leftist grassroots organizations, such as the Coalition of Women for Peace, the Socialist Struggle Movement, Anarchists against the Wall, New Profile and Tarabut-Hithabrut (the Arab-Jewish Movement for Social & Political Change), together with a very few political parties including the Da'am Workers' Party and Balad and several Palestinian groups who were active mostly in Tel Aviv, but also in the major mixed Palestinian-Jewish cities such as in Jaffa, Haifa and Lod.

In opposition to these political initiatives, over the summer of 2014, slogans saying 'death to Arabs' and 'death to leftists' became common (Scheindlin 2014; Zonszein 2014) and, as reported by several interviewees, radical leftist activists experienced violent assaults from supporters of organized right-wing groups, such as Lehava, who are against any kind of assimilation between Jews and Palestinians, Shadow's Lions led by a well-known rapper named 'Shadow', and also from some more spontaneous right-wing factions, in some cases related to soccer fans' clubs, who began to frequently attack Israeli Jewish left-wingers in the streets during public demonstrations (Mualem 2014).

Regarding the peculiarity of the internal political debate among radical leftist activists, some of my interviewees have preferred to define themselves as either 'non-Zionist' or 'anti-Zionist', seeing Zionism as one of the major objects of their political struggle. On the other hand, in further cases, activists have not really felt the need to define themselves by means of exclusive references to Zionism, and they have preferred to use broader self-definitions of the diverse, and parallel, narrative identities with which they have engaged. However, generally speaking, the political perspectives articulated by several Israeli Jewish leftists I met have confirmed a general sense of isolation within their society and sometimes also among their families and friendships, as described in the following words:

> sometimes I define myself as a political and cultural refugee, exiled in my own community, sometimes a Jew from occupied Palestine/apartheid Israel. I do not define myself either as an Israeli or as a Palestinian Jew, although I could do in the future, but I do not now. This is my home on the emotional level, but I do not have any narrative, any story to identify with, I am anti-nationalist anyway. I learn to live on very basic identity food, my relationships, my actions, my places. The stories, the narratives, the symbols, the songs I do not identify with, it is a kind of cut off. I do not have a new identity to compensate for what I lost. It is disturbing to be isolated, but it is not disturbing to be without a national narrative I identify with. I do not need it. (Aviyah 2014)

In connection with the demise of the Oslo 'peace process', the present crisis of Israeli left-wing activism provides evidence of how the relationship between the Zionist Left and the Palestinian struggle can be described as an historical oxymoron rather than a source of real support for the Palestinian people in striving to achieve self-determination. In fact, most of those Israelis who have been involved in peace-oriented initiatives throughout the 1990s have questioned neither the hegemonic Zionist consensus within Israel nor any feasible change of Israelis' consciousness towards the Palestinian cause. Such a perspective has been reinforced by the fact that both the Labor and Meretz parties[8]:

do not want to deal with anything through which they could lose votes. In particular, they do not want to have a clear position on the conflict since they would lose votes. They do not do anything, they do not have any perspective on the conflict. They do not have an alternative socio-political plan as well, because this would lead them into losing votes. (Yahni 2014)

As a consequence, this has implied a reduction in numbers participating, kinds of mobilization and the articulating of effective proposals for alternative pathways to be taken and has also led to the development of a deeper sense of frustration experienced by many radical left-wing activists. For example, the majority of my interviewees, who belong to diverse backgrounds among the Israeli Left political scenario and often express multiple narrative identities, have experienced the complexity of being outsiders from within their own society, from which so little internal criticism has risen up. On this subject, some of them have pressed for action inside Israel to explain to the Israeli people that it is still possible to work on societal changes from within and to push the Israeli government itself to take another strategy; on the other hand, other activists, who no longer have any hope for internal transformation, have continued to be involved, suggesting something different could only come from abroad.[9]

Another significant consequence of similar collective as well as individual conditions experienced by the majority of activists from the radical Left has arisen due to a sense of alienation. In addition to the sense of isolation previously mentioned, this is an aliena-tion that is related to the huge disillusion felt with regard to any possible change in the near future. This has caused a disconnection from everyday life that the activist Guy Butavia from Ta'ayush (the Arab Jewish Partnership where a number of Israelis and Palestinians struggle together with the aim of ending the Israeli military occupation and of reaching full civil equality by means of everyday nonviolent actions) has described as follows:

I am living in a bubble, it is like the activists' family, I have only relationship with people whose views are more or less the same as mine; also with family it was hard, now I have disconnected relationships with most of my larger family which have totally different views, many of them are settlers, so it is very hard to have relationships with them. In my view, activism is not like one part of my life, but it is surrounding me, it is very hard to separate parts of life from others. (Butavia 2015)

If historically a few examples of dissident political activism towards the Zionist hege-mony have arisen in Israel, such as the most well-known group called Matzpen in the 1970s and 1980s (Davis 2003; Greenstein 2014), the ongoing climate of fear and intimidation against Israeli leftists has become commonly accepted in a society increas-ingly dominated by the silencing of dissent and, in particular, of alternative political discourses growing up from some of the most marginalized actors within Israel. As will be also discussed in the next paragraph, many of these contributions have confronted controversial concerns about the increase of power asymmetries and can be considered a testimony to the attempt to spread critical debates inside Israel and to oppose the 'passive Left scenario' (Scheindlin 2014).

4. From the margins to the core of alternative politics

At least, the most current political events inside Israel have enabled us to get a clearer view of the real nature of the Zionist Left and also helped us to speculate on whether Israel can be a democracy for its Jewish citizens, although it is apparent that it is not for the non-Jews, since it is becoming even more repressive especially for Palestinians (Gordon 2015). Nonetheless, as I mentioned at the beginning of the paper, and in spite of its emergence from very different backgrounds and histories, alternative politics advocated by marginalized actors and directed towards the Zionist hegemony, along with the intersecting ethnic, national, class and gender narrative identities of these actors, require further examination with reference to the present Israeli political context.

Starting with the analysis of the most historic marginalized community inside Israel, namely the Palestinian citizens of Israel, in March 2015 a relatively unexpected electoral result was achieved by the Palestinians inside Israel, who created a united front called the Joint Arab List by involving the Democratic Front for Peace and Equality (Hadash), the United Arab List, the National Democratic Assembly (Balad) and the Arab Movement for Renewal (Ta'al) to pursue the cause of full democracy and equality within Israel. With participants coming from diverse political traditions, such a unity has required the identification of common tasks and specifically a national common front to overcome their internal divergences. In contrast with past initiatives that resulted in disillusion, and as a result of what has been defined as 'the winter of despair, but also the spring of hope' (Diab 2015b), in 2015 elections they reached a third position without signing either an agreement with the Zionist Camp or one with Meretz, as the Palestinian leaders claimed that those parties have only represented an intra-Jewish discourse.

Seen as a political transformation among '48 Palestinians, as the Palestinian citizens of Israel prefer to define themselves, the united front of the Joint Arab List has been also considered as a potential tool to counter the calls to boycott the elections that have frequently been made in previous times. In order to achieve this strategic aim, one of their major focuses has continued to be the Palestinian national identity, since this is the core issue which determines their methods of resistance and internal struggle, and this approach is especially supported by generations of Palestinians who have increasingly identified their social as well as political objectives in terms of a collective national struggle of non-Jews in a majority Jewish society.

In support of this political initiative, several Israeli Jewish radical leftists voted for the Joint List. The discourse surrounding these developments owes much to those activists who have gone on fighting against the exclusive status of Israel, in which only a powerful section of society has rights and privileges and calling for a state that will be able to adopt an inclusive vision among all its citizens. With the primary aim of questioning the idea of Israel as a place only for Jews, but also going beyond their common feeling of disillusionment, this push for political transformation has obtained significant encouragement from within the Israeli radical left-wing, in spite of uncertainty as to whether it represents a real change. By speaking on behalf of the most oppressed people within Israel, they have declared themselves to represent not only the interests of the Palestinian citizens of Israel, but also of Israeli Jewish voters supporting a political project through which Israel will move from being a Jewish state to a state for all its citizens. For such reasons, several Israeli Jewish radical leftists have given their vote to the Joint List, as Guy Butavia has confirmed in this statement made prior to the election:

> generally I do not believe that change will come from within the Israeli public, I do not see any change coming from the next elections. The only thing that has changed is that the Arab parties are united, it is good, but I am not sure it will be really effective. I do not know if it is good to be part of this game or not, it is also a question for myself. I'm going to vote because of this Joint Arab List, but I am not sure if we will create any difference. (Butavia 2015)

Although this list looked beyond the deterministic idea that '48 Palestinians cannot be represented by prominent leaders and cannot influence the Israeli political structure, a number of critical statements have been expressed from different perspectives, calling attention to the role of Palestinian political parties as well as grassroots movements inside Israel. First, what has emerged from the 2015 elections has demonstrated how the Joint List can be considered an important step forward, but more in terms of symbolism than as a real transformation based on the effective representation of Palestinians within the state of Israel. Second, such a political challenge has been questioned saying that 'the List is the wrong antidote, addressing the symptom rather than the root cause' (Sultany 2015) since the enthusiastic celebration of the Joint List has moved the prospect from the issue of inclusion and active participation to a slow but relentless process of exclusion from the Israeli social and political scene, at both formal and grassroots levels. Third, even though the List will not produce any substantial impact on Israeli politics, its role could partially influence the Palestinian Authority, as a result of the evident demise of the two-state solution and its consequential necessity to undertake a new strategy in line with an intra-Palestinian agreement that includes Palestinians from the West Bank, Gaza Strip and also from inside Israel (Pappé in Diab 2015b).

Another major marginalized community of Israeli society, the Mizrahim, have represented heterogeneous standpoints rather than distinctive positions, placing themselves between leftists and rightists, between religious and secular people, and between Palestinians and Ashkenazi Jews (Chetrit 2010; Shenhav 2006). In general terms, the Zionist Left, mainly led by middle-class Ashkenazi Jews, has historically delegitimized the Mizrahi claim, focusing more on the Palestinian cause, on the conflict and on the military occupation, and pretending that there has been not a social, economic, political and cultural gap between Ashkenazim and Mizrahim due to the power asymmetry of the former over the latter (Dahan-Kalev 2004; Ghanem 2010; Lavie 2014; Shenhav 2012). Also, by means of an orientalist approach, the Mizrahim have often been perceived as people coming from underdeveloped countries and without adequate tools, both economically and socio-culturally speaking, to have an influential role in the Left as well as in Israeli society in general. As explained by one of the leading Mizrahi feminist activists and director of Achoti ('Sister' in Hebrew) – for Women in Israel, Shula Keshet:

> there is a huge difference between the situation, the way of living in the Mizrahi, Palestinian and Ethiopian periphery if you compare them to the white Jewish colonies. We are the majority of Israeli society, both Jews and non-Jews, the colored community, such as the Mizrahi, Palestinian, Ethiopian, are being neglected, oppressed, getting a very small percentage of the state budget, while the rich hegemony is white Jewish Ashkenazi, they have always got the most of the state budget. The whole power structure is on their behalf.

> The gaps are in all spheres of life, social, cultural, educational, housing. It's not that the gaps and the oppressions are only in a few issues, they go throughout everything. There are no equal opportunities in the Israeli state, even though they say Israel is the only democracy in the Middle East, the reality is another. (Keshet 2014)

Further to such marginalization and controversial patronage from within the panorama of the Israeli Left, the divide between Ashkenazi and Mizrahi leftists has increasingly enlarged in the most recent years. If solidarity with the most deprived parts of society should have been considered as one of the main founding pillars of the left-wing, on the other side such a socio-economic, political, cultural and ethnic disparity has represented a demagogic discourse – used mainly by the Zionist Left – that has not provided any solution to the problem of power asymmetries inside Israel.

A similar reality has become even more difficult for those Mizrahi radical activists, as told by a few of my interviewees, who are living in between two challenging and, in several cases, opposite narrative identities, namely being leftists and belonging to a community in which the huge majority sustain right-wing and nationalist visions.[10] Accordingly, this has explained the reason why Mizrahi left-wingers have never held influential positions in the Israeli Left arena, though a few Mizrahi political initiatives have been historically recognized, such as the Black Panthers which grew up in the 1970s and is still represented by one of its founders, Reuven Abergel, who called for boycotting of the 2015 elections (Abergel 2015), and the Mizrahi Democratic Rainbow Coalition that has attempted to overcome the separation established among Mizrahim, Palestinians and other marginalized communities experiencing common struggles against analogous inequalities and discriminations.

Another significant component that has been silenced in the Israeli political scenario, and in a few cases excluded from the leftists' voice too, has been represented by women's and feminist movements. Whilst struggling not only for advancement of their rights, but also to recommend an alternative view of society, they have problematized the major challenges women have to face every day, due mainly to ethnic, social, national and economic disparities. Such activists have attempted to bring their differences out, although internal asymmetries have continued to exist among them, as demonstrated by the leading position taken by Ashkenazi middle-class feminists towards women activists coming from the most marginalized communities (Dahan-Kalev 2001; Lavie 2011; Shadmi 2003). In addition, as some of my interviewees have highlighted, a number of feminist activists have suffered from panic and depression following episodes of gender-based violence and sexual harassments that have occurred within the left-wing groups themselves as well as from the attacks of right-wing groups, as happened during the breaking out of extreme violence throughout demonstrations in the summer of 2014, when many of them were standing up against the military operation in the Gaza Strip (Raz 2014; Scheindlin 2014).

Through both the institutional and the grassroots discourse, the building up of a solid relationship and mutual cooperation between women feminist activists and the Zionist Left has been at times problematic. In the specificity of the most recent elections in 2015, even with the increasing number of female member of Knesset elected, especially those belonging to the left-wing, the integration of women's narratives from diverse political groups and identities into decision-making positions has not been feasible, since a gender-focused agenda has been put on the table in a very few occasions (Salaime 2015).

What's more, in relation to the transformation of women's role within social and political movements in the last decade, apart from the most well-known feminist initiatives such as the Coalition of Women for Peace founded in 2000 by the union of nine feminist organizations, examples of the most recent ones, such as those called 'Courage' and 'Women Wage Peace', have suggested the enlargement of women's participation beyond past paradigms and approaches. Whilst the current forms of women's feminist mobilization have been sometimes put into question by the most historic ones, the intersection of plural narrative identities has needed to accompany any development of women's feminist political activism in the direction of improvement of a broader opposition to the present situation of ongoing violent dehumanization by way of a gendered specific awareness, as underlined by one of the participants in historic feminist activism, Edna Zaretsky-Toledano:

> I really feel that we must bring the very humanistic basic concepts and terminology back, I feel that we as women – although we have also very right-wing women – must work on the concept of humanistic perception. My dignity is your dignity. If I reduce you and de-humanize you I am de-humanizing myself. If there is not security for you, there is not security for me. If we are not going towards the right direction, if we are part of the perception of a Jewish state then we are doomed. I feel responsibility, I am trying to see who we can mobilize, even though we need the help of the world to put pressure on Israel. The situation is exploding, our society has become indifferent to the 'Other', not only the Palestinians, but many 'Others'. (Zaretsky-Toledano 2014)

Such a discourse has also been relevant in relation to the internal debate growing up inside Israeli women's and feminist organizations dealing with asymmetric relationships based on class, ethnic and national disparities and among the women activists them-selves. Therefore, in parallel with what has happened in general terms between the Ashkenazi white middle-class left-wingers and activists from marginalized communities inside Israel, discriminatory actions among and within different women's and feminist backgrounds have taken place (Lavie 2011). On the other hand, and in contrast to the creation of further 'peripheries' defined by geographical, ethnic, political, socio-economic, educational and gendered divisions across the country, many of these women and feminist activists have sustained the necessity of recognizing connections among the numerous forms of power asymmetry that have remained in existence up to the present time.

Among other groups that have often been ignored by the political agenda of the Israeli Left,[11] African migrants and asylum seekers – mostly from Eritrea and Sudan – have experienced extreme difficulties inside the state of Israel, living with threats of jail and deportation by the Israeli authorities. By occupying one of the worst and lowest places in the Israeli societal ranking, especially since the beginning of 2014, when hundreds of protesters demonstrated against the dreadful conditions of detention and difficulty in obtaining refugee status, African asylum seekers have asked recognition as political actors. In such a context, the so-called Marches for Freedom have set out alternative ways of resisting those policies developed by the Israeli government that are hostile to the refugees (Sheen 2015). At the same time, as the Zionist Left has not been involved in such issues, just a few Israeli leftist organizations have provided legal and political assistance to them. One of the activists working in the strategy team to help asylum seekers for logistics, authorizations, and contacts with media, Tamar Aviyah, described:

> they very quick pushed out Israelis, they wanted to run their own struggle. This was the first time I saw Israelis working in total support of, without being involved in the strategy. I was very proud of it. But it fell apart very quickly. [...] The Sudanese activists made very strong campaigns about the great violations of international law these people had to pass through (and also regarding the issue of missing passports), the diplomats were shocked. I do not know any country that sends back its asylum seekers to the exact country where they run away from, only Israel does it. This was ignored by the Israeli NGOs and was not part of the public debate. (Aviyah 2014)

As the above testimony proves, only a tiny group of radical left-leaning activists, along with a few human rights organizations such as Physicians for Human Rights, the Hotline for Refugees, and Assaf – the Aid Organization for Refugees and Asylum Seekers in Israel, have backed the African refugees' voice as a part of the widespread intersectional struggle against oppression and discriminations inside Israel. On the whole, such forms of activism are essentially concentrated on achieving a recognized role in the Israeli political scenario, as an essential step towards obtaining a full citizenship status that does not relegate them to the margins of society.

5. Conclusion

The Israeli current reality has shown an ongoing exclusivist conception of politics, through which it has been possible to preserve considerable gaps of economic, political and cultural power among its citizens. According to the latest electoral results in March 2015, what has become clear is the unfeasibility of reaching internal change in the near future as well as of making progress forward the historical two-state solution (Pappé 2015). Although this outcome has confirmed the trend in the Israeli political panorama which is moving much more towards a narrow-minded neoliberal and ethno-nationalist view, it has also provided a glimpse of some new options that cannot be ignored as potential for managing alternatives to the present impasse.

Whilst in some cases the inclusion of more heterogeneous voices can generate a consequential difficulty in recognizing further internal disparities (Young 1986), I believe a comprehensive analysis of the relationship between the Zionist Left and the most marginalized components of Israeli society is still required in order to understand whether and, if so, in which way, its political legitimacy has progressively declined. In this sense, such a story of hierarchies, divisions and exploitations has been strictly correlated with people's identification with their own class, gender, ethnic, national and political narratives and has created further types of domination and, by contrast, of resistance. In particular, the role of the Zionist Left has been significant in creating the current regime in terms of Ashkenazi Jewish white middle-class hegemony.

Although such a standpoint has been marginal both in the political and academic environments, I argue that this paper can be considered a further contribution towards a workable analytical pathway to be taken to explore the positions of the least visible political players inside Israel, following the lead of the most prominent of the recent works that have critically put into question the contemporary status of Israeli society and politics.[12] In going along with such a prospect, I have primarily questioned the current political legitimacy of the main strategies taken by the Zionist Left since the failure of the Oslo process. Overall, by discussing those alternative political responses to the left-wing mainstream coming from the most marginalized communities and groups, I have attempted to demonstrate that the heterogeneity of these forms of activism can be considered as one of the most valuable tools to be deployed in order to overcome such a particular moment of crisis within Israeli politics.

An important crossroad now seems to have been reached, from which it is possible to look at Israeli internal criticism and give relevance to the different political perspectives emerging from this fragmented scenario, and this can also provoke thought about the way through which such political alternatives might enable transformation from within. In fact, since the end of the 1990s, the Zionist Left has mostly ceased to focus on a just resolution of the conflict and internal issues regarding socio-political struggles against increasing inequalities. On the contrary, it has directed its major political efforts to widen its electorate, with the attempt to include voters from center and other Zionist parties as much as possible, but it has consequently decreased its original political legitimacy, following a common trend occurring in many other countries across the world.

On the other hand, a number of grassroots leftist struggles have still developed alternative political initiatives, which have primarily included the support to the Boycott, Divestment and Sanctions campaign, demonstrations led by popular resistance committees in the occupied Palestinian territories, civil disobedience actions against Israeli governmental decisions and international networking. If a one-state regime has already been set up, and is based on asymmetries of power and privileges, the reversal of this situation is complicated by the fact that such deep-seated asymmetries would be difficult to uproot. Nevertheless, in opposition to this reality, as has been demonstrated by many of my interviewees, a minority inside Israel still believes that it is not time to close the door to looking forward to something different from the present, something that will reverse the current gap between the possible and the existing scenario.

Notes

1. In the end, and by means of a final anti-Arab incitement (Abunimah 2015), Likud won the 2015 elections (30 seats), followed by the Zionist Union (24 seats) and the Joint Arab List (13 seats).
2. In spite of being mostly explained by the spatial and societal dimensions (Cullen and Pretes 2000; Jussila, Roser, and Mutambirwa 1999; Rutledge 2005), I refer to the concept of marginality within the Israeli context to understand the way through which the Zionist hegemony has built up internal divisions and deep gaps among its citizens in relation to social, economic, ethnic, national and gender discriminations. This also concerns the notion of minority that requires to be problematized in relation to what happened in 1948, and, as Hannah Arendt stated, 'the solution of the Jewish question merely produced a new category of refugees, the Arabs, thereby increasing the number of stateless and rightless by another 700,000 to 800,000 people' (Arendt 1951, 290).
3. With reference to both the fieldwork methodology and the political standpoints from which axes of power at the base of class, political, economic, ethnic, national and gender differences in defined historical moments and locations need to be analysed, I have mostly used the 'intersectionality' approach (Crenshaw 1989; Hancock 2007; McCall 2005; Yuval-

Davis 2006, 2011) in order to highlight how various forms of inequalities are strictly intertwined within Israeli society and in the Israeli Left context as well. As regards my fieldwork, in the end of 2014, I have conducted more than thirty open-ended semi-structured interviews with representatives of what I have defined as marginalized communities and groups along with differing class, ethnic, national, age, and gender narrative identities, and who had been involved in diverse initiatives both in relation to the end of the Israeli military occupation in the West Bank and to the most challenging internal issues emerging from within Israel. In addition to the material resulting from my interviews, I have also used the documentation from conferences, initiatives and demonstrations organized by such political actors. If it was necessary to participate in some initiatives during my fieldwork in order to maintain the quality of information I was producing, I did this whilst maintaining awareness of my own background and my positionality towards the core of this study.

4. Israeli society has been historically composed of the hegemonic Ashkenazi elite and of other marginalized communities including the Palestinian citizens of Israel, the Mizrahim, the Russian-speaking community, Ethiopians, African asylum seekers and foreign workers.

5. By following the Palestinian call for the BDS – Boycott, Divestment and Sanctions – campaign launched in 2005 (see note 9), Israeli Jewish activists have also decided to support this struggle from within Israel.

6. Founded in 1977, Hadash – the Democratic Front for Peace and Equality – has been based on the aim of uniting 'most of the supporters for peace, equality, democracy and workers' rights, Jews and Arabs, in order to create a political alternative to the government's policy of occupation and exploitation' (from their web site http://www.hadash.org.il/english/). It has represented the party for which Palestinian citizens of Israel have traditionally voted. In 2015 elections, it has participated in a new political entity, known as the Joint List, in partnership with the United Arab List, the National Democratic Assembly (Balad) and the Arab Movement for Renewal (Ta'al).

7. The research centre 'Who Profits from the Occupation' has conducted several studies on the multifaceted boundaries among the settlement industry, economic exploitation and control over population. Their analyses are available at the following web site: www.whoprofits.org/ (accessed 7 September 2015).

8. Although it has maintained a residual formal representation after 2015 elections, this party, which represented a central position within the Zionist Left in the 1990s, has effectively been crushed by the migration of most of its former supporters to either the Zionist Camp or the Joint List.

9. This debate is mainly related to the BDS campaign (Boycott, Divestment and Sanctions) that has represented an economic as well as political initiative, through exertion of strong international pressure. Considered as a primary challenge to be accomplished by many Israeli radical leftist activists since 'it is a rights-based approach, rather than a solution-based approach' (Barkan 2014), this struggle has been initially a Palestinian campaign, before it became international. Since its launch in 2005 by the Palestinian civil society, when its initial statement described it as a 'call for a campaign of boycott, divestment and sanctions against Israel until it complies with international law and Palestinian rights', it has been founded on demands for equality for Palestinians and preventing participation in the mainstream peace negotiations that have only continued to delay the discussion of rights, which is needed in order to achieve a just conflict resolution.

10. In the 2015 electoral scenario, alternative options from the Mizrahi background have emerged for voters: Shas, the ultra-orthodox political party, has used a very powerful electoral message directed towards the large variety of 'invisible Israelis' (Diab 2015a), and Kulanu, a new political party founded by a former Likud member, has focused on socio-economic issues and in particular on the cost of living of the most marginalized people (Omer-Man 2015).

11. Being out of the scope of political interest of the mainstream Left, foreign workers' rights have not been taken into consideration in the public debate at all, even if the numbers of such workers have increased in the past few years, especially those coming from China, Nigeria, Romania, Thailand and the Philippines.
12. Among the most significant works based on critical analyses of the current Israel and on perspectives of alternative politics, see those by Butler (2012), Tikva Honig-Parnass (2011), Smadar Lavie (2014), Ilan Pappé (2014), Shlomo Sand (2014), and Yehouda Shenhav (2012).

Funding

This work was supported by the Centre for Research on Migration, Refugees and Belonging (CMRB) of the University of East London.

References

Abergel, R. 2015. "Israeli Black Panther: Mizrahim Must Boycott the Elections." *Haokets*, February 20.
Abunimah, A. 2015. "On Election Day, Israeli Leaders Step Up Anti-Arab Incitement." *The Electronic Intifada*, March 17.
Arendt, H. 1951. *The Origins of Totalitarianism*. Cleveland: Meridian Books.
Aviyah, T. 2014. "Author interview." Jerusalem, December 3.
B'Tselem. 2015. *Black Flag: The Legal and Moral Implications of the Policy of Attacking Residential Buildings in the Gaza Strip, Summer 2014*. Jerusalem. http://www.btselem.org/download/201501_black_flag_eng.pdf
Barkan, R. 2014. "Author interview." Brussels, October 29.
Bar-On, M. 1996. *In Pursuit of Peace: A History of the Israeli Peace Movement*. Washington: United States Institute of Peace Press.
Butavia, G. 2015. "Author interview." Florence, March 6.
Butler, J. 2012. *Parting Ways: Jewishness and the Critique of Zionism*. New York: Columbia University Press.
Chetrit, S. S. 2010. *Intra-Jewish Conflict in Israel: White Jews, Black Jews*. London: Routledge.
Choudry, A., and D. Kapoor, eds. 2013. *NGOization: Complicity, Contradictions and Prospects*. London: Zed Books.
Crenshaw, K. 1989. "Demarginalizing the Intersection of Race and Sex: A Black Feminist Critique of Antidiscrimination Doctrine, Feminist Theory and Antiracist Politics." *University of Chicago Legal Forum* 1989 (1): 138–167. Article 8.
Cullen, B. T., and M. Pretes. 2000. "The Meaning of Marginality: Interpretations and Perceptions in Social Science." *The Social Science Journal* 37 (2): 215–229. doi:10.1016/S0362-3319(00)00056-2.
Dahan-Kalev, H. 2001. "Tensions in Israeli Feminism: The Mizrahi-Ashkenazi Rift." *Women's Studies International Forum* 24: 669–684. doi:10.1016/S0277-5395(01)00206-0.
Dahan-Kalev, H. 2004. "The *Mizrahim*: Challenging the Ethos of the Melting Pot." In *Who's Left in Israel? Radical Political Alternatives for the Future of Israel*, edited by D. Leon, 161–167. Brighton: Sussex Academic Press.
Davis, U. 2003. *Apartheid Israel*. London: Zed Books.
Derfner, L. 2015. "The Silent Majority of Complacency." *+972 Magazine*, March 14.
Diab, K. 2015a. "The Visible Links between Israel's Invisible Citizens." *Ha'aretz*, February 3.
Diab, K. 2015b. "Palestinians and the Israeli Elections: Spring of Hope amid Winter, of Despair." *Ha'aretz*, March 19.
Filc, D. 2010. *The Political Right in Israel: Different Faces of Jewish Populism*. London: Routledge.
Ghanem, A. 2010. *Ethnic Politics in Israel: The Margins and the Ashkenazi Center*. London: Routledge.

Gordon, N. 2015. "The End of Liberal Zionist Façade." *Counterpunch*, March 20–22.

Gordon, U. 2012. "Israel's 'Tent Protests': The Chilling Effect of Nationalism." *Social Movement Studies* 11 (3–4): 349–355. doi:10.1080/14742837.2012.708832.

Greenstein, R. 2014. *Zionism and Its Discontents: A Century of Radical Dissent in Israel/Palestine.* London: Pluto Press.

Grewal, I., and V. Bernal. 2014. *Theorizing NGOs: States, Feminism, and Neoliberalism.* Durham: Duke University Press.

Grinberg, L. 2010. *Politics and Violence in Israel/Palestine: Democracy Versus Military Rule.* London: Routledge.

Grinberg, L. 2015. "The Three Bullets that Killed Israel's Left-wing Bloc." *+972 Magazine*, February 25.

Hancock, A.-M. 2007. "Intersectionality as a Normative and Empirical Paradigm." *Politics and Gender* 3 (2): 248–254.

Hermann, T. S. 2009. *The Israeli Peace Movement. A Shattered Dream.* Cambridge: Cambridge University Press.

Herzog, H. 2008. "Re/visioning the Women's Movement in Israel." *Citizenship Studies* 12 (3): 265–282. doi:10.1080/13621020802015420.

Hever, S. 2010. *The Political Economy of Israel's Occupation: Repression Beyond Exploitation.* London: Pluto Press.

Honig-Parnass, T. 2011. *False Prophets of Peace: Liberal Zionism and the Struggle for Palestine.* Chicago: Haymarket Books.

Jad, I. 2004. "The NGOization of the Arab Women's Movements." *IDS Bulletin* 35 (4): 34–42. doi:10.1111/j.1759-5436.2004.tb00153.x.

Jussila, H., M. Roser, and C. C. Mutambirwa. 1999. *Marginality in Space – Past, Present and Future: Theoretical and Methodological Aspects of Cultural, Social and Economic Parameters of Marginal and Critical Regions.* Farnham: Ashgate.

Kaminer, R. 1996. *The Politics of Protest: The Israeli Peace Movement and The Palestinian Intifada.* Eastbourne: Sussex Academic Press.

Karpf, A., B. Klug, J. Rose, and B. Rosenbaum. 2008. *A Time to Speak Out: Independent Jewish Voices on Israel, Zionism and Jewish Identity.* London: Verso.

Kemp, A., D. Newman, U. Ram, and O. Yiftachel. 2004. *Israelis in Conflict: Hegemonies, Identities and Challenges.* Eastbourne: Sussex Academic Press.

Keshet, S. 2014. "Author Interview." Haifa, December 2.

Kimmerling, B. 2008. *Clash of Identities: Explorations in Israeli and Palestinian Societies.* New York: Columbia University Press.

Lang, S. 2013. *NGOs, Civil Society, and the Public Sphere.* Cambridge: Cambridge University Press.

Lavie, S. 2011. "Mizrahi Feminism and the Question of Palestine." *Journal of Middle East Women's Studies* 7 (2): 56–88. doi:10.2979/jmiddeastwomstud.7.2.56.

Lavie, S. 2014. *Wrapped in the Flag of Israel: Mizrahi Single Mothers and Bureaucratic Torture.* New York: Berghahn.

Leibner, G. 2012. "An Israeli Spring? Critical Reflections on the Israeli Mass Protests." http://www.tarabut.info/en/articles/article/summer-of-protest-2011/

Leon, D., ed. 2004. *Who's Left in Israel? Radical Political Alternatives for the Future of Israel.* Brighton: Sussex Academic Press.

Levy, G. 2009. "Does Zionism Legitimize Every Act of Violence?" *Ha'aretz*, February 12.

Levy, G. 2011. "The Tent Protesters Must Graduate to Second Grade." *Ha'aretz*, July 28.

McCall, L. 2005. "The Complexity of Intersectionality." *Signs: Journal of Women in Culture and Society* 30 (3): 1771–1800. doi:10.1086/426800.

Mualem, M. 2014. "Intolerance Becoming All Too Common in Israel." *Al-Monitor*, July 14.

Neiman, O. 2014. Author Interview. Sheikh Jarrah, November 26.

OECD. 2014. "Society at a Glance 2014 Highlights: Israel OECD Social Indicators." March. http://www.oecd.org/els/soc/OECD2014-SocietyAtAGlance2014.pdf

Ohayon, S. 2011. "Speech at the Tel Aviv Rally." August 6. http://www.kibush.co.il

Omer-Man, M. S. 2015. "Does Herzog Have a Chance at Unseating Netanyahu?" *+972 Magazine*, February 22.

Pappé, I. 2001. "The Decline and Fall of the Israeli Left." *Al-Ahram Weekly*, September 27- October 3.

Pappé, I. 2014. "Israel's Incremental Genocide in the Gaza Ghetto." *The Electronic Intifada*, July 13.

Pappé, I. 2015. "The Messages from Israel's Election." *The Electronic Intifada*, March 20.

Pappé, I., and J. Hilal, eds. 2010. *Across the Wall: Narratives of Israeli-Palestinian History*. London: I.B. Tauris.

Pedahzur, A. 2012. *The Triumph of Israel's Radical Right*. Oxford: Oxford University Press.

Piterberg, G. 2008. *The Returns of Zionism: Myths, Politics and Scholarship in Israel*. London: Verso.

Ram, U. 2011. *Israeli Nationalism: Social Conflicts and the Politics of Knowledge*. London: Routledge.

Raz, O. 2014. "'Unprecedented' Violence Stalks Anti-war Demos across Israel." *+972 Magazine*, July 29.

Reider, D., and A. Abu Sarah. 2011. "In Israel, the Rent Is Too Damn High." *The New York Times*, August 3.

Rutledge, D. M. 2005. *Marginality, Power, and Social Structure: Issues in Race, Class and Gender*. Oxford: Elsevier.

Salaime, S. 2015. "More Female MKs Doesn't Mean a More Feminist Knesset." *+972 Magazine*, April 1.

Sand, S. 2014. *How I Stopped Being A Jew*. London: Verso.

Scheindlin, D. 2014. "What Israelis Really Mean When We Talk about the Left." *+972 Magazine*, October 13.

Shadmi, E. 2003. "Being a Feminist Peace Activist—and Ashkenazi." *Nashim: A Journal of Jewish Women's Studies & Gender Issues* 6: 52–55.

Shafir, G., and Y. Peled. 2002. *Being Israeli: The Dynamics of Multiple Citizenship*. Cambridge: Cambridge University Press.

Sheen, D. 2015. http://www.davidsheen.com

Shenhav, Y. 2006. *The Arab Jews: A Postcolonial Reading of Nationalism, Religion, and Ethnicity*. Stanford: Stanford University Press.

Shenhav, Y. 2012. *Beyond the Two State Solution: A Jewish Political Essay*. Cambridge: Polity Press.

Sherwood, H. 2011. "Tel Aviv's 'Tent City' Protesters Dig in to Demand Social Justice." *The Guardian*, August 4.

Shlaim, A. 2005. "The Rise and Fall of the Oslo Peace Process." In *International Relations of the Middle East*, edited by L. Fawcett, 241–261. Oxford: Oxford University Press.

Sultany, N. 2015. "The Joint List: The Fetishism of Representation and the Illusion of Influence." *Jadaliyya*, April 15.

Veracini, L. 2006. *Israel and Settler Society*. London: Pluto Press.

Veracini, L. 2010. *Settler Colonialism: A Theoretical Overview*. Basingstoke: Palgrave Macmillan.

Wolfe, P. 1999. *Settler Colonialism and the Transformation of Anthropology*. London: Cassell.

Yiftachel, O. 2006. *Ethnocracy: Land and Identity Politics in Israel/Palestine*. Philadelphia: University of Pennsylvania Press.

Yahni, S. 2014. *Author interview*. Jerusalem, November 30.

Young, I. M. 1986. "Deferring Group Representation." In *Nomos: Group Rights*, edited by W. Kymlicka, and I. Shapiro, 349–376. New York: New York University Press.

Yuval-Davis, N. 2006. "Intersectionality and Feminist Politics." *European Journal of Women's Studies* 13 (3): 193–209. doi:10.1177/1350506806065752.

Yuval-Davis, N. 2011. *Power, Intersectionality and the Politics of Belonging*. FREIA Working Paper Series n. 75. Aalborg: Feminist Research Center in Aalborg (FREIA), Aalborg Universitet.

Zaretsky-Toledano, E. 2014. "Author interview." Haifa, November 20.

Zonszein, M. 2014. "How Israel Silences Dissent." *The New York Times*, September 26.

The Israeli left: part of the problem or the solution? A response to Giulia Daniele

Lana Tatour

This is a reply to:

Daniele, Giulia. 2016. "Looking for a new legitimacy: internal challenges within the Israeli Left?" *Global Discourse* 6 (3): 470–486. http://dx.doi.org/10.1080/23269995.2016.1152789.

In her paper, 'Looking for new legitimacy: internal challenges within the Israeli Left', Giulia Daniele explores the legitimacy crisis of the Israeli Zionist left. Daniele overviews the long-standing legitimacy crisis of the Israeli Zionist left since the failure of the Oslo Accords, focusing in particular on the aftermath of the 2015 Knesset elections. This crisis in the Israeli left is not new. In fact, the Israeli left has consistently been out of power since the 1977 Begin Likud Government, except for two short periods, namely the Rabin-Peres Government during 1992–1995 and the Barak Government between 1999 and 2001. The Rabin-Peres Government came to an end with the assassination of Prime Minister Yitzhak Rabin after the Oslo Accords, and the Barak Government marked the beginning of the 'no Palestinian partner for peace' paradigm. Today, as the recent elections show, there are no real prospects of the Zionist/centre left returning to power in the foreseeable future. A recent poll conducted by Pew Research Centre, a Washington-based think tank, shows that only 8% of Jewish Israelis consider themselves to be 'leftists' (Pew Research Centre 2016). As Smadar Lavie points out, 'in Israel today, there is virtually no political left' (Lavie 2014, 64).

As Daniele convincingly argues, this crisis is rooted in the left's failure to represent and promote issues of intersectional injustice amongst Israel's most marginalised communities. Daniele then proposes that the recent flourishing of alternative political organising by marginalised groups, such as the Mizrahi, the Palestinians in Israel and the 'new' radical left,[1] offers insights into revitalising a new counter-hegemonic force within the Israeli left. This mobilisation of the most marginalised groups within Israeli society, Daniele argues, has 'called into question the Zionist hegemonic structure of Israeli society' (3). In Daniele's view, carving a space for the most marginalised to articulate their critical points of view 'could enable the building up of a new and broader legitimacy within the Israeli leftist political arena' (1). But do any of these political mobilisations have the potential to become viable alternatives? And is the answer to Israeli settler colonialism the revival of the Israeli left? Are all the marginalised groups that Daniele identifies committed to 'opposing the Zionist hegemonic mainstream' (3)? I argue that the left's pursuit of cross-sector alliances is not a solution. It fails to see the ways in which marginalised Israeli groups such as the Mizrahi are invested in the settler-colonial state. It also fails to acknowledge the uniquely vulnerable position that Palestinians occupy as an indigenous population. As opposed to revitalising the Israeli left, I suggest, we need to look more radical demands for decolonisation and deracialisation.

Daniele's compelling focus on race, ethnicity, nationality, class and gender as intersecting axes of inequality, marginalisation and exclusion offers new insights into how alternative political organising of the most marginalised may have a counter-hegemonic role in Israeli politics. However, Daniele's analysis, I argue, overlooks the important distinction between resistance to Ashkenazi hegemony and resistance to Zionism as a supremacist settler colonial project. This is a fundamental distinction in settler colonial contexts. While the former is a project of state reformism premised on a demand for inclusion as equals into the settler regime, the latter more radically demands both decolonisation and deracialisation of the Israeli state.

Daniele's assumption that all forms of alternative political organising necessarily equates to rejecting Zionist hegemony reveals a slippage between marginality and anti-Zionism. This slippage is particularly evident in Daniele's analysis of Mizrahi political organising. It is questionable whether Mizrahi mobilisation could be applauded as a significant political alternative to Zionism. Indeed, Zionism as a white settler colonial project marked by the 'nexus of racial and colonial power' (Morgensen 2014) has been complicated by the ambivalent folding of non-white Mizrahi Jews into the larger racial category of 'Jewishness', albeit as inferior to Ashkenazi Jews. However, while analysing the ambivalent and liminal position of Mizrahim in Zionism does help to reveal racial structures that shape the Zionist settler project and the political, economic and cultural subaltern positionality of Mizrahim in Israel, the possibility of translating their positionality into a political programme of decolonisation is slim. Moreover, while the spirit of Mizrahi-Arab solidarity has long been part of the history of Mizrahi (radical) organising (Roby 2015; Samuel 2016), movements such as the Mizrahi Democratic Rainbow and the newly established Mizrahi Palestinian Partnership[2] are not grounded in Mizrahi communities. These movements remain limited to the realm of political symbolism and only speak to small elite.

Daniele's characterisation of the Mizrahim struggle as counter-hegemonic to Zionism is a common tendency in postcolonial studies on Mizrahim. This tendency fails to recognise how the Mizrahim remain ideologically committed to Zionism. Daniele's characterisation of the Mizrahi struggle also overlooks how over time Mizrahim have become 'more establishment, more traditional and more Zionist' (Tubul 2015, translation from Hebrew). As Nissim Mizrachi (2011) argues, the Mizrahi's support of the Israeli right is not just a counter-reaction to Ashkenazi domination and decades of political, economic and cultural repression, nor is it a mere form of 'false consciousness' as often suggested in critical studies (see Filc 2010; Shalom-Chetrit 2006; Shohat 1988; Swirski 1981). Rather, Mizrahi rejection of the liberal grammar of human rights is deeply rooted in a communitarian and political commitment to safeguarding the racial boundaries of the Jewish national collective (Mizrachi 2011).

Mizrahim are simultaneously both victims and perpetuators of Zionism. They are simultaneously racialised not only as inferior Arabs but also as superior Jews. The latter is no less significant than the former. Mizrahim, therefore, share a Zionist orientalist epistemology that views Jews as racially superior to Arabs. Zionism is not leveraged as a form of strategic essentialism so to gain access to power. It rather reflects the ways in which Mizrahi struggles have internalised and naturalised Zionism as intrinsic to Mizrahi subjectivity. Mizrahi mobilisation and activism is thus about undermining an Ashkenazi hegemony *not* a Zionist one. It is a struggle to expand the category of Jewish entitlement to ensure Mizrahi Jews are as privileged as Ashkenazi Jews. As the slogan of *Tor Hazahav* (The Golden Age) proclaims – a Mizrahi movement recently formed by leading young Mizrahi activists, intellectuals, artists and journalists – 'It is Now Our Turn'.[3]

This trajectory of the Mizrahi struggle – as well as other political movements within Israeli society – calls for our critical consideration of both the viability and the ethics of the radical left's project of seeking new cross-sector political alliances. The 'new' radical left – dominated by Ashkenazi activists – persistently emphasises the need for cross-sector alliances and the 'interlinking of a series of grassroots struggles' (3). Cross-sector alliances, it is argued, is necessary to the formation of a counter-hegemonic meaningful political alternative. For example, on the occasion of the 2015 Land Day, Oren Yiftachel, a prominent Israeli critical scholar, wrote:

> In the 2015 Land Day, it is necessary to think about spatial justice as the flagship for joint struggle that will signify a goal and new hopes for both the social and political left. This struggle will begin by making Land Day into a protest day shared to all the citizens and residents of the state that suffer from the housing, borders and land systems/policies. Such a 'holiday' day will begin to institutionalise a cross-sectoral struggle, and will ensure what is common sense – that an equal form of Arab-Jewish partnership, together with creating an political umbrella that joins Ashkenazi-Mizrahi-Russian and even religious communities that will work together for a just society – is a necessity to stop the colonisation and privatisation that harm most of the nation. Only this way we can change the government. (Yiftachel 2015, translation from Hebrew)

However, as Vine Deloria, a prominent Native American intellectual has argued, 'to bring about a radical change in present structure … depends upon how clearly those people advocating change want a change and *understand the system they are facing*' (Deloria [1970] 2007, 67, emphasis added). Daniele does not seem to consider that politics of solidarity and alliance cannot be disassociated from the fundamental question of the legitimacy of the Israeli settler colonial regime. It also cannot overlook the power relations and racial hierarchies between the different groups that make up the alternative left. The end game is a regime change, not merely a change of government as suggested by Yiftachael. The demand of the Israeli left for joint resistance and cross-sectoral alliances asks Palestinians (and Mizrahim, though in different ways) to carry the Ashkenazi (white) radical left burden, and is characterised by an orientalist and romanticised pursuit of an alliance with – and between – people of colour.

Furthermore, the radical left's pursuit of cross-sector alliances is often done at the cost of failing to destabilise the racialised settler colonial project. This illuminates the insidious ways in which 'the contours of political solidarity continue to be indelibly shaped by race' (Hooker 2009, 4). The Israeli left's political projects are marked by, in Juliet Hooker's terms, a 'racialised solidarity'. The 'social fact of race shapes the practice of solidarity and the challenges this poses to the project of achieving racial justice' (4). The expectation that Palestinians join groups committed to entrenching rather than displacing settler agency is a manifestation of racialised solidarity. How can Palestinians be asked to support Mizrahi demands for redistribution of state (Palestinian) land to the Jewish population? How can they be asked to support calls for 'affordable housing' which overlook the history and present reality of ethnic cleansing and dispossession? With no feasible prospects of forming a meaningful leftist political alternative, it is no coincidence that the privileged Ashkenazi radical left (in collaboration with a small number of colonised Palestinian intellectuals) emphasises the necessity of intersecting struggles. As Audri Lorde has pointedly stated:

> this is an old and primary tool of all oppressors to keep the oppressed occupied with the master's concerns [in this case the master's fantasies] … This is a diversion of energies and a tragic repetition of racist patriarchal thought. (Lorde 1984, 113)

Furthermore, focusing on politics of alliance as way to rebuild a new radical Israeli left rests on the problematic assumption that Palestinians are on par with other groups in Israeli society. Reading Palestinian struggle as part of an Israeli left project risks appropriating Palestinians into Israel's settler national body politic and normalising settler sovereignty. If we are to take the structure of settler colonialism seriously, we need to acknowledge the unique position that Palestinians occupy as an indigenous population in a settler-colonial state. Palestinians – as opposed to all Jewish populations regardless of their marginal position in Israeli society – are neither part of the settler collective agency nor the multiethnic make-up of Israeli society. Settler colonialism, as Frantz Fanon reminds us, 'is a world cut in two': settlers and natives (Fanon 1963, 38). The necropolitics of settler colonialism as a project of elimination (Wolfe 2006) renders the indigenous Palestinians to 'the status of living dead' (Mbembe 2003, 40). Thus, the struggle of Palestinians is a unique one that cannot be assimilated within a broader narrative of cross-sector mobilisation. The Palestinian experience is that of indigenous peoples governed by racialised regime of citizenship where political and civil rights are bifurcated along racist lines (Mamdani 2015).

Rebuilding the Israeli left through the 'alliance paradigm' is not the panacea for Palestinians living under extreme conditions of colonial violence. Indigenous Palestinians who are subjected to discrimination, ethnic cleaning, occupation, apartheid, inhumane sieging and death do not have the luxury of waiting for a 'transformation from within' (15) because 'it is not the time to close the door' (16). For the most part, the Israeli left's 'alliance paradigm' only offers a racialised solidarity. True decolonisation, as Frantz Fanon reminds us, is nothing less than 'a complete calling in question of the colonial situation' (Fanon 1963, 37).

Notes

1. Daniele's classification of the radical anti-Zionist leftist groups as one of the most marginalised communities in Israeli society is puzzling. While they are a very small minority targeted by right wing politicians, groups and Israeli media for their anti-Zionist political stance, it is hard to justify their classification as a disadvantaged population, certainly not in relation to axes of race, ethnicity or class. Intersectionality shapes not only disadvantage but also privilege. The radical Israeli left is constituted of, by and large, privileged Ashkenazi activists who enjoy access to power and political, economic and cultural capital. Even more so, Ashkenazi radical leftists often point that their privilege comes with responsibility. They, therefore, argue that it is their duty to use their privileged position as an asset in order to challenge the differentiated

rights regime that is at the heart of the Zionist racial project. Thus, their marginal position within Israeli society is limited to their anti-Zionist stance and their characterisation as enemies of the state and the nation. Similarly, commitment to intersectional approach should lead us to question the extent to which Ashkenazi leftist anti-Zionist feminist women are in a marginalised position in Israeli society, especially when compared with Arab, Ethiopian, Mizrahi, migrant, refugee and asylum-seeking women *and* men. Nonetheless, by being anti-Zionist, the radical left is an important counter-hegemonic force in Israel.

2. For more information on the newly established Mizrahi–Palestinian partnership, see Noy (2016). For their political manifesto, please see Declaration: The Joint Mizrahi Initiative (2016).
3. For more information, see Galili (2016). Also see Tor Hazahav website, http://www.tor-hazahav.org, accessed 20 April 2016 (Hebrew).

References

Daniele, G. 2016. "Looking for a New Legitimacy: Internal Challenges within the Israeli Left?." *Global Discourse* 6 (3): 470–486. doi:10.1080/23269995.2016.1152789.

Declaration: The Joint Mizrahi Initiative. 2016. "Haokets: Critical Platform on Socioeconomic, Political, Media, Cultural and other Issues in Israel and Beyond." March 15. (Hebrew). Accessed April 20, 2016. http://www.haokets.org/2016/03/15/%D7%A7%D7%95%D7%9C-%D7%A7%D7%95%D7%A8%D7%90-%D7%99%D7%95%D7%96%D7%9E%D7%94-%D7%9E%D7%96%D7%A8%D7%97%D7%99%D7%AA-%D7%9E%D7%A9%D7%95%D7%AA%D7%A4%D7%AA-%D8%A7%D9%84%D8%B4%D8%B1%D9%82%D9%8A%D8%A9-%D8%A7/

Deloria, V. [1970] 2007. *We Talk, You listen: New Tribes, New Turf*. Lincoln: University of Nebraska Press.

Fanon, F. 1963. *The Wretched of the Earth*. New York: Grove Press.

Filc, D. 2010. *The Political Right in Israel: Different Faces of Jewish Populism*. London: Routledge.

Galili, L. 2016. "Meet the Israelis Calling for a New Golden Age." *i24 News*, February 25. Accessed April 20, 2016. http://www.i24news.tv/en/news/israel/society/104107-160225-meet-the-israelis-calling-for-a-new-golden-age

Hooker, J. 2009. *Race and the Politics of Solidarity*. Oxford: Oxford University Press.

Lavie, S. 2014. *Wrapped in the Flag of Israel: Mizrahi Single Mothers and Bureaucratic Torture*. New York: Berghahn Books.

Lorde, A. 1984. *Sister Outsider: Essays and Speeches*. New York: Crossing Press.

Mamdani, M. 2015. "Settler Colonialism: Then and Now." *Critical Inquiry* 41 (3): 596–614. doi:10.1086/680088.

Mbembe, A. 2003. "Necropolitics." *Public Culture* 15 (1): 11–40. doi:10.1215/08992363-15-1-11.

Mizrachi, N. 2011. "Beyond the Garden and the Jungle: On the Social Limits of Human Rights Discourse in Israel." *Maasei Mishpat* 4: 51–74. (Hebrew).

Morgensen, S. L. 2014. "White Settlers and Indigenous Solidarity: Confronting White Supremacy, Answering Decolonial Alliances." *Decolonization, Indigeneity, Education and Society*, May 26. Accessed April 19, 2016. https://decolonization.wordpress.com/2014/05/26/white-settlers-and-indigenous-solidarity-confronting-white-supremacy-answering-decolonial-alliances/

Noy, O. 2016. "Meet the Mizrahi Activists Who Support the Joint List." *+972*, March 19. Accessed April 19, 2016. http://972mag.com/meet-the-mizrahi-activists-who-support-the-joint-list/117952/

Pew Research Center. 2016. *Israel's Religiously Divided Society*. Washington, DC: Pew Research Center.

Roby, B. K. 2015. *The Mizrahi Era of Rebellion: Israel's Forgotten Civil Rights Struggle, 1948-1966*. Syracuse, NY: Syracuse University Press.

Samuel, S. 2016. "The Mizrahi-Palestinian Intersectionality Nobody's Talking About." *Forward*, March 13. Accessed April 19, 2016. http://forward.com/opinion/335609/the-mizrahi-palestinian-intersectionality-nobodys-talking-about/

Shalom-Chetrit, S. 2006. *The Mizrahi Struggle in Israel between Oppression and Liberation, Identification and Alternative 1948-2003*. Tel Aviv: Am Oved Publishers LTD. (Hebrew).

Shohat, E. 1988. "Sephardim in Israel: Zionism from the Standpoint of Its Jewish Victims." *Social Text* 19: 1–35. doi:10.2307/466176.

Swirski, S. 1981. *Orientals and Ashkenazim in Israel: The Ethnic Division of Labour*. Haifa: Notebooks for Research and Critique. (Hebrew).

Tubul, O. 2015. "Athalta De-Geula: The Mizrahi Discourse Looks at Itself in the Mirror and Sees Itself for the First Time." *Haokets: Ctirical Platform on Socioeconomic, Political, Media, Cultural and other Issues in Israel and Beyond*, May 7 (Hebrew). Accessed April 19, 2016. http://www.haokets. org/2015/09/07/%D7%90%D7%AA%D7%97%D7%9C%D7%AA%D7%90-%D7%93%D7%92% D7%90%D7%95%D7%9C%D7%94-%D7%94%D7%A9%D7%99%D7%97-%D7%94%D7%9E% D7%96%D7%A8%D7%97%D7%99-%D7%9E%D7%A1%D7%AA%D7%9B%D7%9C-%D7%91% D7%9E%D7%A8%D7%90%D7%94/

Wolfe, P. 2006. "Settler Colonialism and the Elimination of the Native." *Journal of Genocide Research* 8 (4): 387–409. doi:10.1080/14623520601056240.

Yiftachel, O. 2015. "Land Day - A Day of Struggle for Spatial Justice for All." *Haokets: Ctirical Platform on Socioeconomic, Political, Media, Cultural and other Issues in Israel and Beyond*, March 30 (Hebrew). Accessed April 20, 2016. http://www.haokets.org/2015/03/31/%D7%99%D7%95% D7%9D-%D7%94%D7%90%D7%93%D7%9E%D7%94-%D7%99%D7%95%D7%9D-%D7%94% D7%9E%D7%90%D7%91%D7%A7-%D7%9C%D7%A6%D7%93%D7%A7-%D7%9E%D7%A8% D7%97%D7%91%D7%99-%D7%A9%D7%9C-%D7%9B%D7%95%D7%9C%D7%9D/

Body politics and legitimacy: towards a feminist epistemology of the Egyptian revolution

Lucia Sorbera

ABSTRACT

In this essay, I discuss political legitimacy from a feminist perspective, analysing the experience of women political activists in Egypt. Building on Linda Alcoff's work on memory, testimony and decolonizing epistemology, my analysis focusses on two intertwined issues: women's political representation and the public debate about sexual harassment. Data collected by Egyptian feminist organizations reveal that, after one century of women's political participation and 60 years after universal suffrage, the gender gap remains wide. Furthermore, both feminist and human rights organizations denounce that authoritarian regimes use sexual harassment to intimidate democratic activists. Although the right to equal political participation has been a main concern for the Egyptian feminists since 1923, the achievement of universal suffrage in 1956 did not provide a viable solution to the gender gap in Egypt, and women are still fighting to find a way out from the binary co-optation/exclusion. Significantly, as I discuss in this essay, women political activists are the main targets of harassment. In addition, women in general and discourses about sexual violence and sexual morality remain highly controversial in Egypt.

Introduction

Public discussion about political legitimacy in Egypt has historically intersected discourses about identities, which are an integral part of the history of Arab political thought. During each period of social reform and reorganization of the political system, the debate over women and their bodies has always been central to and afforded an insight into broader politics and forms of power in Egypt as elsewhere (e.g. Baron 2005 on the 'querelle des femmes' and Egyptian modernity). In seeking to assert and to reinforce patriarchal views of gender and of political legitimacy, and to silence women's political agency, ruling elites and their religious counterparts have attempted to redefine and discipline the spaces for women's social and political visibility through women's bodies themselves. As a result, both feminist critiques of both indigenous and international patriarchal visions of power and the alternatives these critiques foreshadow have been largely concealed from outside observers, overshadowed by culturally essentialist and Orientalist discourses.

One of the hallmarks of the January 2011 revolution was precisely to negotiate multiple identities and to articulate an inclusive notion of political legitimacy, acknowledging the demand for social justice and rejecting patriarchal deployments of arguments about the secular–religious divide. This rejection helped shed new light on a range of alternative actors, from a new wave of feminists, post-ideological youth movements to independent trade unions. As such, it was central to the revolutionary attempt to reorganize the body politic. Unfortunately, this inclusive and nonidentity master-signifier did not last for long, soon challenged by a renewed identity politics the function of which was to help prevent the fulfilment of revolutionary demands for inclusiveness across classes, religions, gender and generations. Significantly, sexual violence against women political activists and women generally, coupled with their marginalization in formal political institutions, again became routine in Egypt. Like any attempt at marginalizing a particular dissenting/alternative voice, this move to silence/discredit reveals the regime's (sense of its own) weakness, both in general and specifically with regard to the revolution and to women.

In this essay, I relate women's experience of political activism in the 2011 revolution to the concept of political legitimacy, and I argue that the religious versus secular opposition is not productive in understanding gendered power relations in Egypt. I suggest that women are simultaneously key subjects and objects of political discourses and that efforts to define and discipline women's bodies reveal attempts to legitimize or delegitimize both women activists and issues, and competing political actors attempt to keep or make women subservient far beyond politics.

This research is influenced by Linda Alcoff's contribution to feminist epistemology, especially her focus on experience, testimony and memory. When talking about women's experience, their testimony and memories, truth is always questioned and their experience as episteme is challenged. Memory is not just the product of experience but it is affected by the socio-politics of each discourse at a specific epoch of history. As Alcoff puts it:

> The pursuit of truth will be enhanced if we come to a better understanding of how the domains of knowledge emerge, are delimited and constrained by the peculiar ways in which concepts are formed in different historical moments, this means that we can make an epistemic evaluation of contrasting notions of the relation between sexual practices and identity. (Alcoff 2011, 222)

The notion of testimonial episteme can be productively related to the specific context of the Egyptian revolution. Collective memory is a space of continuous and politicized contestation, and post-2011 Egypt is no exception, with competing political forces claiming the legitimacy of the Revolution. Under the current military regime, which is increasingly now violently targeting intellectuals, researchers, journalists and writers, there is a concerted effort by the new regime to rewrite the collective memory of the history of the 2011 uprising. While those versions might encounter popular scepticism, and while the memory of the events of 2011 is alive with those who took part in the protests, what will be consigned to collective memory risks remaining closer to the former than to the latter. A feminist epistemology of the Revolution challenges authoritarian narratives. My work of collecting women's oral and written testimonies of the Egyptian Revolution is part of a broader and collective feminist work to contrast the counter-revolutionary narratives and the male-dominated militarization of political space. Feminist oral history does not exclude male testimonies, but it situates the latter at the intersection of class, ethnicity and gender relations, structures of power and people's resistance to them (Sangster 1994). The feminist focus on experience, testimony and memory allows investigation of how power shapes the construction of historical memory and contributes to reformulate historical questions. The same reformulation of questions occurs in feminist epistemology (Alcoff 2000, 842), where the focus on memory and on subjective experience allows for questioning the normative definition of legitimate political authority, traditionally conceived as a result of consent within a constitutional frame, and critiquing the notion that the legal domain is the only venue for justice.

During several phases of fieldwork in Cairo between 2011 and 2014, I conducted numerous interviews with women and men activists and conducted participant obser-vation of feminist conferences and workshops, continuing the conversation when I was away from the field through my collection of women's memoirs of the revolution, media and social media interventions, NGO reports and academic analyses. I study and inter-pret these sources in the context of Egyptian political history, charting the experiences of contemporary political women's activism. Through this empirical research, I address a theoretical question that, as I argue, transcends the Egyptian national space, investing the global public sphere: in times of deep political crisis of representative institutions, what is the relationship between power and politics, and between authority and accountability? Gender is a useful category to address these questions, and Egypt, whose current regime claims legitimacy on continuous calls to maintain the country's stability and to ensure its security through the militarization of the public sphere, is a key space to understand these processes.

I will focus on the intersection of two highly debated issues: 'sexual harassment' or, as Paul Amar aptly puts it 'the sexualized assault and terrorizing of women activists' (Amar 2013, 200), and women's political participation and representation. I will discuss the entanglements between these two issues to show the link between sexuality and politics in current political discourse about legitimacy.

Disciplining women's bodies and policing people: the decline of Mubarak's regime

Henri Lefebvre writes that 'A revolution takes place when and only when … people can no longer lead their everyday lives' (Lefebvre 1991, 75). This observation fits Egypt, where the crisis of political legitimacy exploded in 2011 and is entrenched in a spiral of economic, socio-political and cultural changes that need to be analysed in their histor-ical context. The long-lasting effects of the *infitah* policy – a program of economic liberalization initiated by President Anwar al-Sadat in the early 1970s – and the accel-eration of the neoliberal experiment in the 1990s made Egypt a champion of neoliber-alism and privatization. The rate of poverty among the population reached a very high peak, differences in wealth among people became striking (Marfleet 2009, 17–20) and the State's recourse to violent repression, including torture, against any form of dissidence became routine over the 1990s and the early 2000s (Seif El-Dawla 2009, 120–136). Significantly, it is in this period that the regime advanced a 'pseudo-feminist discourse' (Abouelnagha 2015, 40).

In 1994, Cairo hosted the UN International Conference on Population and Development (ICPD). One year later, the government sent official delegations to the Fourth UN World Conference on Women in Beijing, and then to the Beijing + five Conference in New York.

> Through its official participation in all the relevant regional and international conferences, Egypt has sought to make a serious and effective contribution to international cooperation relating to women in all fields. (CEDAW 1996, 14)

The government was clearly trying to monopolize and to manipulate the international agenda on women, projecting to those outside of the country an image of commitment to women's rights. However, in the background of this politics was a civil society, which, even if harshly repressed by the *nizam*,[1] was acting underground or in the 'other spaces' untouched by the regime.

At the turn of the twenty-first century, feminism in Egypt had matured following a long history where women activists had experienced a range of patriarchal regimes: colonial, liberal, military and socialist. Mubarak's neo-liberal authoritarianism was the last of a long line. In the late 1980s and early 1990s, one decade after the emergence of 'second-wave feminism', a new generation of 'gender activists' (Badran 2009, 242), many of them intellectuals and professionals in the fields of the humanities, health and development, was part of the scene. In the lead-up to the ICPD, the government was compelled to give them space to promote their progressive and feminist agenda (Badran 2009, 295; Human Rights Watch 2005, 1). In this context, women's bodies became the centre of controversial politics, as illustrated by the discourse around female genital mutilation (FGM). In 1994, the Female Genital Mutilation Task Force was instituted and, after 2 years of controversy, decree 261/1996, which reinstated the ban on FGM in hospitals, was issued (Badran 2009, 312). Ironically, in 1991, one of the targets of the regime was the feminist intellectual and activist who first denounced FGM in the 1970s, Nawal al-Saadawi. In 1991, the Arab Women's Solidarity Association, funded and chaired by Saadawi, was forced to close, after its president and other members protested against the Gulf War (Badran 2009, 226, 267).

The double standard adopted by the regime towards women illustrates the link between patriarchy and authoritarianism. Women – like men – could be supported when their claims were not perceived as openly political, and were part of a segregated agenda, not when their approach was intersectional, and questioned the nature of the regime. In addition, women, represented as custodians of national honour, could be supported when the threat was coming from 'uncivilized/pre-modern' practices (such as FGM), which constituted harm to the construction of the image of the modern nation, but not when their presence in the public space subverted modern-patriarchal social norms. It was certainly easier to be anti-FGM than anti other forms of violence against women.

During the 1990s, the political elites tried to delegitimize independent feminist voices. This was very clear in 1996, when a young woman was brutally raped by a group of men at al-Ataba bus station in Cairo. In the growing atmosphere of social conservatism, encouraged by the State and by the Islamists, when the young woman dared to denounce the rape, she was blamed by the national media and the court (Zuhur 2001, 81). The masculine hegemony dominated the approach of the court, where women's testimony and knowledge of self was censured, and masculine juridical/moral legitimacy was imposed.

The tension between women political activists, whose agenda was political, intersecting women's issues with human rights and workers' struggles, and the regime, which was trying to neutralize the impact of women's political participation, again escalated in 2005. That year witnessed the famous constitutional amendments that allowed for the first multicandidate presidential elections in Egypt's history. In addition, 2005 saw the people's Assembly elections where the Muslim Brotherhood won around 20% of the seats for the first time. This coincided with the peak of the *Kifaya* (Enough) movement, a broad democratic mobilization, of which women were an integral part. Significantly, that year there was an intensification of serious episodes of sexual harassment of women political activists. On 25 May 2005, also known as 'Black Wednesday' (*Al-Ahram* 2013), women journalists were sexually assaulted when protesting constitutional amendments, which strengthened Hosni Mubarak's position in power (Al-Nabaa 2005). The regime acted along the same lines as 10 years earlier, blaming the victim. National media conducted a campaign against one of the victims of the assault, the journalist Nawal Ali (Abouelnaga 2015, 39).

Activists remember this episode as the first time they saw sexual harassment organized in a group:

> No one can forget the tragedy of 5/25/2005 when security forces cleared the way for 'thugs' and their men, donning civilian clothes, to violate women in front of Saad Zaghlul's memorial and the Press Syndicate. We cannot forget the words of a policeman to a female protester on that day explaining the violence used against female protesters, 'so you would stop taking part in demonstrations again' (Adly 2013, 2).

Activist testimonies confirm the link between security politics, authoritarianism and economic alignment with the neo-liberal imperialism embraced by the Mubarak regime. Here, the intersection between gender and class representation played a key role in the construction of the regime's narrative. Sexual harassment was either denied, as during the incidents of the 2006 Eid, notwithstanding the documentation by independent bloggers (Abdelmonem 2015, 24), or it was represented as a casual routine of urban working class young men. In the latter case, reasons advanced were social frustration, crisis of marriage, and cultural attitudes, which needed to be censored using unprecedented operations by the police, as occurred in relation to the Eid al-Fitr incident in 2008. The use of sexual harassment as standard operating procedure by security forces was concealed. In the years immediately preceding the 2011 revolution, the regime tried to reduce the issue of sexual harassment in public spaces to a social and cultural problem, in order to avoid the obvious link between sexual harassment, State violence and highly documented violations of human rights by the security apparatus (Abdel Aziz 2007). In these years, and under pressure by international donors, the government's approach to violence against women focussed on domestic violence and FGM, deflecting attention from the State's violence against women in the public space.

Under these circumstances, civil society played a central role in shifting the issue of sexual harassment from the margins to the centre of political debate, as underlined by one of the cofounders of Harrassmap, an initiative launched in 2010 by a team of four young Egyptian and foreign women:

> In 2005 and 2006, when I started volunteering for the Egyptian Centre for Women's Rights (ECWR), the term itself was a taboo, we could not even name it. There was social and political denial back then [...] In those years the Egyptian Centre for Women Rights [ECWR] took the lead. They started doing research and asking women how they experienced the issue. At the time there was nothing on the issue. (Interview, Cairo, 17 October 2014)[2]

The initiative built upon a decade of work carried out by human rights organizations. The main concern of independent women's initiatives and organizations was to research, map, lobby and keep the issue of sexual harassment on the agenda in order to increase people's awareness around the issue and to influence legislators.

In 1994, the New Woman Research Foundation together with El Nadeem Center contributed to the preparatory activities of Egyptian civil society organizations for the 1995 Beijing conference on women by carrying out the first field research on women's perceptions of violence against women. In 2008, ECWR released a study where high rates of exposure to sexual harassment were reported: 83% of Egyptian women and 98% of foreign women experienced sexual harassment in Egypt (Hassan, Shoukry, and Abul-Komsan 2008, 16). The issue came again to public attention in 2008, when young filmmaker Nuha Rushdi was sexually assaulted in the street and decided to file a lawsuit. Unlike what happened 12 years earlier, Nuha Rushdi won the case. At the end of 2010, a few months before the Revolution, Mohamed Diab's film *Cairo678*, inspired by this story and the testimonies collected by ECWR, for the first time brought women's agency to the silver screen in order to contrast the reality of sexual harassment with its denial by the male-dominated political, media and security apparatus.

The National Council for Women (NCW) responded to the ECWR's report, drafting a law against sexual harassment (Hassan, Shoukry, and Abul Komsan 2008, 9), but the initiative did not find institutional support. While civil society was experiencing a season of unprecedented vitality, people appeared disaffected by the electoral process, which appeared void of meaning. This disillusionment was mirrored in the turnout at the 2005 Presidential election, which dropped to 23%.

While independent NGOs denounced women's marginalization at all levels (political, legal and social), the government could hear only international pressures (especially from the United States) to reduce its violations of women's rights and human rights. This resulted in top-down initiatives, such as appointing to leadership positions, some figures who were not perceived as challenging by the regime. In the first decade of the 2000s, Hosni Mubarak appointed the first female judge, a university president, and several cabinet ministers. The regime was attempting to simultaneously stifle political dissent within Egypt and pander to international political agendas by co-opting women's rights issues. Thus, while the new law on divorce, passed in 2000, crowns a long history of feminist activism, on the other hand independent women's associations, like all civil society organizations, were suffocated by restrictive legislation and 'state corporatism' (Human Rights Watch 2005, 1). The NCW, which was established in 2000 by Presidential decree and was chaired by the First Lady, launched two projects, in 2003 and in 2006, to reintroduce a quota system in the elections.[3] However, the atmosphere of political oppression that accompanied these top-down programs made them ineffective. In June 2009, women's quotas were finally reintroduced in Egypt, and 64 seats were allocated to women, increasing the number of seats in the People's Assembly to 518. The goal was to ensure 12% of seats went to women in the forthcoming 2010 elections (in 2005 it was 1%). The mechanism of the electoral law, where women ran in specially designated constituencies, favoured candidates of the hegemonic National Democratic Party. According to Nehad Abu el-Komsan, Chairwoman of the ECWR, who at that time had been lobbying for a women's quota for at least 15 years, this mechanism only reinforced the notion that women should compete separately from men: 'A proportional system would guarantee that women are not isolated; they would be part of the group and this would force the parties to look for active candidates, and to train women and support them at all levels' (Mc Grath 2009).

The debate about the quotas continued after the 2011 Revolution, when the Supreme Council of the Armed Forces (SCAF) repealed the women's quota in the new electoral law.

Women activists' reaction to this measure reveals the ambiguities of the transitional phase. An activist of the National Council for Human Rights associated the 2010 law on the women's quota with the leadership of the former head of the NCW and ex-first lady:

> It was introduced by Suzanne Mubarak ... She wanted to show off.... it was just for herself... And these women candidates in 2010 were not qualified, they didn't have any vision, any plan for the elections. They don't make campaigns for women for example; they were not really interested in serving. (Interview, National Council for Human Rights, Cairo, 7 December 2011)

At the same time, the interviewee appeared concerned about the cancellation of the quota in the electoral law issued by the SCAF: 'I was against the quota system at the beginning, but after the revolution I am concerned about women's situation; without that system it would be too difficult'.

Overall, between the 1990s and 2011, in an atmosphere of growing political oppression and State violence, the regime conceived gender politics as one tool among many to enforce its control over the population and to consolidate its international legitimacy. During that period, independent and oppositional women activists were marginalized, if not repressed. The NCW tended to monopolize the women's agenda, framing it as family-related issues, and tending to neutralize the subversive potential of feminist activism.

Under these circumstances, the space for political agency in formal institutions was very limited, and many feminists brought their experience into civil society. Bringing their second-wave feminist perspective into these organizations, women developed a political approach to gender issues, intersecting sexual violence with economic issues, health and human rights. In the years leading up to the 2011 revolution, the workers and labour movements became spaces where women's activists emerged. ECWR reports that in 2007, a year of extraordinary strikes and protests throughout the whole of Egypt, 3000 women participated in textile workers' strike in El-Mahalla el-Kubra[4]:

> Women's participation in the different strikes reached 75% as was seen in Mahalla, Kafr El-Dawar, Aspanya, and El-Hendawy. Due to the large presence of women in these strikes,

people raised the slogan 'where are the men, the women are there'. Women played a prominent role in urging their colleagues to participate in the strike as what happened in El-Mahalla El Kobra. The recent strikes reflected the strengthening of 'the women's labour role' which has a strong effect on the workers in the factories and mills. Furthermore, it especially reflected that these women refused financial bribery, which is frequently used with male workers. Women reacted strongly against board members when they made illusory promises to them on the condition that they end the strike. Moreover, women are more courageous in demanding rights for workers, because most women are the breadwinner of most households and contribute with their salaries to the household sphere. (ECWR 2008)

Determined to contest the patriarchal discourse on gender which was promoted by the regime, and capable of linking women's issues to broader political, economic and social issues, women NGO-independent activists, feminist intellectuals and workers challenged the legitimacy of the Mubarak regime. They all contributed, from different positions, to disseminating a culture of dissidence, from where the Revolution would eventually flourish.

Body politics against politics of the body in the Egyptian Revolution

The dynamics of resistance against patriarchy, which are rooted in one century of Egyptian feminist history (Badran 1996, 2009), exploded in 2011. In the 18 days of the Egyptian revolution, the images of Tahrir Square showed a renewed – though not new – protagonism by young people in general and women in particular. Multiple and intersecting women's narratives of the Egyptian revolution were displayed from the outset. The first narrative described Tahrir Square in the 18 days as a utopian, inclusive and safe space, an experience that contrasted with the practices of repression, co-optation and violence of Mubarak's regime.

Hundreds of young girls walk free, chanting – and no one has been sexually harassed or molested. The chants are for freedom, dignity and equality–and many are led by women – with men following. Coptic Christians are side by side with Muslims. Even some of the youth of the Muslim Brotherhood told me, 'We disagree with some of your writings but love you because you did not change opportunistically, you have been consistent'. (Saadawi 2011)

The narrative of Tahrir as a safe space for women resonates also in a number of oral history accounts.

Actually I think that in those 18 days there was a Tahrir country inside Egypt. I think I can call it that way because it had its own food and security and no leaders actually… it was like a big complex that they had to protect, the way people were dealing with each other in Tahrir must be in the whole country, that's what I think. I think that they are all one to make it better, because now they are all thinking about their own interests. No sexual harassment or stolen things whatever… no violence except the police against the protestors… it was just amazing … I don't know how people talked about sexual harassment inside the square (Interview, Cairo, 3 December 2011).

Acknowledging the credibility of these memories, as I do, should not lead to an assertion that this was a velvet revolution. Amnesty International reported that in January 2011 'at least 840 people were killed and 6,467 others were injured, according to Ministry of Health and Population sources, and thousands were detained, many of them tortured' (Amnesty International 2011a, 8). These data are confirmed by the

Egyptian NGO El-Nadeem, which published a report with hundreds of testimonies on the violations to which Egyptian people were subjected by the authorities in 2011 (El-Nadeem 2012). In the light of these data, one could question the representation of the revolution as inclusive and women-friendly, and whether it relates to the reality on the field. However, this does not seem to be a relevant issue. These multiple narratives do not appear to be mutually exclusive, but respond to different needs and to different moments. It can be argued that the aim of the utopian narrative was not necessarily to mirror actual reality, not even that of the 18 days: it was rather a conscious revolutionary act, aimed at shaping a new future. This narrative was genuinely optimistic, spontaneous and enthusiastic: it was also strategic, and it became a source of legitimacy for the revolution. Against a mainstream representation of the public space as unsafe, violent and women-unfriendly, it presented the icon of an inclusive and peaceful square, occupied by 'the peaceful people' as opposed to 'the violent regime'. Simultaneously, the act of situating the violated body at the centre of the political struggle against the Mubarak regime was revolutionary and was the core of the oppositional movements that led to the Revolution. The 6 April movement, Kefaya, and the Know Your Rights Campaign mobilized public opinion against police torture (Lesch 2012, 37).

The 2011 revolution has been a space for feminist narratives about the public space, to which the SCAF, the Muslim Brotherhood and Sisi's regime established a counter-narrative of Tahrir Square as a hyper-masculine space for mob assaults, with the aim of 'restoring order' and delegitimizing the revolution. From a feminist perspective, this is a disempowering narrative, which reduces women political activists to victims of violence, neglecting their agency and silencing their voices. This counter-narrative was accompanied by a significant shrinking of the space for women's political action and indeed political action more generally.

March–November 2011: sexual violence under the rule of the SCAF

As early as March 2011, the gendered nature of the securitarian and authoritarian policy promoted by the SCAF, and its attempts to neglect and to attack women political activists, was palpable.

Women were excluded from the first Constitutional Assembly and forbidden to run for elections in the governorates, under the pretext of concerns for their security. In March 2011, the demonstration for International Women's Day was brutally attacked, without any intervention of security forces to forbid it, and 'virginity tests' were inflicted on women political activists arrested on the 9 March. At that time, Amnesty International reported the comment of a General – who later was revealed to be then-Marshal al-Sisi – on the incident, which reveals the SCAF's attitude towards women revolutionary activists:

> The girls who were detained were not like your daughter or mine. These were girls who had camped out in tents with male protestors in Tahrir Square, and we found in the tents Molotov cocktails and drugs. We didn't want them to say we had sexually assaulted or raped them, so we wanted to prove that they weren't virgins in the first place. None of them were. (Amnesty International 2011b)

The epistemological violence of this statement is self-evident. There is no focus on the crime (the rape), and the morality of the victim is questioned. The victim is not considered reliable, she does not deserve any trust, her testimony is delegitimized and her rebel voice silenced by patriarchal speech.

Unanimous solidarity was expressed by feminist activists for Samira Ibrahim, who sued the army officer who had harassed her. The officer was eventually acquitted by a military court, a clear sign that male-dominated justice would prevail, and the counter-revolution was already there.

In 2011 and 2012, violence against women political activists was paralleled by the tendency to exclude them from political institutions. This connection was highlighted in a document issued in September 2011 by a group of women's organizations, the Feminist Coalition, titled: 'Ignoring Women is Unacceptable Particularly at this Critical Stage of Our National History' (NWF 2011). Here, the exclusion of women from the transition process was criticized and the use of violence against women as a political anti-revolutionary weapon was denounced. Claiming the 'long tradition of Egyptian feminism', the statement argued for 'women's partnership in the revolution and in the political process' and rejected women's exclusion from formal political institutions.

At this stage, revolutionary women's action maintained a broad intersectional spectrum. For instance, in March 2011, University professor Leila Sueif and her daughter Mona found out that a civilian was under military trial. They started investigating the issue, and they discovered many similar cases. From there, a campaign developed: *No to Military Trials for Civilians*, which addressed State violence under the SCAF and subsequent regimes. Throughout 2011 and 2012, the centrality of body politics became more and more evident, as illustrated by the public debate around the above-mentioned case of 'virginity testing' and the experiences of the visual artist Alia Mahdi, who in November 2011, a few weeks before the parliamentary elections, posted on her blog a self-portrait where she was naked, to protest against sexism and violence in Egyptian society. Widely discussed, and echoed in popular cultural productions such as graffiti, the two cases show the tension between a delegitimized patriarchy and women who have experienced the revolution. These women were willing to speak about violence and sexuality publicly and 'to transgress the limits placed on their bodies' (Hafez 2014, 184).

While the elections were still ongoing, another episode of violence destined to become iconic took place: a veiled young woman demonstrator was violently dragged and beaten in Tahrir Square by the Egyptian military; she was stripped of her *abeya* (loose full-length robe) and they left her stripped down to her blue bra. The 'blue bra incident' revealed the gendered nature of State violence. Women's reaction was multi-layered: a large demonstration was organized in the days following the incident, and the most prominent feminist creative artists and intellectuals – including Baheia Shehab (2012), Mona Abaza (2013), Ahdaf Soueif (2011), and Laila Soliman (Hussein 2015, 364) – voiced women political activists' outrage. Blue bras became also quite popular in the street market in Cairo, and both Egyptian and international women bought them to express solidarity with the unnamed woman who was attacked.

The violence experienced by women in 2011 led an emerging generation of artists and intellectuals to discuss the relationship between sexual harassment, rape and political domination in their works. Laila Sulaiman's theatre play, *Hawa I-Huriya/Whims of Freedom*, stages an intense parallel between women's experience in the 1919 anti-

British uprisings and the 2011 revolution. In this play, official historical narratives, collected in State archives, are continuously challenged by folk and oral history sources, and the generally neglected narrative produced by women experiencing sexual violence in the context of revolution shifts from the margin of political history to the centre of the stage.

2011 and 2012 were years of continuous mobilization, and women activists challenged the legitimacy of military rule. The chant of the 25th of January (*Yaskut, yaskut ya Mubarak!*/Down, down, to Mubarak) became *Yaskut, yaskut hukm al-askari* (Down, down to military rule) and new oppositional practices took shape. Violence escalated, and confrontations between different components of the revolutionary front, the supporters of the Muslim Brotherhood, and the security forces became more intense.

On the 9 of October 2011, a protest against anti-Coptic sectarianism had set off from Shubra Cairo district, having its final destination Maspero, the State television building. It ended in a brutal massacre, where more than 25 protesters were killed either by the army's bullets or under the wheels of military tanks. One year after the massacre, freelance journalist and blogger Wael Eskandar questioned the legitimacy of the Muslim Brotherhood government, which failed to bring justice.

> Morsi released 1500 protesters not just because his 100 days are over and he has nothing to show but to divert attention from the fatal failing of a regime he is supposed to lead. The failing is reflected in the first memorial of a massacre. One year on and we have not altered our path. The real murderers are still free, some promoted and some retired honorably. Morsi pledged in his speeches that they wouldn't be touched, but his supporters are too adamant to listen to what his words actually mean. They mean that the current state of affairs will be maintained. That hatred and impunity will rule, that soldiers and officers can be free to run us over and that injustices to minorities will prevail. (Eskandar 2012)

Maspero became an open wound in the memory of revolutionary activists (Abdelfattah [2011] 2014; Atallah 2014; Carr 2013; Eskandar 2011; Gaber 2013; Toma 2015), and it was the prelude to more tragedies to come. Between 19 and 24 November 2011, more than 40 people died in clashes on Mohammed Mahmud Street; on 17 December, the Cabinet sit-in was dispersed and 17 people died; on 1 February 2012, after the Egyptian premier league football match in Port Said between al-Ahli and al-Masri, Al-Ahli's supporters were attacked: 74 were killed and 1000 wounded (Hamdi and Karl 2014, 132). Following this series of tragic events, and building on the experience of the collective of media activists *Mosireen* (We are Determined), the campaign *3askar Kazeboon* (Military Liars) was launched. Volunteers took to the streets, not to protest, but to document episodes of violence by security forces and by army officers, and to organize public screenings to show these episodes to a wider audience (DailyNewsEgypt 2012).

These actions aimed at contrasting the dominant narratives, which tended to blame women for being assaulted and raped. The situation escalated until 2013, when some members of the Shura Council (at that time dominated by the Muslim Brotherhood and the Salafi), called for separating men and women during protests to prevent sexual harassment, blamed women for mingling with men during protests and represented men protesters as 'thugs and street inhabitants', adopting a narrative that aimed at restoring class and gender normative boundaries (*Daily News* 2013). The fact that in all these circumstances there were women activists challenging the legitimacy of political authority in office was completely wiped out from the political debate.

In the context of growing State violence and exclusion, new forms of resistance were generated, and new political discourses about gender and political legitimacy were produced. Women activists rejected the idea of victimization and they produced their own narratives of that period. *Words of Women from the Egyptian Revolution*, a series of video interviews of women activists from across the political spectrum, provided an effective counter-narrative to the official ones. Even the words used by women activists to describe their experience shaped a new discourse. For instance, all the documents produced by Nazra for Feminist Studies and by Egyptian Initiative for Personal Rights refer to women who experienced sexual violence and rape as 'survivors' rather than 'victims', while it is evident that the political space is becoming more and more oppressive and the patriarchal State is trying to reappropriate feminist discourses.

Feminist women and men together have challenged normative visions of gender and of security. To protect themselves against sexual mobs during the demonstrations, they set up their own unarmed security groups. Tahrir Bodyguard and OP-Anti-sexual harassment were created out of emergency in 2011, to face sexual mobs. In this context, the State was perceived as sponsoring sexual harassment to intimidate and to delegitimize political activists, or at least as covering it up by its complicity (Kirollos 2013). A discussion developed also among revolutionary activists, on the approach to be taken with regard to sexual harassment. Some of my interviewees told me that they were afraid that denouncing the episodes would have discredited the Tahrir Square protest and undermined the revolution. Others had a different view and said that denouncing sexual violence in the Square should be an integral part of the revolutionary commitment.

At the turn of 2013, the revolutionary narrative of Tahrir Square as a safe space evolved into new representations, where the Square became an area that could be perceived as safe only through a continuous revolutionary agency, with women and men equally committed to combat violence. The most recurrent carillon-call of that time was '*al-thawra mustamirra*/the revolution continues'.

From the 2011/12 elections to the fall of the Muslim Brotherhood. What kind of democracy for women?

When the parliamentary elections in December 2011 and January 2012 were held, a debate was opened among revolutionary activists. Radical activists called for a boycott, asserting that it was not possible to lead elections under military rule.

More than 40 political parties and coalitions applied for the elections, and the overall figure of female candidates included in the lists was 658 candidates compared to 3590 male candidates, equivalent to 15.5% (Nazra 2013). Even fewer women were elected.

Having women in parliament is not a guarantee of women's rights per se. However, having less than 2% of women parliamentarians in a country where women are the breadwinners in at least 33% of the families should raise some questions about representativeness, if not legitimacy.

The election results and women's exclusion from the political scene in the aftermath of the revolution have been strongly criticized by feminist activists (ECWR 2012), and projects to promote women's success in the future elections have been put in place. The women's political academy, launched by Nazra in 2012, is one of the projects through which feminist organizations are trying to develop new women's approaches to politics, avoiding mechanisms of co-optation and trying to transform the political system from a procedural to an actual democracy.

2012 heralded the year of Morsi's presidency, which presented new challenges for women political activists. The candidate's statement during the electoral campaign 'We work on supporting and empowering the Egyptian woman and paving the way for her in social and political participation' (AllAfrica.com 2012) was never translated into an actual plan and reveals the Muslim Brotherhood's patronizing attitude towards women. Throughout the twentieth century, the Muslim Brotherhood has 'reframed not reformed their gender agenda' (Tadros 2011), and the year they were governing Egypt was no exception. For instance, they threatened to repeal the Personal Status Law, and the divorce law (Al Ahram 2012), which they labelled as a 'Suzanne's Law', neglecting the work produced by women's activists over the previous decades to promote it.

With regard to sexual harassment, no measures were taken during this period to contain it. On the contrary, in their oral history accounts, women activists blame the Muslim Brotherhood for continuing the practice by previous regimes, of infiltrating protest demonstrations, practicing torture (El-Nadeem 2013) and organizing sexual mobs.

In this period, official government discourse tended to promote religious, 'pious' women as the only legitimate political actors, when they did not invite women to resume their 'traditional' roles. Women candidates for the Salafi party al-Nur were not even represented in the electoral posters, their face replaced with a rose. Once again, feminist human rights activists denounced the gendered violence of the regime. In March 2013, El-Nadeem published a collection of live testimonies on sexual torture in Tahrir Square and surrounding neighbourhoods. In an insightful comment, Dr. Magda Adly wrote:

> Publication of the testimonies is a method of resistance, of shaming the perpetrators and paralyzing their hands from continuing with their heinous crimes.
>
> Publication is a way of responding to their message…our will shall not be broken…we will not be ashamed, for shame should only be felt by authoritarian regimes that commit crimes against humanity and challenges the will of nations to create a state built on justice, freedom, dignity, and equality. Publication is a way of showing our solidarity with our daughters and sisters who paid this high price from their mental and physical health, just as the women and men of this nation have been paying their lives, sight, and health for a span of two years.
>
> Publication is a way to confront the state with its responsibilities to protect all its citizens and to present the phenomenon with its painfulness, lets a government authority of a parliamentarian understand the importance of introducing legislation to penalize violence and discriminations against women, seeing that the Egyptian constitution lacks articles that prohibit against discrimination and violence and establishing equality between men and women in all areas of life. (El-Nadeem 2013, 4–5)

The gradual loss of legitimacy of the Muslim Brotherhood was due to political and economic instability. Their perceived ineptitude in government lead to the *Tamarrud* (rebellion) campaign, which was followed by the oceanic demonstrations on 30 June 2013, and to the ousting of President Morsi on 3 July. Revolutionaries' perceptions of the June and July events shifted dramatically after the massacre of Raba'a and al-Nahdah Squares (14 August 2013) where, according to Human Rights Watch's investigation, 'at least 817 and likely more than 1,000 demonstrators were killed' (HRW 2014). At the time of writing, no one has yet been held accountable for these lives. What followed was a vast campaign of arrests targeting both the Muslim Brotherhood and political activists from across the political spectrum. If in the first months only the Muslim Brotherhood were referring to the ousting of Morsi as a 'coup', at the end of the year, leftist and liberal revolutionaries, including women, also adopted the expression. That being said, many did not acquiesce in it and continued to insist it was a revolution. One of my interviewees, at the end of 2013 said: 'well… it was a …popular coup'.

Where do we go from here? Women's political activism under the regime of al-Sisi

On 30 July 2013, the Egyptian Women's Union, an informal reading and online activism group convened by Nawal el-Saadawi, published a photo that went viral on social networks. The photo represented an old woman standing in a Cairo street in July 2013 – during the days following the removal of President Morsi and the eruption of the violent spiral that followed the events of the 3 July – and holding a sign: 'As long as an Egyptian's blood is cheap, then down, down with any President'.

To those who are familiar with the iconography of the Egyptian Revolution and its representation in popular arts, particularly graffiti, the face of the old women brings to mind the mothers of those martyred in the Revolution, a group who have become iconic in the last 4 years. Even more importantly, this image shows an underrepresented side of Egypt's 2013 events. While international commentators tended to divide the field between followers of the Muslim Brotherhood, labelled as terrorists or traitors, on one side, and supporters of the Army, labelled as *feloul* (remnants of the old regime), on the other, this picture pays homage to what a number of Egyptian activists and intellectuals defined as 'The Third Square', with reference to a segment of the society that is against any form of dictatorship and of political violence. This counter-narrative is shared also beyond the intellectual field, as witnessed by the words of a young Egyptian woman activist: 'Egyptians, believe it or not, there are people who oppose Morsi, his supporters, the army, and police brutality all at the same time'. (M.K. 28 July 2013)

Women's bodies continue to be a site of contestation under the regime of al-Sisi. A report by *I Saw Harrassment Initiative* indicates an increase in cases of sexual violence and harassment nationwide during the first 100 days under Sisi (Mada Masr 2015), and the government's initiatives to deal with the problem are not considered sufficient by women activists. In June 2014, following a serious case of sexual harassment at Cairo University, only a few days before leaving his interim office, former President Adly Mansour approved an amendment to the Penal Code to criminalize sexual harassment and fight the widespread abuse of women. This amendment was received with a mix of satisfaction and concern by feminist activists (El-Rifae 2014). On one side, they agreed that a law was necessary and they saw this 'as result of continued pressure by feminist groups and organizations on the necessity of holding perpetrators of sexual violence accountable' (Nazra 2014). However, they also called for a holistic approach to the problem.

Feminist activists that I interviewed between September and December 2014 expressed scepticism towards the law's framework and, although not completely dismissing it, as they all agreed that it was indeed good that sexual harassment was considered a crime, they pointed out that the law does not reflect the complexity of the issue:

> You need to educate people, to let them understand that sexual harassment is something wrong. Most importantly, you need to instruct policemen, judges, nurses and doctors about sexual harassment. They are not trained and, when a woman goes to hospital or to the police station after she has been sexually harassed, they don't support her, actually, they blame her.... (Interview, Cairo, 16 October 2014)

This distrust is also motivated by the simultaneous crackdown against civil society, which in the first months of 2015 has forced the closure of more than 380 NGOs (Mada Masr 2015), the recourse to mass death sentences against Muslim Brotherhood supporters by the judiciary and the prosecution of high-profile human rights and labour activists.

It would be safe to argue that the current amendment reflects, more than a genuine concern regarding sexual violence, a wider securitarian approach to politics and militarization of the public space, and it avoids dealing with the issue at its roots.

In this context, feminist organizations have deployed a range of strategies to keep alive a public discussion about sexual abuse committed by security forces and to change society's attitude towards sexual harassment.

In October 2014, the launch of the first issue of the magazine *al-Shamghiyya*, organized by Nazra for Feminist Studies and hosted by the French Cultural Centre in Cairo, saw a wide participation by feminist and human rights activists. The magazine featured a collection of comics against sexual harassment and an analysis by the feminist activist and artist Fatma Mansour, which discussed sexual harassment as a crime (Mansour 2014). Here, the public debate about sexual harassment intersects the discussion on women's equal political representation and the role played by cultural actors to promote it.

Again, in women activists' testimonies, the debate about sexual harassment intersects with broader political debates, such as women's political participation and the reform of the Constitution. Feminist activists were critical of the composition of the Constitutional Committee, which included only 5 women out of 50 members. However, this is the first one where gender equality is explicitly mentioned. The scholar and member of the Constitutional committee Huda el-Sadda invites us to read this important gain in its broader context (El-Sadda 2015), where, again, processes of legitimacy play an important role. Yet at the writing, El-Nadeem, a leading Human Rights organization in Egypt, which was founded in the 1980s by prominent second-wave feminist activists, is under attack by the Ministry of Health and is at high risk to be shut down. These developments are clear evidence that the trajectory of women's political participation and the fight against violence is not linear.

The violence exercised by present and past regimes against women political activists demonstrates that the relevance of independent women's political activism to legitimacy, democracy and human rights goes far beyond the 'pseudo-feminist discourse' promoted by the current and the past regimes.

Conclusion

The Egyptian revolution is a deep and historically rooted crisis of political legitimacy, which is still unfolding. It is an experience that has led Egyptian women and men with diverse political visions to challenge, not only the legitimacy of the Mubarak regime, but also the mainstream liberal notions of political legitimacy as the result of ballots and the balance of power between modern patriarchal political elites, both secular and religious. The focus on women's bodies as a battle site for competing political actors, and on women's practices of resistance to their objectification, highlights once again the fundamental feminist questioning of one of the main principles of liberal ideology: the dichotomy between the private and the public.

By setting the analysis of the developments having occurred in the past 4 years in a *longue durée* perspective, it can be seen that, notwithstanding the present-day masculinization and militarization of the public space, alternative discussions on gender and sexualities are ongoing. Emerging feminist movements are challenging polarized visions of politics and gender and in doing so are contributing to the shaping of a new political culture. Feminist activists reject identitarian politics and are trying to escape the conundrum of legitimacy–delegitimation.

Since the first phases of the revolution, feminist and democratic groups have been facing the competition of two counter-revolutionary and patriarchal forces to occupy the public space: the Army, which represents itself as the hero of national unity and security, and the Islamists, which represent themselves as the legitimate opposition to the military order. A feminist analysis shows that these counter-revolutionary forces are not antithetical, at least in relation to patriarchy or 'restored masculinities' (Kandiyoti 2013). They rather share the same anti-democratic and patriarchal notion of political power, they have both exercised violence to control revolutionary women and they both tend to mobilize identities – the Islamist or the nationalist – rather than political ideas and projects. Therefore, the binary religious versus secular opposition is not productive for understanding the gender balance of power in Egypt before, during and after the 2011 Revolution.

On the contrary, there is a long continuity between the Mubarak regime, the SCAF, the Muslim Brotherhood and the current regime: women political activists from the opposition are targeted, they are sexually harassed and their testimony is delegitimized. Public authorities are not accountable for these crimes. This should raise many questions about political legitimacy and about the rhetoric on security and stability that is endorsed by the current and the past regimes, and their international allies, to legitimate their power.

In fact, a feminist analysis of the Egyptian Revolution and the counter-revolution highlights the necessity to go beyond the modern tradition of orthodox Western epistemology, which is still mainstream today in Anglo-American thought. Going back to Alcoff's decolonial feminist epistemology, the significance of theorizing testimony, and acknowledging gender-related and racial experience, is key to understanding the current Egyptian crisis.

Notes

1. Nizam in Arabic can indicate both 'regime' in the narrow sense of a set of people or groups who wield power, and 'system' in the sense of a particular form of power, a set of informal norms governing political, economic and social spheres.
2. All the interviews quoted in this article have been conducted by me in Arabic and in English. I have translated and edited them. The interviewees, who are all knowledgeable people in the field of women and gender rights, prefer their names not to be disclosed.
3. Egypt was among the first countries in the world to introduce women's quota (law No. 21/1979). This law, which in less than 10 years raised the number of women in the Parliament from 3 to 36, was repealed in 1987 by the Supreme Constitutional Court, which 'deemed it to be contrary to the constitutional principle of equality among citizens' (Nazra 2013, 4).
4. El-Mahalla el-Kubra is home to the largest public sector Egyptian textile company, and since 2006, it has been a centre of workers protests.

Acknowledgments

Part of the research to write this article was undertaken in September–November 2014, while I was a visiting fellow at the NVIC Institute in Cairo. I would like to express my appreciation for the Institute, its Director and staff, for their generous hospitality and insightful intellectual exchange. I wish to acknowledge the many valuable suggestions made by the anonymous reviewers, by my colleagues Bronwyn Winter and Andrea Teti, and by my research assistants Rosemary Hancock and Shima Shahbazi. This research would have not been possible without the generous support of a number of feminist scholars and activists in Egypt, who shared their experiences and their stories with me. Given the current backlash against the intellectuals and the broader civil society, I prefer not to name them, but I would like them to know that I am grateful for their care and encouragement.

Disclosure statement

No potential conflict of interest was reported by the author.

References

Abaza, M. 2013. "Intimidation and Resistance. Gender in Cairene Graffiti." *Jadaliyya*, June 30. Accessed July 31, 2015. http://www.jadaliyya.com/pages/index/12469/intimidation-and-resistance_imagining-gender-in-ca.
Abdel Aziz, B. 2007. "Torture in Egypt." *Torture* 17 (1): 48–52.
Abdelfattah, A. 2014. "Living with the Martyrs." *Mada Masr*, October 10. (First published in *al-Shourouk*, October 20, 2011). Accessed August 2, 2015. http://www.madamasr.com/opinion/politics/living-martyrs.
Abdelmonem, A. 2015. "Reconceptualizing Sexual Harrassment in Egypt: A Longitudinal Assessment of *el-Taharrush el-Ginsy* in Arabic Online Forums and Anti-Sexual Harrassment Activism." *Kohl: A Journal for Body and Gender Research* 1: 23–41.
Abouelnaga, S. 2015. "Reconstructing Gender in Post-Revolution Egypt." In *Rethinking Gender in Revolutions and Resistance: Lessons from the Arab World*, edited by M. E. Said, L. Mehari, and N. Pratt. London: Zed Books.
Adly, M. 2013. "Introduction." In El-Nadeem, *Live Testimonies on sexual tortures in Tahrir Square and surrounding neighborhoods*. Accessed February 1, 2016. http://alnadeem.org/en/node/426
Ahram online. 2013. "Activists Commemorate Eighth Anniversary of Black Wednesday." *Al Ahram online*, May 25. Accessed February 1, 2016. http://english.ahram.org.eg/NewsContent/1/64/72300/Egypt/Politics-/Activists-commemorate-eighth-anniversary-of-Black-.aspx.

Al Ahram. 2012. "After Reconsidering the Khula (Divorce Initiated by Women) and Custody Laws: Women are between Two Fires! the Custody: Conflict between Couples and Children are the Victims." (in Arabic) April 6. Accessed April 7, 2016. http://www.ahram.org.eg/archive/Women-Child/News/141610.aspx.

Alcoff, L. 2000. "Philosophy Matters: A Review of Recent Work in Feminist Philosophy." *Signs: Journal of Women in Culture and Society* 25 (3): 841–882. doi:10.1086/495484.

Alcoff, L. 2011. "Experience and Knowledge: The Case of Sexual Abuse Memoires." In *Feminist Metaphysics: Explorations in the Ontology of Sex, Gender and Identity*, edited by C. Witt. New York: Springer.

AllAfrica. 2012. "Egypt: Presidential Candidates on the Role of Women and Their Rights." Accessed August 1, 2015. http://allafrica.com/stories/201205211299.html

Al-Nabaa Information Service. 2005. "Al-Taharrush bil-munazaharat fi masr: hatk 'ard al-Muwatanat hatk lilwatan." June 2. Accessed August 5, 2015. http://www.annabaa.org/nbanews/47/261.htm

Amar, P. 2013. *The Secutiry Archipelago: Human-Security States, Sexuality Politics, and the End of Neoliberalism*. Durham, NC: Duke University Press.

Amnesty International. 2011a. "Egypt: Military Pledges to Stop Forced 'Virginity Tests'." Accessed July 31, 2015. https://www.amnesty.org/en/press-releases/2011/06/egypt-military-pledges-stop-forced-virginity-tests/

Amnesty International. 2011b. "Not like Your Daughter or Mine: Forced 'Virginity Tests' in Egypt." Accessed July 31, 2015. http://www.amnesty.org.uk/blogs/press-release-me-let-me-go/not-your-daughter-or-mine-forced-virginity-tests-egypt

Atallah, H. 2014. "Remembering Those Who Were Slain." *Mada Masr*, October 9, 2014. http://www.madamasr.com/opinion/politics/remembering-those-who-were-slain.

Badran, M. 1996. *Feminists, Islam, and Nation: Gender and the Making of Modern Egypt*. Princeton, NJ: Princeton University Press.

Badran, M. 2009. *Feminism in Islam. Secular and Religious Convergences*. London: Oneworld.

Baron, B. 2005. *Egypt as a Woman: Nationalism, Gender and Politics*. Berkeley: University of California Press.

Carr, S. 2013. "Why Is Maspero Different?" *Mada Masr*, October 10. Accessed August 2, 2015. http://www.madamasr.com/sections/politics/why-maspero-different

Committee on the Elimination of Discrimination against women (CEDAW). 1996. "Consideration of Reports Submitted by States Parties under Article 18 of the Convention on the Elimination of All Forms of Discrimination against Women." *Third Periodic reports of States parties*. Accessed February 1, 2016. http://www.un.org/womenwatch/daw/cedaw/cedaw24/cedawcegy3.pdf

DailyNewsEgypt. 2012. "Kazeboon Street Campaign Aims to Expose SCAF Lies." January 16. Accessed August 5, 2015. http://www.dailynewsegypt.com/2012/01/16/kazeboon.street.campaign

DailyNewsEgypt. 2013. "Shura Council Members Blame Women for Harrassment." February 11. Accessed August 5, 2015. http://www.dailynewsegypt.com/2013/02/11/shura-council-members-blame-women-for-harrassment

Egyptian Centre for Women Rights. 2008. "Egyptian Women's Status Summary Report 2007." Accessed August 2, 2015. http://ecwronline.org/?p=4556

Egyptian Centre for Women Rights. 2012. "Egyptian Women's Status Summary Report 2011." Accessed August 2, 2015. http://ecwronline.org/?p=4556

El Sadda, H. 2015. "Article 11. Feminists Negiotiating Power in Egypt." *OpenDemocracy*, January 5. Accessed August 1, 2015. https://www.opendemocracy.net/5050/hoda-elsadda/article-11-feminists-negotiating-power-in-egypt.

El-Nadeem. 2012. "Diaries of a Revolution Under Military Rule." Accessed February 1, 2016. http://alnadeem.org/en/node/426

El-Nadeem. 2013. "Live Testimonies on Sexual Tortures in Tahrir Square and Surrounding Neighborhoods." Accessed February 1, 2016. http://alnadeem.org/en/node/426

El-Rifae, Y. 2014. "Egypt's Sexual Harassment Law: An Ineffective Measure to End Sexual Violence." *Middle East Institute*, July 17. http://www.mei.edu/content/at/egypts-sexualharassment-.

Eskandar, W. 2011. "The Maspero Massacre on 9 October 2011." *Notes from the Underground*, October 10. Accessed August 2, 2015. http://blog.notesfromtheunderground.net/2011/10/maspero-massacre-on-9-october-2011.html.

Eskandar, W. 2012. "Remembering the Maspero Massacre." *Notes from the Underground*, October 9. Accessed August 2, 2015. http://blog.notesfromtheunderground.net/2012/10/remembering-maspero-massacre.html

Gaber, S. 2013. "Maspero and Memory." *Mada Masr*, October 9. Accessed August 2, 2015. http://www.madamasr.com/opinion/maspero-and-memory.

Hafez, S. 2014. "The Revolution Shall Not Pass through Women's Bodies: Egypt, Uprising and Gender Politics." *The Journal of North African Studies* 19 (2): 172–185. doi:10.1080/13629387.2013.879710.

Hamdi, B., and D. Karl. 2014. *Walls of Freedom. Street Art of the Egyptian Revolution*. Berlin: From Here to Fame Publishing.

Hassan, R. M., A. Shoukry, and N. Abul Komsan. 2008. "Clouds in Egypt's Sky. Sexual Harrassment: From Verbal Harrassment to Rape. A Sociological Study" ECWR. Accessed August 5, 2015. http://egypt.unfpa.org/Images/Publication/2010_03/6eeeb05a-3040-42d2-9e1c-2bd2e1ac8cac.pdf

Human Rights Watch. 2005. "Egypt: Margins of Repression State Limits on Nongovernmental Organization Activism." Accessed August 3, 2015. https://www.hrw.org/reports/2005/egypt0705/index.htm

Human Rights Watch. 2014. "World Report 2013: Egypt." Accessed August 2, 2015. https://www.hrw.org/world-report/2014/country-chapters/egypt

Hussein, N. 2015. "Gestures of Resistance between the Street and the Theatre: Documentary Theatre in Egypt and Laila Soliman's No Time for Art." *Contemporary Theatre Review* 25 (3): 357–370. doi:10.1080/10486801.2015.1049822.

Kandiyoti, D. 2013. "Fear and Fury: Women and Post-Revolutionary Violence." *Open Democracy*, January 10. Accessed August 3, 2015. https://www.opendemocracy.net/5050/deniz-kandiyoti/fear-and-fury-women-and-post-revolutionary-violence

Kirollos, M. 2013. "Sexual Violence in Egypt: Myths and Realities." *Jadaliyya*, July 16. Accessed February 23, 2016. http://www.jadaliyya.com/pages/index/13007/sexual-violence-in-egypt_myths-and-realities.

Lefebvre, H. 1991. *Critique of Everyday Life*. New York: Verso.

Lesch, A. M. 2012. "Concentrated Power Breeds Corruption, Repression, and Resistance." In *Arab Spring in Egypt. Revolution and Beyond*, edited by B. Korany and R. El-Mahdi. Cairo: American University in Cairo Press.

Mada Masr. 2015. "With Latest Crackdown, State Dissolves 380 Ngos in Just 2 Months." March 18. Accessed August 5, 2015. http://www.madamasr.com/new/latest-crackdown-state-dissolves-380ngos-just-2-months

Mansour, F. 2014. "'al-Taharrush Garima' (Sexual Harrassment Is a Crime)." *Al-Shakmagiyya*, No 1.

Marfleet, P. 2009. "State and Society." In *Egypt. Moment of Change*, edited by R. El-Mahdi and P. Marfleet. Cairo: The American University in Cairo Press.

Mc Grath, C. 2009. "POLITICS-EGYPT: Women Get Help on Road to Parliament." Accessed February 1, 2016. http://www.ipsnews.net/2009/06/politics-egypt-women-get-help-on-road-to-parliament/

Nazra for Feminist Studies. 2014. "Egypt: Statement from Nazra for Feminist Studies about Mob Sexual Assaults." Accessed April 7, 2016. http://yfa.awid.org/2014/06/egypt-statement-from-nazra-for-feminist-studies-about-mob-sexual-assaults/

Nazra For Feminist Studies. 2013. "She and the elections. Report. Mentoring on the Ground With the Candidates 2011/2012." Accessed August 4, 2015. www.nazra.com

New Women Foundation. 2011. "Ignoring Women Is Unacceptable Particularly at this Critical Stage of Our National History." Accessed July 31, 2015. http://nwrcegypt.org/en/?p=5203

Saadawi, N. 2011. "Egyptian Feminist Nawal El Saadawi in Cairo's Tahrir Square: The City in the Field." *MS Magazine*. Accessed July 31, 2015. http://msmagazine.com/blog/2011/02/07/egyptian-feminist-nawal-el-saadawi-in-tahrir-square-i-saw-with-my-own-eyes-the-barbarism/.

Sangster, J. 1994. "Telling Our Stories: Feminist Debates and the Use of Oral History." *Women's History Review* 3 (1): 5–28. doi:10.1080/09612029400200046.

Seif El-Dawla, A. 2009. "Torture: A State Policy." In *Egypt. Moment of Change*, edited by R. El-Mahdi and P. Marfleet. Cairo: The American University in Cairo Press.

Shehab, B. 2012. "A Thousand Time NO." Accessed July 31, 2015. http://www.ted.com/talks/bahia_shehab_a_thousand_times_no/transcript#t-171421

Soueif, A. 2011. "Image of Unknown Woman Beaten by Egypt's Military Echoes around World." *The Guardian*, December 19. Accessed July 31, 2015. http://www.theguardian.com/commentisfree/2011/dec/18/egypt-military-beating-female-protester-tahrir-square.

Tadros, M. 2011. "The Muslim Brotherhood's Gender Agenda: Reformed or Reframed?" *IDS Bulletin* 42 (1): 88–98. doi:10.1111/idsb.2011.42.issue-1.

Toma, S. 2015. "My Survivor's Guilt: Coping with the Trauma of Loss." *Mada Masr*, July 22. Accessed August 2, 2015. http://www.madamasr.com/opinion/politics/my-survivors-guilt-coping-trauma-loss.

Zuhur, S. 2001. "The Mixed Impact of Feminist Struggles in Egypt During the 1990s." *Middle East Review of International Affairs Journal* 5 (1): 78–89.

De-orientalizing sexual violence and gender discrimination in Egypt

Nancy Okail

This is a reply to:

Sorbera, Lucia. 2016. "Body politics and legitimacy: toward a feminist epistemology of the Egyptian revolution." *Global Discourse* 6(3): 493–512. http://dx.doi.org/10.1080/23269995.2016.1188461.

Lucia Sorbera's (2016) 'Body politics and legitimacy: toward a feminist epistemology of the Egyptian Revolution', is one of the most important papers on gender relations in Egypt as well as globally. Sorbera's discussion of a very critical moment in the battle over equal rights and access to public space for women in Egypt sheds light on the dynamics of power relations under authoritarian rule and how they play out in the struggle against all forms of repression. In this respect, I would like to draw on the significant examples that Sorbera has analyzed in her paper in order to unpack some of the conventional misconceptions about the nature of the struggle and the challenges that women face in Egypt as well as globally. The main problem is not that oriental patriarchal culture that undermines women, as that exists in the west as well. Rather, it is the culture of impunity and absence of rule of law and accountability that is the biggest problem and the main difference in the two contexts.

One of the ostensibly significant battles won in Egypt that Sorbera cites is the criminalization of Female Genital Mutilation (FGM). It is worth clarifying why the criminalization of the law passed, as it reveals the dynamics of repression and discrimination in Egypt. As the paper suggests, the law was not accepted because FGM was considered to be a barbaric act. For example, Egyptian society would resist the idea of addressing domestic rape (rape within marriage), let alone criticizing it. The FGM law was adopted because it was endorsed by the regime and particularly the first lady, Suzan Mubarak who wanted to show an achievement – rather a progressive achievement – that the western world would applaud her for. Albeit symbolically significant, these efforts were superficial and never attempted to address the roots of the problem or delegitimize FGM through deconstructing the structural foundations in society that allows this practice.

As an evaluation consultant for foreign aid projects, I witnessed many women enroll in the anti-FGM courses promoted by the government and funded by foreign aid. During the evaluation observation visits, they would reel off all the disadvantages of FGM. However, they were doing so as a favor for the project officer with whom they have mutually dependent power relations. Yet following the courses, as I chatted with women who had attended over tea at their houses, they would completely dismiss the idea of abandoning the circumcision of their girls, and stress the necessity of FGM for their daughters to be married. FGM was no exception. This was symptomatic of many aid-funded projects endorsed by the regime, represented by the President and his wife for a cosmetic effect, while in reality they hardly ever had the political will to change the very roots that led to these problems.

The same applies to the sexual harassment law that the author referenced which has actually been passed since the paper was published. It is still ineffective, and civil society organizations that support it are being threatened and prosecuted. In fact, Ms Mozn Hassan, the director of Nazra organization for Feminist Studies and who is referenced in the paper, is among the civil society leaders who had their assets frozen by a Cairo court in 17 September 2016.

Under the authoritarian regime, the target of oppression is not woman per se but marginalized groups in society who have no means of achieving accountability or justice. The paper references black Wednesday where police coordinated the sexual assault of Ms Nawal Ali who was protesting in 2005 over the constitutional amendments. As Sorbera notes, 'Activists remember this episode as the first time they saw sexual harassment organized in a group'. However, this happens all the time to the more vulnerable groups in society. Although Nawal Ali's case was public, it was not different from the sexual assault in the same year by the police on the microbus driver Emad Al Kabeer who was raped by a stick. The incident was captured on camera and went viral on social media. Both Al Kabeer and Ali were subject to the same type of violation and the same power relations dynamic: a powerful authoritarian institution (the police force) acting brutally outside of the law, knowing that they can get away with it, in the complete absence of impartial rule of law. The subjects of oppression here are not a man and a woman. The subjects of oppression are members of marginalized groups who had no recourse to justice in a culture of impunity.

This is a point that the author alluded to when explaining that 'the intersection between gender and class representation played a key role in the construction of the regime's narrative' in the context of discussing the sexual harassment phenomena in Egypt around public holidays and Eid festivities. Although it is indeed a class issue, it is not in the way that the regime presents it (as intra-class abuse). It is a class issue in the sense of the regime abusing the weaker in the power relation (the marginalized men and women). Although similar issues may occasionally happen to upper-class women, the difference here is that elite women have capacity for recourse, not through the law but through impunity and their connections and access to the power circles. To further elaborate on the class gender and marginalized group dynamics, this year, an 80-year-old Coptic woman from the upper Egyptian governorate, El Minya, was stripped naked and dragged around the town by 300 men, because she was the mother of a young man who was allegedly involved in an affair with a Muslim woman. Now, this is not just an old woman from a lower-class group, but also a person belonging to a religious minority which places her lower in the power relation than other, Islamic women from similar socioeconomic backgrounds. Instead of holding those men accountable, she was later forced to claim on video that she had forgiven all that had happened.

The same dynamics apply when it comes to access to power. Sorbera makes an excellent point when showing rightly how 'independent and oppositional women activists were marginalized, if not repressed. The NCW tended to monopolize the women's agenda, framing it as family related issues, and tending to neutralize the subversive potential of feminist activism.' This shows that it is not the issue or the cause that is of the Government's concern but rather the appearance and appeal to the international leaders and donors to present the illusion that something positive and progressive has been achieved.

Operationally, projects, programs and legal bills are not designed to actually address the roots of the problem as shown from the author's paper and the examples listed above. As for political legitimation when it comes to addressing sexual violence and gender discrimination, there are two dynamics at hand that hinder real change.

On the national level, the Government is very keen to apply cosmetic reforms which please the international community while, at the same time, do not upset the conservative cultural structure, but actually preserve it. The conservative structure is not important for the regime per se, but it is the structure that the Government needs to play on when they need to defame women activists or at least guarantee that there is no public decry when such women are sexually assaulted. A conservative society would be more receptive to the Government's claims (and its state controlled media machine) that it is primarily the fault of such deviant women who took to the streets and subjected themselves to such harassment. At the same time, the regime gives the superficial impression that they are reformist and working to combat the regressive society (who is also susceptible to radicalization) and the struggle they face to enforce laws which match and appeal to western values.

On the international level, the problem with legitimation is driven by western leaders who adopt and buy into the narrative of 'the cultural specificity of the Muslim world', and that accordingly they should not interfere with or criticize practices which they frame as patriarchal relations.

Now, is this cultural specific? No. There are several critical issues with the cultural specificity argument and it could not appear starker than when seen within the current context of the US elections and the scandal of Presidential Candidate Donald Trump's lewd tape in which he brags about sexually assaulting women.

The difference is that, in Egypt, there are more structural barriers and no access to independent media or impartial legal channels. While the situation is not ideal in the US either, because of power and media manipulation, at least there is a greater chance of accountability being achieved.

The irony could not be sharper when we see the close similarity in the discourse propagated by Trump and his supporters in the US and Sisi and his supporters in Egypt. When asked about the lewd tape during the US Town Hall debate on 9 October 2016, Trump briefly apologized and repeatedly responded that we now have to address the priority challenges facing the nation: fighting ISIS. This is not at all different from the discourse in Egypt. When Egyptian women took to the street on Women's International Day 8 March 2011, they were not only assaulted and beaten up, the next day the state-controlled media rolled out tens of articles with a core message of 'let's focus on the priorities of the country first'. When there was a public outcry over a video of a women being gang-raped by 50 men in Tahrir square in Egypt on the day of President Sisi's inaugural speech in 2014, the response to any criticism is that the Sisi is fighting terrorism. This is similar to Sorbera's claim that sexual harassment and other gender-related issues are seen as secondary to stability – as if they are mutually exclusive – because women are seen as marginal to the core of society for the west and in Egypt. Also similar is the response of Trump and Sisi. The latter took a bunch of flowers to the rape victim and gave it to her on camera, expressing regret over such an 'individual' incident, while the former took to the second Presidential Candidate debate the female accusers of Bill Clinton and expressed sympathy for their experiences. Clearly, in both cases, it was about their own political battle not the victims. As Sorbera aptly put it, 'women's bodies continue to be a site of contestation'. Obviously, that is not specific to Egypt.

Yes, it is not up to Western powers to dictate a specific cultural code to the orient. It would be hypocritical given all forms of inequality that women still face in the West and what has been revealed by the behavior of a Presidential Candidate and the response of his supporters to revelations regarding his actions. Rather, it is expected to at least not contribute to the problem by validating these criminal acts by framing them in culturally specific terms. What is needed is not the imposition or endorsement of specific moral codes, but the support for national civil society actors so that they can enforce their own accountability mechanisms, document abuses, push cases in court and aim to reach the minimum impartial form of justice that exists in the democratic world.

Women's human rights and Tunisian upheavals: is 'democracy' enough?

Bronwyn Winter

ABSTRACT

The regimes that came to power (in some cases ephemerally) in the wake of the so-called 'Arab spring' claimed democratic legitimacy as a primary means of credentialling their political agenda in international and even local eyes. Yet, how legitimate some of these new regimes have been is open to question. So-called 'moderate' Islamist movements have been criticised as using democratic processes to introduce new forms of theocratic authoritarianism and/or for not paying sufficient attention to strengthening and resourcing the political, legal and civic institutions, which make democracy effective. Moreover, women's rights have been under fire in both overt and covert ways. Through a study of Tunisia, touted as one of the success stories – indeed the only one for the moment – of the 'Arab spring', this article investigates the question of 'democratic legitimacy' from a feminist perspective.

The UN's 'global issues' webpage on Democracy and Human Rights asserts that 'democracy provides the natural environment for the protection and effective realisation of human rights' and that conversely, respect for human rights and freedom are essential values of democracy.[1] This argument echoes those made by Habermas (1989, 1996) that democracy (or popular sovereignty) and human rights (expressed as a combination of communicative public liberties and personal autonomy) are 'cooriginal': one cannot properly exist without the other. On the same UN website, under the subhead 'Supporting transitional democracies', the UN proclaims, in relation to the 'recent' Arab world uprisings, that the 'calls for transformational change are a popular cry for choice, participation, transparency and respect for people's legitimate quest for democratic space. These events have reaffirmed the pivotal importance of democratic governance as a system premised on inclusion, participation, nondiscrimination and accountability. At the time of this writing – that is, some 4 years down the track from the UN statement – the extent to which that accountable and inclusive democratic governance is in operation or even in the active process of being created remains open to question. The impacts of unachieved democracy

Note: this article has been amended slightly since original online publication to correct a typographical error. For more details, see Corrigendum http://dx.doi.org/10.1080/23269995.2016.1168674

on the traditionally most excluded populations are severe, and women, as usual, are paying the highest price. Unsurprisingly, it is feminist activists whose voices are among the loudest in calling regimes in the Middle East and North Africa (MENA), longstanding or transitional, to account. They have shown through their protests that a democracy that does not include the full 'civic engagement' of women in decision-making – alongside their personal liberty – or that lacks the political will to ensure the 'transparency and accountability' of government and institutions in the areas of women's rights and socioeconomic participation, is weak and its claims to political legitimacy questionable.

This article looks at this aspect of 'political legitimacy' through discussion of Tunisia, which is not only the trigger site of Arab-world uprisings, with spontaneous and nationwide demonstrations that followed the self-immolation of street vendor Mohamed Bouazizi in Sidi Bouzid on 17 December 2010, but it is the only flashpoint site of the uprisings that has peacefully – or relatively so – transitioned from one regime to another *six times*.

Tunisia's 'Arab spring' thus appears to have well and truly sprung, and indeed blossomed into a relatively functional democracy, having survived its revolutionary transition and handled Islamist challenges better than its Maghrebian neighbours Egypt or indeed Algeria in the 1990s, and certainly better than either Libya or Syria. The entry of Tunisia into its Second Republic following the 2014 adoption of its new constitution would seem to augur well for the strengthening of democracy. As such, Tunisia is a worthy case study for the women's rights litmus test.

But first, a little background on the abovementioned six transitions, and on the situation of women in Tunisia prior to and during them.

14 January and after

Tunisians today speak of a 'before 14 January' and 'after 14 January', as it was on that date in 2011 that leader Zine El-Abidine Ben Ali fled the country, marking the first transition. Rachid Ghannouchi, (leader of Ennahda – 'Renaissance', the Islamist party that immediately positioned itself as the inheritor of the revolution), returned from exile in the United Kingdom at the end of the month. His namesake, Mohamed Ghannouchi, remained prime minister at that time. Further protests, involving trade unions and human rights organisations and a sit-in by young people in the Kasbah square in Tunis, called for Mohamed Ghannouchi's removal and the election of a Constituent Assembly, tasked with writing a new Constitution. In February, in response to those protests, the second transition occurred: the prime minister was replaced by former Bourguibist minister Béji Caïd Essebsi, who headed up a caretaker government responsible for first, dissolving Ben-Alist institutions and second, organising the election of the Constituent Assembly in October (third transition).

In terms of democratic participation in the lead-up to that election, Tunisia's was effervescent to the point of confusion, as one commentator put it in September of that year, at a public meeting organised in Paris by the secular and feminist left party Pôle Démocratique Moderniste. On 23 October 2011, Tunisians went to the polls to choose from among 11,686 candidates, representing a total of 1517 lists, in a country of only 10.6 million. Only around 54% of the potential 7.5 million voters, however, registered to vote and not all of these ended up voting. Ennahda obtained a clear majority in the election with some 37% of the recorded vote and 89 of the 217 seats. Given the election was single-round and proportional, the party did not win enough seats to govern alone, and so formed a coalition, known as the Troika, with two Social Democrat Parties, Ettakatol (Democratic Forum for Labour and Liberties) and the Congrès pour la République (of which some leaders had previously been members of Islamist groups), which together won another 15% of the vote and 55 seats. Although the three Troika members initially enjoyed a cosy relationship, Troika partners criticised Ennahda over its increasingly autocratic style and its refusal to cede any of the five core ministries of Defence, Foreign Affairs, Interior, Justice or Finance to them, despite the less than stellar performance of the Ennahda nominees. These last were increasingly implicated in both escalating political and social violence in Tunisia (including violence against women) and in the inefficiency or corruption of the justice system and various levels of administration.

The opposition, in the meantime, made alliances of its own, with splinter left parties joining forces in new coalitions, of which the main ones were the Front populaire and a three-way coalition between social democrat Al Massar (la Voie Démocratique et Sociale) – itself an amalgamation of several other groups including the Pôle Démocratique Moderniste – the neo-Bourguibist party Nidaa Tounes (Bourgiba was the first president of independent Tunisia) and the centrist social liberal party the Parti Républicain. It was the 2013 assassination of two leaders of the Front populaire – Chokri Belaïd (Parti Unifié des Patriotes Démocrates) and Mohamed Brahmi (Mouvement Populaire) – within 6 months of each other that would trigger the fourth transition.

By the end of 2012, time at which the new Constitution was supposed to be in place, the Constituent Assembly was deadlocked over key issues, such as human rights and freedom of speech and conscience, and some Ennahda-authored drafts contained provisions that were seen as opening a backdoor to introduction of sharia law in a country that had historically been an Arabo-Muslim world leader on women's rights (Tunisia's personal status law, effective from 1957 and amended in 1983 and subsequently, remains the most progressive in the Muslim world). In mid-2013, Deputy Karima Souid, who had resigned from Troika partner Ettakatol earlier that year, stated in an open letter to the vice president of the Constituent Assembly, Meherzia Laabidi (Ennahda), that the objectives of the revolution had been 'hijacked, forgotten, held in contempt and denigrated'.[2]

After Brahmi's assassination on 25 July 2013, with the same gun that had killed Belaïd, some 60 deputies walked out of the Constituent Assembly and began a sit-in in the Place du Bardo just in front of it (and of the museum that was to become the site of a terrorist attack in March, 2015). The murder weapon was traced to a Salafist jihadi cell that according to the participants in the sit in was either encouraged or tolerated by sections of Ennahda, but according to Ennahda, was the author of 'cowardly' acts 'targeting the revolution and national unity, and obstructing the democratic transition process'.[3]

These murders are not the only incidence of Salafist violence in Tunisia since the 2011 election, and there have been reports of salafisation of mosques and other cultural and educative institutions. In response to the political crisis of mid-2013, a 'quartet' of the trade union Union Générale des Travailleurs Tunisiens (UGTT), the employers' organisation Utica (these first two organisations were not previously known for working in concert), the Tunisian Human Rights League and the Order of Lawyers, drew up a 'roadmap' for the replacement of the Constituent Assembly with a caretaker technocrat government that would oversee the finalisation of the new Constitution and organise the subsequent general election, maintaining public order and public services (which had seriously deteriorated between 2011 and 2013) in the meantime. Parallel to the work of the quartet (which subsequently received the Nobel Peace Prize, in 2015), US Secretary of State John Kerry also pressured the Troika to stand down. In late September 2013, Ennahda agreed to the roadmap but it was almost another 3 months before the technocrat government was formed. The new Constitution was finally voted on 26 January 2014.

Even though Islam remains the state religion, as it does in the constitutions of all Muslim-majority countries in MENA except Turkey, the Constitution also defines the state as civil, guarantees freedom of speech and conscience and the political neutrality of education institutions, places sovereignty in the hands of the people, and encodes formal equality between men and women, including protection of already existing rights and electoral parity, and commits the state to talking all necessary measures to eradicate violence against women. On the downside for women, the family (where most violence against women occurs) is protected as the essential unit of society – as it is, for that matter, in the 1948 Universal Declaration of Human Rights (Article 16, paragraph 3, which is encoded almost word-for-word in the new Tunisian Constitution). The 'right to life' is also deemed sacred and inviolable, which is problematic for women's reproductive rights, but the Constitution is light years from the more regressive documents that Ennahda had attempted to introduce. On 1 May 2014, an electoral law was signed, ushering in a new caretaker government (transition five), setting up lasting institutions of government and providing for elections by the end of 2014, which took place in October (transition six).

In that election, the neo-Bourguibist party Nidaa Tounes gained the majority (close to 40% of the vote and 85 seats), as well as the presidency (Béji Caïd Essebsi, who had also been caretaker prime minister in 2011), and Ennahda gained the second largest number of votes and 69 seats. As in 2011, however, few electoral lists were headed by women in 2014. Women's electoral score nonetheless increased, with women winning 68 out of 217 seats (31.3%), as opposed to the 49 won in 2011 (22.6%, which represented, in fact, a lower percentage than before the departure of Ben Ali: women represented 28% of deputies following the 2009 parliamentary election). While 42 of the 49 seats went to Ennahda women in 2011, in 2013, the political turnabout following disillusion with the 'hijacked' revolution saw 35 seats going Nidaa Tounes women and only 27 to Ennahda.

The mood in the months following the elections appeared to be one of moving beyond the divisions of 2013. In February 2015, President Essebsi appointed a 'unity government' of 27 ministers and 17 undersecretaries led by Prime Minister Habib Essid (independent). Yet, the unity in question does not reflect the proportion of the legislative vote won by the various parties. Many see it as cosmetic or tokenistic, and in particular as an attempt to appease Ennahda, which in December 2014 put out a press release calling for a national unity government, without which it claimed there would be no political stability.[4] The coalition government included 21 independents and five parties: Nidaa Tounes, Ennahda, the Free Patriotic Union, centrist liberal party Afek Tounes, the National Salvation Front, rebadged the National Tunisian Movement, a broad left-leaning coalition. The Popular Front, the fourth largest group in parliament with 15 seats, refused to join any coalition involving Islamist parties and is thus not a member of the government.

The biggest early challenge faced by the new government was 'security'. The Salafist violence that had been a key factor in the 2013 walkout and sit-in hit the new government hard on 18 March 2015, when two armed men, after trying unsuccessfully to break into parliament during debate of a new antiterrorist bill, instead went into the next-door Bardo Museum, the most prestigious in the country, killing 21 tourists and a security guard and taking several hostages. In the operation to free the hostages, they themselves were killed. The attack was claimed the next day by Islamic State. On 24 March, the Tunisian Prime Minister sacked the chiefs of police of Tunis and of the Bardo and arrested one of the Bardo security guards for undisclosed reasons, but one factor in the success of the terrorist attack had been that security at the Bardo was very lax. Even in the face of these attacks, President Essebsi publicly stated in an interview with French newspaper Le *Monde* on 6 April 2015, on the eve of a visit to France, that it was 'not a matter of transforming Tunisia into a police state', in an oblique reference to the politics of the pre-14 January regime. Subsequent attacks at a hotel in the beachside resort town of Sousse (June 2015) and against a bus carrying members of the Presidential Guard in Tunis (November 2015), have sharpened the security focus.

Economically, however, Tunisia has remained in the doldrums, with very weak growth and high unemployment (discussed below). That, and ongoing conflicts both within Nidaa Tounes and between Nidaa Tounes and Ennahda (notably over the removal of many Salafist or Islamist imams as part of the 'security' measures), led to a ministerial reshuffle in January 2016, with a smaller number of ministries and a more 'technocratic' profile.

'Successful' post-Arab spring Tunisia, then, at the time of this writing, is in the difficult situation of trying to protect its new constitutionally guaranteed liberties and equalities in a politically and economically fragile context, while at the same time, fighting terrorist violence that, although not unheard of pre-14 January, has significantly escalated since.

A snapshot of women's rights in Tunisia and in MENA, 2008–2013

There are many indicators and sources one could use to provide snapshots of women's rights in MENA; I will start here with the yearly themed UN Development Reports. The 2010 edition of the report, the theme of which for that year was 'the real wealth of nations', showed variable outcomes for women in MENA, which mostly did not tally with the overall development rate in the countries (UNDP 2010). The criteria used for measuring gender equality were maternal mortality, underage pregnancy rate, percentage of seats in parliament, proportion of population aged 25 or above with at least secondary education, use of contraceptive methods, antenatal care levels and births attended by skilled professionals. While one may question some of the criteria as Western-centric or otherwise inadequate – and the UNDP itself notes that it does not include data on a number of important aspects of inequality such as level of land or business ownership, or violence against women – factors, such as maternal mortality, parliamentary representation and education levels are generally agreed to be significant albeit not the only criteria for measuring women's participation in society and safety within it. Wealthier MENA countries identified in the high or very high human development category for 2008, such as the UAE, Bahrain, Saudi Arabia, Iran and Qatar, were ranked significantly lower (sometimes more than twice as low) in terms of gender equality. Tunisia (ranked 81st on the Human Development Index [HDI] near the bottom of the 'high development' list, in human development, but 56th on the Gender Development Index [GDI]) was among the notable exceptions to this mismatch among high development MENA countries, showing gender equality rates to be as good as – indeed, much better than – overall human development (UNDP 2010, 156 ff).

The UNDP report noted, emphatically, that 'good things don't always come together', stressing in particular that 'a high human development does not mean democracy, equality or sustainability' (UNDP 2010, 65–66). The report did, however, note a world-wide trend over the previous 30 years towards greater democratisation, which tends to indicate that equality and sustainability were the greater problems. More tellingly for our concern here, the report noted that Islamist groups were in some cases using demo-cratic process to move towards theocratic rule and suggested that the greatest 'democ-racy deficit' was in the Arab world. Little wonder, then, that the 'Arab spring' was hailed in the West and within the United Nations as 'opening greater space for civic engage-ment' (UN website cited above). The report also noted the possession or otherwise of significant oil reserves as playing a role in enabling states to 'resist pluralist tendencies': 'the political economy allows the state to insulate itself through far-reaching patronage networks and a weighty security apparatus' (UNDP 2010). On the other hand, countries such as Tunisia, more dependent on foreign aid, were deemed more open to external political influence in favour of democratisation (UNDP 2011, 69), although the extent to which this influence was truly exerted at the time is debatable. France in particular and the European Union (EU) more generally supported authoritarian pre-Arab spring regimes in both Tunisia and Egypt, for example.

More disturbingly, the 2010 report noted that reported levels of human rights violations had not diminished over 40 years. It concluded that 'democracy' is not always synonymous with accountability and will not necessarily improve it (UNDP 2010, 71), and noted that women remain systemically and systematically disadvantaged overall, with progress in some areas or regions being countered by traditionalist regressions in others (UNDP 2010, ch. 4 & 5).

A 2013 article on governance and health in the Arab world, published in medical journal *The Lancet*, paints a similar picture: 'In democratic states, elections are a frequent operative instrument of accountability, but they neither always serve that role nor do they hold a monopoly on accountability' (Batniji et al 2014, 344). The authors note that accountability of governments is lacking in most of the Arab world, that public spending and human development do not automatically correlate outside Organisation for Economic Co-operation and Development (OECD) countries, and that transitional democracies may in fact take a step backwards in this area because the new institutions are unstable and often weak. Moreover, informal Islamist patronage networks, including within social justice activities, often carry over into government institutional structures once Islamist parties accede to power.

Tunisia nonetheless presented in 2008 as one of the better performers in the region: more or less democratic (ostensibly) with relatively good gender equality outcomes. By 2013, the UNDP rankings had changed somewhat, but not necessarily in the ways one might have expected. In the 2014 Human Development report, on the theme of 'vulnerabilities', the UNDP showed that more countries had entered the high human development club but Tunisia's HDI ranking had slipped to 90. Its GDI had nonetheless continued to improve, moving Tunisia to 48 in the ranking, although the improvements were more modest in absolute terms, which indicates that other countries did not improve as much or indeed did worse than 5 years earlier. Turkey, for example, had risen to 69th place on both HDI and GDI rankings, with improvements in GDI being fairly slight, but Egypt had backslid dramatically on both indicators.

Notwithstanding the somewhat encouraging overall figures, for women at least, in Tunisia, the 2014 UNDP report nonetheless stressed that 'globally, women suffer the most pervasive discrimination' and that many countries maintained several forms of legal discriminations against women (UNDP 2014, 74). It further pointed to the 'epidemic proportions' of violence against women (VAW), which inhibit women's ability to participate socially, economically and politically in a range of areas (UNDP 2014, 75), although this 'epidemic' is still not factored in to the UNDP's GDI assessments, one reason given being that it is very difficult to measure accurately. The *Lancet* study cited above also added intimate partner violence to the areas in which women in Arab countries fare far worse than their sisters in other regions of the world, the others being political representation, education and general health (Batniji et al 2014, 347).

These findings on VAW are further reinforced by a World Health Organisation (WHO) study published around the same time, which shows the incidence of violence against women to be higher in low- and middle-income regions, and identifies Africa, the Eastern Mediterranean and South East Asia as the regions among these where the rates of violence are the highest, at 36.6%, 37% and 37.7%, respectively. This is slightly higher in all cases than the estimate, produced over the last few years from a number of research sources, that one in three women will experience male violence in her lifetime, mostly intimate partner or ex-partner violence (WHO 2013; UNICEF 2014; UNODC 2014). Of the total of the world's women killed in any 1 year, roughly half die at the hands of intimate partners or family members (UNODC 2014).

Poverty and VAW in Tunisia

The combined impact of poverty and violence is always more pronounced for women, as women are the majority of the poor and as the UNDP tells us, the victims of violence of 'endemic proportions'. So, how is Tunisia doing in this area? On socioeconomic indicators, it regressed significantly between 2011 and 2013, which is no doubt to be expected given the difficult transitional period. At the same time, the socioeconomic issues were a key trigger factor in the December 2010 uprisings, so Tunisians hopeful of a revolution would logically expect improvement in this area. Instead of that improvement, Tunisians faced socioeconomic degradation, which has proven to be more lasting than originally hoped.

In a lengthy report published in April 2013, the National Association of Tunisian Economists (ASECTU) attributed Tunisia's socioeconomic malaise to the political one, drawing attention to the absence or perceived absence of the rule of law and incompetent management of public services, dwindling investment, sharply rising cost of living and increasing insecurity and violence (Haddar 2013). Figures provided by the National Institute of Statistics in Tunisia show that unemployment in Tunisia was running at around 15% at the end of 2014, which was lower than 16.7% at the end 2012, but worse than before the revolution, in 2010 (13%).[5] When disaggregated by sex or age, the statistics are even more alarming. In mid-2015, the average unemployment rate for women was 21.6%, compared to 12.5% for men during the same period. Young people's unemployment skyrockets to above 30%, and is most severe among graduates; again, the rate is significantly higher for women. Youth unemployment was one of the social driving forces of the 2010–2011 uprisings, but no significant progress has been made.

According to the ASECTU report, the post-14 January debates in Tunisia over the theoretical, cultural and ideological issues of the relationship between sharia and positive law, women's rights and gender equality, freedom of conscience, thought and expression had become political fixations that deflected attention from the more pressing socioeconomic issues that are determinant for the country's fate (Haddar 2013, 18). The report also argued, however, that Ennahda realised its aim of conserving and consolidating its power through mobilising religious identity politics at all levels. In such a context, women's rights and the theocratisation of society are not simply political abstractions and distractions to be debated only by elites in and around the Bardo. A number of grass root women's groups, some women-only, some mixed, many functioning with the financial support of European NGOs, started working throughout urban and rural Tunisia to support women's health, 'civic engagement' and provide information and education to women about their rights. Among the poor and the marginalised in Tunisia as anywhere else, women are the most so, and the question of their rights is integral to any discussion of socioeconomic inclusion.

As indicated above, however, the biggest of the many problems faced by women in the Arab world, and indeed in the world more generally, is male violence, which in a post-Arab spring context has increasingly come from both religious militants and public authorities. Following the 2011 election, and even before it, ideas of 'public decency' and 'blasphemy' were used to justify increased violence and intimidation against women and against any who defended women's rights. In October 2011, in the lead-up to the Constituent Assembly election, for example, Nabil Karoui was arrested for having screened Marjane Satrapi's popular animated film *Persepolis* (2007), dubbed in Tunisian Arabic dialect, on his channel Nessma. The film was considered blasphemous because it represented God as a human figure; it also, of course, took a stand against the Islamicisation of society and subjugation of women. The outraged Islamist hardliners who physically attacked the TV station and Karoui's home were not, in contrast, charged. Karoui was tried for 'attack on sacred values', and the plaintiffs were represented by 140 lawyers. One of them, Maître Laâbidi, told the press that 'depiction of divinity is blasphemous in itself, because God must under no circumstances be depicted' (cited in Le *Monde*, 20 April 2012).

In September 2012, an incident that was to become an even greater *cause célèbre* among the many in Tunisia at the time featured conservative notions of 'decency' and 'morals' as a pretext for VAW committed by public authorities. In the evening of 3 September, a woman subsequently known to the public by the pseudonym of Meriem Ben Mohamed was sitting with her fiancé in a car in Tunis, when the car was approached by three police officers. One of them held the fiancé while the other two repeatedly raped Ben Mohamed. The policemen also attempted to extort money from the young couple. When Ben Mohamed went to register her complaint against the police officers for rape and extortion, she found herself arrested and tried for 'indecent behaviour': according to a spokesperson for the Minister for the Interior, she and her boyfriend had been in an 'immoral position' when the policemen found them (*TF1* 29 November 2012; *Libération* 1 October 2012).

Amnesty International, in a press release issued on 27 September, stated that laying such charges against a rape victim 'instead of protecting her against intimidation and prejudice' were at best evidence of the inadequacies of the Tunisian legal and penal systems, and at worst evidence of a 'pernicious manoeuvre to discredit a rape victim and to protect those she has pointed to'. The Amnesty spokesperson, MENA region deputy-director Hassiba Hadj Sahraoui, added that 'rape committed by security forces, often used as a tool of repression, constitutes a form of torture and should quickly be the object of an in-depth inquiry' (Amnesty International 2012).

The case against Ben Mohamed was thrown out in November 2012 due to insufficient proof, and the police were put under investigation for rape. On 31 March 2014, the police officers' sentence was handed down: seven years' prison for the two policemen accused of the rape, and two years and a 20,000 dinar (around 9000 euro) fine for the third one, found guilty of having extorted money from Ben Mohamed's fiancé. Ben Mohamed's lawyer commented over the phone to French newspaper Le *Monde* that the sentence was lenient, of the sort usually handed down when there are extenuating circumstances, and that no consideration was given to the suffering endured then and subsequently by Ben Mohamed (Mandraud 2014).[6]

Ben Mohamed subsequently wrote a book about her experience, published in France in early 2013. In that book, she extrapolates her own story to the story of Tunisian women who suffer sexual violence: the difficulty in being heard by authorities, in even obtaining a medical examination; and the dishonour that falls on the woman among her friends and family, to the extent that it becomes 'about' the father and brothers and no longer about the victim herself. This taboo around sexual violence existed well before the 2011 election and will likely continue to exist well after that of 2014. Tunisian feminists have in fact consistently maintained that violence against women, and its handling by families, police and the courts, is an enormous problem even in a country that is perceived, notwithstanding post-2011 regressions, as one of the most progressive and secularised in the Arab world, particularly for women.

A study conducted in 2010 and published in 2011 by the Tunisian national office of family and population (ONFP) concluded that 47% of all Tunisian women have suffered some form of violence in their lives. Although rural women (especially those in the remote south-west) and poorly educated women are more likely to suffer violence, the rate does not alter significantly according to whether or not women are working outside the home. According to the study, the overwhelming majority of violence occurred in the home, but it is arguable that violence outside the home has increased since 2011, as Meriem Ben Mohamed's story appears to indicate. Already, the 2010 study suggested that psychological violence (intimidation, harassment and so on) was on the increase.

On 23 April 2013, Ahlem Belhadj, President of the Association Tunisienne des Femmes Démocrates (ATFD, one of Tunisia's oldest feminist organisations, founded in 1989) published on the independent and progressive Tunisian news and commentary site *Nawaat* a declaration against all forms of violence against women and for the pluralism of women's expression. For Belhadj, the sources of the violence were multiple: imams and lay preachers, media, spokespersons for political parties, police, militia and everyday citizens 'giving free rein to their machism that has at last been "liberated"' (Belhadj 2013). In particular, she opposed any use of 'morals' to justify an obsessive precoccupation with women's bodies and women's behaviour, or of religion to justify winding back women's rights. She refused 'political legitimacy' or 'electoral majority' or even 'transitional phase towards democracy' as justifications for either legitimating, even encouraging, such violence or doing nothing to combat it.

The issue of VAW continues to dog the new regime. On the occasion of Tunisian women's day on 13 August, 2014, the then Undersecretary for Women's Affairs, Neila Chaâbane, presented to the Constituent Assembly a new framework law against VAW. Tunisia became the first country in the region to adopt such a law; Algeria followed suit in March 2015, amidst much controversy over the provisions concerning sexual violence within marriage. As in Algeria, conservatives in Tunisia opposed the law; they included conservative women such as Ennahda deputy Mounia Ibrahim, who had also earlier opposed the parity provisions in the new Constitution. Ibrahim claimed, during a parliamentary debate on the 2015 public finances law held on 10 December, 2014, that Chaâbane was 'spending the state budget on a law that is undermining the foundations of the Tunisian family and the institution of marriage in Tunisia' (cited by Labidi 2014). She continued at some length on the damage this new law against VAW would do to the family.

Moreover, according to some commentators reacting to the introduction of the law on VAW, it would be ineffectual unless the policing and particularly legal infrastructure in Tunisia was to be vastly improved. Writing in *Nawaat* on 14 August, 2014, academic and lawyer Riadh Guerfali argued that the legal arsenal devoted to combating various forms of violence, and not only against women, which had permeated all aspects of life in Tunisia, would be condemned to relative failure because 'the main structural flaw in combating violence is the legal machine', which was underresourced to the extent that it was the one of the major disasters of Tunisia at the time. Without a functional justice system that is 'given the means commensurate with its mission', he wrote, 'we will continue to talk of problems related to violence for years' (Guerfali 2014). His voice joined that of many others who, in writing and in conversation, had been speaking in 2012 and 2013 of increasing infrastructural and systemic failure in Tunisia as the Troika placed senior administrators in public service roles who had neither the experience nor the real political will to provide efficient management of services that were already overstretched and underresourced, not to mention frequently corrupt. Such ongoing bad management was directly implicated in, among others, the failure to prevent the March 2015 attack at the Bardo Museum. It remains to be seen, at the time of this writing, whether the government sworn in at the beginning of 2015 and reshuffled a year later will have the political will and the means to address these issues. If it does not, however, the impacts for women will continue to be disastrous, compounding the effects of the ideology of 'morals' – already part of the sociocultural landscape prior to the uprisings, the 1957 Personal Status law notwithstanding – and of theocratic incursions into public life and indeed, women's bedrooms.

Such political will is unlikely to be found, however, unless progressive women are given access to the means to drive it – such as a meaningful voice in politics.

Descriptive and symbolic versus substantive representation

With 22.5% of seats held by women following the 2011 Constituent Assembly election, Tunisia appeared on the face of it to be doing better than comparator countries on the political participation indicator of gender equality – except for Algeria, where around 36% of lower house members of parliament (MPs) were women at that time. In Egypt following the 2012 election, for example, only 2% of seats were held by women. One of the coalitions that subsequently formed Al Massar, the Pôle Démocratique et Moderniste (now disbanded following various realignments of political alliances), had been the only party at the time of the 2011 election to completely respect the principle of electoral list parity to which all lists were supposed to conform (and which is now encoded in the Constitution). Of the 33 lists presented by the Pôle, 16 were headed by women, although as the Pôle received less than 3% of the vote, the impact on the numbers of women in parliament was minimal, with only one woman elected (Nadia Chaabane, member for one of the diasporic French seats).

Ennahda made much of its female deputies, such as Mounia Ibrahim, who argued so passionately in opposition to the law against VAW discussed above. However, while these deputies may have *descriptively* represented women in that they shared characteristics with the demographic 'woman' (Pitkin 1967), *substantively* represented an ultra-conservative and ultimately anti-woman position, thus helping perpetuate the time-honoured tradition of divide-and-conquer. Another Ennahda star of the moment was Souad Abderrahim, the so-called 'unveiled face' of the party as she did not wear hijab. Her critics quickly nicknamed her 'Souad Palin' because of her conservative views, likening her to former US Vice-Presidential 'Tea Party' Republican candidate Sarah Palin. Abderrahim was particularly notorious for having claimed, shortly after her election, that single mothers did not deserve the protection of the state.

When thousands of women took to the streets in August 2013, in the middle of the political crisis, to demand justice and protection of their rights and joined the Bardo sit-in, a few hundred Ennahda women – 2000 at the very most, according to community news site Tuniscope[7] – prayer mats at the ready, enjoined women to support the regime in place and Tunisia's 'Muslim identity'. The slogan put out by Ennahda to rally women differed little from that of the regime it replaced, or indeed any regime seeking to harness women's rights to a nationalist cause: 'Tunisian women are the guarantors of democratic transition and national unity'.

The 2013 march took place on Tunisian Women's Day on 13 August: the anniversary of Bourguiba's 1956 beylical decree that became the personal status law on 1 January 1957. A leading presence in the march was the post-14 January group Hrayer Tounes (Free Women of Tunisia): part of the 'new wave' of Tunisian feminism. In a press release cited by *Nawaat*, Hrayer Tounes called on 'all those who believe in a civil State, a social democratic State of which the substance is liberty, dignity and justice, in complete and effective equality and in respect for the right to difference' to demonstrate 'against any attempt to wind back Tunisian women's rights'.[8]

The opposing Islamist and feminist demonstrations on 13 August 2013 throw into sharp relief the limitations of quotas and parity measures: they ensure nothing beyond representation at the most basic formalistic and descriptive levels. Increased presence may have symbolic importance, especially in contexts where women have not previously been visible, but symbolism is insufficient to guarantee material outcomes for women. Ennahda women, in fact, are mainly handmaidens to their male Islamist counterparts.

One area where parity models do have a slight advantage over quotas is that they are more likely to generate 'critical masses' of women in public institutions, which may over time exert influence in matters of concern to all women (such as childcare or violence), whatever their political leanings. For that to happen, however, the parity system has to be used effectively. If women are placed at the head of party lists in mainly unwinnable or difficult-to-win seats, then the outcome will not necessarily be more women in parliament, and in fact, it usually is not. Moreover, the capacity of women in parliament or government to effect change depends not only on 'critical mass' that *may* in some cases help generate a *rapport* de *force* – a sufficient balance of power to cause shifts in the way politics is done and in political priorities – but also on *which* women are there. As we have seen, feminism is not genetic: women can be conservative and many internalise misogynist worldviews. More generally, the right and extreme right have been able to manipulate quota and parity systems to court the female vote by 'feminising' their political profile. The women placed on electoral lists are often, in fact, 'good girls': obedient women who will toe the party line and help the party to police other women.

The 'good girl' syndrome is even more the case with women selected as ministers. In September 2013, for example, the Minister for Women and the Family with the former Troika government, Sihem Badi, sacked historian Dalenda Largueche from her post as the Director of the long-existing Centre de Recherche, d'Études, de Documentation et d'Information sur la Femme (CREDIF). She judged Largueche, who also headed up the women's studies program at Manouba University – a progressive university that had been the object of Salafist agitating – to be too 'modernist'. Among other things, in 2012 Largueche had publicly criticised the Salafist popularisation of orfi marriages, that is, short-term or 'customary' marriages, in Tunisia as breaching not only Tunisian law but even sharia law, and as a form of prostitution or polygamy by another name. Badi had originally responded that orfi marriages were a matter of 'personal freedom' exercised by the women but subsequently retracted that statement (Arefi 2012). Largueche's sacking may be remembered as the only decisive action taken by a Minister otherwise judged completely ineffectual in advancing women's rights.

Even if constitutional implementation of parity slightly increased the percentage of women in parliament after Tunisia's 2014 election, and the political power balance shifted away from religious conservatism, there is still no guarantee that those women – or women appointed as ministers – will act decisively to advance women's rights, or be supported in doing so by their male colleagues. A case in point is the Minister for Women appointed in the new government at the beginning of 2015. Feminist Khadidja Cherif, outspoken defender of complete equality between men and women and advocate for the separation of all public institutions from religion, was passed over in favour of the far more moderate Samira Marii. As writer Sophie Bessis put it:

> it's the symbolism that matters here. The women's ministry cannot be run by a feminist, it's too serious an affair … Once again, this episode of Tunisian political life reveals that the

situation of women represents the deepest dividing line between those who champion freedom and those who champion social immobilism' (Bessis 2015, my translation).

In short, the increased 'descriptive' participation of women is minimalist and although welcome, does not in itself mean that women's interests will be represented in terms of greater social and economic gender equality, increased protections against violence and so on. On this matter as many others, the jury remains out on the success of Tunisia's democratic transition for women, and thus on the 'legitimacy' of the Tunisian state and political processes in feminist terms.

A 'stolen' revolution retrieved?

'Legitimacy' was the catchcry for Ennahda as it was for the Muslim Brotherhood in Egypt – yet Ennahda, and most particularly its leader Rachid Ghannouchi, claimed a victory in 2011 that had not been theirs. As Janine Gdalia wrote in her collection of interviews with Tunisian feminists, published in 2013, the reaction of many who had put all their 'effervescence' into a new hope of a democratic Tunisia, were devastated by Ennahda's success at the polls on October 23: their revolution had been 'stolen' (Gdalia 2013, 13). Indeed, many of those who took to the streets during the 2013 sit-in brandished placards and banners with that message of betrayal. Of the many photographs of the 13 August march circulating on the Web, one is particularly eye-catching. It shows headscarf-wearing older women lamenting, immediately in front of a younger woman who holds up a placard with the words in French: 'Bilan d'une révolution volée: femmes violées, petites filles voilées' (result of a stolen revolution: women raped, little girls veiled). The slogan clearly plays on the assonance of the three verbs voler, violer and voiler. For many feminists in Tunisia as elsewhere, the claim by Islamist parties that they were the 'popular' and 'legitimate' alternative to authoritarian states was little more than a pretext for the reimbrication of religion and politics, and for sending women back to what theocrats have decided is their place.

As French political philosopher Geneviève Fraisse has pointed out, however, while religion is discursively useful for justifying marginalisation of women, it is simply a convenient smokescreen – albeit one of the more useful ones – masking a more entrenched 'existential fear felt by men confronted with sex equality' (Fraisse 2011, my translation). As soon as positive law is made subservient to whatever the ruling class has decided is transcendent law, or the 'natural' order of things, then law becomes an even more than usually difficult mountain to shift. This is terribly bad news for women.

As in many other parts of MENA over the last three decades, Tunisian women have been caught in the middle in a battle between a largely secularised and modernist but authoritarian state and a so-called 'moderate' and so-called democratic Islamist opposition which in some cases itself subsequently became the authoritarian state. In Tunisia, however, that battle has now shifted to a new terrain, with neoliberal technocrats walking the middle of the political road in a socioeconomic context that remains far from encouraging.

At the same time, legal and constitutional guarantees do matter: even if the laws are not systematically or equitably applied, their very existence creates spaces in which women are able to interact and organise. As in Kemalist Turkey, women's rights were harnessed in Bourguibist Tunisia to a nationalist project, and this has had its downsides. The benefits for women, however, have been far more than simply rhetorical or state-serving, and have had lasting impacts, even if they are more pronounced among elites than among other women (which is also the case elsewhere in the world).

The risk now, however, is that the Tunisian centre-left and centre, having organised themselves to challenge Ennahda, will fail to deliver on their promise to Tunisian women, and to Tunisian people more generally, or that Ennahda will find new ways to pull Tunisia to the religious right. Already in 2013, Rachid Ghannouchi was spin-doctoring the end of Tunisia's political crisis to the international press, not as the product of internal and external political pressure after two and a half years of government corruption and ineptitude, of socioeconomic regression, of violence and of cultural salifisation, but as a 'consensus' of which Ennahda was supposedly one of the key architects. Tunisia was, in short, the new Turkey, the latter country having lost its glowing Islamist-democratic 'model' status as its government became more deeply corrupt, authoritarian and neglectful of human rights issues on its own doorstep. Now, Tunisia is being held up as the model for Turkey to follow.

As African American lesbian feminist poet Pat Parker once famously reminded us, in the groundbreaking feminist anthology *This Bridge Called My Back*, revolution 'isn't neat or pretty or quick' (Parker 1981). It happens unevenly and messily, and its progress towards any sort of change is never guaranteed to be linear. It took the French revolution, for example, almost a century to produce a Republic of which the fundamental institutions would endure (barring a rather nasty interruption between 1939 and 1944). Just as the Second Republic produced on the wave of the so-called 'European spring' of 1848 was ephemeral, so the regimes produced by the 'Arab Spring' (so named by Westerners nostalgic for 1848, or perhaps for the Prague spring of 1968) have to date proven to be, and may still be in Tunisia. Revolutions take time, and as Batniji et al remind us in the *Lancet* article, cited earlier, transitional periods are often those in which human development and indeed human rights may take a backward step.

Moreover, as we have seen time and again (the case of Iran in 2009 comes to mind), uprisings do not necessarily produce revolution and even if they do, the latter may not necessarily be progressive (again, Iran comes to mind: the Iran of 1979). Transitional 'backward steps' may in fact be more enduring, in forming the basis of the new regime, and any perceived gains (such as constitutional gender equality) may simply be carry-overs from previous regimes. In other words, they continue *in spite of* whatever happens after the 'revolution' and not *because of* it.

A stated allegiance to democratic values and social justice – even a constitutionally encoded one – does not automatically translate into material realisation of social justice and again, it most especially does not for women. Talk is easy enough: actions require a political commitment of quite another order. In a global context where politics continue to be declined in the masculine by default, any sort of professed commitment by political actors to the advancement of women should be treated with a goodly amount of scepticism in the first instance. Promises are easy, and as Guerfali noted, even laws are relatively easy; it is practices that need to change, in more than cosmetic ways.

Caution is even warranted when some statistics may suggest that equality is being realised. Women's political participation, health and education levels are key components of the Gender Development Index, which leads to the assumption – also made by many feminists – that if enough women are educated and enough women are elected to parliament, things are necessarily going to look up. Outside the OECD (and even sometimes inside it), this assumed correlation simply does not hold. Iranian women, for example, are among the best educated and healthiest in MENA, but on practically every other indicator of gender equality they are doing very badly: low workforce participation, hardly any women in parliament, and high rates of violence against women, much of it condoned and even encouraged by law. It is unlikely that there will be more women in Iranian parliament or the workforce before the issues of violence and domestic subjugation are addressed.

Conclusion: Tunisian feminism reclaimed

Prior to 2010, there existed in Tunisia, for all its problems, a sense of rights and justice – *including for women*, and a longstanding feminist movement with a strong sense of civic and political engagement. Even if new groups formed since the Sidi-Bouzid revolution have often taken some critical distance from the 'historic' feminists associated with organisations such as the Association Tunisienne des Femmes Démocrates (ATFD), they have nonetheless benefited from that political and women's-rights education. Some new groups have even formed alliances with the 'historic' feminists, as in the case of lesbian cultural and audiovisual media group Chouf, which organises events with ATFD's support.

What did change were the forms that activism took, with more use of new media and cultural expressions, such as in the case of Chouf, as well as individualised and Web-based expressions and a heavy use of social media, as has been observed elsewhere with relation to new generations of political activism. As one 'post-Arab-spring' iconic young blogger, Lina Ben Mhenni, put it: 'the Web is a dream instrument for direct democracy and citizenship. We want a world without leaders or bosses, where everyone can participate in decision-making, where everyone can have an effect on reality' (Ben Mhenni 2011, 31).

Ben Mhenni's words may appear overly and simplistically idealistic, and her actions overly individualistic, but in a context where it could be easy to become cynical, sighing *'plus ça change…'*, such initiatives are salutary. Ben Mhenni is, moreover, not a lone example. Others include cartoonists such as Nadia Khiari, author of *Willis from Tunis* (2012) (Willis being a rather sarcastic cat who comments on unfolding events), or Amina Sboui, who became for a short time the Tunisian face of controversial Ukrainian group Femen (of which the key members are now based in France). On 1 March 2013, within the context of protests over the assassination of Chokri Belaïd, Sboui (then using the pseudonym Amina Tyler), posted a photograph of herself, bare-breasted, on social media. On her chest, were written, in Arabic, the words: 'my body belongs to me and is the source of nobody's honour'. She was also overtly critical of then women's minister Sihem Badi, discussed above, and was briefly imprisoned for having spray-painted graffiti on a cemetery wall. Sboui later, however, distanced herself from Femen when the latter group's self-appointed leader, Inna Shevchenko, tweeted 'Can you think of anything more stupid than Ramadan or anything uglier than Islam?' Sboui judged this comment to be Islamophobic and severed her connections with Femen, a group that is problematic in any case on many levels, for reasons I do not have the space to discuss here. As for Sboui's actions, they were controversial in Tunisia and feminists were divided over their effectiveness, but they do demonstrate a new spontaneous individualisation and even a new form of transnationalisation of activism among young feminists that, while not unique to the Tunisian context, is nonetheless now a part of the post-Arab-spring scenario.

The Tunisian 'success story', then, is far from fully written as yet. The country has a Constitution and a new government, which happened with *relatively* little bloodshed, and evidence of new forms of feminist engagement, both individual and collective, that build upon the old. But for Tunisia to pass from a weak democracy with only the shell elements of a Constitution, and institutions in need of rebuilding, to a strong democracy where rights and freedoms are guaranteed in the act as well as in the letter of the law, there remains much work to be done. And that work must start with, and for, its women. Only then can Tunisia pass from 'national disenchantment', as Hélé Béji titled her well-known critique of the postcolonial Tunisian state (1982), to real political legitimacy.

Notes

1. https://www.un.org/en/globalissues/democracy/human_rights.shtml, accessed 25 May 2014.
2. 'Karima Souid clashe Meherzia Laabidi', Mosaïque-FM, 13 August 2013. http://www.mosaiquefm.net/fr/index/a/ActuDetail/Element/24746-karima-souid-clashe-meherzia-laabidi, accessed 20 April 2014.
3. Cited by *The Independent*, 26 July 2013. http://www.independent.co.uk/news/world/africa/tunisia-shocked-by-assassinations-opposition-leaders-mohamed-brahmi-and-chokri-belaid-killed-with-the-same-gun-8733972.html, accessed 13 August 2013.
4. As reported by Tunisie Numérique, 14 December 2014. http://www.tunisienumerique.com/tunisie-ennahdha-pas-de-stabilite-politique-sans-gouvernement-dunite-nationale/241641, accessed 19 April 2015.
5. http://www.ins.tn/indexfr.php, accessed 9 February, 2016.
6. http://www.lemonde.fr/international/article/2014/04/01/la-justice-tunisienne-prononce-un-verdict-clement-pour-des-policiers-violeurs_4393473_3210.html, accessed 26 May 2014.
7. http://www.tuniscope.com/index.php/article/29760/actualites/partis/ennahdha-lachee-femmes-253220#.Ugrrq1NgCL0 (accessed 14 August 2013).
8. Source: *Nawaat*, 12 August 2013. http://nawaat.org/portail/2013/08/12/13-aout-journee-nationale-de-la-femme-le-face-a-face-des-manifestations/, accessed 13 August 2013.

References

Amnesty International. 2012. "Tunisia: Woman Allegedly Raped by Police Faces Prosecution." *Amnesty Intenational website.* Accessed 15 October 2012. https://www.amnesty.org/en/articles/news/2012/09/tunisia-woman-allegedly-raped-police-may-face-jail-time/

Arefi, A. 2012. "Tunisie: La Révolution Sexuelle Des Salafistes." Le *Point*, February 20. Accessed 9 February 2016. http://www.lepoint.fr/monde/tunisie-la-revolution-sexuelle-des-salafistes-20-02-2012-1433357_24.php

Batniji, R., L. Khatib, M. Cammett, J. Sweet, S. Basu, A. Jamal, P. Wise, and R. Giacaman. 2014. "Governance and Health in the Arab World." *The Lancet* 383 (9914): 343–355. doi:10.1016/S0140-6736(13)62185-6.

Béji, H. 1982. *Désenchantement National. Essai Sur La Décolonisation*. Paris: Maspéro.

Belhadj, A. 2013. "ATFD: Nous Femmes Tunisiennes, Restons Debout!" *Nawaat*, April 24. Accessed 25 May 2013. http://nawaat.org/portail/2013/04/24/atfd-nous-femmes-tunisiennes-restons-debout/

Ben Mhenni, L. 2011. *Tunisian Girl: Blogeuse Pour Un Printemps Arabe*. Montpellier: Indigène éditions.

Ben Mohamed, M. 2013. *Coupable D'avoir Été Violée*. Paris: Michel Lafon.

Bessis, S. 2015. "Khadija Cherif, La Femme Qui Fait Peur Au Pouvoir Tunisien." Le *Monde*, February 2. Accessed 9 February 2015. http://www.lemonde.fr/idees/article/2015/02/09/khadija-cherif-la-femme-qui-fait-peur-au-pouvoir-tunisien_4572721_3232.html

Fraisse, G. 2011. "Révolutions Arabes: La Démocratie Est-Elle Incompatible Avec Le Droit Des Femmes?" Le *Nouvel Observateur*, November 3. Accessed 20 May 2013. http://leplus.nouve lobs.com/contribution/210393-revolutions-arabes-la-democratie-est-elle-incompatible-avec-le-droit-des-femmes.html

Gdalia, J., ed. 2013. *Femmes Et Révolution En Tunisie*. Montpellier: Chèvre-feuille étoilée.

Guerfali, R. 2014. "Bientôt Une Nouvelle Loi Contre La Violence Faite Aux Femmes: Encore Une "Tartine" Législative À Collectionner!" *Nawaat*, August 14. Accessed 21 April 2015. http://nawaat. org/portail/2014/08/14/bientot-une-nouvelle-loi-contre-la-violence-faite-aux-femmes-soit/

Habermas, J. 1989. *The Structural Transformation of the Public Sphere: An Inquiry into a Category of Bourgeois Society*. trans. Thomas Burger and Frederick Lawrence. Cambridge, MA: MIT Press.

Habermas, J. 1996. *Between Facts and Norms: Contributions to a Discourse Theory of Law and Democarcy*. trans. William Rehg. Cambridge, MA: MIT Press.

Haddar, M. 2013. *Les Défis De La Transition*. Tunis: ASECTU. Accessed. 15 May 2014. http://www. asectu.org/Documents/PDF/LES%20DEFIS%20DE%20LA%20TRANSITION.pdf

Khiari, N. 2012. *Willis from Tunis: Chroniques De La Révolution*. Paris: La Découverte.

Labidi, N. K. 2014. "Tunisie: La Députée Monia Ibrahim S'oppose À Un Projet De Loi En Faveur Des Droits Des Femmes." *Huffington Post Maghreb*, December 10. Accessed 21 April 2014. http:// www.huffpostmaghreb.com/2014/12/10/monia-ibrahim-neila-chaaban-_n_6302752.html

Mandraud, I. 2014. "La Justice Tunisienne Prononce Un Verdict Clément Pour Des Policiers Violeurs." Le *Monde*, April 1. Accessed 26 May 2014. http://www.lemonde.fr/international/arti cle/2014/04/01/la-justice-tunisienne-prononce-un-verdict-clement-pour-des-policiers-violeurs _4393473_3210.html

Parker, P. 1981. "Revolution: It Isn't Neat or Pretty or Quick." In *This Bridge Called My Back: Writings by Radical Women of Color*. edited by C. Moraga and G. Anzaldúa. New York, NY: Kitchen Table Women of Color Press.

Pitkin, H. 1967. *The Concept of Representation*. Berkeley: University of California Press.

UNDP. 2010. *Human Development Report 2010*. New York, NY: UN.

UNDP. 2013. *Human Development Report 2013*. New York, NY: UN.

UNDP. 2014. *Human Development Report 2014*. New York, NY: UN.

UNICEF. 2014. *Hidden in Plain Sight: A Statistical Analysis of Violence Against Children*. Accessed 3 February 2015. http://www.unicef.org/publications/files/Hidden_in_plain_sight_statistical_analy sis_Summary_EN_2_Sept_2014.pdf#sthash.1LezM9Ry.dpuf

UNODC (United Nations Office on Drugs and Crime). 2014. *Global Study on Homicide 2013: Trends, Contexts, Data*. Vienna: UNODC. Accessed 15 March 2015. http://www.unodc.org/gsh/

WHO (World Health Organization). 2013. *Global and regional estimates of violence against women: prevalence and health effects of intimate partner violence and non-partner sexual violence*. Accessed 13 February 2014. www.who.int/iris/bitstream/10665/85239/1/9789241564625_eng

A reply to 'Women's human rights and Tunisian upheavals: is "democracy" enough?' by Bronwyn Winter

Hajer Ben Hadj Salem

This is a reply to:

Winter, Bronwyn. 2016. 'Women's human rights and Tunisian upheavals: is "democracy" enough?' *Global Discourse* 6 (3): 513–529. http://dx.doi.org/10.1080/23269995.2016.1155299

For more than five decades following its independence, Tunisia has been singled out as the flagship of women rights in the Muslim world and treated as an exception by foreign observers and scholars interested in the study of women rights in the region. However, this sense of celebrated exeptionalism was shaken after the uprisings of December 2010 and January 2011 as Tunisian women and an increasing number of feminist scholars became wary of the political transition. Their worries became more acute as news stories of salafists intimidating unveiled women on the streets and attacking women gatherings spread across the country. They reached a peak as the power vacuum became infiltrated with returning religiously zealous ex-pats, who back in the 1980s and 1990s had fought a relentless war to repeal the Code of Personal Status and reinstate a Shari'a-based family law. As they won the majority vote in the 2011 elections, they tried to resume implementing their suspended agenda, dominating the National Constitutional Assembly and key ministries of a state apparatus that had for more than five decades advanced and protected progressive gender policies in a patriarchal society. While the globally celebrated ratification of the January 2014 Constitution, securing basic legal guarantees for gender equality, dissipated some of the fears of many foreign women rights observers who hailed the birth of the first 'moderate Islamist-led democracy in the Muslim world', it failed to mislead feminist scholars, who had developed a deep understanding of the Tunisian context both pre- and post-2011.

Bronwyn Winter critically evaluates the 'moderate Islamist-led' transition period from a feminist perspective. Upon scratching at the surface of what she qualifies as 'the upheavals' that befell Tunisia under Islamist rule, which have calamitously affected the context structures (political, economic, legal systems) upon whose strength depends the soundness of any claims for a democratic form of governance that rests on promoting the human rights of women, the author questions the 'moderate Islamists' claim for 'democratic legitimacy,' which was brandished as 'a primary means of credentialing their political agenda in international and even local eyes.' The work does not directly engage the long arc of the Tunisian struggle for democracy and women rights in general to gauge advances and setbacks in promoting women human rights in Tunisia before and after 2011, but it focuses on the immediate years that followed to the ousting of Ben Ali, and, in particular, the coming to power of the Islamists, which remains still critically under-examined. However, what Winter's work loses in not delving into the history of the in-tandem struggles for women rights and democracy in Tunisia and the regressive role that transplanted political Islamism had in the four decades that preceded 2011, it gains in experimentalism. This feature is epitomized in the author's unconventional feminist approach to the concepts of democracy, human rights, legitimacy, women rights, and thereby to UN gender development indicators.

Also distinct from many studies of women rights in Tunisia post-2011, Winter's work does not attempt to reinforce the neo-Orientalist and Western mass-mediated global romance of the 'Arab Spring's' only success story, the heroes of which are the 'moderate Islamists' who abandoned their theocratic-undemocratic package of the 1980s and 1990s and adopted a new 'democratic' package that recognizes electoral legitimacy, succession, pluralism, universal human rights, including women rights. Nor does it rehash the concomitant neo-Orientalist myth that increased Islamist women representation in the National Constitutional Assembly (NCA) accounts for whatever legal guarantees for gender equality inscribed in the new Tunisian constitution. The author rather challenges these myths from a feminist perspective. Additionally, Winter's work is poised to stand apart for the authors' willingness to embrace the complexity, and relative uncertainty, of the current status and the future of women rights by smartly addressing multiple dimensions (legal, economic, political) affecting the question of women rights in Tunisia while focusing essentially on two main indicators to measure gender development in Tunisia: one is part of UN standards and the other is not. These are respectively women representation in politics and violence against women. Winter's work does a good job addressing these two issues. But still, the best of the work is geared toward raising the long-silenced and provocative issue of violence against women in Tunisia. This issue keeps the work close in spirit to the sort of insider accounts of the drama of women rights in Tunisia despite the author's heavy reliance on international reports and secondary sources.

Given the author's smartly conceived and multi-dimensional approach to the question of democracy and of women rights in Tunisia, I will break down my review into sections that reflect key concepts upon which the author built her main argument. These include the trio democracy-women rights-legitimacy, violence against women (VAW), women representation, and 'stolen revolution.' As such, it is geared toward a dialogic interaction with the text, rather than conveying my own perspective on the subject.

Poverty and VAW in Tunisia

In focusing on VAW in Tunisia, the author sheds light on a topic that had been considered a taboo by the pre-2011 regime, which wanted to build a success story by marketing the image of Tunisia as the flagship of women rights and did not refrain from persecuting the Tunisian women rights activists who had repeatedly wanted to divulge this endemic phenomenon since the early 1990s (Charrad 2001). In this respect, Winter's work is poised to redirect the study of gender equality in Tunisia to a ground that has only recently come under academic investigation and make a contribution to the field from an outsider perspective. At the same, time she experiments with a new gender development indicator that the UN does not use in their GD assessments on the grounds that 'it is very difficult to measure accurately.' As such, one would expect the author to suggest empirical tools that would help advance the state of research in the field and ways to overcome some of the methodological hurdles that still impede the accurate measurement of this worldwide phenomenon that cripples women's advancement. However, Winter rather reoriented the study toward tracing the festering socioeconomic and legal tapestry that accounts for the rise of violence against women, which she neither translated into numeric terms nor managed to reflect through on-sight ethnographic research, but through heavy reliance on secondary sources.

Even though insider empirical studies of the question of violence against women are in the process of development, some nongovernmental feminist organizations, such as the *Association Tunisienne Des Femmes Democrates* (AFTURD), which set up the first call center to offer legal support for women victims of violence as early as 1993, and *l' Office National de La Famille et de La Population* (ONFP) already offered alarming statistics on violence against women in Tunisia both before and after 2011. After almost two decades of independent feminist activism, in 2010, the ONFP conducted a national survey on violence against Tunisian women under the auspices of the UN Population Fund. The study showed that 47.6% of Tunisian women had been victims of violence (for the most part intimate-partner violence) and that the percentage increases dramatically according to age and regional variables as it reaches 72% in the poor South Western cities. On 2 March 2016, the *Centre de Recherches, d' Etudes, de Documentation et d' Information sur La Femme* (CREDIF) held a press conference to announce the arresting findings of a study they had been conducting on violence against women since 2011. Even though the study reflects the same regional and age variations of the 2010 study, it went far beyond focusing on intimate partner violence studied in the 2010 report and the UN reports quoted by Winter in her work. It focused on violence against women in the public spaces between 2011 and 2015. It showed that 78.1% of the interviewed women reported that they had been victim of psychological violence in public spaces, 41.2% had been victim of physical violence, and 75.4% had been victim of sexual violence. The study also shows that these figures vary with the educational level and professional level of the women. It shows that 88.5% of the students, 67.3% of the working women, and 75.3% of women senior managers reported that they had been victim of violence, compared to 43% of housewives.

Of the many conclusions that can be drawn from this groundbreaking study of violence on women in the public spaces since 2011 is that violence targets essentially the women who have achieved a high degree of social, economic, and academic success and therefore represent telltale signs of the success of the postindependence modernist societal project that hinged on the liberation of Tunisian women from the crippling shackles of traditionalism and dealt a powerful blow to a perennial patriarchal mentality that has kept resurfacing in the society in the past four decades with cyclical social and economic crises and fed by rising cyber and satellite versions of global political Islamisms.

Descriptive and symbolic versus substantive representation

Like violence against women, women representation in politics and elected bodies is used by the author as a yardstick to gauge democratization in Tunisia post-2011 from a feminist perspective. Again, compared to other Muslim countries on the political participation indicator of gender equality, the author notes that Tunisia fared well after the 2011 elections. In reality, this does not represent a greater foothold in electoral success as prior to 2011 women comprised 22.7% of the 214-person chamber of deputies, 13% of the 112-seat Chamber of advisers, and 7 members in the government and unanimously supported the women-oriented statehood model. Quantitative representation aside, the author's qualitative assessment of women's representation in Tunisia in the aftermath of the 2011 elections is insightful and challenging. It raises questions about overtly romanticized conceptions of Islamist women as protectors of women rights in the Muslim world that not only Islamist parties have been promoting inside Tunisia, but also Western sponsors of the 'moderate Islamist' experiment through a public relations campaign that predates 2011 (Ben Hadj Salem 2016). This worldwide campaign reached a crescendo with the ratification of the constitution as Western media outlets, print and electronic press diffused the photo of a group of veiled Islamist NCA women hugging each other on the ratification ceremony attended by many world leaders and diplomats, sending a misleading message to the world that these very 'anti-women rights' Islamist women, as demonstrated through Winter's work, were key agents in writing what came to be qualified as 'the most progressive constitution' in the Muslim world. Winter's work debunks this myth by delineating the anti-women rights record of the Islamist women during the transition period reflected in their participation in anti-woman rights demonstrations in 2013, opposition to the anti-violence against women bill introduced at the NCA in 2014.

Winter has perhaps made a good choice by focusing on Islamist women opposing pro-women policies during the Islamist-led phase of the transition period to substantiate her argument that the Islamist women 'represented an ultra-conservative and ultimately anti-woman position,' that they are 'obedient women who will toe the party line and help the party to police other women,' and, as such, their representation is descriptive rather than substantive. However, I believe that there is something more substantive that the author could have explored to give more strength to her argument. It is how Islamist women supported an unremitting flow of anti-women rights project laws and constitutional articles proposed by their ultra-conservative male leadership and would have led, if not denounced and opposed by civil society and opposition NCA non-Islamist members, to the establishment of one of the most theocratic dictatorships in the Muslim world. Their desperate and protracted fight for the cause of Shari'a as a source of law, of gender complementarity rather than equality, along with a series of other proposals directly and indirectly targeting the CPS compound the impending risk of regression and endanger the integrity of the Tunisian modernist project with which the author concluded her work.

Disclosure statement

No potential conflict of interest was reported by the authors.

References

Ben Hadj Salem, H. 2016. "Anabaptized 'Moderate': 'Moderate Islamists,' American Think Tanks, and the Roadmap to the 'Jasmine Revolution' and the 'Arab Spring'." *International Journal of Humanities and Cultural Studies* 2 (4): 358–383.

Charrad, M. 2001. *States and Women's Rights: The Making of Postcolonial Tunisia, Algeria, and Morocco.* Los Angeles: University of California Press.

Index

INDEX